GLIDER PILOTS IN SICILY

GLIDER PILOTS IN SICILY

Mike Peters

Pen & Sword
MILITARY

First Published in Great Britain in 2012
and reissued in this format in 2025 by
Pen & Sword Military
an imprint of
Pen & Sword Books Ltd
Yorkshire - Philadelphia

ISBN 978 1 03615 088 4

A CIP catalogue record for this book is available from the British Library.

Typeset in 10/12pt Palatino by Concept, Huddersfield

Printed and bound in England by CPI Group (UK) Ltd, Croydon, CRO 4YY

MIX
Paper | Supporting responsible forestry
FSC® C013604

The Publisher's authorised representative in the EU for product safety is Authorised Rep Compliance Ltd., Ground Floor, 71 Lower Baggot Street, Dublin D02 P593, Ireland. | www.arccompliance.com

For a complete list of Pen & Sword titles please contact

PEN & SWORD BOOKS LIMITED
47 Church Street, Barnsley, South Yorkshire, S70 2AS, England
E-mail: enquiries@pen-and-sword.co.uk
Website: www.pen-and-sword.co.uk

or

PEN AND SWORD BOOKS
1950 Lawrence Road, Havertown, PA 19083, USA
E-mail: uspen-and-sword@casematepublishers.com
Website: www.penandswordbooks.com

Contents

Acknowledgements

I decided to write this book following the 50th anniversary of Operation HUSKY in 1993. I remember listening to the very vivid accounts of two Glider Pilot Regiment (GPR) veterans who had survived Operation LADBROKE, Jock East and Les Howard; sadly, both passed away some years ago. It was their personal stories that inspired me to write this book, which includes all the contributions of those other glider pilots who, over the years, have shared their at times painful memories so freely with me. I remain grateful to Wallace Mackenzie, Harry Howard, Robin Walchli, Mike Hall, John McGeough, Les Howard, Jock East and Tom Davidson. More than 300 officers and men of 1st Airlanding Brigade lost their lives off the coast of Sicily and in the subsequent battles of July 1943, all leaving bereaved families behind them. I am indebted to those family members who have contributed their personal memories and letters, among them Mike Barrie, Patricia Woodcock, Mrs Dorothy Brown, Graham Coulson and Nigel Clifton. I extend my sincere thanks to them all.

The planning, preparation and execution of the airborne landings on Sicily was a complex and challenging task for all of those involved, generating vast tomes of information and files. Sourcing and verifying the research material for this book has thus been difficult at times. Fortunately, I have had the benefit of enthusiastic assistance and advice from John Howes, a skilled and pro-active researcher whose hard work and technical advice has saved me many weeks of time and effort when researching Operations BEGGAR, LADBROKE and FUSTIAN. In addition to providing invaluable assistance as a researcher, he has also allowed me to make use of previously unpublished extracts from his father's account of the weeks leading up to the landings, including personal memories of LADBROKE and its immediate aftermath. John's father, Sergeant Norman Howes, was a member of the 2nd Battalion The South Staffordshire Regiment.

Many of the anecdotal accounts from GPR veterans included in this book were drawn from *The Eagle*, the excellent magazine of The Glider Pilot Regimental Association (GPRA). Thanks must therefore go to the editor, David Brook, whose willingness to allow the publication of these accounts, has provided an unprecedented insight into the first large-scale glider operation undertaken by the British Army. I am also grateful for the support, time spent proofreading, and the encouragement offered so freely by fellow historians and GPRA members, Luuk Buist (my co-author on *Glider Pilots at Arnhem*), Steve Elsey and Steve Wright.

Researching distant campaigns can be difficult and costly. Fortunately however, through the generous support of Alain Chissel and Alison Biegel of Anglia Tours, I have had the privilege of leading a series of battlefield tours on Sicily which gave me the invaluable opportunity to walk over the landing zones and objectives many times, verifying my research and gaining a feel for the ground in the process. On most of those tours I was working with my good friend and fellow battlefield guide and author Tim Saunders, to whom I am extremely grateful for sharing so generously his extensive knowledge of the island and the campaign that took place on it in 1943.

Closer to home, I have been extremely fortunate in receiving much practical help and advice from fellow Airborne historians and International Guild of Battlefield Guides members Jo Hook, Tim Lynch, John Greenacre and Bob Hilton to whom I am indebted for proofreading and checking the draft chapters, and for allowing me to bounce my ideas off them. I must also mention Andrew Duff and Tom Dormer of Battlefield History TV who, along with Tim Saunders, sent me to Sicily to record and tell the story of the gliderborne operations on camera – providing me with another opportunity to walk the Airborne battlefields and cemeteries of Sicily.

Access to archives and museums is critical to any author's research, and I have relied heavily on the support of the Airborne Assault Museum at Duxford. Its ever-patient curator Jon Baker, the assistant curator Becks Skinner, and Tom Lusby have been a great help throughout the writing of this book. I unreservedly recommend the museum and its archive to anybody interested in the history of airborne forces. In a similar vein, I also have to acknowledge the continued support of Stuart Eastwood and the staff at the King's Own Royal Border Regiment Museum and thank them for allowing me to use source material from their archives. The Prince Consort Library in Aldershot has also been very supportive, as has Mark Hickman of The Pegasus Archive. I must also single out Chantal White, the librarian of the recently closed Army library at Wattisham Flying Station, to whom I am most grateful for her patience and unending enthusiasm, particularly when ordering on my behalf a seemingly endless list of reference books and source material.

Maps and photographs of the Sicily operations are very difficult to find, and in this respect I owe particular thanks to Robert Sigmond, Bob Gerritsen and Ian Blackwell for their great support in sourcing several of them for me.

Speaking of patience, I have to salute Henry Wilson, the commissioning editor at Pen and Sword Ltd, who really does deserve a medal for coping with my constant shifting of the projected completion date for *Glider Pilots on Sicily*. I extend my thanks to him and to my editor, the accomplished military historian and good friend, Peter Harclerode.

Finally, and most importantly, I must acknowledge the support and endless patience of my wife Karen, and two sons Adam and Tom, who have put up with me spending hours every evening and weekend researching and writing when I could have been spending time with them. I can now also apologise publicly to Karen for suggesting a 'family holiday' to Sicily and then revealing that it was in fact a reconnaissance of the island's battlefields. To my wider family and colleagues at work I also extend my grateful thanks for reading and commenting on my draft chapters, and for their continual interest and encouragement.

Mike Peters
Suffolk 2012

Prologue

Greeks and Romans

The Combined Chiefs of Staff have resolved that an attack against Sicily will be launched in 1943, with the target date as the period of the favourable July moon (Code designation HUSKY).

Operation HUSKY, the Allied invasion of Sicily in July 1943, was the largest operation of the Second World War, being almost greater in scale than the Normandy landings that took place less than a year later in June 1944, and dwarfing any of the numerous amphibious landings mounted during the island-hopping campaign carried out by United States forces in the Pacific.

In order to understand the part played by The Glider Pilot Regiment and 1st British Airborne Division, we must spend some time reviewing the wider strategic picture as it appeared to the Allies in early 1943. It is important to remember that prior to HUSKY, Allied airborne forces were still very much in an embryonic state. The British Army Air Corps had only been in existence since the summer of 1942, while the fledgling Glider Pilot Regiment was established in name on 24 February the same year; this was followed by the formation of The Parachute Regiment on 1 August 1942. In spite of their collective lack of operational experience at this level, both would be at the forefront of the first large-scale Allied airborne operation of the Second World War. By examining the events leading up to the decision to invade Sicily, we will gain some insight into the thought processes that led to the involvement of British and American airborne troops in the landings.

Prior to HUSKY, the battles fought across the deserts of North Africa had been the focus of British military effort, the campaign there having remained prominent in Britain's strategic priorities since the autumn of 1940. Any German advance towards Egypt and the Suez Canal was viewed as a knife being thrust toward the already exposed jugular of the hard pressed British Empire. Moreover, following the fall of France in June 1940, the desert was also the only remaining arena where the British Army could engage the Italian, and subsequently German, armies toe-to-toe on any meaningful scale. Free from the hindrance of large cities and the movement of mass populations, large armoured formations from both sides had ranged back and forth across a vast sterile battlefield. Lacking the combat power to mount a landing on the French coast and maintain a foothold against numerically superior German forces, the British had thus remained focused on the desert war. The campaign in North Africa had enduring strategic, political and military significance to the British, while the Italians also placed some importance on the campaign. The German, American and Soviet high commands, however, largely took the view that it was a distraction. The decisive British victory at the second battle of El Alamein in October 1942 finally placed an Axis victory in North Africa out of reach. This was followed within weeks on 8 November 1942 by Operation TORCH, the Allied landings in Algeria and Morocco, the arrival of American troops in the North African theatre only eleven months after the Japanese attack on Pearl Harbour being an impressive achievement. In spite of the presence of close to 230,000 Axis troops in North Africa, it shifted the strategic initiative in North Africa irrevocably in favour of the Allies. Despite dogged, well-organised Italian resistance, it appeared to be only a matter of time before the Axis forces collapsed. The fighting in Tunisia continued until the surrender of both German and Italian forces on 13 May 1943, this marking the end of a 32-month long struggle for dominance of North Africa. In the months leading up to that surrender, Allied victory seemed certain and the stage was set for the opening of a new front in Europe. However, the question of where and when to open a second front was not as straightforward as it first appeared. Each of the Allies had opposing views on what should be the next objective after the long-awaited victory in North Africa.

The next step in Europe was one of many points to be discussed at a historic ten-day conference that took place in the Moroccan city of Casablanca, under the code name of Operation SYMBOL, beginning on 14 January 1943. Initially intended to be a 'Big Three' conference attended by all three Allied leaders, instead it became a meeting of 'The Big Two' when the Soviet leader, Josef Stalin, declined the invitation to attend. With his country besieged by both Hitler and the severe Russian winter, he did not feel that he could risk travelling to North Africa. The absence of the Soviet dictator was viewed very much as an opportunity by the British delegation. The Soviets were suspicious of Allied intentions in the long term and wanted a direct attack on Germany through a second front in North-West Europe. Anything other than a large-scale offensive in France was likely to be viewed as verging on a betrayal by the capitalist west.

There had never been any doubt that the British Prime Minister would attend the conference, Winston Churchill being renowned for his willingness to travel wherever necessary in order to further British aims. The absence of the famously obstinate Soviet leader gave him the freedom to manoeuvre he needed with the American delegation and so he travelled to Morocco with a large well-briefed staff and a very clear agenda. One of his prime objectives was to convince the American President, Franklin D.R. Roosevelt, that the next step after the imminent victory in North Africa should be the opening of a second front in the Mediterranean. Churchill and the British Chiefs of Staff had long favoured the region, along with the Balkans, and the Chief of the Imperial General Staff, Field Marshal Sir Alan Brooke GCB DSO*, articulated the logic behind the British strategic vision in his personal papers:

> The soft underbelly of Europe was the whole of southern Europe including a portion of southern France, the whole of Italy and the whole of Greece, all of which Germany was defending, and all of which is difficult to defend. It's like a series of fingers spread out into the sea. In order to defend it you've got to disperse your forces through it ... By defeating the Italian forces and wiping them off the map, forcing German detachments to take over the jobs that the Italians had been doing and to detain forces in Italy was the idea.[1]

The American view on the undertaking of any further operations in the Mediterranean theatre was well-known to the British before their arrival in Casablanca. They were pre-warned and briefed in detail by Field Marshal John Dill GCB, CMG, DSO, the Chief of the British Joint Staff Mission in Washington D.C. The first briefing took place within hours of the arrival of the British delegation in Casablanca. Dill possessed a great flair for diplomacy and was eventually to become the senior British representative on the Combined Chiefs of Staff. A trusted confidant, he fully understood the mindset of the American military chiefs and his insight into American thinking, combined with collective experience of fighting the Germans since 1939, gave the British a distinct edge over their American counterparts. The British had also deployed significant administrative resources to Casablanca to support their delegation. They had positioned HMS *Bulolo* in port nearby; a 6,000 ton pre-war liner, she had been converted into a floating headquarters and command ship for combined operations and thus provided communications with Whitehall, as well as clerical support and an extensive archive of papers supporting the British case for Sicily. The American delegation possessed no such facilities and so the presence of the *Bulolo*, together with her complement of specialist staff, gave the British a distinct advantage.

From the outset, the Americans' view contrasted starkly with that of the British: they saw no advantage in any further involvement in the Mediterranean theatre which they considered to be a sideshow to the main campaign that had to be opened in France. General George C. Marshall, the Chief of Staff of the US Army, noted his misgivings: 'I think the Mediterranean is a kind of dark hole into which one enters at one's peril.' Prior to Casablanca, any proposal for a Mediterranean or Balkan offensive received no support from the US Chiefs of Staff. Admiral Ernest King, the US Navy's Commander-in-Chief Fleet and a known Anglophobe, believed that the British would never consent to a cross-channel assault. During a series of angry exchanges he resisted any potential transfer of resources from the Pacific theatre while consistently lobbying for reinforcements for that theatre. Furthermore, he was particularly determined to retain every landing craft and support vessel he could for use against the Japanese.

This lack of enthusiasm remained prevalent in spite of some sympathy for the British argument on the part of Roosevelt. The US Chiefs of Staff and the Soviet High Command both strongly advocated the opening of a Western Front in North-West Europe in 1943. Their view was that only Operation ROUNDUP, the plan for an Allied assault on northern France, would draw significant German forces away from the Eastern Front. The polarisation of Allied opinion on what the next strategic move should be, following the surrender of German and Italian forces in North Africa, had to be resolved. It was thus hoped that the Casablanca conference would see the first steps toward the formulation of a joint Allied strategy to secure victory over Germany, Italy and ultimately Japan.

The conference was essentially a gathering of the British and American Combined Chiefs of Staff. Both delegations' thoughts on the next phase of the war were shaped by their own national histories. The Americans, headed by General George C. Marshall, were adamant that the quickest way to end the war was to invade France and advance directly into Germany. Believing France was where the decisive battle would have to be fought, they pushed for an invasion to be undertaken in 1943. The horrific casualty figures of the protracted and costly American Civil War, together with their views on the attrition of the First World War, had convinced them that a direct assault would shorten the war. With the Japanese campaign also prominent in their minds, they believed that a shorter war in Europe would be less costly and would in turn release men and resources for the Pacific theatre.

The British were also influenced by their own ghosts of battles past. The direct frontal approach suggested by the Americans conjured up visions of the stalemate and carnage associated with the trenches of the Western Front in the minds of the senior British officers present. As young officers, they had witnessed first-hand the horrors of such tactics and were determined not to be responsible for any return to a war of attrition, and thus forcefully and repeatedly argued that none of the pre-conditions for a landing on the coast of France yet existed. The Battle of the Atlantic was far from over; the Luftwaffe had yet to be defeated; the logistic infrastructure for the immediate support of an invasion did not exist; and Allied air forces were not yet capable of maintaining air supremacy over any proposed landing area.

During the negotiations, the British deployed their 'big guns' in support of the Sicily option over all others under discussion. They highlighted a number of strategic advantages to their plan that would have a positive benefit in other theatres. Admiral Sir Dudley Pound GCB, GCVO, the First Sea Lord, was first to speak to General George C. Marshall and his assembled staff. He emphasised the fact that with Sicily firmly in Allied hands, Allied shipping would be able to transit safely through the Mediterranean to the Suez Canal thus removing the need to bypass the Mediterranean and make the lengthy journey around Africa. This significant reduction in sailing time would free up 252 merchant ships and their much-needed cargo-carrying capacity for additional tasks. With the Battle of the Atlantic still raging, every one of these merchant ships were of great value.

The Chief of the Imperial General Staff, General Sir Alan Brooke, then landed what proved to be the overriding argument of the entire session by pointing out that the German Army's known strength in France stood at 42 divisions without reinforcement. Such a force could comfortably deal with any Allied invasion force without weakening German forces on the Eastern Front. He concluded that if the Allies could knock Italy out of the war, it would force the German High Command, the Oberkommando Wehrmacht (OKW), to occupy the Italian mainland and replace the Italian formations in the Balkans. These reinforcements would have to come from Russia or occupied France. Brooke further strengthened his argument by speculating that once Allied preparations for an invasion of Sicily became visible to the Germans, they would have to respond by dispersing their forces to meet the threat. Any relocation of German ground forces would require a corresponding reconfiguration and dispersion of Kriegsmarine vessels and Luftwaffe units to protect the redeployed ground formations. The defence of such a wide area would require much larger numbers of troops and equipment to be moved from Russia than if the Allies threatened an amphibious landing on the coast of France.

As the conference wore on, it became apparent to both sides that the Allies were collectively ill-prepared for the massive task of assaulting and breaching Hitler's 'Atlantic Wall'. An operation of such magnitude would not realistically be possible until 1944 as the assembly and training of a force capable of mounting a cross-Channel invasion, along with its supporting air and naval components, would take many months. Moreover, any offensive in North-West Europe would have to be preceded by extensive preparatory operations to reduce the German capacity to resist. A sustained bombing campaign to disrupt Germany's war industry would also have to be integrated into the operation. Such a campaign would be extensive and lengthy in nature; it could not be concluded before 1944. As the assembled staff officers delved into the detailed logistics of mounting an operation of such scale, it became obvious that the Americans' expectations were unrealistic and thus they were faced with some hard facts: there was not enough shipping available to transport Allied combat troops from North Africa to southern England within the required timeframe; furthermore, there would not be sufficient landing craft in existence to deliver them on to French beaches until 1944. A multitude of other planning constraints that would hamstring any attempt to open a second front in North-West Europe that year also bubbled to the surface.

The imminent victory in North Africa, coupled with the ever-present need to do something to relieve pressure on the hard-pressed Soviets, drew the Allied planners inexorably toward the conclusion that the Mediterranean theatre was the only option for a second front. Gradually, with each passing day, even those who had been entrenched in their opposition to the British proposal reluctantly accepted that a major offensive in Southern Europe was the only realistic option available in 1943. Once the southern option had been agreed, a series of meetings and at times heated discussions followed about alternative objectives to Sicily. Operation BRIMSTONE, the proposed invasion of the island of Sardinia, emerged as the main alternative, but General George C. Marshall and General Sir Alan Brooke both supported Operation HUSKY and insisted that Sicily must be the next objective of Allied forces.

The British mix of superior staff work, together with well-rehearsed and considered arguments, had eventually prevailed. They had won nearly every major argument on strategic policy with their American counterparts. There would be no major landing on the French coast in 1943; instead the Allies would invade Sicily that summer. The Americans took some consolation from the fact that HUSKY would be commanded by one of their number, General Dwight D. 'Ike' Eisenhower, who was appointed to the prestigious post of Supreme Allied Commander in the Mediterranean. In the interests of political balance, the mantle of deputy commander and ground commander was given to Churchill's favourite commander, General Sir Harold Alexander GCB, CSI, DSO, MC. If further evidence of British dominance at Casablanca was needed, the composition and configuration of the remaining command structure told the tale. Command of the combined Allied Naval fleet was given to Admiral Sir Andrew Cunningham GCB, DSO**, the commander of the British Mediterranean fleet. The other key appointment, that of Commander-in-Chief Mediterranean Allied Air Forces, was given to Air Chief Marshal Sir Arthur Tedder GCB of the Royal Air Force.

Eisenhower was unhappy with the new command structure but had little choice but to soldier on and influence the planning process as it progressed. He was not alone in his dissatisfaction. After ten long days the conference drew to a close, the American delegation to a man feeling that they had been manipulated and out-manoeuvred by their allies. They vowed that they would never allow the British such an advantage again – they never did. With the decision on the second front finally made, the plan to invade Sicily could at last be formulated.

As the Casablanca conference drew to a close the 1st Battalion The Glider Pilot Regiment (GPR) had yet to pass the milestone of twelve months in existence. All over England, the officers and soldiers who had left their parent units to volunteer for the new regiment were undergoing training on the ground and in the air, all of them unaware of the momentous decisions taken thousands of miles away in Morocco. The motto of The Glider Pilot Regiment was 'Nothing is Impossible'. Six short months after Casablanca, the newly qualified pilots of the regiment were destined to pay a terrible price living up to it.

Note

1. Papers of Lord Alan Brooke, 9/3/8, NBC Television Interview, 1958.

CHAPTER 1

Nothing is Impossible

I realised what a dodgy game I was in and that I ought not to expect to survive the war.

On 10 May 1940, the day designated by Adolf Hitler as 'A' *Tag*, the shocked defenders of the Belgian Fortress at Eben Emael witnessed the birth of a new weapon of war – the assault glider. In the early hours of dawn, a small assault force of Luftwaffe parachute engineers landed in gliders on the fortress roof on which they positioned explosive charges to blow their way into the fortress and neutralise its Belgian garrison. What followed over the next few hours was Operation GRANITE, an audacious German assault on what was reputed to be the most impregnable fortification in the world. Thus it was in such spectacular fashion that the glider made its debut as a weapon of war.

Winston Churchill had been among those who observed with horrified awe Germany's use of *Blitzkrieg*, of which one of the most dynamic components was the use of airborne forces. The airlandings and parachute drops in Norway, the parachute assault on The Hague in Holland and the successful glider coup de main on Eben Emael during 1940 in particular caught his attention. The fortress at Eben Emael was the lynchpin of Belgium's defences; garrisoned by 1,200 well-trained troops, it was intended to act as an unassailable obstacle blocking the path of any invading force. Its powerful guns were inside steel-reinforced concrete casemates and surrounded by well-sited machine gun positions, anti-tank guns and anti-aircraft batteries. Indeed, such was the much-vaunted impregnability of the fortress that German planners had predicted casualties of 6,000 men if they attempted to capture it using conventional means.

The Fallschirmjäger; of Sturmgruppe Granit were landed silently and with pinpoint accuracy in nine small DFS 230 assault gliders. The highly trained 78-strong force of parachute engineers, commanded by Oberleutnant Rudolf Witzig, was equipped with specially developed shaped demolition charges that were used to blast through the concrete casemates, collapsing their roofs and putting the guns inside out of action. All external entrances and exits were also attacked with explosives, sealing the garrison inside and preventing it from mounting a counter-attack. Meanwhile, three other glider-borne coup de main attacks were being mounted against three key road bridges over the Albert Canal, all of them proving successful.

The raid on Eben Emael was a phenomenal success achieved at the relatively light cost of six German casualties. Having swiftly grasped the potential of airborne forces, Churchill wasted no time in issuing a directive on the subject; on 22 June, he issued one of his famous minutes ordering the creation of a British airborne capability:

> We ought to have a corps of at least 5,000 parachute troops, including a proportion of Australians, New Zealanders and Canadians, together with some trustworthy people from Norway and France. I see more difficulty in selecting and employing Danes, Dutch and Belgians. I hear something is being done already to form such a corps, but only I believe on a very small scale. Advantage must be taken of the summer to train these forces, who can, nonetheless, play their part meanwhile as shock troops in home defences. Pray let me have a note from the War Office on the subject.[1]

In fact, work on such a corps had begun already. Nine months prior to Operation GRANITE, in September 1939, a conference had been convened at the Air Ministry in London. The need for gliders and trained military pilots to fly them had already been agreed, the initial concept involving the use of RAF/Army co-operation squadrons to assist in the training of the fledgling force.

The training syllabus required the volunteer aviators to complete three solo sorties prior to moving on to a glider training school. Three solo flights and landings was, however, a totally inadequate amount of flying instruction for a military pilot, so it can only be assumed that there was a plan for some form of continuation training. A major limitation was that the only gliders available at the time were little more than sailplanes and thus totally inadequate. The military glider would of necessity be a larger much heavier aircraft requiring a longer and far more comprehensive course of instruction to fly and land it.

Further British development of the military glider concept was interrupted by the German campaign launched against the Low Countries in the summer of 1940, the battle to save France and Belgium from the German juggernaut drawing the Britain's RAF/Army co-operation squadrons over to France away from their training role. Their deployment, and the resulting losses of aircraft and instructors during the campaign, delayed the implementation of the new glider programme and formation of training establishments until December 1940, although research had continued into the composition of an airborne force and how it would be equipped.

In June 1940, the Central Landing School (CLS) was established at Ringway Airport near Manchester. Squadron Leader Louis Strange DSO, MC, DFC* was appointed as the commandant and he arrived at Ringway on 21 June 1940 on the official formation of the CLS. He was joined by Squadron Leader Jack Benham as the chief instructor responsible for development of equipment and techniques. Major John Rock of the Royal Engineers was to be the senior Army officer at the CLS, and subsequently would play a significant role in the development of the fledgling Glider Pilot Regiment.

The first gliding school was eventually established at Haddenham (renamed RAF Thame), near Aylesbury in March 1941. It was commanded by Squadron Leader H.E. Hervey MC whose staff of instructors consisted of pilots from all three services who had flown gliders as a hobby before the war. As there were no true military gliders available to equip the school in those early days, the first students were taught to glide using civilian sailplanes that had been donated or requisitioned from all over the country; ironically a number of them were of German manufacture. Prior to undergoing glider training, however, each student pilot was required to undergo elementary flying training at RAF flying schools where they learnt to fly in the Miles Magister trainer and the iconic De Havilland Tiger Moth, the latter also being employed as a tug aircraft. At the end of this powered aircraft phase of his training, each student was expected to have accumulated an average of 130 flying hours in his logbook.

Although small in scale, this early development of a British glider force made good initial progress. On 26 September 1940, a demonstration was mounted using two First World War vintage Avro 504 trainers towing two of the civilian sailplanes, being followed in October by a night flying sortie using four sailplanes. Later in the same month, 66 men from No. 2 Commando, all of whom had declared some form of previous flying experience, were selected for training as 'Glider Coxswains'. In December 1940, the new Glider Wing was officially established with its Army pilots included in its order of battle. The new unit, however, immediately created controversy as its formation was not welcomed in certain quarters. On 11 December 1940 Air Marshal Sir Arthur Harris AFC made the following sceptical statement that was to become infamous within the GPR:

> The idea that semi-skilled, unpicked personnel (infantry corporals have, I believe, even been suggested) could with a maximum of training be entrusted with the piloting of these troop carriers is fantastic. Their operation is the equivalent to forced landing the largest sized aircraft without engine aid – than which there is no higher test of piloting skill.[2]

The Army's General Staff, however, did not share Harris's opinion; it believed that an experienced soldier who was trained to fly had clear advantages, and countered with the following argument:

> The glider coxswain [pilot] on touching down will be the only man present who will know exactly where the landing has been made and in which direction the troops should go. He has the best forward view, he is highly trained in map reading and studying ground from the air, and he will have noted the lie of the land to the objective. Even if only a corporal, he will be the one to lead the other 23 officers and men to the right place.[3]

The need for an airborne force of any size or composition was the subject of fierce and protracted inter-service debate and correspondence. Many within the RAF were loathe to squander valuable aircrews, aircraft and resources on the development of a capability that might never be used. This wrangling hindered any real progress toward the creation of the 'Airborne Corps' envisaged by Winston Churchill in his original minute, and the woeful lack of progress was made evident to him in the spring of 1941.

Churchill himself came to inspect progress personally on 26 April 1941, accompanied by Mrs Churchill, US Ambassador Averill Harriman, Major General Hastings Lionel Ismay CB, DSO and Air Marshal Sir Arthur Sheridan Barratt CB, CMG, MC, the Air Officer Commanding-in-Chief at Army Co-operation Command. A combined demonstration was staged by the now renamed Central Landing Establishment (CLE) and the Parachute Training School (PTS) involving a formation of six Whitleys dropping 40 paratroops and their equipment on Ringway. The drop was accompanied by an equally small formation landing of five single-seat gliders and a demonstration by the newly delivered 8-seat General Aircraft Ltd Hotspur troop-carrying glider. Following this demonstration, Churchill expressed himself as being reasonably satisfied with the progress made in difficult circumstances. Only a month later the argument for the creation of British airborne forces received a boost from a most unexpected quarter – none other than the Germans themselves.

On 20 May 1941, the Luftwaffe mounted a huge airborne operation to capture the Mediterranean island of Crete. The massed landings, using over 3,000 paratroops, gliderborne troops and airlanded infantry overwhelmed a much larger British and Commonwealth garrison and placed the strategically important island under German occupation. Despite the very heavy casualties suffered by the German airborne troops, this nevertheless reinvigorated Churchill's determination that Britain must at least achieve parity in airborne forces with the Germans. He called for immediate action, and it was agreed that the Army would supply glider pilots with the RAF taking responsibility for qualifying them.

Some weeks later, in June 1941, the first deliveries took place of the production variant of the Hotspur. Designed as a small assault glider capable of carrying a section of infantry into battle, it was destined never to be used in action. However, after some initial production teething problems had been solved, it proved to be an ideal training aircraft. Meanwhile, the birth of military gliding and the training of soldiers to fly was being regarded by many as a dangerous novelty. Such a degree of suspicion and wariness existed at the time that whenever gliding was in progress at Thame airfield, notice of a ten-mile exclusion zone was circulated to other airfields.

In August 1941, the Air Ministry finally acceded and agreed that glider pilots should be fighting soldiers, further conceding that they could be officers or NCOs and that they would be seconded to the RAF for training. The decision was also taken to formalize the training of glider pilots by the creation of Elementary Flying Training Schools (EFTS) that would train the pilots. In late 1941 the War Office approved the formation of an Army Air Corps, which would be the parent formation for The Glider Pilot Regiment. The next step was to recruit the soldiers required; notices had begun to appear in unit orderly rooms all over England:

> **THE AIRBORNE FORCES OF THE BRITISH ARMY CONSIST OF PARACHUTE TROOPS AND GLIDERBORNE TROOPS OF ALL ARMS OF THE SERVICE.**
>
> Officers and men in any Regiment or Corps (except RAC), who are medically fit, may apply for transfer to a parachute or glider-borne unit of the Airborne Forces ... A limited number of officers and other ranks are urgently required for training as glider pilots. Applications for transfer or further information should be made to unit headquarters.

In December of the same year, the RAF's Flying Training Command was directed to administer the training of ab-initio Army students on powered aircraft. There was however an initial delay due to a lack of students as the Army was unable to provide them, the first students for the new course not being available until January 1942. On 24 February of that year, The Glider Pilot Regiment officially came into being.

Meanwhile, that same month, Britain's newly-formed airborne forces scored their first major success when Major John Frost led 'C' Company of 2nd Parachute Battalion in a successful raid on a German radar station at Bruneval on the coast of northern France, removing vital top secret components and spiriting them away back to England. The use of paratroops in such an operation was a significant milestone in the development of this new type of warfare being adopted by the British Army.

Further progress was made when The Glider Pilot Regiment Depot was opened at Tilshead camp on Salisbury Plain in Wiltshire. The pilots, who were all volunteers, had to pass the RAF selection boards for standard aircrews. During that first year, when the regiment had little idea of its employment, it was structured on the traditional infantry model, being formed into a battalion comprising companies. The first commanding officer was Lieutenant Colonel John Rock, who previously had been the Army liaison officer at Ringway where he had written a series of papers on the strategic and tactical employment of parachute forces. He had also 'staffed' a number of ideas for the development of specialist clothing and equipment for the new force. As the regiment's commanding officer, he would be among the first of the students that would learn to fly under the new system.

The regiment would need company and flight commanders as well as its own staff officers to lead the freshly trained glider pilots. In advance of the first intakes, the 'Officers Course' formed up at No. 16 EFTS at Burnaston on New Years Day 1942. The eight students comprised Regular Army captains and majors, each of whom had been personally selected by Major General Frederick 'Boy' Browning, the commander of the newly formed 1st Airborne Division. Assisted by two staff officers, Browning had interviewed 30 candidates before choosing the eight for the course. After the results of the selection board had been published, an amendment was issued. The post of second-in-command of the 1st Battalion GPR had initially been offered to Major Willoughby of the Highland Light Infantry, but was subsequently withdrawn and given to Major George Chatterton, a former RAF pilot and infantry officer. As second-in-command of the regiment, his responsibilities included training and the running of the depot at Tilshead. Previous experience as a fighter pilot, and later as an infantryman in France, had given Chatterton very clear views on the skills and qualities required in a glider pilot. This extract from the opening address delivered by him to new intakes of recruits gives some indication of the priorities he set for his depot staff and the recruits in their charge:

> The Glider Pilot Regiment is established from volunteers of all regiments, which have grown out of the traditions heretofore mentioned. It is the most unusual unit ever conceived by the British Army. A soldier who will pilot an aircraft, and then fight in the battle, a task indeed.
>
> It must start from nothing, and weld its own name. However, let it not fail to see that within its ranks are the material and tradition of years. This being so, it must set itself the highest standards of spiritual endeavour. From the parade ground to the air, let it only be in the highest rank. Let the Esprit de Corps be second to none, and the bearing and discipline of all, be that which can only be admired. Let manners, and humour and sympathy predominate, and above all, let loyalty to all, be the mainstay of the regiment. Let there be no limits to the ambition of its material feats.
>
> With every kind of weapon will the regiment fight, and let the traditions and experiences of the Royal Air Force be its standard as airmen.[4]

The basic principles outlined in the opening address were formalised in the training notes later produced by Chatterton when he later assumed command:

> There is no doubt, that, to produce the type of advanced soldier necessary for the Glider Pilot, a good grounding is essential, and is in the early stages that the character and faith in the Regiment is born.
>
> Operational commanders have found that a well disciplined, well trained, and smart Glider Pilot is an asset, whereas a stubborn and casual type is definitely a liability, both in the air and on the ground. A great deal of individual initiative is required in order that the complex situations and varying operational tasks may be faced and successfully overcome. A weakness in morale can mean disaster to the individual and to all concerned.
>
> It is therefore suggested that the Glider Pilot must have the following simple principles instilled, during his progress from the Regimental Depot to the Glider Training School:
>
> - Recognition of the high standards that will constantly be required.
> - Importance of bearing, saluting and drill.
> - Highest standard of knowledge of Infantry weapons.
> - Full appreciation of the responsibility of his rank.
> - The vital importance of the ground subjects taught by the RAF.
> - That the Regiment will only tolerate men of the highest principles and ideals.

The instructors who would instil these standards in the trainee pilots were drawn almost exclusively from the Brigade of Guards. Chatterton had been attached to the Grenadier Guards during the Dunkirk campaign and the bearing and discipline of their warrant officers and sergeants had made a deep impression on him. He had been able to persuade Major General 'Boy' Browning, himself a Grenadier, to use his influence to secure Guards instructors for the new depot. The resulting level of discipline and 'bull' at Tilshead, however, was not what many of the new GPR recruits had anticipated when they volunteered to fly. A large number were 'Returned To Unit' by the training staff or voluntarily withdrew their papers and left the depot. Many glider pilots still have vivid memories of the intensive training regime that they underwent at the camp out on Salisbury Plain, not all of which were pleasant. Each potential pilot developed his own survival strategy to ensure that he progressed beyond Tilshead, as later recalled by Corporal Joe Michie. A Londoner who had left The Worcestershire Regiment to join become a glider pilot, he had no intention of failing at the first hurdle and arrived for training in Wiltshire in December 1942 with the simplest of plans:

> I knew that if you shut up and did everything you were told – no matter what – you would get through. I knew what this meant when RSM Jim Cowley arrived, having been away sick, bellowing 'Make way for a soldier!' Were his tunic buttons really sewn on with wire?[5]

The opening of The Glider Pilot Regiment Depot at Fargo Camp, Tilshead, in Wiltshire, was followed in May 1942 by plans to train and maintain a force of 1,200 glider pilots to support airborne operations. The pace of the expansion programme was maintained with the opening of three new Glider Training Schools by the end of July 1943. At the same time, the Heavy Glider Conversion Unit at RAF Brize Norton was also opened to introduce glider pilots to the intricacies of handling the Horsa and later the Hamilcar. Sergeant Bob Boyce was among the first to volunteer for service in the new Army Air Corps:

> Soon after Christmas in 1942, I was summoned to the Adjutant's office: Captain Lewis was a young officer, wearing a coronation medal ribbon, who had served in a commando unit and taken part in the raid on the Lofoten Islands. He told me that as I had been selected by an RAF selection board for pilot training and that all transfers were stopped, I was eligible to apply to a new Army unit, which was being formed to fly gliders. I remember his words, 'If you decide to apply, I think you'll find it quite exciting,' he said, 'you can have 48 hours leave and think it over.[6]

Many other likely candidates were mulling over the idea of escaping from the monotony of home defence duties and applying to join the new regiment; among their ranks was Corporal Mike Hall who had enlisted in the London Irish Rifles, a Territorial Army unit, in April 1939. He volunteered for The Glider Pilot Regiment and arrived at the depot in March 1942:

> The first few weeks at Tilshead were spent in square bashing, physical training, cross-country runs and assault courses. We were always told that the aim of the Regiment was to make us 'total soldiers' who, once we had delivered our glider loads into battle, could turn our hands to most aspects of fighting, so we had lectures on tanks, artillery and of course infantry. During these weeks on most afternoons we attended lessons on air navigation, meteorology, aircraft recognition, which were all very interesting.[7]

Those students that were not RTU'd during initial training at Tilshead were anxious to get into the air. Pilots were separated into batches and posted to EFTS dotted around the country, although early in the summer of 1942 the majority of these training schools were still far from operational. In May 1942, Staff Sergeant Mike Hall was among one of the first batches of pilots to leave Tilshead to begin his flying training. He and his comrades were posted to the No. 16 EFTS at RAF Burnaston near Derby:

> My instructor for the whole of the course, which lasted until 12 August, was a quiet RAF sergeant pilot, a Scot called Menzies, and we got on

well together. The Magister aircraft was a single wing, dual control plane with the instructor in the rear seat, and it was easy to fly. It must have been easy for on 12 June, just 13 days and 10 hours 10 minutes instruction, I did my first solo flight, after passing my solo test. The experience of being alone in an aircraft and completely in charge is something I will never forget, it was wonderful.

After the first solo flight the exercises became more adventurous. Aerobatics, stalls, spinning, side slipping to lose height quickly, landing into and across wind, instrument flying where we had a hood over the cockpit and could see nothing except the flight instruments. I was not particularly keen on the aerobatics, for to deliberately fly the aircraft vertically until it stalled, flipped over and dived straight down spinning like a top was not a thing I would do for fun, but of course it was necessary to learn the procedure for getting out of the spin.

In August, we started night flying, which was something else. It was very interesting because with the countrywide blackout in operation, it was not easy to recognise the surrounding countryside. Of course the airfield had paraffin flares to mark the grass runway and there were flashing markers placed at various places. which we had to learn to recognise. As Burnaston was very near Derby, the home of Rolls Royce, the area received attention from the Luftwaffe and as soon as a raid warning was received all aircraft had to land immediately to enable the lights to be put out. If you were some distance from the airfield it could get a bit scary in getting back quickly.[8]

The trainee pilots soon learnt that, in addition to wayward Luftwaffe intruders, there were other hazards with which they would have to contend. 20-year old Sergeant Harry Lansdell reported to No. 16 EFTS at RAF Burnaston as a student on No. 7 Elementary Flying Course and was to become familiar all too soon with the dangers of flying. He and his fellow students on the course were billeted in the nearby Repton School within reach of the field at Burnaston. As normal, the day began in traditional Army manner with a healthy dose of early morning physical training, followed by a quick breakfast and then a bus journey from the billet at Repton to RAF Burnaston for flying training:

My instructor was Sergeant Evans, a married man with two young children. He took me through much of my training. We got on well and I admired him. Once he took me low flying along the meanders of the River Trent with steep turns at each bend of the river. Then simulated forced landings at the satellite airfield. This whole army caper was great fun. Then on 5 June after a forced landing exercise at the satellite airfield my instructor and fellow pupil took off to do the same. When they were due back I bought them an ice cream each. As they became more overdue their ice creams melted and I was cross, but they were

> both dead ... crashed into the satellite field. I was a pallbearer for the funeral at Repton Parish church. The pupil's mother stood looking so tiny by the graveside and tottered at the noise of the rifle volley salute.[9]

Another who experienced tragedy during his training at Burnaston was Sergeant Harry Lansdell:

> My next flying instructor was Pilot Officer Grantham whose thighs were so fat that there was hardly any space for aileron movement on the stick. I flew with him eight times; the last was for spinning and side slipping exercises. Then he too crashed and was killed. His pupil that time was not killed but was seriously injured that we never saw him again. That was just before my twenty-first birthday and I began to grow up. After losing my first two instructors there was another fatal crash while I was at Burnaston, I realised what a dodgy game I was in and that I ought not to expect to survive the war.[10]

Constant improvement of aircraft, equipment and instruction by Flying Training Command resulted in a reduction of the length of the entire gliding course from eleven weeks down to eight but with students logging more flying hours than previously. On completion of the EFTS phase of their training, glider pilots moved on to one of the newly established Glider Training Schools. There they got to grips with the challenges of flying and, equally importantly, landing an unpowered aircraft. The Glider Schools were staffed and equipped to train a course of 66 pilots in three weeks, with each student working a five-and-a-half day week and making an average of 33 day landings during the course. The grass strips used by these schools were in fact exceptionally active airfields; a single course would rapidly log over 2,000 landings in the three weeks of training. The tug pilots would log an identical number of take-offs and landings, an average of 180 sorties per day from each airfield.

Lieutenant John Prout remembers progressing through the training programme. Although flying gliders was a serious and at times risky business, there were the occasional lighter moments:

> The airfield at Stoke Orchard was at the top of a hill, with a public road running along the edge, and the members of the general public used to come on Saturdays and Sundays to stand on the road and watch the flying. So we used to make a dive approach into the valley below and then climb from directly below and behind the spectators and scare the living daylights out of them by coming in silently from behind them and approaching just over their heads.[11]

On completion of their flying training and conversion to heavy gliders at Brize Norton, the newly qualified pilots were posted to 'Battle School' to develop their infantry skills. Many of them were regular soldiers who had seen active service with the BEF in France, while others had served in the Territorial Army prior to the outbreak of war. Major George Chatterton's 'Total Soldier' concept required every pilot to be able to fight on the battlefield immediately after emerging from the cockpit of his glider, so The Glider Pilot Regiment established its battle schools to hone the skills and tactics required to turn the newly qualified pilots into the Total Soldier. The first of these new facilities was Southbourne Battle School, which came into being in Bournemouth during the winter of 1942. Its headquarters was located in the Overcliffe Hotel, which also doubled up as a barracks, while the Warrant Officers and Sergeants Mess was set up in Crawford's Café.

The staff for the school consisted of glider pilots who had previously served as sergeants in infantry battalions. Staff Sergeant Ken Barratt was appointed as the senior instructor and tasked with establishing the school, while the first commandant was Captain Hamilton O'Malley of the Irish Guards. The training syllabus provided instruction in all British, and a number of German, infantry weapons. Much time was spent practising the arts of patrolling, bayonet fighting and fighting in built-up areas, described at the time as 'Street Fighting'. All these skills would be put to great use in due course by glider pilots in Sicily and on the streets of Arnhem and Oosterbeek later in the war.

The Total Soldier ethos was heavily emphasised throughout this phase of training during which glider pilots were expected to fight as individuals or as formed bodies of troops. It was outlined in The Glider Pilot Regiment training pamphlet, which included this description of the qualities required of the GPR staff sergeant:

> He must be a soldier of the highest type, fully trained in all methods of warfare, confident to take on anything, anytime, and be constantly ready to use his initiative, from being an ordinary rifleman, to commanding a platoon.

One of the roles envisaged for gliders from the outset was the carriage of heavy weapons and vehicles on to the battlefield. If glider pilots were to be of use after landing, Major Chatterton's view was that they had to be trained to operate them. Clear direction was also available from the training pamphlet published on the subject:

> The Glider Pilots' load may be Anti-Tank Guns, Machine Guns, Mortars, Light Artillery – it may be tanks, carriers, or wireless. Here again the Glider Pilot will train as the unit requires, and must be able to operate his load. This calls for complicated, specialist and individual training – all Glider Pilots will have attended courses in their squadrons.

Further to a directive on individual training, the role of the regiment after landing its loads of troops and stores was also explained:

> The Glider Pilot Regiment once landed will be generally concentrated as a light infantry regiment, its task being mainly a defensive one. All commanders and Other Ranks must be prepared to fight as battalion, company, and platoon. Therefore squadrons will constantly train as a normal infantry company – from individual to company training. The Regiment will be practised in the field as a two-battalion brigade, and must be prepared to fight as such.

In October 1942, a tragic event occurred that was to change the character, ethos and overall direction of the regiment: the death of Lieutenant Colonel John Rock during a training exercise. Captain Philip Cooper, a Royal Artillery Officer also undergoing glider training, wrote an account of the events surrounding the loss of the first Commanding Officer of The Glider Pilot Regiment:

> I was taking my turn as second-in-command and had to investigate the accident afterwards. 'Robby' Robson and his squadron were doing their turn of flying at Shrewton, trying out an operational flare path of one gooseneck flare to enable tug and glider pilots to locate the flare path, and resin lights put out to windward from this flare path in an 'L'.
>
> The weather was dull, frosty with patches of fog. On that evening, the first trial of the night with a full load of ballast was to be made. Robby was flying the Hotspur but Rock, who was of course on the strip to see how the trial went, said 'I'll come with you Robby' and climbed into the second pilot's seat. The tug took them off and did a circuit; but at the end of it, visibility had become bad, a swathe of fog having swept across, the tug pilot had difficulty in finding the flare path. When he did see it, it was about 200 feet below him, and the tug pilot turned a little sharply towards it.
>
> Robby in the glider lost position, the towrope slackened and broke on tightening again; and the glider was left almost vertically above the landing strip at 200 feet. Quite rightly, he made no attempt to get down on the strip with a fully loaded Hotspur, but turned away to land on the open plain to the northward. Here he could pick up the ground in the light from the nose-mounted combination navigation lamp when a few feet above it. The gliders had been fitted with car spotlights for use as emergency landing lights; but these had been decided to be of no practical use and removed only the week before.
>
> Unfortunately he struck the top of the only line of telephone poles crossing that part of the ranges with the root of the port wing. The machine turned over, and crashed upside down. Robby was hurled out through the nose as it burst, and went to hospital for a long spell with a

> fractured skull, concussion and multiple injuries, though he eventually returned to flying.
>
> Rock was trapped behind the first pilot's seat and his own stick, and took the load of ballast sandbags in the back. He was taken to the American Hospital at Tidworth, where amongst other injuries he was found to have ruptured his intestines in three places. They operated to deal with this, and he was conscious and cheerful when I saw him (He looked up and said to me 'Don't look so worried, Philip. I'm coming out of here.') But peritonitis of course developed, which they tried to control with sulphonamide, then a new drug. They pushed it too hard, and got it crystallising in the kidney tubules and blocking them. He died after about five days from anaemia.[12]

Lieutenant Colonel John Rock passed away on 8 October in the American military hospital in Tidworth, as a result of injuries incurred in a flying accident during a night flying exercise at Shrewton on 27 September, and was buried in the military cemetery there. Immensely popular, he was replaced by his second-in-command, the newly promoted Lieutenant Colonel George Chatterton. The 'Total Soldier' concept would now become the foundation stone on which The Glider Pilot Regiment would be built and Chatterton's determined intent in that respect is captured in another extract from one of his opening addresses:

> We will forge this regiment as a weapon of attack ... Not only will we be trained as pilots, but in all we do ... I shall be quite ruthless ... Only the best will be tolerated. If you do not like it, you can go back whence you came.

With the selection and training process for the glider pilots taking shape, the need for gliders increased. By January 1941, Air Speed Limited was already assembling jigs in preparation to meet an initial order for 440 of the newly introduced Horsa, an aircraft designed to meet specification issued in October 1940 for a glider that could carry 25 fully equipped troops into battle. Production got underway in August of that year and the Horsa, which would become the workhorse of British gliderborne forces, was cleared for daylight operations from June 1942; within months it was also cleared for use at night. It is testament to its design and construction that it was only modified once during its service history.

From the outset, the vulnerability of lightly armed airborne forces to armoured counter-attacks and heavy weapons was appreciated fully. In October 1940, a further specification was issued for a larger glider that could deliver large anti-tank guns or light tanks on to the battlefield. The development and production of a glider that was as large as a four-engined bomber was controversial. Lieutenant Colonel Rock had advocated adapting loads for carriage in the smaller Horsa, as he believed that any glider built to meet this new specification would be ungainly and vulnerable to ground fire. Such a heavy glider was developed, however, in the form of the Hamilcar. While it would never be produced in the numbers as the Horsa, it would nevertheless play a significant part in the landings in Normandy, Arnhem and ultimately on Operation VARSITY – the Rhine crossing in March 1945.

In late 1942, The Glider Pilot Regiment carried out its first operation, codenamed FRESHMAN. On 19 November two Horsas, towed by Halifax bombers, took off from RAF Wick in Scotland carrying a detachment of sappers of 9th Field Company (Airborne) RE and 261st Field Park Company (Airborne) RE, from the 1st Airborne Division. Their mission was to attack the German heavy water plant at Vermork in southern Norway that was playing a pivotal role in the Nazi programme to develop an atomic bomb.

The first glider-tug combination to take off at 1745 hours was a Horsa flown by Staff Sergeant Malcolm Strathdee and Sergeant Peter Doig, and towed by a Halifax piloted by Squadron Leader Arthur Wilkinson. The second combination took off at 1800 hours, the Horsa being flown by two Royal Australian Air Force pilots, Pilot Officers Norman Davies and Herbert Fraser. Its Halifax tug was flown by Flight Lieutenant Arthur Parkinson of the Royal Canadian Air Force.

Each glider carried fifteen sappers, under the command of Lieutenants Alex Allen and David Methven GM respectively. What was already an intimidating prospect was further complicated by the relative inexperience of all those on board the gliders. The distance to the landing zone (LZ), the inadequate mapping of the LZ area, and the poor weather conditions at that time of year, increased the already significant risks. The weather that night was bad over Scotland but promised to improve over Norway.

The first combination decided to fly over the cloud all the way, while the second decided to fly below the cloud until nearing the coast, and then climb in the better weather nearer the target. For some unknown reason the low-flying Halifax flew into a mountain at Helleland, Rogaland, killing its crew. Its glider had been cast off but made a very heavy landing approximately 2.5 kilometres north-east of Lensmannsgard, 400–500 metres north-west of Gasetjern and some four kilometres north from where its tug crashed. Most of its occupants were killed or seriously injured.

The first combination meanwhile approached the Norwegian coast at 10,000 feet, but was unable to find the LZ despite an improvement in the weather. With fuel running low, the Halifax turned for home with its glider still in tow. On crossing the coast, however, the combination ran into heavy cloud and suffered icing up. The air became very bumpy and eventually the towrope parted. The glider crash-landed at Fylgjesdal near Lysefjord, but the Halifax succeeded in returning safely to Wick.

The survivors from both gliders were captured and almost immediately fell into the hands of the Gestapo at whose hands they perished. The four pilots and 21 of the Royal Engineers are buried in Stavanger (Eiganes) Churchyard, Norway, while five other sappers are buried in Oslo Western

Civil Cemetery. The remaining four, however, have no known graves. The members of the second Halifax's crew are interred in the churchyard in Helleland.

The failure of Operation FRESHMAN was a painful lesson that illustrated just how much more development was needed before British gliderborne forces could be deemed to offer the same offensive capability as their counterparts in the newly formed parachute formations. Such development would however take time and resources, both of which were in extremely short supply in wartime Britain. Nevertheless, the embryonic Glider Pilot Regiment was soon to be put to the test.

Notes

1. NA, CAB 120/262, Churchill to War Office, 22 June 1940.
2. Otway, Lieutenant Colonel, T., *Airborne Forces*, IWM, London, 1990, p. 35.
3. NA, AIR 32/2, CLE paper, 14 November 1940.
4. Opening Address by Colonel Chatterton to GPR recruits, undated.
5. Michie, Staff Sergeant, J., 20 Flight, B Squadron GPR, by permission of *The Eagle*.
6. Boyce, Sergeant, R., 2 Squadron, 1st Battalion GPR, by permission of *The Eagle*.
7. Hall, Corporal, M., 1 Squadron, 1st Battalion GPR, by permission of *The Eagle*.
8. Hall, Corporal, M., 1 Squadron, 1st Battalion GPR, by permission of *The Eagle*.
9. Lansdell, Sergeant, H., 1st Battalion GPR, by permission of *The Eagle*.
10. Lansdell, Sergeant, H., 1st Battalion GPR, by permission of *The Eagle*.
11. Prout, Lieutenant, J., 1st Battalion GPR, by permission of *The Eagle*.
12. Cooper, Captain, P., 1st Battalion GPR, by permission of *The Eagle*.

CHAPTER 2

Orders to Embark

Then, embarkation to where? Both 2 and 3 Companies incognito, no red berets, no stripes, no wings, just a bunch of private soldiers, destination North Africa, but they knew not why.

The death of Lieutenant Colonel John Rock had immediate repercussions for The Glider Pilot Regiment. The loss of a commanding officer inevitably will have a major impact on a unit, but Rock's tragic death could not have come at a worse time. Popular with all ranks of the regiment, he was also highly respected as a leader who never asked his men to do any task that he was not prepared to perform himself beforehand. He was renowned for always 'testing the risk' and had survived a number of near misses when trying out new parachutes and gliders.

With potential operations looming, changes took place almost immediately. Lieutenant Colonel George Chatterton had only recently been appointed to command the newly established 2nd Battalion GPR at Tilshead; now he was ordered to leave Tilshead and to assume command of the 1st Battalion. After the war he would admit that he had some reservations about the reception he would receive from the officers of the battalion, suspecting that they were loyal to Rock and would resist his different style of command. Whatever his concerns about his new command, however, he was even more anxious about those above him in the chain of command.

Weeks of uncertainty at Fargo Camp ended on 7 April 1943. A warning order was received by the 1st Battalion GPR to be prepared to deploy its headquarters, together with Nos 2 and 3 Companies, overseas. There was disappointment, however, for some as the majority of the men of No. 1 Company were ordered to remain in England, being tasked with supporting the training and development of the newly formed 6th Airlanding Brigade. Others were detached from the company, together with a number from the then embryonic No. 4 Company, to reinforce Nos 2 and 3 Companies.

On receipt of the warning order, Chatterton visited Headquarters 1st Airborne Division to request a postponement for the deployment of the battalion. His concerns were twofold: firstly, no information was available on the availability of gliders in North Africa; secondly, the significant lack of flying hours and experience among his pilots was uppermost in his mind. The lack of dedicated tug aircraft to support training had resulted in a dire lack of flying hours in the 1st Battalion, the majority of whose pilots had only flown six to twelve hours in the past six months.

Supported by Group Captain Tom Cooper, the senior RAF staff officer on the divisional staff, he raised his concerns. Instead, he and Cooper proposed a period of concentrated flying in England to build up the experience of the glider pilots to an acceptable level. On completion of this work-up training, the battalion could then be flown out to North Africa to join the division. This suggestion, however was rejected by Brigadier George 'Hoppy' Hopkinson OBE MC, the commander of 1st Airlanding Brigade, who insisted that the glider pilot companies would embark for North Africa with the rest of 1st Airborne Division; there would be no time for any further much-needed flying training prior to embarkation.

Chatterton returned to his own headquarters with much to think about:

> It was a strange experience, and I was full of foreboding. I knew that headquarters had no idea what they were driving up to as far as the Glider Pilot Regiment was concerned, but no effort of mine succeeded in bringing even a glimmer of light into their darkness. There was indeed a great gulf between those in authority and myself as to our proper role in battle.[1]

The battalion spent the following days in a frenzy of activity punctuated by speculation, the issue of tropical clothing and vaccination parades fuelling rumour and counter-rumour. This continued until the issue of a movement order detailing a date of embarkation and movement instructions for a move by rail to a port of departure. The bulk of 1st Battalion GPR would travel to North Africa as part of a large troop movement under command of 2nd Parachute Brigade.

After boarding trains outside Bulford and Tidworth respectively on 13 April 1943, Nos 2 and 3 Companies eventually sailed from British waters on 16 April 1943. The battalion war diary states the number of pilots involved in the move to be 26 Officers and 254 Other Ranks. Lieutenant Colonel George Chatterton's name also appeared on the nominal roll for the move; he had intended to remain at Tilshead to oversee the training of the remaining crews but once again his plans were overruled:

> I had been informed that I was to detail two companies of glider pilots to stand by; the rest of the battalion was to follow. I detailed this force to be commanded by my second in command, Major Maurice Willoughby, but Brigadier Hopkinson insisted that I myself should command the first group and go out with 1st Airborne Division to Africa.[2]

The majority of 1st Airborne Division took the same route by troop train and then boarded ships at the Scottish port of Gourock, near Glasgow. They then sailed in an escorted convoy through the straits of Gibraltar to Algeria and the port of Mers-el-Kebir; in the interest of security the exact details of the final destination of the convoy remained secret at this stage. Sergeant Geoffrey Fowell later gave an insight into the weeks leading up to the sailing and the nature of some of the security precautions surrounding the battalion move:

> ... Netheravon for Tiger (Moth), Hotspur and Horsa flying and so to Bulford and Fargo and a series of exercises, flying and non-flying, then embarkation to where? Both 2 and 3 Companies incognito, no red berets, no stripes, no wings, just a bunch of private soldiers, destination North Africa, but they knew not why.[3]

Any irritation felt by Fowell and his comrades at the removal of their hard earned chevrons, flying wings and Pegasus insignia would pale into insignificance once at sea. Conditions on board the troop ships were far from pleasant; many of the ships were never intended to offer any degree of comfort to passengers. Staff Sergeant 'Dusty' Miller was among those of the 1st Battalion GPR who arrived by train in Greenock to embark for North Africa that night in April:

> We detrained, marched across a pier and on to a small tug-cum-transport boat which left a few minutes later, heading out towards the large ships in the harbour. As we transferred to one of the huge towering boats, I caught the name '*Boissevain*' in small letters up on the bow. She turned out to be a Dutch passenger/cargo vessel, and it was not long before she had been firmly condemned by all who travelled on our trip as the 'Hell Ship'. Men were crammed into every possible corner. By night we almost stifled in the sweat-laden air. The food, when we eventually got it, was not bad but invariably cold by the time a place had been found in which to eat it. Almost the whole of every day was spent on deck in order to recover from the nights in the foetid sealed innards of the heaving ship.[4]

The battalion was split between the MS *Boissevain* and the SS *Nieuw Holland*, both of which belonged to the Dutch Orient-Java-Africa Line; they were certainly not cruise liners. Some GPR veterans believe to this day that the removal of their badges of rank resulted in them being allocated less salubrious lower deck accommodation. Staff Sergeant 'Andy' Andrews had vivid memories of the routine aboard ship. As with all soldiers in transit, his frustrations and concerns were largely focused on the menu and finding somewhere comfortable to sleep:

> You guarded your lifejacket with your life. Almost inevitably men lost or misplaced theirs and would pick up the next one available, and so it went on. To sleep at night without tying the lifejacket to your waist became more important than cleaning your teeth ... It seemed that we spent the entire journey in a queue – if it wasn't for the toilet or to wash, it was for food. If you were the mess deck orderly; if not for chocolate or other cookies, it was for other items which we hadn't seen for a long time in England. There were strange contrasts – white bread with butter for breakfast, and rice with maggots for lunch. There was sugar in the tea, but the tea was never warm nor sufficient to drink in the hot, stuffy atmosphere ... We were not allowed on deck at night, and only during the day if there were no danger of submarine or air attacks.[5]

Not every passenger was dissatisfied with life on board; Staff Sergeant Tom Davidson was a lot happier with conditions on the *Nieuw Holland*. The cheerful Scot had a different perspective on the journey:

> We embarked on the *Nieuw Holland* in the Clyde. I remembered it was the Clyde because Staff Sergeant Jim Tigar told me that his father owned a small hotel in Dunoon so he got the nickname, because of his stylishness, 'Duke of Dunoon'. He was a native of the Edinburgh village of Blackhall, as was I. On the boat was great! There were comfortable hammocks and freshly baked bread for breakfast.[6]

On Easter Sunday, 22 April 1943, six days after leaving the Firth of Clyde and following a tedious sea voyage, the convoy approached the North African coast. The ships would disembark troops and stores at the old French naval harbour of Mers-El-Kebir, a few miles outside the town of Oran. The forlorn, blackened wrecks of the French battle fleet, reluctantly destroyed at anchor by the Royal Navy in July 1940, still lay rusting and silhouetted in the harbour.

During the sea voyage, the battalion's two companies had been redesignated as squadrons, each comprising three flights. The men of No. 2 Squadron disembarked at 2300 hours, while their comrades in No. 3 Squadron made their own landfall in Africa at 0300 hours on the following morning.[7] 2nd Parachute Brigade, commanded by Brigadier E.E. 'Eric' Down, and 1st Battalion GPR were declared complete on shore on 24 April 1943.

The 1st Battalion GPR war diary records the battalion's first location in Algeria as being at Tizi, situated in the minor Atlas hills just seven miles south of the town of Mascara, a famous wine growing region prior to the war and one that remains so today, whose name means 'Mother of Soldiers'. In 1943 the town was surrounded by vineyards and boasted a number of cafés and bars, and thus it caused little surprise when the divisional headquarters established itself there, with the battalion's headquarters based in a requisitioned hotel nearby. The town had been a focal point for Arab resistance against conquest by France for fifteen years, and had been levelled by the French after their invasion and rebuilt in colonial style. Beyond the town the terrain was described as ideal glider country, similar in nature to southern Spain. The absence of low walls, hedges and trees made the environs of Mascara a perfect training area.

Nos. 2 and 3 Squadrons continued south beyond Mascara to Tizi as part of the 2nd Parachute Brigade road move, travelling 60 miles inland from the docks at Mers-El-Kebir in US Army transport. Many of the pilots' personal accounts comment on the fact that every six-wheeled 'deuce and a half' truck in the seemingly endless American convoy seemed to be driven by a negro soldier chewing on a huge cigar. This was not uncommon at the time and would not have raised any eyebrows in the US Army. Racial segregation of black and white troops was US Army policy at the time, with negroes frequently relegated to support roles such as drivers and not permitted to serve in front-line combat units.

Initial impressions of the camp at Tizi were positive, the local scenery even being described by some of the pilots as quite beautiful. It was seen as a pleasant respite after days of confinement at sea and the dusty road journey through the desert. Formerly a prisoner-of-war camp, it had been re-roled by the US Army into a reception centre for the incoming British troops. The reception and administration of the new arrivals went exceptionally smoothly. So impressed was Brigadier Eric Down with the administrative efficiency of the US Fifth Army, that he published a congratulatory order of the day complimenting the Americans on the whole operation.

This favourable impression, however, would not last long. Conditions in the camp were basic with all troops living under canvas, crammed two or three into very small American pup tents. The camp was sub-divided into barbed wire compounds, originally intended to contain German prisoners; on moving into the camp, 1st Battalion GPR was allocated one compound per flight.

Unaware of the high-level decision-making that had resulted in their being located in Tizi, the pilots swiftly adapted to their surroundings and wasted little time in acclimatising to them. A battalion route march took place on 25 April 1943, followed by a detailed briefing from Lieutenant Colonel Chatterton on the next day. Two days later, an advance party of two officers and 21 pilots then departed from Tizi by road, their destination a site close to a new US Army Air Force (USAAF) airstrip at Froha. Once in place they were directed to begin work establishing a tented camp to accommodate the two squadrons during the forthcoming training and work-up phase of the operation. Staff Sergeant Alec 'Fanny' Waldron was detached from his post as the Intelligence Senior NCO in Battalion Headquarters to join the Froha advance party:

> Morale rose steeply ... As far as I was concerned, it was a welcome return to the camaraderie of squadron life, even though our activities were centred on such practicalities as digging latrines, laying out a tented camp and erecting a large marquee to serve in due course as our

> Sergeants Mess. Try digging a regulation latrine six to seven feet deep, requiring a rickety ladder for access and egress in the final stages! The sharing in humorous but purposeful activities, albeit of a very physical and basic nature, did much to restore our sense of purpose. Doubtless this was aided further by a few days of perfect weather.[8]

However, with no gliders yet available to fly and therefore no immediate prospect of flying training, ground training became the priority. A programme of physical training, infantry tactics and map reading exercises was initiated, with route marches and battle runs extending further afield each day as men became acclimatised. It is testament to the overall fitness of both squadrons that in spite of the prevalence of mosquitoes no cases of malaria were reported during this phase of the operation. There were, however, cases of heatstroke, migraines and stomach cramps attributed to dehydration. Much discussion centred on the most likely cause of 'gippy tummy' that was inevitably prevalent. The prime suspect was the Mecrapine anti-malaria tablets that were supposed to be taken four times a week. Other suggestions ranged from the drinking water and the ever-present flies, to the fine dust and even the US Army tinned rations. There were, however, more serious problems than heatstroke and 'gippy tummy' to contend with at Tizi.

On 29 April 1943, just when it seemed that things could not become any worse, the camp was subjected to a violent thunderstorm. In what was described by many as the worst storm of their lives, tents were whipped off the ground by high winds and washed away in the resulting flood. This was to become a regular occurrence over the coming weeks and the pilots of 1st Battalion GPR quickly adapted their morning routine to include the drying of uniforms, bedding and equipment in the hot morning sun. The favourable first impressions of Tizi evaporated with the steam from the wet clothing and canvas. Major John Place, commanding No. 3 Squadron, endured the conditions at Tizi with his men. A Dubliner not known to exaggerate, he entered this vivid description of the conditions at Tizi in his diary:

> Ask any Airborne soldier, who was there, how he enjoyed Tizi Camp and you will hear his views in terms that will scorch your ears like flame. For three weeks we existed in the hell that was Tizi. It was not yet the end of the rainy season and very soon the camp became a sea of glutinous mud. Bivouac tents were the only shelter available for the troops. Never, as long as I live, shall I ever forget the storms we had, storms which went on for hours. The thunder crashed like siege guns and the lightning blazed with every colour of the rainbow. It sizzled and crashed and sparked until at times it seemed we were crouched in a giant powerhouse with every insulator smashed. And the rain it didn't fall, it cascaded in blinding walls of water. Within two hours a scarcely visible dry hollow became a swirling and reddish-brown flood, carrying

> with it tent pegs, boots, groundsheets – an assortment of equipment from sodden, waterlogged and wretched bivouacs. One night during such a storm, a river more than one foot deep and 20 feet wide, swept through all of our tents. When daylight came the havoc was almost too much to look at. A great sea of mud, and in the morass, hundreds of scarecrow figures groping for missing kit and hanging sodden blankets on the barbed wire fences to dry ... When the weather cleared, squads of men with picks and shovels dug watercourses and, even amidst this chaos and discomfort, there was cheerfulness and good humour.[9]

Sergeant Tom Davidson also recalled one of the later rainstorms at Tizi quite clearly:

> We were called to the cookhouse in a hayshed. Not long after this, the heavens opened with amazing thunder and lightning and torrents of rain. The shed was hit from time to time and we all felt shivers of electricity passing through. We had a good meal and watched the red mud stained water running through our tents. There followed a day of drying bedding and trying to beat the red grit out of everything.[10]

Regardless of the appalling weather conditions, work continued on new American airstrips at Froha, Matmore, Thiersville and Relizanne in spite of the fact that the pre-war French Air Force had rejected the sites as unsuitable for flying operations due to high levels of malaria infected mosquitoes. The risk of malaria and effects of intense heat, however, were outweighed by a number of other significant considerations and so the US Army engineers pressed on with carving out and marking runways, dispersal parking and taxiways to support glider and tug operations. The very fine, light and sandy red dust, and its detrimental affect on engine performance and visibility, was a concern from the outset. Aware of the potential hazard of dust clouds to aircraft while manoeuvring on the ground, the engineers soaked the runway and taxiways with heavy waste oil. Other areas were covered with metal panels pegged into the ground to give traction and stability. These rudimentary methods proved partially effective, but the fine dust continued to impede visibility during all aircraft moves.

Although sheltered from the physical hardships of the storms in his headquarters in the hotel, Lieutenant Colonel Chatterton was very aware of their potential affect on his unit's morale. The following comment from Staff Sergeant Dusty Miller expressed his own concerns:

> For a while I wondered why we were out here. It seemed to me that we had missed the boat. Stagnancy set in. Every night found the camp empty, except for those on duty, while the village of Tizi, and especially the town of Mascara echoed with the singing of our men while the North African wines flowed freely ...[11]

The extreme weather and the potential for his men to lose operational focus were not the only things on the Chatterton's mind. He remained very concerned about the lack of recent flying hours and experience in tactical formation flying among his crews, and the immediate lack of gliders and tug aircraft to support training in Algeria only served to deepen his anxiety. He could not accept the prospect of his men stagnating in the Algerian desert without training.

Within days of his arrival, however, he was summoned to Algiers where among others he met Colonel Ray Dunn USAAF, the commander of the 51st Troop Carrier Wing of the US XII Troop Carrier Command, who understood the British way of thinking better than most of his own fellow countrymen as his wing had earlier supported 1st Parachute Brigade in Tunisia.

The purpose of the meeting was to discuss the provision of tug aircraft by US XII Troop Carrier Command for pre-operational training and during forthcoming operations. The Command itself was not yet fully operational; only one of its component formations, the US 51st Troop Carrier Wing, was flying from the new desert strips. In fact it had been operational for some months, having dropped elements of 1st Parachute Brigade during the Tunisian campaign. In spite of its familiarity with British operating procedures, however, the Wing was not scheduled to support 1st Airborne Division. Instead, the aircraft of 52nd Troop Carrier Wing, under the command of Colonel Harald L. Clark, had been allocated the task. Moreover, neither Wing was available to engage in any form of joint training with the glider squadrons.

Colonel Ray Dunn explained that his own aircraft were currently allocated to routine transport operations, moving personnel, casualties and combat supplies back and forth across the expanse of North Africa. The aircraft and personnel of 52nd Troop Carrier Wing, however, were only just beginning to arrive in Algeria, and thus the Wing would not be operational until the middle of May. Once both Wings were in place, Brigadier Paul L. Williams would assume command of XII Troop Carrier Command.

The 52nd Troop Carrier Wing was a logical choice to support British glider training and any subsequent operations. It had worked closely with the US 82nd Airborne Division for three months during its work-up training in America which had incorporated numerous gliderborne exercises, during which the Wing's pilots had accrued extensive experience of towing the CG-4A WACO glider. During the meeting, Lieutenant Colonel Chatterton stressed the need to get his pilots on to airstrips and back into their glider cockpits as soon as possible. In spite of his efforts in Algiers, however, he could not locate even a few gliders for his men:

> I still could not find out if there were any gliders, and this distressed me, for I was becoming really concerned about the morale of my aircrews.

> No one could tell me about the arrangements that had been made and there had been no sign of General Hopkinson the Divisional Commander, for weeks.[12]

There was a reason for the absence of gliders for training. It was no accident; in fact it was in accordance with the early planning for Operation HUSKY completed by Task Force 141. The arrival of 2nd Parachute Brigade and the concentration of 1st Airborne Division in North Africa was part of the wider HUSKY plan. Both the division's parachute brigades featured prominently in the thinking of Task Force 141 and so were being rapidly drawn together.

Two weeks after the arrival of the first convoy the surviving veterans of 1st Parachute Brigade, under Brigadier Gerald Lathbury, were also due to arrive in the area of Mascara from Tunisia to take part in HUSKY; they were actually in place on 10 May 1943. The 'Red Devils', as they had been dubbed by their German opponents in Tunisia, were battle-hardened troops who had experience of combat drops, the extremes of the Tunisian climate, and of fighting an equally experienced enemy. Nevertheless, they had suffered heavy casualties and were well below strength, and thus would need significant reinforcement and re-equipping before they could be committed to battle again. The official history of Airborne Forces paints this brief snapshot of the condition of 1st Parachute Brigade's battalions on their withdrawal from the front line in Tunisia:

> By then the battalion was reduced to between sixty and seventy men a company. They were almost barefoot, the barrels of their rifles and Bren guns were worn, and their wireless sets were no longer serviceable. The other two battalions were in the same case ...[13]

The impressive number of gallantry awards accumulated by 1st Parachute Brigade gives some indication of the intensity of the fighting during the Tunisian campaign. The outgoing brigade commander, Brigadier Edwin 'Ted' Flavell MC**, was awarded the Distinguished Service Order. Other recipients in the brigade accrued a further eight Distinguished Service Orders, no less than fifteen Military Crosses, nine Distinguished Conduct Medals, twenty-two Military Medals, three Croix de Guerres and one Legion of Honour. A large number of replacements required to restore 1st Parachute Brigade to full strength were drawn from the newly arrived 2nd Parachute Brigade. This resulted, however, in neither brigade reaching its full fighting strength; the shortfall was particularly felt in the attached combat support specialists such as Royal Engineers and the Royal Signals.

A calendar month later, on 26 May 1943, 1st Airlanding Brigade and the second sea convoy was also due to be established in Tizi. The airlanding infantry battalions and the brigade's supporting arms would then be reunited with the glider crews that would fly them into battle. In turn, each of the component brigades of 1st Airborne Division would move through the tents of Tizi and another staging camp at Fleurus before subsequently moving onto the Mascara Plain.

Meanwhile, 4th Parachute Brigade was also due to further augment the strength of 1st Airborne Division. It was based in Haifa in Palestine where it had faced a continual struggle to secure aircraft to complete its parachute training. Shortly after a visit by Major General 'Boy' Browning on 12 April 1943, the brigade received orders to join the division in North Africa. The move was not completed until June later that summer when it arrived in Tunisia.

The selection of the Mascara Plain as a location for the initial forming up and training area for 1st Airborne Division was based on a number of tactical, logistic and climatic considerations. The overriding requirement was for the division and its supporting aircraft to be positioned within striking distance of Sicily, but in an area that would not indicate that it was the intended area of operations. An airborne formation so far to the west could logically be expected to pose a threat to areas across the western reaches of the Mediterranean or even to mainland Italy; in fact, the Allies made every effort to convince the Germans and Italians that the target was the island of Sardinia.

Another major factor was that the airfields in eastern Tunisia originally intended for use on Operation HUSKY were deemed to be too congested to accommodate 1st Airborne Division. In fact, the whole area between Algiers itself and Sousse was heavily occupied by Allied formations, and the limited road network linking these forward bases with the coastal ports that supplied them were already operating beyond full capacity.

Furthermore, the airspace in Tunisia was also very busy. The prospect of hundreds of trainee glider and tug combinations transiting over active air defences and through established air corridors was not an attractive or practical one for all concerned. The only alternative offered to the Mascara option was a group of three airstrips fifty miles to the north but these were widely dispersed in what was classed as a climatic 'hot belt', even by Algerian standards. It was thus thought unsuitable for extended operations.

In view of these factors, it was therefore logical to keep 1st Airborne Division and its supporting aircraft from 52nd US Troop Carrier Wing out of Tunisia for as long as practicable. The use of the Algerian airstrips would hopefully mask the true Allied intentions and deceive German intelligence until the airborne formations were trained and ready to play their part in the assault on Sicily.

There was, however, a drawback to this decision. The British First and Eighth Armies' areas of operations were hundreds of miles to the east of Mascara and the cluster of four airstrips on which the 1st British Airborne Division was centred. Consequently, communications with the British chain of command were consistently difficult and frequently tenuous. This, combined with an initial shortage of dedicated Royal Army Service Corps (RASC) and Royal Electrical and Mechanical Engineers (REME) units to provide direct logistic and mechanical support, complicated matters further. In a classic oversight, the supply and logistic specialists were not available, or had not been allocated berths on the first convoy to North Africa, and thus the British were forced to rely predominantly on the US Fifth Army for logistical support. The latter did its best to meet British demands, but so much of 1st Airborne Division's equipment was unique that the Americans were often hard pressed to meet them. Specialist stores and British equipment had to be brought west across the desert from Tunisia along extended supply lines, or landed by sea from England. In addition to providing support for 1st Airborne Division, US Fifth Army was also directed by Allied Force Headquarters to establish an airborne training centre and headquarters at Oujda. This was intended to co-ordinate air support to the training activity of 1st Airborne Division and the US 82nd Airborne Division in Algeria, but the desired level of co-ordination was never really achieved.

The numerous higher level headquarters that would play a role in the planning and execution of Operation HUSKY were spread right across North Africa in locations from Morocco to Egypt. Headquarters 1st Airborne Division had the unenviable task of maintaining communication links with the command structures of the Allied air and ground commanders whose wide dispersal of their locations had been dictated by the need to co-ordinate previous campaigns in the region. The British centred on Egypt, as a result of their need to protect the Suez Canal during their lengthy desert struggle with Field Marshal Erwin Rommel's Afrika Korps, while the newly arrived Americans and the British First Army were established further west after landing on three separate beachheads as part of Operation TORCH in November 1942.

Algiers would be the home of the combined Allied (Expeditionary) Force Headquarters, which had the complex task of co-ordinating the efforts of Allied formations positioned all across North Africa. The Supreme Commander Allied (Expeditionary) Force, Lieutenant General Dwight D. Eisenhower, and his staff were still overseeing Operation TORCH while the British First Army and US Fifth Army were still in Tunisia dealing with remnants of German and Italian units that continued to offer stubborn resistance to the vastly superior Allied formations. Task Force 141, under the command of General Sir Harold Alexander, had positioned itself close to the Allied headquarters in the city of Algiers. Meanwhile the British Eighth Army, commanded by General Bernard Montgomery KCB DSO, maintained a headquarters and a planning staff in Cairo.

None of these headquarters had any experience of conducting airborne operations as prior to HUSKY there had been no attempt at large scale use of airborne troops. Although the British had indeed mounted five combat operations to date, they had no experience with using paratroops beyond battalion level. Moreover, large-scale gliderborne or airlanding operations had never been attempted before. The Americans had an even steeper learning curve to negotiate as they had no operational experience of airborne operations whatsoever, and thus HUSKY would be the first use of their airborne forces.

This inexperience in the use of airborne troops shaped Allied thinking in 1943: all drops and landings would be limited to brigade levels. Early versions of the plan did not envisage the use of airlanding troops during the initial assault, while parachute brigades would drop in advance of the landings to neutralise coastal defences. It was thought that once troops were ashore and pushing inland, USAAF gliders could possibly be used in a cargo ferrying role, and this dictated the priority for the shipping of USAAF gliders and their pilots to North Africa. Consequently, it was not until late March 1943 that an order to ship 500 CG-4A WACO gliders from the United States was issued. Events during the first week of May 1943, however, would force alterations to this plan and see gliders being allotted an assault role.

Notes

1. Chatterton, Lieutenant Colonel, G., CO, 1st Battalion GPR, by permission of *The Eagle*.
2. Chatterton, Lieutenant Colonel, G., CO, 1st Battalion GPR, by permission of *The Eagle*.
3. Fowell, Sergeant, G., 2 Company, 1st Battalion GPR, by permission of *The Eagle*.
4. Miller, Staff Sergeant, V., 3 Company, 1st Battalion GPR, *Nothing Is Impossible*, Spellmount Ltd, 1994, p. 20.
5. Andrews, Staff Sergeant, H.N., 3 Company, 1st Battalion GPR, by permission of *The Eagle*.
6. Davidson, Staff Sergeant, T., 2 Company, 1st Battalion GPR, by permission of *The Eagle*.
7. War Diary 1st Battalion GPR dated: April 1943. National Archives file WO 175/118.
8. Waldron, Staff Sergeant, A., HQ, GPR, *Operation Ladbroke*, Woodfield Publishing, Bognor Regis p. 38.
9. Place, Major, J., OC, 3 Company, 1st Battalion GPR, by permission of *The Eagle*.
10. Davidson, Staff Sergeant, T., 2 Company, 1st Battalion GPR, by permission of *The Eagle*.
11. Miller, Staff Sergeant, V., 3 Company, 1st Battalion GPR, *Nothing Is Impossible*, Spellmount Ltd, 1994, p. 21.
12. Chatterton, Brigadier, G., CO, GPR, *Wings of Pegasus*, Battery Press, Nashville, 1982, p. 39.
13. Ministry of Information, *By Air To Battle*, HMSO, London, 1945.

CHAPTER 3

Monty's Excalibur

In my opinion the operation as planned in London breaks every common- sense rule of practical battle fighting and is completely theoretical. It has no hope of success and should be completely re-cast. Have given Dempsey letter for you stating my views as to lines on which planning should proceed.

At the conclusion of the Casablanca conference, the Allied Combined Chiefs of Staff had formally agreed on Sicily as their next strategic objective. A few days earlier, on 19 January 1943, they had issued a memorandum titled *Conduct of the War in 1943*. The memorandum contained the broad strategic reasoning behind forthcoming operations in the Mediterranean theatre and what they hoped to gain:

- The occupation of Sicily with the object of:
  - Making the Mediterranean line of communication more secure.
  - Diverting German pressure from the Russian front.
  - Intensifying the pressure on Italy.

The memo also alluded to the possibility of Turkey entering the conflict on the Allied side in the event of an Italian collapse. With Italy out of the war and Hitler's southern flank then exposed, Germany would be vulnerable to an Anglo-American offensive up the spine of Italy. The advancing Allies could then launch their armies into Central Europe. The British were convinced that such an exploitation of Italy's surrender would shorten the war dramatically; even if not fully successful, they argued, it would draw significant German forces away from the Eastern Front, thus relieving pressure on Soviet forces. Suspicious of Stalin's post-war intentions, Winston Churchill wanted to keep the communists as far out of Europe as possible. The Americans, however, remained less convinced of the merits of any operation against Sicily or of the value of any campaign in Italy.

As Supreme Allied Commander, Lieutenant General Dwight Eisenhower was ultimately responsible for the conduct of Operation HUSKY. He had been given clear and detailed direction from the Combined Chiefs of Staff outlining his objective and the command structure that would be in place to support him. The directive was issued on 23 January 1943; it opened with the following preamble:

> The Combined Chiefs of Staff have resolved that an attack against Sicily will be launched in 1943, with the target date as the period of the favourable July moon (code designation HUSKY).[1]

The directive was the trigger that initiated the planning of what was to be the largest, most controversial and yet least well-known operation of the Second World War. Timing would be critical, and Eisenhower's staff wrestled with the variables generated when mounting a combined operation, not least the challenge of balancing the conflicting meteorological requirements of the air and naval forces that were to support the invasion. The naval commanders needed darkness to mask their approach and convoy movements close in to the Sicilian coast, while over the same time period the air force commanders wanted good levels of moonlight that would aid their navigation and formation flying at night. The meteorological analysts had identified the second quarter of the July moon as the optimum period for the operation. During that period there would be enough moonlight early in the night to aid night flying and airborne operations; then after midnight the moonlight would fade, leaving near complete darkness to cloak the movement of ships.

At the end of January 1943, the war in North Africa was far from concluded. Understandably Eisenhower and many of his leading staff officers remained focused on fighting the German and Italian armies that were still contesting command of the Tunisian desert. Nevertheless, the second quarter moon of July and the target date for HUSKY were only six short months away. Planning thus had to get underway and quickly. During the last week of January a separate planning staff was established to draw up the plan for the invasion. The first meeting of the HUSKY staff, designated Task Force 141, took place at the Saint George's Hotel in the city of Algiers, taking its name from the number of the room in which it was held. The size of the staff expanded rapidly over the coming weeks and months, quickly outgrowing the hotel and moving out into a French school nearby.

Task Force 141 remained under the direct command of Allied Force Headquarters, the word (Expeditionary) having been dropped by then, and functioned as part of the G3-Operations Section until the end of the Tunisian campaign. From the outset, however, indecision, inter-Allied rivalries and inter-service wrangling hindered the planning process. Furthermore, the conduct of the Tunisian campaign continued to distract the senior Allied commanders from the preparation of the Sicily plan. Command of Task Force 141 and ownership of the HUSKY plan had been temporarily delegated to the senior British staff officer at Headquarters Task Force 141, Major General Charles Gairdner, until the North African campaign was over, and thus it was only after the surrender of the Axis forces in Tunisia on 13 May 1943 that General Alexander assumed full-time command of Task Force 141. With

North Africa cleared of enemy forces, the other Allied senior commanders were also now free to scrutinise the emerging HUSKY plans.

The initial directive given by the Allied Combined Chiefs of Staff to Eisenhower, now promoted to full General following the success of TORCH, had included an outline order of battle for HUSKY. The invasion force was to be split into two separate inter-service task forces. The Western Task Force, designated Task Force 543 and centred on the US Seventh Army under General George S. Patton Jnr, was to be entirely American with its headquarters in Rabat, Morocco, while its Eastern Task Force counterpart was a British/Canadian formation commanded by General Bernard Montgomery and formed around the British Eighth Army. Designated Task Force 545, its headquarters were based in Cairo.

Confusion was inevitable given the distances between the numerous headquarters and commands. The Sicily landings would also involve formations that would travel direct to the island from the United States and from Britain. This resulted in the involvement of planning headquarters in both Washington and London in addition to those in North Africa. With five major planning centres working thousands of miles apart from each other, confusion and debate were regular. Nevertheless, despite all of the complications and difficulties involved, an outline plan for HUSKY began to take shape.

It was almost immediately apparent to the planners that the key to Sicily was the seizure of the city ports of Palermo and Messina, on the northwestern and north-eastern coasts respectively. The capture of these two ports, in particular Messina, would block the only escape routes for the Axis forces from the island. Prior to the surrender of Axis forces in Tunisia, the hard-pressed staff of Task Force 141 had produced a total of eight successive versions of the HUSKY plan. Each was submitted with Alexander's approval but was robustly challenged by the waspish Montgomery who considered the whole concept of operations for Sicily to be fundamentally flawed, unrealistic and potentially doomed to failure. In March 1943 he wrote to Major General Charles H. Gairdner, making his views abundantly clear:

> In my opinion the operation as planned in London breaks every commonsense rule of practical battle fighting and is completely theoretical. It has no hope of success and should be completely re-cast. Have given Dempsey letter for you stating my views as to lines on which planning should proceed.[2]

At this stage, the outline plan for HUSKY proposed that the US Seventh Army should land in the north, close to Palermo. Concurrently, the British Eighth Army would land along the eastern and southern coastline to the south of Messina. The crux of Montgomery's objection to the plan was that the Allied armies would be put ashore on opposite sides of a 150-mile wide mountainous island. He argued that they would have little hope of co-ordinating their efforts or supporting each other. He also advised against the proposed landing plan, a plan that would disperse the assault brigades across multiple beaches over a wide front. The Task Force 141 staff had anticipated only weak resistance from a thin crust of defences, hence their dispersed landing plan. Once again Montgomery raised objections, believing that the plan underestimated the Italian Army and German forces; he had very recent experience of dogged and well-planned Italian resistance in the closing battles in Tunisia and thus expected fierce and determined resistance from Italian troops fighting to defend their own homeland from invasion. With this in mind, he strongly advocated parallel US/British landings on the south coast of Sicily and a narrowing of the Eighth Army frontage, pulling all of the bridgeheads tighter together.

At the very early stages of planning, the exact role of the airborne forces was unclear but a pre-emptive drop of parachute troops was assumed probable. As the plan developed, an audacious operation was proposed which involved the landing of airborne troops on the toe of Italy to prevent or disrupt the reinforcement of Sicily from the Italian mainland. It is likely that any such operation on the Italian coast, no matter how well executed, would have been ill-fated without effective fighter cover and, close naval support.

The plan was developed further, to include a more realistic use of 1st Airborne Division that would mount a series of brigade-sized landings, in advance of the main seaborne landings, behind the coastal defences identified on Sicily. The proposed drop zones (DZs), however, were dispersed over a wide strip of coastline; not the best method of deploying lightly armed airborne troops. In the light of the scale of the coastal mission, it was decided that the division would be reinforced for the operation with a third parachute formation. Brigadier Shan Hackett DSO, MC and his 4th Parachute Brigade were thus to be moved from Haifa in Palestine to North Africa, Headquarters 1st British Airborne Division being made aware of this plan in March 1943.

On 7 March 1943 the commander of 1st Airlanding Brigade, Brigadier 'Hoppy' Hopkinson, travelled to North Africa in company with Wing Commander 'Wally' Barton DFC, a staff officer from 38 Wing RAF. Their task was to advise the HUSKY planners on the capabilities of 1st British Airborne Division and the level of support it would require in North Africa prior to the operation.

Brigadier Hopkinson was left in no doubt that the neutralisation of the coastal defences was vital to the success of the invasion; 1st British Airborne Division had now become an indispensable part of the overall plan. Its impending arrival, and that of its associated transport aircraft and gliders, would require a significant amount of organisation and preparation beforehand. The presence of the division's hierarchy in North Africa was reinforced a few weeks later with the arrival on 29 March 1943 of the divisional commander himself, Major General 'Boy' Browning. He was accompanied by

Air Commodore Sir Nigel Norman RAF and a brace of other staff officers to plan the arrival of the division and the aircraft of 38 Wing RAF. Halfway through April, however, Brigadier Hopkinson was promoted to the rank of major general and assumed command of 1st British Airborne Division. Browning remained in North Africa where he assumed the role of Airborne Advisor to the Allied Force Headquarters.

This change of command was destined to have a dramatic effect on the overall airborne plan and that of the role of the 1st Battalion GPR within it. Major General Hopkinson was a strong advocate of the assault glider as a new 'wooden Excalibur' that should be at the forefront of the role of airborne forces. Prior to the formation of airborne forces in Britain, he had been an amateur glider pilot, learning to fly while working in the oil fields of the Middle East. He was a dynamic character with an impressive Airborne pedigree that stretched back to the beginning of the war when he had formed and commanded No. 3 British Air Mission during the 1940 campaign in France, its role being the gathering of intelligence and reporting back to Headquarters Advanced Air Striking Force. The Mission was later redesignated No. 1 GHQ Reconnaissance Unit, this subsequently being changed to Phantom GHQ Liaison Regiment.

On 31 October 1941, Hopkinson assumed command of the fledgling 31st Independent Brigade Group when it shed its complement of mules and re-roled as 31st Airlanding Brigade – ultimately being re-designated 1st Airlanding Brigade. During his tenure as the brigade's commander, he preached the airlanding gospel with missionary zeal to all who would listen to him. He also underwent parachute training; unfortunately he later dislocated his neck on a practice jump and thereafter vowed to stick to gliding.

By the time he assumed command of 1st Airborne Division, Hopkinson was well known as an ardent exponent of the advantages of the use of gliders over delivery of troops by parachute. He was determined that 1st Airlanding Brigade should be blooded for the first time as part of the Sicily landings and, as the divisional commander, was in the perfect position to ensure that the gliders and infantry of his old brigade would be in the vanguard of the invasion of Sicily. The move by Montgomery to break the stagnant malaise that he felt afflicted the HUSKY plan would present Hopkinson with the opportunity he desired.

Montgomery's plan to land both task forces on parallel beachheads within reach of each other created another potential use for the British and American airborne formations. He argued that condensing the frontage of the entire operation would allow his brigades and divisions to offer each other mutual support, and that the resulting concentration would direct a more dynamic force against the Axis defences. Very familiar with the realities of modern warfare, he also highlighted a critical weakness in the draft plans to land close to Palermo and Messina – primarily an absence of air cover over the landings. Allied fighter cover could not be projected over the beachheads from Malta or the established North African airfields while Messina, in particular, was well within range of German and Italian aircraft. Lack of air cover would render the beachheads extremely vulnerable and dramatically hinder the ability of Allied naval forces to maintain supplies to the proposed beachheads. The grim spectres of the debacles of Dunkirk, Dieppe and Crete loomed large in recent British military memory. An army without effective air and naval support would not exist for long.

Montgomery continually opposed any version of the HUSKY plan that separated the Eastern and Western Task Forces over what he considered unworkable distances and terrain. Believing that the staff assembled at Task Force 141 lacked experience and that his superior, Alexander, was a 'fence sitter', he argued for the appointment of a single commanding general on the ground. Buoyed by his victory in North Africa, he believed he had the necessary experience and drive to take sole command of the Allied invasion force in Sicily. Convinced that the early plans were flawed he wrote in typically forthright style to Alexander:

> Planning to date has been on the assumption that resistance will be slight and Sicily will be captured easily. Never was there a greater error. Germans and Italians are fighting well in Tunisia and will repeat the process in Sicily. If we work on the assumption of little resistance, and disperse our effort as is being done in all planning to date, we will merely have a disaster. We must plan for fierce resistance, by the Germans at any rate, and for a real dogfight battle to follow the initial assault.[3]

With the fighting in Tunisia drawing to a close, Montgomery and the staff of Eighth Army began to work up their own alternate HUSKY plan, which envisaged both Allied armies making amphibious landings on the south coast of Sicily. These would be made under the protective umbrella of Allied fighter aircraft based on Malta. The US Seventh Army would land and concentrate along a 20-mile front between the towns of Licata and Gela, thus placing the Americans' beachhead in the centre of the southern coastline where they would be in a position to seize Italian airfields. The British Eighth Army, meanwhile, would land 50 miles to the east on the south-eastern tip of the island. The British invasion assault brigades would establish beachheads along the 35-mile long strip of coast between the ancient port of Syracuse and the small town of Pachino.

In spite of the distance that Montgomery's plan placed between the invading troops and the city of Messina, it was underpinned with sound military logic. The proposed beachheads were within reach of Allied air cover and therefore viable for naval re-supply and naval gunfire support. Moreover, once the beachheads were secure, the lead elements of both invading armies would be within striking distance of much-needed Italian airfields. With these airfields in Allied hands, fighter endurance over the island and range across the wider Mediterranean would be dramatically increased. The denial of these airfields to Axis squadrons would also reduce the reach of Italian and German aircraft that were currently operating against Malta and Allied shipping in the Mediterranean.

Montgomery's influence over the plan grew as the months passed and D-Day drew ever nearer. In the absence of firm direction from Eisenhower and his deputy, Alexander, the headquarters of US Seventh Army and their British and Canadian counterparts in Eighth Army continued to work up their own separate plans. This lack of overall co-ordination and firm leadership inevitably hindered progress toward the formulation of a robust and cohesive plan.

Frustrated with what he viewed as indecision and inefficiency, Montgomery set about selling his plan to Alexander and ultimately to Eisenhower. In broad outline he intended to push his Eighth Army rapidly north from its beachhead up the island's east coast. His intention was that this direct thrust along the heavily defended and well-fortified coast road would capture Messina and trap the Italian Sixth Army on the island with its German supporting divisions. As the battle progressed north on the coast road, the US Seventh Army under General George Patton would move in parallel, shielding the British left flank. Montgomery's plan, however, would depend on Patton keeping any counter-attack at bay while the British drove hard for Messina. Once the American spearhead reached the north coast, the island would be cut in half and all enemy forces to the west trapped with no port from which to evacuate. Such a threat to the Axis escape route across the straits of Messina would immediately undermine the position of the Axis forces facing the Eighth Army.

Montgomery's plan envisaged the British and Canadian forces pushing north out of their bridgeheads crossing the Catania Plain, seizing key ports and airfields as they went and capturing the towns of Syracuse, Augusta and Catania. The axis of advance to each, however, involved crossing a series of rivers and analysis of the terrain revealed that there were a number of natural obstacles that could be utilised to great effect by even a half-hearted defender to disrupt and delay the advance on Messina.

Immediately after landing, the Eighth Army would have to push out from its beaches to capture the first of its objectives: the port of Syracuse. The River Anapo and the Mammaiabica Canal crossed the route from the beaches to the town and its vital harbour. The coastal road that would be the axis of Eighth Army's advance north crossed the twin water obstacles by means of two connected bridges known as the Ponte Grande. Located two miles south-west of the town, it was a significant feature with a combined span of 600 yards. The prospect of the Ponte Grande being blown, and a well-established defence line being formed using the natural line of the river and the canal, was not an attractive one. Any setback at the first hurdle after the initial landing would pin the invasion force down, potentially adding weeks or even months to the campaign, and so the Ponte Grande would thus have to be seized intact in advance of the seaborne landings. The rivers further north presented similar challenges to the Eighth Army planners and their counterparts in Task Force 141.

The capture of this series of river crossings in advance of the Eighth Army's thrust north was identified as a potential task for airborne forces. Until now, the British had only used parachute forces on a meaningful scale; gliders had not even been used extensively during exercises in England. If Montgomery did make his voice heard and the Sicily plan was re-shaped, it appeared likely that it would be the parachute brigades that would be committed to battle first. With few commanders understanding the technicalities and logistics of employing airborne forces, it was however difficult at this stage to predict what level of airborne involvement would be required.

During April, Montgomery visited both Alexander and Eisenhower personally in attempts to persuade them to modify the HUSKY plan and focus all staff effort on the invasion of Sicily. Although he was given no written direction to the effect, the Eighth Army commander came away from both meetings under the impression that he had won the argument. He believed that he had persuaded Eisenhower and his deputy that his consolidated landing plan was the only way to approach the Sicily invasion. He was also convinced that he should be given overall command of both the Eastern and Western Task Forces.

It was on Saint George's Day, 3 April 1943, as the 1st Battalion GPR was disembarking at Mers El Kebir, that Montgomery visited the headquarters of Task Force 545 in Cairo. He had come to be briefed in detail on the outline Sicily plan by his own Chief of Staff, Major General Sir Francis de Guingand CB, DSO. The Cairo briefing heightened Montgomery's concern; he was further horrified by what he saw and heard of the proposed operation. The next day, exasperated by the whole HUSKY mess, he nailed his colours firmly to the mast and made a high risk and controversial gamble. Putting his considerable reputation at stake he signalled Alexander, informing him that if the plan remained in its present form, he would take no part in it. Amid the resulting storm of controversy generated by his ultimatum, Montgomery directed his staff to begin detailed planning to support his concept of HUSKY – a blitzkrieg-style drive north along the coast road and across the Catania Plain, punching through to Messina.

On that same day, oblivious of Montgomery's ultimatum and the resulting high level friction taking place in Algiers and Cairo, the men of 1st Battalion GPR were arriving at Tizi. Like chess pieces on a board, other events were also falling into place around them. Unbeknown to the glider pilots, the first consignment of 500 crated WACO CG-4A gliders was being unloaded on to the dock side at Oran; at the same time, a handful of American-piloted WACOs were approaching Algerian airfields after a lengthy flight from Ghana. Individually these events were insignificant but as a whole they would result in the propelling of the 1st Battalion GPR to the forefront of Operation HUSKY.

Regardless of the outcome of Montgomery's gamble, or whichever plan was finally adopted for Operation HUSKY, the date and the objective had been set and preparations were already underway. Aware that Axis intelligence would identify Sicily as the Allies' most likely next objective, the British mounted a deception operation to convince the Axis high command that Sicily was not about to be invaded. The Allies realised that any significant German reinforcement of the Italian Sixth Army that garrisoned Sicily would dramatically reduce their chances of success. A German armoured counter-attack launched against a still-forming and fragile beachhead was the nightmare scenario that haunted the planners. Sicily was, however, a very obvious potential objective that even the most inept Axis intelligence analyst would include in his analysis of Allied intentions.

Less than a week after the Cairo briefing on 30 April 1943, the Royal Navy submarine HMS *Seraph* surfaced off the coast of neutral Spain, near the port of Huevla. The British have a long and successful history of clandestine operations designed to deceive their enemies, and Operation MINCEMEAT would prove to be one of the most spectacular.

Under cover of darkness a specially selected and carefully prepared corpse dressed in the uniform of a major of the Royal Marines was slipped over the side of the submarine. According to the identity documents it carried, the body was that of Major William Martin, a courier who had perished when the aircraft in which he was travelling had been forced to ditch in the sea. The meticulous preparation of the body, its clothing and personal effects, added credibility to the falsified Top Secret documents in a briefcase attached to 'Major Martin's' body. These were designed to convince the German High Command that the Allies, aware that Sicily was such an obvious target, intended to mount only a diversionary attack on the island. They also suggested that the Allies intended to carry out their main offensive further afield in the form of large-scale amphibious landings on the island of Sardinia and the southern coast of Greece.

As was intended, the pro-German Spanish authorities soon discovered Major Martin and reported the find to Adolf Clauss, the son of the German consul and the resident agent of the Abwehr, the German military intelligence service, in Huelva. The documents were copied by the Germans and the information in them transmitted swiftly to Berlin where it was analysed by German intelligence. In spite of some suspicion among senior German commanders, the information was judged genuine by Hitler and many of his closest aides. Consequently, a significant number of German divisions were re-deployed to positions in Sardinia and Greece, their deployments being monitored by the British via ULTRA intercepts. Some weeks later in May, Winston Churchill was informed, 'Mincemeat swallowed whole'. As a direct result of this highly successful operation, the German presence on Sicily remained at only two divisions.

Meanwhile, Major General Hopkinson travelled all over North Africa gathering information on possible tasks and objectives for 1st Airborne

Division, so much so that his extended absences from his headquarters at such an important time attracted much comment and speculation. Events would show, however, that he was determined to influence the structure of the evolving plan. Lieutenant Colonel George Chatterton shared the opinion of many of the divisional staff as to the motivation for Hopkinson's continual absences:

> There had been no sign of General Hopkinson, the divisional commander, for weeks! General Browning had also lost him. I found out afterwards that Browning had waited in North Africa for as long as he was allowed, in order to discuss the impending operation with General Hopkinson, but the latter had kept out of General Browning's way.[4]

The absence of Hopkinson on the particular occasion referred to by Chatterton is worthy of closer scrutiny. Hopkinson had left British shores in March as the brigade commander of 1st Airlanding Brigade with Major General 'Boy' Browning as his immediate superior as commander of 1st British Airborne Division. The responsibilities of commanding the division, however, extended beyond those normally expected of an officer commanding a formation of that size. Indeed, experience had already proved that there was a real need for an air planning staff separate from the divisional headquarters.

All through his tenure as divisional commander, Browning had lobbied hard for an independent 'Commander Air' and a staff of officers to support him. He had found the constant demands of developing policy, doctrine and equipment for the newly formed airborne forces a continual distraction for himself and his staff. He drafted a series of papers and reports arguing for a new headquarters that would deal with all of these issues while the divisional commander and his staff focused entirely on directing day-to-day operations. The experience of 1st Parachute Brigade during the 1942 campaign in Tunisia reinforced further the argument for a higher airborne command echelon and so, on his return from a visit to the brigade in January 1943, Browning pressed even harder for the establishment of it. He appears to have implemented the proposed new command structure on an unofficial basis, thus giving Hopkinson a licence to roam and develop his own plans.

Approval for a 'Headquarters Major General Airborne Forces' finally came on 1 May 1943, coinciding with approval for the establishment of a second British airborne formation in England: the 6th Airborne Division. It was no surprise to anybody in Airborne circles when the post of Major General Airborne Forces went to Browning while the vacated appointment of General Officer Commanding (GOC) 1st Airborne Division and promotion to major general went to Hopkinson who officially assumed command on 6 May 1943.

Hopkinson wasted little time in seeking an audience with Montgomery, meeting the latter at the headquarters of Task Force 141 in Algiers on 7 May

1943. The latter was flushed with success, having at last secured approval for a dramatic remodelling of the HUSKY plan to conform to his concept of parallel Anglo/US landings. The Eighth Army drive across the Catania Plain was on. Seizing the opportunity, Hopkinson pounced. Already well-briefed on the airborne element of HUSKY, and determined to ensure a prestigious role for his gliderborne troops in the first Allied assault on occupied Europe, he arrived well-prepared for the meeting.

By this stage, the plans for use of 1st Airborne Division had already evolved into three separate, consecutive operations. Paratroops were to be dropped ahead of the advancing armour of Eighth Army, seizing crossings over the rivers barring the route north across the Catania Plain. This three-phase plan bears remarkable similarities to the ill-fated Operation MARKET GARDEN of 1944 and consisted of an airborne carpet of troops that would allow the Eighth Army to cross all of the major obstacles unopposed. If this phase was successful, Eighth Army would maintain its momentum and drive through to Messina as planned. The three operations were codenamed and scheduled as follows:

1. Operation LADBROKE – 9 July 1943, the night before D-Day, objective – Seize the Ponte Grande Bridge, spanning the River Anapo and the Mammaiabica canal. Also capture the port of Syracuse.
2. Operation GLUTTON – 10/11 July 1943, a night operation to capture Augusta and the main road bridge over the River Mulinello.
3. Operation FUSTIAN – Date and time to be set by speed of the Eighth Army advance. Objective – seize the Ponte Primasole Bridge over the River Stimeto south of Catania.

With some justification, Hopkinson advised against the use of parachute troops at night in a coup de main role. Exploiting his new role as the senior airborne commander in Eighth Army, he counselled Montgomery against the risk of a scattered drop of paratroops failing to regroup quickly enough and in sufficient force to seize their allotted objectives with any element of surprise. He then proposed that the prestigious and vital task of mounting Operation LADBROKE should be given to 1st Airlanding Brigade, now commanded by Brigadier Philip 'Pip' Hicks DSO, MC. Arguing that a gliderborne landing would deliver a concentrated force of airborne troops directly on to their objectives, he convinced Montgomery to amend the plan. It was also decided that 2nd and 1st Parachute Brigades would carry out the two later operations respectively. Montgomery left the meeting convinced that the use of gliderborne troops on Operation LADBROKE offered the greatest chance of success.

It is now clear that Hopkinson's overwhelming desire to prove his gliderborne force in battle had clouded his judgement. The original concept for the plan using parachute brigades had been overseen by Browning who, in spite of his own enthusiasm for glider forces, was unlikely to have approved the use of airlanding troops on LADBROKE. He was very aware of the lack of relative experience within The Glider Pilot Regiment and of the shortage of gliders to carry out a landing. British paratroops however had proven themselves in Europe and North Africa; but 1st Airlanding Brigade could only cite the disastrous Operation FRESHMAN as an example of a previous glider operation. Regardless of this, it would appear that Hopkinson was convinced that Sicily would be the ideal proving ground for airlanding troops and his glider pilots.

It is exceptionally difficult to track the exact movements of both Airborne major generals during this period, but there is a wealth of anecdotal evidence that suggests that Hopkinson avoided Browning deliberately for weeks before and after the meeting with Montgomery. Eventually, Browning had to return to England to assume his new appointment, leaving his successor free to implement his own plans. Dr John Greenacre included this assessment of Hopkinson in his thesis on the development of airborne forces:

> During the planning for Operation HUSKY, Hopkinson bypassed the chain of command and approached Montgomery personally in order to try to ensure the participation of his Division during the invasion of Sicily. Despite having commanded an airlanding brigade for eighteen months, Hopkinson's appreciation of the requirements of a mass airborne landing was low. The airborne collective training establishment in Britain had yet to reach the stage where brigade level exercises could be practised. The training available to the glider pilots, in particular in North Africa prior to HUSKY, was insufficient to prepare them adequately for the operation ...[5]

With Montgomery's approval secured for the first ever large-scale British glider operation that he so wanted to see launched, Hopkinson returned to his own headquarters at Mascara where he now had to turn his concept into reality. He and his staff now had to plan LADBROKE in which the gliders and infantry of 1st Airlanding Brigade would spearhead the assault. This was demanding much of Brigadier 'Pip' Hicks and his men, and the successful execution of the operation would hinge on the ability of Lieutenant Colonel George Chatterton's glider pilots. The post-operational report compiled by Chatterton in August 1943 gives a critical insight into the state of preparedness of the 1st Battalion GPR on its arrival in North Africa, just a few weeks before the Ladbroke decision:

> On the 23rd April 1943, 240 pilots of The Glider Pilot Regiment arrived in North Africa. They had been at sea for 12 days and had been awaiting postings for one month. They had not flown for six weeks prior to embarkation. Thus their flying state was deplorable in that they stepped ashore without having been in an aircraft for at least three months. Added to this was the fact that there were no aircraft to fly in North Africa, which was very depressing for the pilots. Nevertheless, they

had been given the basic training of very highly disciplined soldier and were able to interest themselves by military training.[6]

Notes

1. C.C.S. 171/2/D, dated 23 January 1943.
2. Montgomery, Lieutenant General, B.L., Signal 18 AG/MA 126, dated 19 March 1943 to HQ TF 141.
3. Montgomery, Lieutenant General, B.L.
4. Chatterton, Lieutenant Colonel, G., *The Wings of The Pegasus*, p. 40.
5. Greenacre, J.W., *The Development of Britain's Airborne Forces during the Second World War* (Ph.D. Thesis, University of Leeds, 2008), p. 196.
6. Report by Commanding Officer The Glider Pilot Regiment, dated 2 August 1943.

Chapter 4

The Wings of Icarus

If at the end of that time you still think that this is too difficult, you can consider yourself relieved of your command.

In the last week of April 1943, there was one event that had a positive impact way out of proportion to its practical significance on the morale of the advance party at Froha. Literally out of the blue, a lone glider-tug combination appeared on the horizon. The glider was a single USAAF CG-4A WACO flown by Lieutenant Allen, a USAAF glider pilot. In response to orders from the US chain of command, he had flown the only serviceable Allied glider in Africa under tow from a C-47 transport 3,600 miles from the west coast of North Africa, across the Western Sahara to Algeria. Following his arrival, this intrepid officer was soon operating from Thiersville airfield where he gave a few selected pilots of 1st Battalion GPR their first taste of flying the WACO. The delivery of this first glider was the final chapter in what was a saga in itself for the USAAF.

The story began on 24 March 1943 with the arrival by sea of a shipment of CG-4A WACOs at the Ghanaian port of Accra. When the need for troop carrying gliders in Algeria became urgent, American pilots and ground crew were despatched to assemble the shipment and ferry them back to Algeria. However, on arrival, the Americans found the crated gliders to be in a very poor state due to poor maintenance and penetration of the crates by sea water. Most of them were not safe to fly.

It was not until a month later, on 23 April, that four WACOs were assembled from the crates and put into the air. Soon there was more good news. The first consignment of 500 gliders had arrived by sea direct from America. Over a period of days, 50 dismantled WACOs were loaded into crates at docks across North Africa and then moved by road to a USAAF maintenance airfield at Blida outside Oran where USAAF personnel would assemble the gliders. It would be at least a week before the news of the crated gliders would filter through the US/British chain of command to the headquarters of 1st Battalion GPR in Mascara. Problems with the passage of information remained a problem in the North Africa theatre; difficulties with all forms of communication plagued the build-up to Operation HUSKY. Distances were large, terrain was difficult and weather was an unpredictable variable.

As the end of April 1943 approached, the target for the forthcoming operation remained a secret to most. The appearance of Lieutenant Allen and his lone glider from Ghana, followed by news of the crated WACOs, had at least let one proverbial cat out of bag; speculation and rumour abounded. The total absence of British gliders in North Africa and the apparent abundance of crated US WACOs seemed to suggest only one thing: The Glider Pilot Regiment was about to add a new aircraft to its inventory. The pilots of Nos. 2 and 3 Squadrons were now sure that they would be flying the 'Cargo Glider 4A WACO' to their target. Speculation, rumour and counter rumour would, of course, continue about where exactly their objective might be.

The assembly of a single WACO, even with the assistance of tractors and cranes, was estimated to take 30 men a complete day. There were, however, further complications as the parts and major sub-assemblies for each glider were split between five separate crates. Due to poor marking and a lack of logistic control, the crates had been shipped to six different ports across North Africa and then further dispersed when moved by road to one of three USAAF engineering depots for assembly. Confusion reigned from the outset, compounded by the poor marking of the crates, with one depot receiving deliveries of all of the tail units and another all of the nose units. This failure was attributed to the inexperience of the companies building the gliders under contract in America.

Oblivious at this point to the complications faced by the American mechanics assembling the crated gliders, Lieutenant Colonel Chatterton travelled to Algiers where he finally tracked down Major General Hopkinson who had sent for him. While en route, Chatterton was well aware that his superior was keeping a low profile and that Browning, unable to loiter any longer in North Africa, had been forced to return to England. There are no official minutes of the meeting, only the following account recorded retrospectively by Chatterton:

> I met him as arranged. He was in splendid form and had obviously pulled off something that pleased him. 'Hoppy', as he was affectionately called, was an amusing little man. Very short with black wavy hair, he was very ambitious and delighted at having been made up to a General.
>
> He had, I felt, pulled a fast one on General Browning in avoiding him in North Africa, and I wondered, as I waited for him to send for me, just what he had been up to. I was more than certain that he had committed the Glider Force to something and he most certainly had!
>
> 'Well George,' he greeted me. 'It's nice to see you. I have a very interesting operation for you to study.' I looked at him and wondered what on earth was coming next.

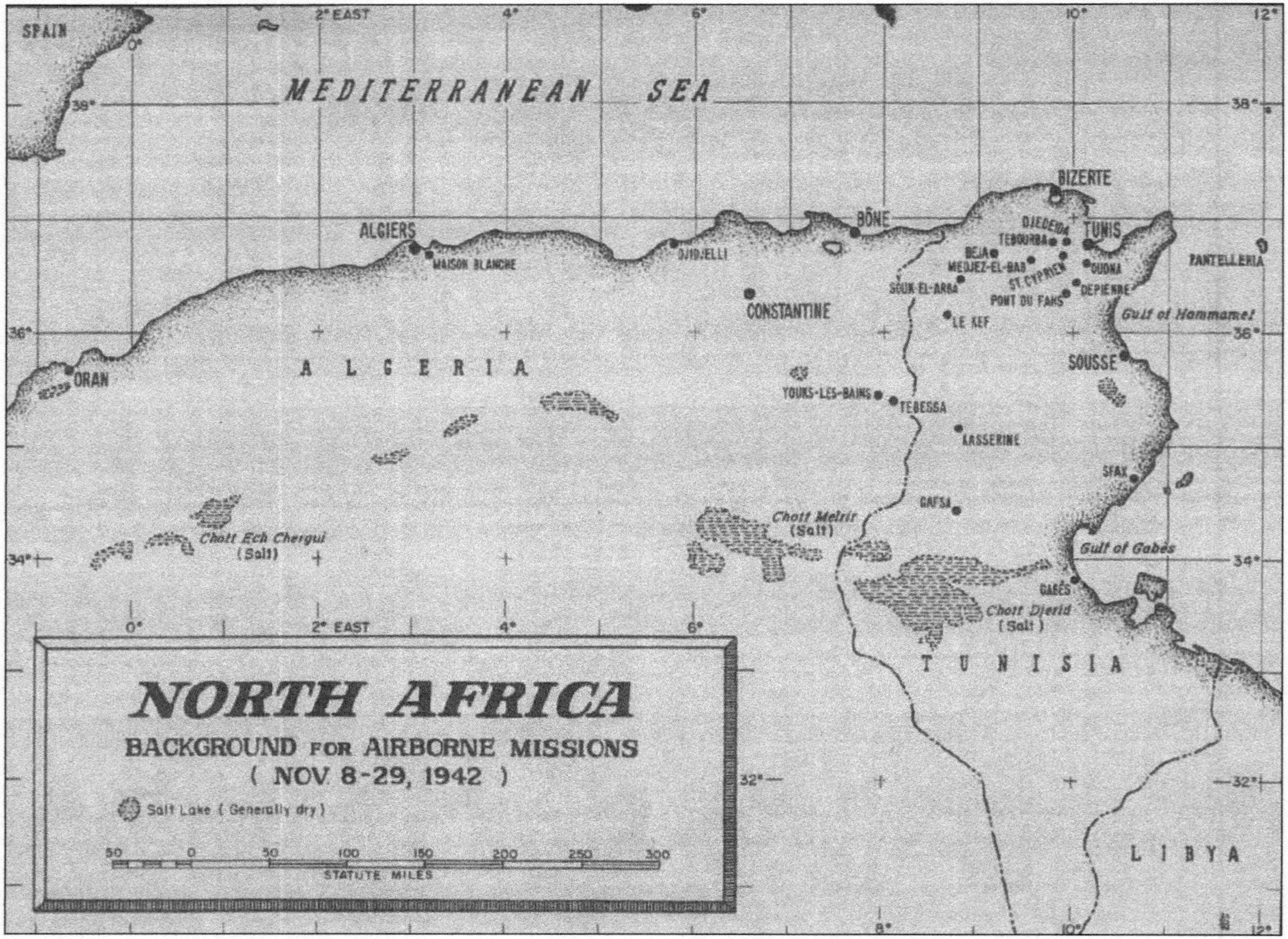

USAAF map of North African theatre of operations

'I've been to see General Montgomery,' he continued, 'and he has agreed to use the 1st Airborne Division on a night assault on Sicily.' I held my breath. I did not like the sound of the developments.

He motioned me to a map of the island that was hanging on the wall.

'I have agreed to land the Airlanding Brigade on the night of 9th/10th July on the beaches in the neighbourhood of Syracuse. Another force of parachutists will be dropped at Catania, and a further force, supported by a glider squadron at Augusta.'

I made a quick calculation ... There was roughly about three [two] months left; no time at all, when one considered there were no airstrips, tugs or gliders.

'Now, let us have a look at these photographs.' And he leaned over a table on which were a number of aerial photographs of the Sicilian beaches. I looked at them and, to my horror, saw that they were rock-strewn with cliffs and that the fields had stone walls.

'Well,' said the General, looking hard at me, 'What do you think?'

I hesitated a moment and then said, 'You know, sir, that the pilots have had no flying practice for at least three months, and little or no experience of night flying at all.'

'Oh,' replied the General, 'We will soon put that right. The US Air Force are going to supply tugs and gliders.'

'American gliders?' I asked incredulously.

'Yes, what difference will that make?'

'Difference sir? Why they hardly know our own gliders, let alone American!'

'Well, you'll have to put up with it, won't you,' he said in some heat.[1]

After further discussion about the proposed glider landing zones, Chatterton's concern and obvious lack of enthusiasm for the whole plan triggered an outburst from Hopkinson who rounded angrily on his subordinate:

> Now look here, Colonel Chatterton, I'm going to leave you for half an hour, and in that time you can study the photographs. If at the end of that time you still think that this is too difficult, you can consider yourself relieved of your command ... Half an hour. You see? I shall then return.[2]

Alone in the room, Chatterton was faced with an 'appalling situation'. His glider pilots, whether kicking their heels in the Tizi camp or still awaiting orders in England, had very little flying experience. They were not trained to land troops in darkness and, as yet, had no experience at all of flying in the Mediterranean heat. If he refused to accept Hopkinson's apparently 'mad' plan and was removed from post, who would replace him? With the flying hours he had amassed in the RAF prior to his crash, he was by far the most experienced officer and pilot in his regiment. The remainder of his officers had no more flying hours than the SNCO pilots under their command:

> The minutes ticked by as I paced up and down and finally I made up my mind that at all costs I must stand by the men, despite the fact that I considered the plan to be mad. The whole situation was astounding, and I felt sure that it had been 'sold' to Monty, with the best salesman's manner, that airborne troops had to be used at all costs, otherwise they might never be used at all!

Having calmed down, Hopkinson went to the room 30 minutes later and the continued presence of Chatterton signalled the latter's assent to the plan. After a brief silence the two men focused on the maps and photographs:

> We continued to discuss the pros and cons. He was like a little boy, he was so pleased.[3]

With the dramatic meeting in Algiers over, Chatterton set off back to his own headquarters in Mascara to begin planning for the operation. Before returning there, however, he visited the La Senia airstrip where, so he had been told by officers from the US Military Air Command, the Americans had delivered gliders for British use. He was relieved to find large packing crates containing gliders scattered across the desert strip. One of his first actions on his return to Mascara was to order the deployment of 50 pilots from Tizi to the airstrip where they set about unpacking the crates and assembling whatever gliders were available for flight. One of their number later described the scene that greeted the small group as they arrived at the airstrip, his description giving a hint of the atmosphere at the time:

> Planes were landing throwing up red dust, hundreds of trucks seemed to be driving about ... more dust ... and no one seemed to be in charge of anything except their own little activity. We hung about for a while and some of the officers tried to find where the WACOs were. After about two hours, we discovered that they were quite close by on the edge of a mass of stores including a lot of tyres. One of the American ground technicians servicing C-47s, a corporal, was sent to help us ... not that he knew much about gliders but he was one of those guys who could turn his hand to anything requiring a spanner. He brought a crowbar to open the first crate and, glory be, there was a handbook inside showing all the parts and how to put them together, and a set of tools for every glider! You'd never have got that with a British issue.[4]

Having examined an assembled WACO, the pilots discovered it to be a totally different aircraft to the Hotspur and Horsa gliders with which they were familiar. The most significant difference was size and capability. The

Horsa was designed around the requirement to carry a platoon of 28 fully equipped infantrymen on to the battlefield. Alternatively, it could carry a Jeep and either a 75mm pack howitzer or 6-pounder anti-tank gun together with its crew. This capability was considered essential to the conduct of airborne operations and it was the first Commanding Officer of The Glider Pilot Regiment, Lieutenant Colonel John Rock, who had stressed this lift requirement during the Horsa's design stages. He had realised that the primary advantage of landing troops by glider, rather than by parachute, was that they would land together as a formed body ready to fight. The Horsa was designed and built around his thinking.

The WACO, on the other hand, was very different in concept and design.

The Weaver Aircraft Company (WACO) of Troy, Ohio, had designed and manufactured the Cargo Glider 4A in response to a statement of requirement from the USAAF issued in April 1941. General Henry 'Hap' Arnold had influenced the thinking that would ultimately lead to the production of the CG-4A, envisaging a glider that was designed and built around a specialist Jeep:

> I would like very much to have a small light Jeep constructed ... to carry two men and have light armour and guns. This Jeep should be designed and constructed with a view to fitting wings to it so that we can take off as a glider and drop as a glider. Having dropped as a glider, it lands on a field somewhere, sheds its wings and goes around as a Jeep.[5]

Production of the WACO began in 1941, the first airframes being delivered in April 1942. It was one of the most significant aircraft programmes of the Second World War; by the end of the conflict almost 14,000 had been built. A total of 13,909 gliders were manufactured by sixteen contractors, making the WACO the fourth most-produced American aircraft of the war. The Ford Motor Company produced 4,190 of the total alone. Each glider cost $18,800 to produce.

By the end of the war the Air Ministry would deliver 750 WACOs to The Glider Pilot Regiment. Naming the aircraft the WACO initially caused a problem; early War Diary and pilot log book entries refer to the WACO as a 'Wako'. To this day many old glider pilots still refer to the CG-4A as the 'Whacko'. This situation was further complicated by the Air Ministry designating the aircraft in British service as the 'Hadrian'. To avoid confusion the CG-4A will be referred to here as the WACO from this point forward.

The aircraft was a strut-braced, high-wing monoplane that was capable of carrying more than its own unladen weight. The wings, two spars and ribs were made of wood, the surface a thin sheet of plywood covered with fabric. The elevators were fabric-covered only, while the wings had elliptical tips and no dihedral. The fuselage was a welded steel tube frame covered with doped fabric while the floor was of honeycomb plywood, a fabricating technique that gave strength and rigidity with little weight. The plywood structure was reinforced under the margins of the floor that bore the load of the Jeep wheels. As simply constructed as it appeared, the WACO nonetheless comprised over 70,000 individual parts.

Although the crates on the desert airstrips did not contain the futuristic weapon system imagined by General Hap Arnold, the WACO's designers had indeed built the aircraft around the Jeep. The glider featured a unique system to allow the vehicle to go into action immediately after landing. After the Jeep was loaded and rigged inside the glider, a cable and pulley system was attached to its rear bumper. The method of unloading the vehicle was simple. Prior to or immediately after landing, the Jeep driver would start the engine; as he did so, the other passengers de-rigged the vehicle by cutting or releasing the straps that secured the load during flight. As soon as practicable after landing, the two glider pilots disembarked from the aircraft, leaving the Jeep driver clear to move his vehicle slowly forward toward the cockpit. The nose section of the glider was attached to the fuselage by hinges; as the Jeep moved forward, the cable attached to the rear bumper came into play and pulled the nose of the glider upward. As it rose, the vehicle's wheels simultaneously pushed down a pair of ramps that allowed it to negotiate the drop from the fuselage to terra firma. There was no requirement for the crew to unhitch the cable from the rear bumper as this happened automatically, as did the locking of the nose section in the raised position. This unloading process could be completed in seconds with a well-drilled crew, and was certainly faster and less complicated than unloading the British Horsa Mk 1.

Any concerns about the potential shortcomings of the WACO had to be put aside. Time was short and Lieutenant Colonel Chatterton, in order to get his pilots into the air quickly, desperately needed whatever gliders were available. His immediate dispatch of 50 pilots to reinforce the 1st Battalion GPR's advance party at La Senia Airfield was the first step toward producing the glider force required to carry out General Hopkinson's plan. The battalion's war diary contains the following entry for 8 May 1943:

> ... On the following day the remainder of the personnel arrived, making a total of 60 pilots. This party started work immediately on the assembly of Wako gliders.[6]

Staff Sergeant Mike Hall remembered his first reaction when he saw the crated WACOs:

> When I saw the first WACO I was not impressed. They were delivered in enormous packing crates like a prefab house, in bits with assembly instructions and we were given the job, in the sweltering heat and some sand storms, to assemble them fit for flying.[7]

The pilots in the advance party were left to unpack the gliders without some technical supervision while a small group of USAAF mechanics were put in charge of the ad-hoc production line at La Senia. Armed with the CG-4A technical manual, they and their glider pilot apprentices set about unpacking the huge crates. Sergeant Norman Howes was with C Company, 2nd Battalion The South Staffordshire Regiment, one of the units of 1st Airlanding Brigade. He watched the pilots working on the glider assembly line with interest and later remembered the American mechanics clearly:

> I also remember fatigue parties being sent to a local aerodrome where the WACOs were being assembled by black American Air Force men. They came in great big crates, about the size of a very large room. And these crates were afterwards being used as living accommodation by these American Air Force men. I remember this black aircraftsman assembling one of these WACOs with a spanner and some sticking plaster and he looked at us and he said, 'Are you's the guys who's gonna fly in this thing?' We said, 'We think so, yes'. And he rolled his great big eyes to heaven as if to say God help you, he was right too.
>
> The glider pilots were there also. I think that they were doing the technical part of the assembly of these WACOs, or sometimes they're called Hadrian gliders. And, of course, as we were getting acclimatised, so were the Glider Pilots.[8]

Within a matter of days, the first assembled gliders were being towed away for test flights by USAAF pilots. Meanwhile, Chatterton's men and the American mechanics had developed an efficient routine. Avoiding the hottest part of the day, they started work at first light in the relative cool of the morning; when the heat of the day or dust storms became unbearable they withdrew to the shelter of the WACO crates in which they were living. Later in the afternoon, when the sun was lower in the sky and the temperature reduced, they returned to their duties. Sergeant Bob Boyce was among them:

> I had begun to wonder if we would ever fly again. Then came the news that some gliders had arrived from the United States and we were to go to the airfield at Oran to assemble them. The weather was pleasantly warm and we lived comfortably in the packing cases that had held the WACO gliders in transit. We began work on the assembly and learned to fly them from the airfield.[9]

In fifteen days the Anglo-US production line assembled 52 gliders that were then flown out of La Senia by USAAF pilots to the airfields at Relizane, Thiersville, Matamore and Froha. The 1st Battalion GPR war diary records the first test flight of the WACO made by a British pilot: 'The Commanding Officer made first flight in a WACO.'[10] This went without incident and

Lieutenant Colonel Chatterton later recorded his initial opinion of the American glider:

> It was entirely different from a Hotspur or Horsa, the British gliders, for whereas these were made of wood, the WACO was made of steel and fabric. Its glide was flat and the whole scheme of flight was different. It was dual-controlled, with a large cockpit capable of carrying thirteen men or one Jeep. The nose lifted up so that the load could be run out of the glider, and it could land on a fixed undercarriage or on skids. It was a pleasant aircraft to fly and handled very easily.[11]

The American vision of an airborne force anticipated the fielding of a 10,000 strong glider fleet, but the training of sufficient pilots to fly this huge number of aircraft against the Japanese in the Far East and the Germans in Europe would be a complex and time consuming process. Time was limited, however, and the US Army was desperate to field an airborne force as quickly as possible. The WACO had thus been designed to be extremely simple to fly, therefore reducing the content of the syllabus for student pilots and consequently shortening the time spent training them. Squadron Leader Lawrence Wright was an experienced glider pilot and one of the first RAF officers from the 38 Wing staff to encounter the WACO; he took a more critical view of it:

> The Hadrian [WACO] proved a disappointment, much inferior to the Horsa. It was easy to fly, in fact all too like a sailplane. But its flat glide and its want of airbrakes made it float on and on before landing, and though it had wheel brakes the run on was far too long. Its so called 'airbrakes' were in fact only spoil lifters above the wing, much less effective than big flaps or true air brakes, especially at high speeds. Side slipping was the routine remedy for an over high approach, but hardly to be recommended with a full load near the ground. The trimmer was awkwardly placed and was sometimes used in the wrong sense. There were no blind-flying instruments. The tail plane attachment was weak, for which reason a towing speed limit of 150 mph was imposed; no problem with the Dakota, but it was not easy to fly the Albemarle below that speed, and the narrow margin was a constant worry to both pilots.[12]

In contrast to the WACO, the Horsa had large flaps with a combined surface area of 116 square feet. These 'barn doors' enabled the pilot to execute rapid and steep descents, followed by a very short landing run. These performance characteristics made the Horsa ideal for the execution of pinpoint landings. The WACO, however, used air spoilers rather than flaps to interrupt airflow over its wings and consequently to lose height. Although an effective method of losing height, spoilers did not enable the pilot to make the steep, aggressive descents sometimes required in a combat situation.

There were other obvious differences in capability that caused immediate concern among the airborne hierarchy. The WACO was a smaller and less robust aircraft than its British counterpart. Payload was of course critical when planning an airborne operation; significantly the WACO had only half the volume and payload capacity of the Horsa. Staff Sergeant Mike Hall remained sceptical:

> The American glider called the WACO was vastly inferior to the Horsa. It had a wing span of 83 ft, length of 48 ft 4 ins and was made of steel tubing covered with fabric and a payload of 7,500 lbs against the 15,250 lbs of the stronger and longer Horsa which was made with a laminated wood construction.[13]

Even as the first WACOs were being put together at La Senia, the staff of Headquarters 1st Airlanding Brigade were already grappling with the issues presented by this dramatic reduction in capability. British airborne doctrine, training and planning prior to North Africa had been developed around the characteristics of the Horsa. which, as mentioned already, could carry a Jeep with a 6-pounder anti-tank gun or 75mm pack howitzer, together with its crew, or alternatively a platoon of 28 men. When deployed by WACO, the same loads had to be split between two gliders. There were also issues with the load-bearing capacity of the WACO cabin floor that created other weight related complications.

Among the units dependent on glider lift capacity were 1st Airlanding Brigade's vitally important units of the Royal Army Medical Corps; the absence of Horsa gliders created a real planning headache for them:

> ... The 181st (Airlanding) Field Ambulance was allotted six WACO gliders. This glider had only half the load capacity of the Horsa glider, and as the movement of the unit had been planned for the use of sixteen Horsas and equipment being designed accordingly, this drastic reduction by type and numbers meant complete reorganisation, involving the cutting down of transport and the breaking down of heavier equipment into man loads. In this the 16th (Parachute) Field Ambulance were able to advise as a result of their practical experience. As the transport was to be reduced to two jeeps, one two-stretcher trailer, two handcarts and three airborne bicycles, the ton of medical supplies was broken down mainly into individual loads of twenty-five pounds.[14]

These planning constraints, though serious, were as yet not prominent in the minds of most of the glider pilots sweating on the La Senia assembly line or those cooped up in Tizi. Well aware of the challenges ahead, Lieutenant

Colonel Chatterton and his battalion staff were working up a training syllabus and formulating a programme to run it. With the July deadline foremost in his thoughts, Chatterton had to find a way to convert his pilots on to a new aircraft, acclimatise them to flying in Africa, prepare them for a night flight over water and, after all of that, ensure they were capable of completing a tactical landing in darkness in enemy-held territory.

Help was at hand, however, as promised by Major General Hopkinson at the Algiers meeting, in the form of American glider pilots who arrived as flight instructors. Fresh from training themselves, the USAAF pilots had even less flying experience than their British counterparts but they knew the WACO extremely well and eagerly passed on their knowledge of the aircraft's characteristics. With the invasion only a month away, flying training had to commence as quickly as possible. The first pilots were in the air almost immediately after Chatterton's WACO test flight on 14 June 1943.

The Americans were drawn from a pool of 110 US glider pilots who were originally part of the US 316th Troop Carrier Group stationed initially near the Suez Canal in Egypt. They had subsequently been transferred to the 60th Troop Carrier Group in Algeria, where, due to a lack of gliders, they had been employed as co-pilots on C-47 transports. In between powered flights, a handful of them had managed to log some glider hours using French sports gliders at Relizon Airfield. These were towed into the air using Jeeps; after a dusty drive down the runway the pilot cast off from the tug at 200 feet and completed whatever rudimentary drills and exercises that could be achieved before landing.

Among the Americans was Flight Officer Sam Fine, a young New Yorker who was desperate to get into the war. He had volunteered to go to Ghana and fly one of the WACO gliders across Africa to Algeria. Not selected for the ferry flight, he felt 'left out' and immediately voiced his disappointment to his flight commander, reminding him that it was almost six months since he had flown a WACO The latter then gave Fine some good news; he had been chosen to join a group of 30 pilots who were going to convert British glider pilots on to the WACO, as he later recalled:

> So off we go, transferred to the British Glider Pilot Regiment ... In a desert field with runways made of metal strips. As an instructor, we had only one flight officer in the right seat and a British glider pilot in the left seat. After that we had to stand behind the pilots and reach over their shoulders to make any corrections. The British glider pilots would alternate seats after each flight.[15]

With Fine and other US pilots adding their weight to the training effort, the situation began to improve. Meanwhile, the pressing need for gliders eventually found its way through the bureaucracy of the Allied command structure. Additional USAAF fitters were deployed and began assembling gliders on the other airfields; production quickly climbed to twelve gliders a day. Crated gliders that had been scattered across airfields and docks all over North Africa, were identified, catalogued and then transported for assembly.

An initial training fleet of 20 gliders was taking shape when Lieutenant Colonel Chatterton took to the air again, this time at night. The 1st Battalion GPR war diary entry for 14 May 1943 recorded the event:

> The Commanding Officer made a night landing in a Wako, accompanied by Major J.W. Place, Major N.H. Leschallas, Captain T.A. Plowman and Lieutenant P.G. Harding. He used only two leading in lights to mark the commencement of the runway.[16]

The trial flight took place over La Senia airfield; Chatterton cast off from his tow at 2,000 feet and made an uneventful approach and landing. The moon state was so good that he compared the landing to flying in full daylight, his confidence boosted by the easy handling of the WACO and the visibility at night. He was concerned, however, about the densities of the dust generated by the tug aircraft during take-off and noted that his pilots would require practice to get used to this. A few days later, he made another flight as recorded in a second entry in the war diary for the evening of 18 May 1943. This involved a longer transit over the desert:

> The Commanding Officer, with Squadron Leader Musgrave as second pilot and the same passengers ... made a remote release of 10 miles over Mascara and made a successful night landing at Thiersville.[17]

The two night flying trials helped the Battalion Headquarters staff to develop the flying training syllabus for the WACO further and gave them the ability to divide the workload in the cockpit between the first and second pilot. The difficult decision as to who would fly as first pilot and who would take the second pilot's seat had already been made before training commenced. Squadron Leader Lawrence Wright recalled the logic behind the pairing of the crews shortly after receiving his first brief on the intended role of 1st Airlanding Brigade in Sicily:

> That gliders were to be used in this way was contrary to all we had learned to date, and to the lesson of Crete, especially with glider pilots trained to the present low standard. About five hundred of them had completed the Horsa course, but with some with so few hours flying that Chatterton had to divide them into first and second pilots, none of the latter being fully experienced even by day. About fifty such crews were resuming their training in Algeria and about sixty more to follow ...[18]

It was decided that the first pilot would handle the aircraft during take-off and landing, while the duties of the second pilot were now defined as:

1. All map reading, pin pointing and general navigation.
2. He must work spoilers and trimmers.
3. On the approach, he must read alternately speed and height until touch down.

The morning after the night flying trial, No. 3 Squadron began its move from La Senia to the airfield at La Relizane where it would be married up with the newly assembled WACOs. The activation of another airfield so soon after the first glider had been assembled was an indication that 1st Battalion GPR's capacity to train pilots was improving. The momentum was maintained; within days No. 3 Squadron was also operational and flying training at La Relizane was underway. A week later No. 2 Squadron was established on Froha Airfield and also putting its first training aircraft into the air. Flying operations at La Senia were closed down during the same week and all pilots who had been living there were moved over to the now active Matamore airfield. In addition, the airfield at Thiersville also began flying operations; this French airfield was to become the training field for the advanced phase of the WACO conversion programme.

Major John Place was the Officer Commanding No. 3 Squadron. He entered a detailed description of the living conditions at La Relizane Airfield, forty miles north east of Mascara:

> My squadron was detailed to go to another strip at Relizane ... where we found half a dozen WACOs waiting for us, and with them Lieutenant Allen. In the meantime our teams of WACO assemblers were sent to the coast to assist in the building of crated gliders. The name Relizane belonged to a small French-cum-Arab town which lay in a large flat bowl of fertile agricultural land over the mountains from Mascara. Three miles east of the town was the airfield. It consisted of a peacetime French colonial air base with permanent buildings and was occupied by the HQ of an American Air Transport Group, which later moved, leaving behind only sufficient staff to cope with the daily courier service to points east and west.
>
> The airfield consisted of a solitary strip or runway of earth and gravel, bordering on a main road which ran east to Algiers and west to Mascara and Oran. The only snag from the gliding point of view, was that a raised concrete aqueduct several feet high, ran from alongside the eastern end of the runway and then slanted south west away from the strip. The aqueduct wasn't going to help if some pilot undershot his approach, especially by night! However we were far too thrilled with our billets, which to us were luxurious after Tizi and Froha, to worry about things like aqueducts.[19]

The pilots of No. 3 Squadron at La Relizane faced a significant challenge. As well as commanding his squadron, Major Place had been allotted the role of Chief Flying Instructor at La Relizane. His orders were to convert a total of 60 crews on to the WACO by day and night within three weeks. There was, however, only a handful of gliders available for training at the start and even less trained ground crew. Lieutenant Allen of the USAAF was the only available technical expert on the new aircraft, while the British pilots had no experience on the operation or routine maintenance of the WACO. The 1st Battalion GPR war diary states that No. 3 Squadron had also detached the best part of its manpower to work on the assembly line at La Senia. In spite of the scale of the task, with the assistance of 51st US Troop Carrier Wing, La Relizane was operational as a training field within two days of the squadron's arrival. Eventually more American glider pilots arrived to act as instructors. In addition, the numbers of C-47 tugs flying in to take part in the flying programme increased every day:

> For the first week several of us went on every shift, averaging two hours sleep in every twenty-four hours, but we had to give that up. The average shade temperature in the daytime was round the 100 degree mark and at times exceeded 105 owing to the low lying country. The humidity was high, and at first caused everyone considerable discomfort. We also had more than our share of mosquitoes, which meant sweltering under a mosquito net during the hours of darkness if we were not on duty night flying. The night shifts had to endure the stinging pests as best they might, and hope that the daily quinine would protect them.
>
> We flew two shifts by day and two by night. The first day shift was from 0700 hours to 1200 hours when the heat and bumps in the air were so violent that we had to stop for a few hours. The second shift began at 1530 hours and ended at 1900 hours. The first night shift began at 2100 hours and finished at 0100 hours, when refreshments in the form of tea and sandwiches were brought to the tow line by the duty cook. The second night shift was from 0200 hours until 0600 hours.
>
> It was a rush against time every moment of the twenty-four hours for those on duty. How did the men stick it I can't think, but they did in spite of the heat, the flies and the mosquitoes, and I cannot remember a case of serious illness or strain. The same sort of work was going on at Froha, and except for a kinder temperature, but in conditions worse than our own. Though the heat may have been a few degrees less on average, the dust and the flies were infinitely worse, and everyone was under canvas. But the dust was the main trouble, Every time a tug and glider took off from Froha a great cloud of yellow dust as fine as flour spread over the whole camp.

> Nowhere could one escape it, it was in one's nose, one's eyes, ears, mouth and clothing and in the food, the water and bedding – everywhere.[20]

The shortage of gliders was the most significant cause for concern right through the month of May. By 5 May only eighteen out of 74 gliders delivered had been assembled and made available for flight. The situation had not improved much a few weeks later. A review on 25 May identified a total of 30 airworthy WACOs available for pilot training from a total of 240. It was about this time that the decision to use gliderborne troops to spearhead the British invasion of Sicily was taken. Almost immediately the shortage of gliders escalated from being viewed as a logistic problem to being categorised as an 'extreme emergency' by General Delmar H. Dutton, commander of XII USAAF Service Command, who directed that the servicing and assembly of WACO gliders was to take priority over ongoing work on P-38 Lightning fighters and other USAAF aircraft. In addition, experienced glider mechanics were detached from Troop Carrier Wing squadrons to increase production capacity at the Service Command depots. These positive measures coupled with a new sense of urgency had an immediate and dramatic effect on glider production. Just three weeks later the total number of WACOs available to 1st Airborne Division had risen to an impressive 346 serviceable airframes. In spite of this logistical feat, however, there was no escaping the fact that valuable training time had been lost due to a lack of gliders. There had, however, been continued progress toward gaining experience on the new aircraft and its characteristics. What was now needed was an understanding of how it would handle on operations.

In spite of the early success in formulating and implementing a basic training programme for the WACO, there was still the question of how it would fly when fully laden, and, most importantly, its performance on landing. These questions had to be answered quickly if 1st Airlanding Brigade was to be ready for its first operation in July. With the basic flying training underway, the focus switched to the development of the next stage of the training syllabus. Once competent in all aspects of flying the WACO, pilots would have to be prepared for the more challenging prospect of operational flying. Landing a fully laden WACO at night in the North African desert was beyond the experience and skills of the majority of the pilots in the battalion and thus the next stage of training was designed to ensure that such landings could be successfully accomplished. The next few weeks would stretch the skills of the pilots.

On 6 June 1943, Lieutenant Colonel Chatterton once again took on the mantle of test pilot. He flew a number of trial flights with the aim of determining the maximum rate 'sink' possible in a WACO without creating a dramatic increase in forward speed. Flying with Major John Place, he found that a combination of air spoilers and maintaining the glider at close to stalling speed, allowed a lightly loaded aircraft to descend or sink at a rate of 700 feet a minute. Maintaining the glider at this attitude produced an airspeed of 65 mph; with the rock strewn landing zones of Sicily in mind, a low speed landing profile was developed and a few days later trialled successfully when a fully loaded WACO landed safely at 65 mph.

While his Commanding Officer grappled with the complexities of the operational use of the new glider, Sergeant Bob Boyce of No. 2 Squadron was among the first to be introduced to the WACO at Froha. The challenges associated with flying it were complicated by the austere conditions present in North Africa:

> Flying a WACO in North Africa was a new experience. I had my first dual with Squadron Sergeant Major Archer: he said, 'Take off is like driving through the Blackwall Tunnel without lights'. The slipstream from the tug stirred up an enveloping cloud of dust and visibility on take-off was nil; find the tug was the name of the game soon after you were airborne. The next stage was night flying and learning to land without a flare path. Unfortunately, the instruments on some WACO gliders were not luminous so whoever occupied the second pilot's seat had a torch – should the torch fail, he had a box of matches. The first pilot was told the airspeed and height and it was interesting to stand on an airfield at night and hear a voice from the heavens call out 'Airspeed seventy, height a hundred feet' and then wait to hear the rumble of wheels on the ground. But not all the altimeters were sensitive to 100 feet and life could be difficult.[21]

Problems with reading cockpit instrumentation in the dark could be further complicated by events on the ground. The flare pots that marked the airfield boundaries and the runways at night were viewed as extremely attractive items by the local Arab population. The poverty-stricken Bedouin living near the airfields thought nothing of extinguishing the flare and making off with the useful metal containers. Even on a very good moonlit night some reference was needed by a pilot to orientate the aircraft to the airfield and confirm his position in the circuit. The sudden removal of a flare at a critical moment over otherwise featureless terrain was less than helpful. Nevertheless, flying progressed well and each of the airfields developed a daily routine around the needs and constraints of the glider crews and their equally important tug crews. The training programme that evolved to convert the pilots on to their new American gliders was basic but effective. Each would hopefully fly a dual circuit under instruction followed quickly by a solo circuit to confirm his competence. With the basic skills assimilated, each pilot completed two remote releases by day and one by night followed by a remote landing using moonlight.

The initially small number of tug aircraft and gliders available for training restricted the volume of training; the majority of pilots underwent half a day's training per day. The relative cool of the evening was used to complete any maintenance required on the tugs and gliders. American ground crew were scarce, the majority were required to service the C-47 tug aircraft, but the pilots pitched in and assisted the few available mechanics detailed to service the gliders for the next day's flying. The increasing tempo of flying training also took a toll on the first batch of WACOs. Anything approaching a heavy landing on the hard baked, rugged surface of the North African airstrips damaged or ruptured the floor of the new gliders. Consequently, as training progressed a small but steadily growing number of unserviceable gliders began to accumulate at the side of the runway.

Meanwhile, as the men of Nos 2 and 3 Squadrons were industriously building and subsequently converting on to their new American glider, thousands of miles away in England, their comrades in No. 1 Squadron were facing a very different but equally dangerous challenge.

Notes

1. Chatterton, Lieutenant Colonel, G., CO 1st Battalion GPR, by permission of *The Eagle*.
2. Chatterton, Lieutenant Colonel, G., CO 1st Battalion GPR, by permission of *The Eagle*.
3. Chatterton, Lieutenant Colonel, G., CO 1st Battalion GPR, by permission of *The Eagle*.
4. Anon Sergeant, 1st Battalion GPR, *The Army In The Air*, A. Sutton Publishing, Bath, p. 79.
5. General Hap Arnold, 1941.
6. War Diary 1st Battalion GPR, North Africa, 8 May 1943.
7. Hall, Staff Sergeant, M., 1 Squadron, 1st Battalion GPR, interview with the author 24 February 2009.
8. Howes, Sergeant, N.D., C Company, 2nd Battalion South Staffs, Transcribe from recorded interview dated 1996.
9. Boyce, Sergeant, R., 2 Squadron, 1st Battalion GPR, by permission of *The Eagle*.
10. War Diary 1st Battalion GPR, North Africa, 12 May 1943.
11. Chatterton, Lieutenant Colonel, G., CO, 1st Battalion GPR, by permission of *The Eagle*.
12. Wright, Squadron Leader, L., Headquarters 38 Wing RAF.
13. Hall, Staff Sergeant, M., 1 Squadron, 1st Battalion GPR, interview with the author 24 February 2009.
14. Cole, Lieutenant Colonel, H., *On Wings of Healing*, Blackwood & Sons Ltd, London, 1963, p. 36.
15. Fine, Flight Officer, S., USAAF by permission of *The Eagle*.
16. War Diary 1st Battalion GPR, North Africa, 14 May 1943.
17. War Diary 1st Battalion GPR, North Africa, 18 May 1943.
18. Wright, Squadron Leader, L., HQ 38 Wing RAF, *The Wooden Sword*, Elek Publishing, London, p. 56.
19. Place, Major, J., OC 3 Company, 1st Battalion GPR, Diary Entry, by permission of *The Eagle*.
20. Place, Major, J., OC 3 Company, 1st Battalion GPR, Diary Entry, by permission of *The Eagle*.
21. Boyce, Sergeant, R., 2 Squadron, 1st Battalion GPR, by permission of *The Eagle*.

CHAPTER 5

Operation BEGGAR – The First Wave

A few weeks earlier the authorities had ruled the flight impossible.

The tactical limitations of the WACO glider remained a serious concern to Lieutenant Colonel George Chatterton and his battalion planning team. The probability of an airlanding anti-tank gun being landed in close proximity to its attendant vehicle by two separate gliders delivered by two separate tugs at night was considered minimal. If this, or indeed, the landing of the equally essential light artillery pieces together with their Jeeps was to be assured, then Horsa gliders were considered vital. However, the nearest serviceable Horsas were 1,350 miles away in England. Delivery of gliders by sea had not been attempted before and technical problems were anticipated in accommodating them aboard ships, even if they were dismantled into sub-assemblies. That was one advantage that the WACO enjoyed over its British counterpart. Even if the Horsa could have been packed in crates and loaded on to merchant ships for transit to North Africa, however, time was running out and cargo space was at a premium as other stores and equipment were shipped to North Africa. There was, therefore, only one viable method of delivery that could realistically provide the Horsa gliders that were so desperately required; they would have to be towed from England to Tunisia.

The concept of long-range glider supply flights was not without precedent. In April 1943, just prior to the death throes of Rommel's campaign in North Africa, the Luftwaffe had attempted to form an air bridge using gliders. Flying from airfields in southern Europe, huge lumbering Me 321 Gigant heavy gliders, packed with supplies, had been towed across the Mediterranean to resupply the beleaguered Afrika Korps. Although some of them reached their destinations with their vital cargo, they were extremely slow and vulnerable. One aerial convoy was intercepted on 22 April 1943, the day before the leading elements of 1st Battalion GPR docked at Oran.

RAF fighters wrought havoc as they tore through the stream of slow-moving, mammoth gliders and their Heinkel tugs, sending a total of sixteen German aircraft down into the Mediterranean in flames.

Initially the War Office treated the 1st Airborne Division request for additional gliders with scepticism and challenged the possibility of such a long-range towed flight. Prior to the 1st Battalion GPR's deployment to North Africa, the maximum practical planning range for a glider tow was thought to be 1,000 miles. Chatterton's request would require a transit flight of nearly half that distance again, a flight way beyond the theoretical range of any glider–tug combination in service. In addition, the route would be fraught with danger as the majority of the journey would have to be flown over the sea, through German-controlled airspace and well beyond the range of Allied fighter escort. Furthermore, the route would have to avoid flying over occupied Europe and therefore cross the Bay of Biscay, which was regularly patrolled by the Luftwaffe. Operating from their airfields on the coast of France, Ju-88 fighter-bombers and Focke Wulf Fw-200 Condor long-range reconnaissance aircraft roamed the airspace over the bay, seeking out Allied shipping and providing support for U-boats en route to and from their hunting grounds in the Atlantic. Any of the glider-tug combinations would be vulnerable to attack and stood little chance in aerial combat as long as the glider remained on tow.

In spite of these obvious difficulties, the request for a reinforcement of Horsa gliders was repeated as Headquarters 1st Airborne Division remained convinced of the need for the Horsas. Lieutenant Colonel Chatterton was certain that he could not complete the mission to seize the bridges outlined to him by Major General Hopkinson without them. Operation LADBROKE and any subsequent coup de main missions would only be successful if Horsa gliders were available. Both Hopkinson and Chatterton knew that any airborne force holding such an objective would inevitably be lightly armed and vulnerable to attack by armour, being at their most vulnerable immediately after landing when they could expect to be subjected to a rapid and vigorous counter-attack. Even the most outdated Italian armour would create chaos among airborne troops who were denied the fire support of airlanded anti-tank weapons. Gliderborne heavy weapons such as anti-tank guns, medium machine guns and mortars were thus deemed critical to the success and survival of an airborne coup de main force. The staff of 1st Airborne Division had articulated a very strong case for a 40-strong force of Horsas to be delivered to Tunisia in time for the planned Sicily operations. The question that remained was how to get them there with less than two months before D-Day.

The practical and logistic problems of any planned reinforcement lift to North Africa would rest with the pilots, aircrew and staff of 38 Wing RAF based at Netheravon Airfield. At this point only four RAF transport squadrons were dedicated to supporting British airborne forces; one of these was soon to be given the daunting task of proving the feasibility of the proposed marathon flights.

The North African mission was initially viewed as impossible by many of those who were briefed on it. The first and most daunting leg of the journey consisted of a 1,350-mile flight over open sea to landfall at Sale in Morocco. After a brief stopover, the glider-tug combinations would then take off from the desert and make a 350-mile flight over hostile desert to the airstrip at Froha on the Mascara Plain. The final leg of this epic airborne odyssey involved a high altitude transit, crossing the Atlas Mountains at 7,000 feet. Once safely over the mountains and at the end of a 580-mile flight, the pilots would cast off and land their Horsas at Kairouan airstrip in Tunisia.

Tactical considerations aside there were also considerable technical constraints, not least of which was the fact that none of the tug aircraft in RAF service had the range to reach North Africa. The task of finding a way to ferry the Horsa reinforcement fleet was given to the surviving tug commander from Operation FRESHMAN, Squadron Leader Peter Wilkinson. The veteran pilot decided to conduct a series of long-range trials and test flights using twelve Halifax Mk V four-engined bombers, converted for use as tugs, and aircrew from 'A' Flight, 295 Squadron RAF. Aware of the urgent need for the Horsas' lift capacity, he set out to find a way to extend the Halifaxes' operating range sufficiently to meet the requirements of Operation BEGGAR, as the flight to North Africa had been named.

The trials were intended to push the 'A' Flight crews and aircraft beyond accepted limits; this alone would prove to be a considerable challenge as many of the 'A' Flight aircrew had only recently converted on to the Halifax. Until then, the squadron had operated antiquated Whitley bombers and conversion to the Halifax was far from complete, with much of the ground support equipment and spares still to be delivered to the squadron's base at Netheravon. Wilkinson's problems were further complicated by a lack of experience among his crews; a number of the pilots were fresh from multi-engined training and had no operational experience at all. Moreover, the initial batch of Halifax tugs to emerge from conversion for towing numbered only three. Wilkinson was in fact the only pilot in the squadron fully qualified on the Halifax. His most trusted and experienced pilot was Flight Lieutenant Buster Briggs, who had amassed only ten flying hours of the 50 solo hours required to qualify on the Halifax. In spite of these problems, however, the process of determining the viability and practicality of the proposed long range tows got underway.

With the tug squadron and its aircrew beginning to form, the next step was to team them up with the gliders and crews they were to deliver to North Africa. Major Alastair 'Babe' Cooper's newly formed No. 1 Squadron was tasked with taking part in the long-range trials and ultimately providing the glider crews for the operation. The fledgling squadron consisted of twelve officers, one squadron sergeant major and eighty-seven rank and file. Its personnel were initially dispersed between Netheravon, Thruxton and

Hurn airfields although ultimately Netheravon Airfield was then deemed unsuitable for the type of night flying required during the training programme. On 1 May 1943, along with the RAF tug crews, No. 1 Squadron moved to RAF Holmsley South and then a few weeks later in June to RAF Hurn near Bournemouth. Sergeant Nigel Brown was shocked when he was briefed on the ambitious plan:

> We were to be hauled non-stop to a place called Sale in Morocco, the whole flight over water, the first three hours at wavetop height. We would be flying, if we made it, up to ten hours.[1]

The Halifax-Horsa long range trials, known as 'consumption tests' were very quickly underway and eventually resulted in the fitting of auxiliary fuel tanks in the bomb bays of all twelve of the 295 Squadron aircraft. Although this modification significantly extended the range of a fully fuelled Halifax, the aircraft were now risky to fly. In the event of a single engine failure, the remaining three engines could not produce the collective power required to allow the pilot to fly the big aircraft out of trouble. In addition, the extra fuel tanks located in the bomb bay greatly increased the risk of fire if the aircraft was forced to make a belly landing. The trials carried out over England and Wales identified a number of technical faults that had not manifested themselves on routine Halifax sorties. The principal risk was that of coolant or oil leaks from connections or couplings that had rattled loose due to long periods of vibration in flight. Such a leak could be catastrophic to an aircraft flying so far out to sea or over the African desert. A modified servicing schedule was thus designed in order to prevent any such potential leaks and a party of 50 ground crew and fitters was despatched to North Africa to be on hand to receive the Halifaxes on arrival, inspect and service them, and then turn them around for their return flight to England.

The programme of flight trials also highlighted the need to reduce drag on the Horsa while under tow. It was thus decided that the undercarriage of the glider should be jettisoned as soon as practicable after take-off. This was a design feature of the Horsa and enabled a safe landing to be made using the central skid, under the fuselage, that remained after jettisoning the undercarriage. The jettison procedure and a confirmatory skid landing were also carried out in England during the work-up trials. Meanwhile, a batch of new Horsa gliders from the Heavy Glider Maintenance Unit at Hurn was earmarked for the operation, each carrying a replacement undercarriage as internal freight for fitting after arrival in Morocco.

Another consideration was the performance of the Horsa after ditching. Air Ministry data suggested that in spite of its wooden construction the Horsa would not stay afloat for long after ditching. It reported that the nose of the aircraft would be likely to break off easily after contact with the sea and that the fuselage would fill with water and sink quickly.

Regardless of all the planning variables and logistical problems, Operation BEGGAR continued to gather momentum. Those glider pilots selected for it were placed under the following warning order drafted by Major Maurice Willoughby, the Second-in-Command of 1st Battalion GPR. The order, issued on 27 May 1943 read as follows:

> These personnel will not be touched or interfered with except under direct orders from Headquarters 38 Wing or 1st Airborne Division. They are on three days notice to move overseas and should not be given more than 48 hours leave.[2]

Among the pilots in 1 Squadron placed on notice to move was a young Scot named Staff Sergeant Wallace Mackenzie who, together with his friend Andy McCullough, had just been posted to No. 1 Squadron. They had begun the year at the Heavy Glider Conversion Unit (HGCU) at RAF Brize Norton, in Oxfordshire, where Wallace and his fellow course members had been introduced to the Horsa. From February to April 1943, they flew training sorties from Brize Norton and Netheravon Airfield in Wiltshire. With their heavy glider training complete, both soon realised the risks present for glider pilots in an operational squadron:

> We were both then based at Holmsley South and spent most of the time there warming up to long distance flights ... ending up with cross-country flights around the UK, each lasting some ten or eleven hours. Andy and I were settled in as a three-man crew with Sergeant Hill and were accommodated in Nissen huts in a magnificent rhododendron forest at the edge of the airfield. One tragic event happened; we returned from a weekend pass to find that a Halifax tug had crashed en route to collect a glider that had been landed on its skid at Hurn. All on board were lost including the glider pilots who were to fly the glider back to Holmsley. They had been the occupants of the other half of our Nissen hut.[3]

The build-up to Operation BEGGAR had not passed without incident. Two long-range flights had ended prematurely with gliders losing their tows and making emergency landings as far afield as Luton and North Wales. The crash referred to by Staff Sergeant Wallace Mackenzie, however, had happened much closer to No. 1 Squadron's home base. It occurred on 16 May 1943, the deaths of the crews involved was tragic and for the glider crew even more so as they were only travelling in the Halifax as a result of one of those cruel twists of fate that tend to surround aircraft crashes. The story was later related by Staff Sergeant Gordon Jenks, an ex-Highland Light Infantryman who was now a glider pilot. He was also based at Holmsley

South where he was crewed with Sergeant Percy Attwood and Londoner Sergeant Harry Flynn:

> One Friday lunchtime the three of us were contemplating whether or not to go up to town for the weekend when we were sent for by Major Cooper. He informed us that the following day we were to do a ten-hour tow, the longest ever attempted by a tug-glider combination. A Halifax tug had been fitted with 'overload' fuel tanks enabling it to carry 2,400 gallons of petrol. The pilot of the Halifax and skipper of the combination was Flight Lieutenant 'Buster' Briggs RAF. Our instructions were to jettison the undercarriage immediately after take-off, and at the end of the tow cast off and do a skid landing at RAF Station Hurn, a few miles away ... We arranged to each do one hour's actual flying in every three hours and twenty minutes each on the final stages of the trip. But in fact, it didn't work out quite that way. Soon after take-off poor Harry became airsick and was ill for practically the whole ten hours. Even Percy succumbed to airsickness after a few hours, with the result that I had to spend seven hours continuously at the controls. It had its compensations however, as I ate the whole of the sandwiches provided for the three of us. Nevertheless I wasn't altogether sorry to see Hurn Aerodrome come into view after a triangular flight of something like 1,400 miles, about 1,000 miles of which I had spent at the controls ... The next morning, we discussed the trip with Major Cooper and suggested one or two improvements to make things easier on future long tows. He was very pleased with the whole affair and told us to get to London on a 36-hour pass. I mentioned the Horsa still at Hurn and he told me not to worry about it as Sergeant Sunter and Sergeant Davies had asked to go over and fly it back.[4]

Administrative flights between the two airfields were by now regarded as routine short hops, the transit time being no more than ten minutes. The Halifax crews of 295 Squadron RAF were certainly familiar with the journey; the pre-flight checks on the four engined bomber probably took longer than the duration of the actual flight itself. It was, however, a good opportunity for a glider crew to log another take-off and landing without the added time of a long transit. No doubt Sergeant Roland Sunter and his two crewmates, Sergeant Francis Davies and Sergeant Ronald Borton, were snapping up the opportunity to gain more experience. Staff Sergeant Gordon Jenks, with the trip to London on his mind, spoke briefly to the volunteer crew:

> I spoke to Geordie Sunter, a short stocky little man from Durham, before he and Sergeant Davies climbed into the Halifax which was to take them to Hurn, pick up the Horsa and tow them back. Harry, Percy and I watched the Halifax as it headed for Hurn which lay just beyond

> some distant trees. It appeared to be in trouble, with smoke coming from the port outer engine.[5]

The plight of the stricken Halifax was also witnessed by an informed local resident. Sid Burt was an RAF fighter pilot who was home on leave in the nearby village of Bransgore.

> I was preparing to go to church on Sunday morning. I heard the increase in revs of a passing 'Halli'. On looking out, it was at about five hundred feet in a very steep turn with the nose down. I remember saying to my Dad, 'That kite is going to prang' and I started to run in the direction across the fields. In fact I was the second person on the spot, the first being a gamekeeper's wife who lived in the area. It actually crashed in the road midway between Shirley and Ripley School – there were no survivors ... a small crowd gathered, oblivious, it appeared, to the danger of exploding ammunition from the aircraft's guns. They came dashing in thinking they could be bloody heroes and we had a job stopping them, but of course there was the heat of the fire and we didn't know what else was on board.

Halifax DG 390 crashed halfway between the two Dorset airfields, at such low altitude, and while constantly losing power, that there was little chance of the pilot recovering. There were no survivors from the four-man RAF crew and the three glider pilots. It was a subdued 36-hour pass in London for Staff Sergeant Jenks and his comrades and a sombre return to Holmsley South for Sergeant Mike Hall and his two fellow pilots. A few days later Staff Sergeant Jenks played the Last Post and Reveille at the funeral service for both crews. The incident and shared loss of life cemented a strong and lasting bond between the RAF and GPR crews that was to be put to the test over coming years.

Very soon after the conclusion of the test flights, the BEGGAR sorties got underway. In order to ensure that every combination got the most out of its fuel tanks, the first leg of the epic flights were to be launched from RAF Portreath in Cornwall, a point as far south-west as possible. This would hopefully give each BEGGAR sortie the longest possible range. Staff Sergeant Mike Hall moved down to the Cornish airfield on 15 May 1943:

> I and a few others were flown in an old Whitley bomber to Portreath in Cornwall. Whilst at the time we knew we were to fly a Horsa out to Morocco we did not have any details of this long operation. As the flight would take nine hours each glider would have three pilots so that at any one time one pilot could rest ...[6]

As work progressed on the preparation and modification of the tugs and gliders, the enormity of the BEGGAR task began to dawn on all involved.

A conference was held on 21 May 1943 at Headquarters 38 Wing RAF to discuss what could realistically be achieved before 9 July 1943. During the conference, the objective of Operation BEGGAR was clarified: the delivery of 36 serviceable Horsa gliders and trained crews to North Africa; in addition, following the ferrying operation, 38 Wing was to have ten Halifax tugs positioned in Tunisia ready for airborne operations against Sicily. All this was to be achieved by a deadline of 21 June 1943. It was agreed that given the pace of the aircraft modification programme and the training required by the aircrews, a projected total of 21 Horsas was altogether more realistic. This revised figure assumed that no aircraft were lost to mechanical failure or enemy action en route. The same meeting also anticipated a total of 30 twin-engined Albemarle tugs from 296 Squadron RAF being in place by the same date.

Squadron Leader Peter Wilkinson and his crew had successfully completed a non-stop flight of 1,500 miles over England and thus theory had now become a reality. The exercise flights had, however, raised the problem of station keeping between tug and glider in cloud or at night, a skill that required maximum concentration from both pilots. Even at full stretch, the towrope between the aircraft only gave 350 feet of separation. Maintaining station behind a tug for the lengths of time anticipated on Operation BEGGAR was thought to be impossible at night or in cloud, requiring great skill and concentration in good visibility by day.

The staff at Headquarters 38 Wing RAF thus suggested a modification that would assist the pilot of each Horsa. An instrument known to the RAF as the angle of glide indicator was to be fitted to all of the BEGGAR Horsa fleet. This gauge measured what was nicknamed the 'Angle of Dangle' and provided the glider pilot with indication of the angle of his tow rope in relation to the tug, confirming whether the glider was in the low or high tow position. In the case of a long-range tow, the 'high tow' was the optimal towing position that maintained maximum fuel economy and reduced turbulence. The powerful Halifax generated a turbulent wake from its four engines, which was most pronounced when a glider was stationed in the low tow position, the Horsa being subjected to a particularly bumpy ride with the narrow speed margin between the two aircraft leaving little scope for error. The angle of glide indicator was described by Staff Sergeant John McGeough:

> In 1942, Farnborough produced what is now known as the Cable Angle Indicator Mk. I. By a direct system of levers it measured the angle of the towrope relative to the fore and aft line of the glider, the datum being the low tow position. Lateral level could be maintained only by reference to the Turn and Bank Indicator. In 1943 they produced another model, the Mk. II, especially for heavy gliders. This incorporated a gyro for assisting the pilot to maintain direction by giving an indication of bank. The direct mechanical means of measuring the angle of the towrope,

> however, was still the basic principle of the instrument and varied little from the Mk. I. The instrument became generally and aptly known as the Angle of Dangle Indicator.[7]

There was a significant risk of collision when blind flying or in the low tow position. The latter did, however, have one use in that it was to be adopted in the event of an attack by German aircraft, the glider holding that position in order to allow the Halifax rear gunner to traverse his turret and bring his four Browning machine guns to bear. Therefore, even once the glide indicator gauge modification had been completed, flying in cloud or at night was to be avoided. All sorties would be flown in daylight and wherever possible in good weather with minimal cloud. Consideration was also given to the factor of crew fatigue. The unprecedented length of the sorties, and the physical effort required to fly a Horsa, resulted in a decision to crew each Horsa with an extra pilot, making a total of three.

The first combinations were in position on 25 May 1943 and ready to set out across the Bay of Biscay to Morocco, but poor weather delayed take-off. The meteorological forecast was critical on such a long flight for all of the reasons discussed previously; one other key variable was of course head-wind. The winds remained unfavourable for a number of days and resulted in a flurry of signals between Headquarters 38 Wing RAF and North Africa where Captain 'Peggy' Clarke was acting as the liaison officer for the 1st Battalion GPR. Eventually a total of four combinations were set to take off from RAF Portreath at ten-minute intervals on 3 June 1943. A fighter escort of Beaufighter aircraft was to be provided by RAF Coastal Command for the first three hours of the flight; this welcome protection did come at a cost, however, as Coastal Command insisted that the whole formation flew as low as possible and no higher than 500 feet. This low-level flight out would keep the formation below German radar height and therefore reduce the risk of the escort being ambushed by German fighters on their homeward leg. The Bay of Biscay and French coastal waters were hazardous places even for a Beaufighter; packs of Ju-88 fighter-bombers had claimed a number of kills in recent weeks.

Finally, with all preparations complete and a relatively favourable 'met' forecast, Operation BEGGAR was declared 'on'. The first of the four Turkey Buzzard, as they were now designated, serials was flown by Lieutenant Robin Walchi, Staff Sergeant Bill Chambers and Sergeant Ron Owen. However, having taken off on schedule at 0800 hours, the combination flew into sea mist and lost visibility almost straight away in fog impenetrable up to a height of 11,000 feet. The combination remained in the air for over seven hours, trying to find a way through the fog, but with fuel running low was forced to abort the flight and return to Portreath, logging seven hours and 30 minutes of flying time.

Meanwhile, due to the operation taking place under the cover of radio silence, the waiting combinations remained unaware of these problems. The

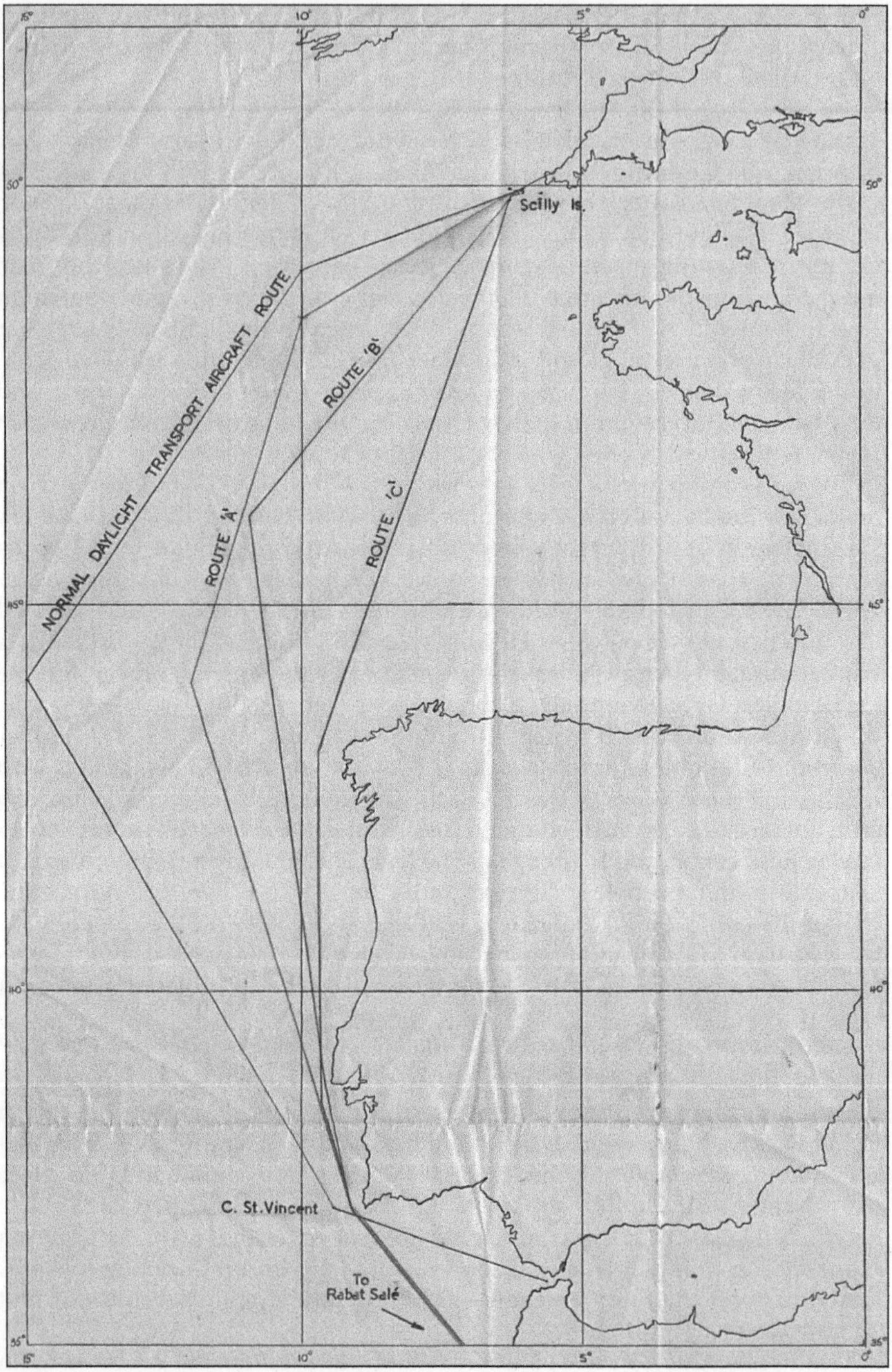

Operation BEGGAR sketch map taken from the operation order

crews of the second combination lined up on the runway and focused on their own impending take-off. Executing a safe take-off from the Cornish airfield required a higher degree of concentration than most of the airfields from which No. 1 Squadron had operated to date. The airfield was located on cliff tops surrounded on three sides by the sea and by hills on its fourth. The take-off had to be well executed as only 300 yards from the end of the runway the land dropped away dramatically to the Atlantic 400 feet below. An engine failure on a fully-laden Halifax was an unthinkable scenario that left little chance of recovery.

The second Turkey Buzzard Horsa was crewed by the squadron commander, Major Alastair Cooper, Sergeant Dennis Hall and Sergeant Sotiris 'Harry' Antonopoulos with the latter at the controls for take-off and the first hour of flying. The glider was packed with freight, two replacement undercarriage jacks and wheels and, of course, the crew's survival pack and dinghy. The weather was by now dull and menacing, with a strong squally wind and a dark cumulus cloud base that was set below 1,000 feet. Finally, the RAF towmaster gave the release signal and the long wait was over, the Halifax engines roaring into life:

> The combination trundled along the runway gradually gathering speed until yards from the end of the runway the tug finally managed to get airborne. Spectators watched in fascination to see the whole combination disappear below the cliff only to appear a minute or so later out to sea struggling to gain height before the glider jettisoned its undercarriage thereby reducing drag and saving fuel.[8]

The second combination slowly climbed away, watched by Staff Sergeant Gordon Jenks from the cockpit of the third Horsa. He later wrote of his relief when it finally began to climb into the dark cumulus cloud over the airfield. A few minutes later the rear gunner of the third Halifax informed him on the intercom that they were about to begin their own take-off run. The heavily laden tug edged forward steadily, taking up the slack in the towrope until with a jolt the Horsa began to move. The crew had remained unchanged since the trial flights, regardless of problems with air sickness, and thus still comprised Jenks along with Sergeants Bernie Attwood and Harry Flynn.

The Horsa lifted from the ground first, followed by the labouring Halifax clawing for height. Leaving the tarmac of Portreath behind, the combination slowly began to gain height. At the point when all appeared to be going well, however, fate typically interceded. The decision to jettison the undercarriage was taken too early, resulting in damage to the glider. The third Horsa was too low at the release point and as the falling undercarriage hit the ground it bounced back up and hit the underside of the wing. Some of the undercarriage framework remained embedded in the starboard wing where it affected the response of the control surfaces making handling difficult and erratic. Only with the controls pushed hard over to port using brute strength could the two pilots maintain the glider in a stable attitude. It was also obvious that, if the unwanted components of the undercarriage remained in situ, they would upset the skid landing at Sale. The leg of the undercarriage that was still hanging from the wing would make contact with the ground before the skid, causing the glider to cartwheel along the runway with potentially catastrophic consequences. As the combination flew on, a brief consultation took place between the two aircraft commanders. The two pilots decided that, all things considered, the best course of action was to press on with the flight and worry later about landing in Morocco.

The additional physical effort now required to cope with the controls resulted in the reduction of 'hands on' time at the controls being reduced from one hour to thirty minutes. Relaxation was, however, short-lived. During Staff Sergeant Jenks's first spell at the controls, the Halifax flew into cloud and the Horsa crew lost visual contact with the tug, only the vee in the tow rope remaining visible. With both aircraft disorientated from each other Flight Lieutenant John 'Buster' Briggs decided to climb up from 500 feet out of the cloud. The damage to the Horsa made a low tow impossible and the glider was rocked violently as it climbed through the turbulent cloud; the altimeter read 2,200 feet and was still climbing. At 3,000 feet Sergeant Attwood took over the controls and the dramatic blind climb thereafter continued to 4,000 feet and beyond.

After a further turbulent passage up through the cloud the Horsa suddenly popped out into bright sunlight at 5,200 feet, but the Halifax was nowhere to be seen. Eventually, however, the huge tug emerged from cloud fifty feet below the glider and extreme care was needed to re-align it behind the Halifax without placing undue strain on the towrope. Under careful guidance from Flight Lieutenant Buster Briggs, the Horsa was gradually re-positioned in the high tow position. Now that the combination had stabilised and with clear skies ahead, the pilots changed over at the controls. Staff Sergeant Jenks could now take the opportunity to leave the cockpit to rest, leaving Sergeant Flynn at the controls with the Horsa now responding well in flight.

The three pilots had taken off from Cornwall in heavy European theatre uniforms, intending to change into lighter tropical dress during the long flight. While changing out of his sweaty battledress, Jenks took the opportunity to look out of one of the fuselage portholes. He scanned the underside of the starboard wing looking for any change in the damage caused by the wayward undercarriage assembly. One of the undercarriage wheels was clearly wedged into the huge starboard flap of the Horsa, so controlling the landing was going to be difficult. Additionally, there was another concern: the parachute pack fitted to the undercarriage to assist with the jettison was still in place. If the canopy was to become inflated in flight or as the glider made its approach to land at Sale, the consequences could be disastrous. There was not much anyone on board the Horsa could do but wait for the landing and hope that the parachute remained inside its pack. Jenks did what any pilot in that situation would do ... he got out his trumpet and played jazz music over the intercom between the two aircraft. It is easy to picture the Horsa hanging in the high tow position behind the Halifax as both crews scan the horizon for German aircraft while listening to their own on-board jazz music.

Elsewhere in the stream of aircraft, unaware of the problems that the other two crews were experiencing and unable to hear the jazz concert, the second combination flew on oblivious. Major Cooper had taken the controls for the second hour of flying and had in turn been relieved by Sergeant Hall. The Beaufighter escort turned back to England at the pre-briefed point and shortly after that Sergeant Antonopoulos began his second stint at the controls of the Horsa. The glider pilots were just beginning to settle into a routine when the Halifax entered cloud, taking the Horsa with it. Almost immediately the pilots lost sight of the Halifax and were unable to orientate themselves on to their tug. They were in trouble and even using the 'angle of dangle' could not maintain the correct towing position. Consequently, the glider was out of position and straining the towrope beyond its capacity. Eventually, it snapped and the Horsa began to descend toward the sea below.

With ditching imminent, Sergeant Antonopoulos remained at the controls ensuring as smooth and controlled a descent as possible while Major Cooper and Sergeant Hall set about cutting escape holes in the roof of the fuselage using their emergency axe. They also prepared the dinghy pack and the emergency rations for use after ditching. Sergeant Antonopoulos meanwhile remained calm as the glider emerged from cloud 100 feet above the choppy sea and much to his credit executed a perfect landing without tipping the aircraft over. No doubt with the Air Ministry assessment concerning the buoyancy of the Horsa after ditching prominent in their minds, the three pilots made speedy exits from the fuselage, clambering out on to the top of the fuselage where they inflated their Mae West lifejackets and their dinghy.

The next few hours were far from pleasant, the sea state was rough and all three survivors suffered from seasickness in the dinghy. Thankfully, the Halifax crew had returned to Portreath with an extremely accurate fix on the ditched Horsa and passed the information quickly to Coastal Command. Later that day Major Cooper's crew heard the morale boosting sound of friendly aircraft engines. On the distant horizon there appeared the welcome sight of a Short Sunderland flying boat carrying out a box search pattern. Cooper fired a Verey flare and the Sunderland quickly located the bedraggled trio in their dinghy. Due to the choppy nature of the sea, however, the Sunderland was unable to land and rescue them. It was, however, able to confirm their location and inform the Royal Navy.

Twelve hours after the ditching HMS *Teviot*, a Royal Navy frigate, arrived to pick them up. Anxious to get back to convoy escort duties and equally keen that they did not remain static long enough to attract the unwanted attention of a prowling U-boat, the crew were enthusiastic in their encouragement of the by now exhausted pilots to make haste up the scramble net on to the frigate's deck. Ironically, although waterlogged, the Horsa had not sunk; in an effort to deny the wreckage and any intelligence to the Germans, the captain of HMS *Teviot* attempted to destroy the wreck with gunfire. When this method failed, depth charges were used but again without success. Eventually, the frigate resorted to the tried and tested method of ramming but the Horsa still refused to sink. Although the fuselage had filled with water, the buoyancy within the glider's massive wingspan had kept it afloat. After extracting her bow from the waterlogged fuselage, HMS *Teviot* set off in search of easier prey.

In the meantime, on board the fourth Horsa in the stream were Sergeant Nigel Brown, Sergeant Dennis 'Galp' Galpin and Sergeant Granger. With Sergeant Brown at the controls they executed a trouble-free take-off and were soon established in the high tow position behind their 295 Squadron Halifax. The combination then followed the flight path of the previous serials and entered low lying, dark cumulus cloud:

> The tug simply disappeared. I could just about make out the 'V' in the towrope. But where the Halifax was I couldn't tell. I didn't think we would get far. Any moment I expected the line to snap, or be shredded on the tug's propeller blades. Suddenly, the radio silence was broken to say one of the gliders was going down.[9]

Although the news of a glider falling out of the stream was disturbing, Brown and his comrades had pressing problems of their own. They were flying in cloud with no visual reference points and desperately trying to keep station on a tug they could not see. If they broke their tow they too would soon be ditching in the rough sea below. Suddenly, without warning and to the relief of all in the cockpit, the Horsa emerged from the cloud into open skies to find the Halifax almost directly below its nose. Slowly and carefully, the two crews worked together to separate the two aircraft and manoeuvre them back to their correct stations with the towrope fully extended. After a series of steady adjustment and numerous corrections passed back and forth along the towrope telephone cable, the two aircraft captains were satisfied and the Horsa was once more stable in the high tow position.

By now, two of the original four combinations were still in the air and beyond the range of German aircraft. The mood on both gliders changed noticeably as the weather and visibility improved. As the two pairs flew further south, they observed Lisbon and the Portuguese coast off to their port side. Eventually, the large cockpit spaces became like greenhouses becoming increasingly warmer as the sunlight streamed in through the perspex panels. Eventually, the pilots were stripped to the waist and wearing sunglasses to reduce the glare of the sun.

After ten long hours of flight the Halifax rear gunner called back to report that the coast of North Africa was in sight. The two combinations circled over Rabat and then approached the American airfield at Sale. The damaged Horsa cast off first at 600 feet with Sergeant Flynn at the controls, Sergeant Attwood as second pilot and Staff Sergeant Jenks looking over their shoulders. Unable to use flaps they made a gentle descent keeping the glide path as shallow as possible on to the runway. The arrival of these unusual aircraft after such a momentous journey attracted large crowds of American personnel and curious Moroccans. They were treated to a dramatic spectacle as the Horsa touched down on the runway amid a cloud of dust at 80 mph. At that critical moment, just as Jenks had feared, the jettison chute caught the slipstream and was whipped open under the starboard wing. The fully inflated chute ripped the undercarriage out from under the wing and then struck the glider's tail plane with its full force, throwing the Horsa violently off track. The glider swung through ninety degrees, tearing up the metal matting as it slewed across the runway. Finally, after what can truly be described as an eventful flight, the first of 1st Airborne Division's Horsa gliders had reached North Africa, although this particular one would need some repair work.

Circling overhead waiting for clearance to cast off from their tow and make an approach was the second Horsa. Casting off from its tug at 600 feet, it made a textbook approach and landing without incident. The Horsa force in North Africa had doubled in size and the Operation BEGGAR route had now been proven to be viable, Although the first Turkey Buzzard mission had only achieved a fifty per-cent success rate, the fact remained that Horsa gliders had reached Africa. The question was, could the required number of gliders run the gauntlet of German aircraft and survive the hazardous long distance flight from England?

The lift capacity of the Horsa was considered critical to the success of the proposed airlanding operations on Sicily, and thus the aircraft was deemed essential to the success of Operation LADBROKE. Accordingly, therefore, the Turkey Buzzard flights would continue. Working against an ever-diminishing number of weeks and days before D-Day, the glider pilots of No. 1 Squadron and the aircrews of 38 Wing RAF proceeded to launch dozens of Turkey Buzzard sorties from Portreath.

Notes

1. Brown, Sergeant, N., 1 Squadron, 1st Battalion GPR, *The Gliders*, London, Arrow Books Ltd, 1982, p. 29.
2. War Diary, 1st Battalion GPR, entry dated 27 May 1943, National Archive.
3. Mackenzie, Sergeant, W., 1 Squadron, 1st Battalion GPR, correspondence with the Author dated 26 May 2010.
4. Jenks, Staff Sergeant, G., 1 Squadron, 1st Battalion GPR, *The Wings of Pegasus*, Nashville, Battery Press, 1962, p. 45.
5. Jenks, Staff Sergeant, G., 1 Squadron, 1st Battalion GPR, *The Wings of Pegasus*, Nashville, Battery Press, 1962, p. 45.

6. Hall, Sergeant, M., 1 Squadron, 1st Battalion GPR, interview with the Author 24 February 2009.
7. McGeough, Staff Sergeant, J., GPR, letter to Luuk Buist dated 1978.
8. Hall, Staff Sergeant, D., 1 Squadron, 1st Battalion GPR, by permission of *The Eagle*.
9. Brown, Sergeant, N., 1 Squadron, 1st Battalion GPR, *The Gliders*, London, Arrow Books Ltd, 1982, p. 30.

Chapter 6

Turkey Buzzards – Running the Gauntlet

An incredibly courageous undertaking that proved to be the greatest long distance combat tow by any nation during the war.

The mixed results of the first wave of Turkey Buzzard combinations had proved that there was sufficient margin for success to risk more gliders and crews on Operation BEGGAR. More crews and Horsa gliders were prepared for the high-risk voyage to Morocco and then for onward flights to reinforce the 1st Battalion GPR at Froha. The ferrying operation was supported by the remaining Halifax flights of 295 Squadron RAF whose Whitleys were employed to ferry factory-fresh Horsas from 38 Wing airfields down to RAF Portreath; the use of the ageing bombers preserved precious flying hours and reduced wear and tear on the small fleet of modified Halifaxes. The Whitleys did,, however, require constant attention and maintenance support to keep them serviceable, with fitters at RAF Netheravon working day and night to keep them in the air. The post-operational report records an eight-day period during which an RAF engineering section consisting of Sergeant Swindells, five engine fitters and three other ground crewmen, worked with little rest to change five Whitley engines.

Staff Sergeant Wallace Mackenzie and his glider crew were employed in ferrying gliders to RAF Portreath, but remained unsure as to the ultimate purpose of their delivery flights. By early June, however, he and his fellow pilots had been briefed fully on their role in Operation BEGGAR and at 1500 hours on 6 June they took off on their own marathon journey:

> I left Portreath with Andy McCullough and Sergeant Hill. Tugs were fully laden with petrol and the take-off involved a full throttle with the brakes on, and then taking off at the very end of the runway, with no ability to increase height for some time. In fact the opportunity was taken to use 300–200 feet that we had above the sea, to put the nose

> down a little bit and gain some flying speed. A fighter escort had been expected but we did not see any of this.[1]

The worrying absence of a Beaufighter escort was the result of a break-down in communications between 38 Wing RAF and Coastal Command. Unbeknown to Headquarters 38 Wing RAF, the Beaufighter squadron was grounded that day while its aircraft underwent urgent engine modifications. The standard operating procedure that had been established for the rendezvous of a glider-tug combination with its fighter escort was for both groups of aircraft to meet over the Bishop Rock. Once recognition codes were exchanged and authenticated, the formation turned out to sea. The co-ordination of this rendezvous procedure proved problematical and a second formation flew from Bishop Rock with no escort. Consequently, later in the operation the procedure and rendezvous point were changed. The Beaufighter flights circled over RAF Portreath and took up their escort position almost from the moment that the glider-tug combinations cleared the Portreath circuit.

On the first occasion that the rendezvous was missed, the Halifax tug was commanded by Flying Officer Muirhead. He adhered to the flight plan timings and made the decision to press on south from Portreath out into the Bay of Biscay. It proved to be a good decision and the passage through German controlled airspace was uneventful, the combination arriving at Sale unmolested by prowling Condors or Ju-88s.

The operation began to develop its own rhythm, albeit the frequency of flights was constrained by a number of variables. The most notable was of course the weather, followed by the constant engineering effort required to maintain the limited number of modified tugs. The RAF ground crews at Hurn and Holmsley South took on the majority of the major engineering, working an average day of sixteen hours a day for week after week to keep the air bridge to North Africa operational. Details of the engineering activity at RAF Hurn between 2 June and 1 July 1943 provide a clear indication of the effort required: the fitters at Hurn completed four 25-hour inspections, seventeen minor inspections, changed three radiator bearings and three engine changes. In addition they replaced two rudder groups, overhauled four complete hydraulic systems, changed eighteen undercarriage oleo leg assemblies and repaired five rudder brackets. All of these major works were carried out in addition to routine pre-flight inspections and servicing.

The engineering effort at RAF Holmsley South was no less impressive and was undertaken in addition to the modification of the seventeen Halifax tugs to the specification required to give them the range to reach North Africa. The logistics of maintaining the Halifax fleet on exposed North African air-strips also required considerable effort by men of 38 Wing RAF. The first 30 Horsas deployed out to Sale were packed with major assemblies and spare engine parts for the 295 Squadron RAF fitters living out in the desert.

Meanwhile, Sergeants Dennis Hall and Harry Antonopoulos had recovered from their Atlantic ordeal and returned to Portreath via Northern Ireland. By 13 June 1943, they were going through a second planning cycle and were ready for another Turkey Buzzard flight. This time they would fly out with Staff Sergeant Paddy Conway as the third pilot. In the meantime, Major Alastair Cooper had been allocated to another Turkey Buzzard crew and had flown out on an earlier sortie.

The Halifax tug that was to tow them from RAF Portreath was flown by Warrant Officer Bill McCrodden. The combination lifted off from the Portreath runway on 14 June 1943 without incident and climbed away steadily from Cornwall. The weather was significantly better than on their first Turkey Buzzard flight and with Sergeant Antonopoulos at the controls the combination headed south. With vivid memories of their previous ditching, both were determined that they would be well equipped if they ended up in the sea again and thus kept their Mae West lifejackets and battledress on. As they flew further south into the Bay of Biscay, however, the spacious Horsa cockpit quickly developed into a Perspex hothouse but in spite of the increasing discomfort, the heavy woollen battledress and lifejackets remained in place.

Sergeant Antonopoulos was back at the controls for a second spell when the situation changed dramatically. Suddenly, tracer rounds streaked past the port and starboard sides of the Horsa fuselage and the rear gun turret of the Halifax opened fire as the gunner engaged two Focke Wulf aircraft as they attacked the lumbering combination. With no fighter escort to defend the British combination this was a very uneven contest; although the outcome was a forgone conclusion, the two crews nevertheless did their best to evade their attackers:

> The two enemy planes (which we took to be Condors) had finally compelled the tug pilot to request us to cast off, after a gallant but hopeless struggle. During the flight I did my utmost to assist the tug by following the twists and turns with all possible accuracy, while Hall in the co-pilot's seat was alert to every move and ready to take control in the case of any failure on my part. As for the third man, Paddy Conway, he had apparently been roused from a quiet rest, while eating a Mars Bar in the back of the glider. Good old Paddy! He dashed up and down the length of the glider, giving us a running commentary on the flight and hits (with epitaphs), and even going so far as to poke his rifle through one of the portholes.[2]

Finally, after a desperate attempt to evade the two German aircraft, the inevitable request came from the Halifax; if the Horsa cast off, at least the tug stood some chance of survival and, if it succeeded in escaping, could report the ditching position of the Horsa. If on the other hand they remained tethered to each other, both aircraft would surely be shot down. Sergeant Antonopoulos was still at the controls and full of fight:

> ... following the tug through some very step turns. Finally, the tow plane pilot spoke over the intercom and said, 'It's no good, would you please pull off?' I pulled the release lever and the Halifax quickly climbed into the clouds and disappeared. One Focke Wulf was just below me, and I dove at him. I don't know what was in my mind, but I thought 'I'll get this bastard'. It must have worried him because he stopped firing and at the last second we both turned away. There was no problem landing – I was the greatest ditcher of all time and had written the definitive report on how to do it.[3]

The Horsa had cast off from the tug at a position roughly 140 miles west of Cape Finisterre, the Halifax meanwhile turning away to the north with its tormentors in pursuit. No longer molested, the glider crew executed a textbook emergency landing and evacuated their aircraft safely. Squashed in their dinghy, the three sodden pilots elected to keep it close to the floating wreck of their Horsa in the hope that the Halifax crew had transmitted an accurate fix of the glider's location to Coastal Command. The Halifax had indeed transmitted the co-ordinates of the incident, subsequently making it safely to Morocco after a running battle with its pursuers; the rear gunner subsequently claimed one Ju-88 destroyed during the action and damage to a further two. After landing, an inspection of the tug revealed 36 cannon shell holes in its fuselage.

Oblivious to the fate of their tug, the three pilots endured a cold, wet and uncomfortable night in extremely cramped conditions. At first light on the second day there was still no sign of rescue on the horizon and the prospect of another day exposed to Atlantic conditions was unattractive. The dinghy was still tied to the Horsa but the sea state was worsening with the glider being lifted out of the water and then crashing back on to the surface. Anxious at the increasing risk of the overloaded dinghy being sunk or that one of them would be crushed, the three pilots held a swift 'Sergeants Mess meeting' and decided to move away from the wreck and make for land. Using a ground sheet, a rope and two planks of wood salvaged from their glider, they rigged up a makeshift sail and, taking a very rough heading from their compass, set off in the direction of the coast of neutral Spain.

The glider crew now become a dinghy crew, dividing their nautical duties between them. Staff Sergeant Paddy Conway was responsible for the all-important Verey pistol and flare cartridges, while also assuming the secondary duty of maintaining morale on board. Having managed to save his harmonica, he did his best to entertain his two comrades by playing popular tunes over the coming days. Sergeant Dennis Hall was in charge of doling out the water and survival rations that they had managed to bring with them, whilst Sergeant Harry Antonopoulos, who had some experience of boats and sailing, took on the role of sailing the dinghy. They would need all of their physical stamina as the sail was estimated to generate a maximum speed of one knot an hour. At this rate, drifting on a very loose south-east heading, they anticipated a journey of at least ten days before landfall.

Back in England meanwhile, the other pilots of No. 1 Squadron, unaware that their three comrades had ditched in the Atlantic, had continued to plan and prepare for their own Turkey-Buzzard sorties. Staff Sergeant Len Wright captured the mood of those waiting their turn to launch from Portreath:

> Portreath was the 'last airfield' in England or the nearest to North Africa. Here the glider crews waited for satisfactory weather reports before the long tow could start. Sometimes crews arrived one evening and were away by following morning; others waited a week or longer. The waiting was quite pleasant from what I remember. The food was good, there was a good beach to sunbathe on when the sun shone, Redruth was only a walk away and there was an opportunity to get in some drinking hours listening to a record of the Ink Spots singing, 'I like coffee, I like tea, I like a java jive, etc, etc.' The snag was it did not pay to drink too much just in case that early morning call came and it was a long way to fly with a thick head.[4]

As the tempo of the operation built up and the weather improved, there were fewer delays and German interference was sporadic. Turkey Buzzard combinations continued to take their chances, setting off from Portreath to run the gauntlet across the Bay of Biscay. In fact by 16 June 1943 the ferrying operation had already succeeded in delivering an impressive total of eighteen Horsa gliders to Sale. The operation now had its own momentum. In mid-June, Staff Sergeant Mike Hall was at Portreath waiting for his own turn to make the epic flight to North Africa. Still unaware of the fate of his comrades adrift in the Bay of Biscay, he and his own crew had some time off:

> We did a certain amount of training each day until 20 June when I and two co-pilots, Sergeants Roberts and Newton, were told we would be off the next day, so off we went into Portreath for a last visit and a cup of coffee. Whilst in the café we were reading the Daily Express and to our horror saw in the stop press a report that the Germans had claimed to have shot down a tug and glider over the Bay of Biscay and we were off the next day.[5]

Out in the Bay of Biscay the crew of Horsa LG 945 had now been adrift for six days in their dinghy. They were enduring the extremes of the open sea and on the fourth day they survived the drama of being capsized by heavy seas. They also had the added frustration of seeing a glider–tug combination pass by in the distance. In spite of their frantic efforts to attract the attention of both crews and the expenditure of a valuable flare cartridge, they remained unobserved. Their frustration was further heightened when a ship passed within 400 yards of their sodden dinghy without stopping, sailing on over the horizon in spite of the pilots firing another of their precious Verey flares.

After eleven days and nights, the elements had worn them down. Staff Sergeant Hall was extremely ill and Sergeants Antonopoulos and Conway were in poor condition. Each of them was suffering from dehydration, exposure, saltwater rash and immersion foot, but they all still continued to battle together against the odds. Day and night they kept the dinghy inflated, using an empty water can to bail out of the dinghy.

Finally, on their eleventh day at sea and having succeeded in bringing their dinghy to within 20 miles of the coast of Portugal, the exhausted trio were becalmed in a bank of thick fog. With no wind to harness, they resorted to paddling until they had expended their last reserves of energy. Then, almost miraculously, from the depths of the fog they heard the welcome sound of a small ship's horn. The exhausted pilots' spirits were instantly lifted and they sat waiting with their aircrew whistles at the ready. They continually scanning the fog bank hopefully as the horn drew gradually nearer. To avoid the risk of scaring the approaching craft away, they decided they would only use their whistles at the last safe moment when the mystery vessel was almost on top of them.

Finally, their desperate prayers were answered when they saw a small fishing boat loom out of the fog. The three men blew their whistles with all of their remaining strength and the boat came to a halt nearby. Soon afterwards, the fishermen pulled each of them on board what they later learned was the Spanish fishing boat *Gaviotta*. Sat on the deck, the three elated pilots opened their last cans of drinking water in celebration and gulped down a can each without stopping.

The Spaniards treated their new guests well, providing them with a bunk below decks, a meal of fish and bowls of hot water and sugar. The *Gaviotta* landed its unusual catch at the Spanish port of Vigo where the local community turned out on the quayside to welcome the intrepid airmen. The initial friendly reception was followed by a probing interrogation by the Spanish police, but fortunately this was interrupted by the arrival of the British vice-consul who extracted the three pilots from a potentially unpleasant experience. This was followed by a short stay in hospital, lightened by a series of visits and overwhelming generosity from the local British community.

As soon as they were fit to travel, all three were discharged from hospital and escorted on their way to the British Embassy in Madrid. The first stage of their journey was by road, in a car driven by a Spanish Air Force officer. They were then placed on a train from Valladolid to the Spanish capital. What followed was a moment of farce amid the serious business of war. Waiting to meet them on the platform at Madrid was not a British diplomat as expected, but a representative of the German Ambassador. Once this confusion was resolved, they were soon on their way to the British Embassy where they remained for a week.

Eventually, after a very warm and jovial audience with the British ambassador, their journey was resumed and the trio began heading south by train. The final leg of their travels across Spain ended in sanctuary within the labyrinth of caves and tunnels underneath the British colony of Gibraltar. A week later, after a thorough debrief, they embarked on a British ship and joined a convoy bound for Liverpool. All three returned to The Glider Pilot Regiment, but played no further part in the Sicily operation. They all flew on later operations and were deservedly awarded the Air Force Medal in recognition of their remarkable exploits.

Meanwhile, as the intrepid crew of Horsa LG945 was making its way across the Iberian Peninsula, the Turkey Buzzard flights continued with Lieutenant Colonel George Chatterton and his staff keeping a close eye on the mounting number of Horsa gliders arriving in North Africa, all being entered in the 1st Battalion GPR war diary: on 30 June 1943 the total sat at 25, and by 7 July 1943 stood at 27. Overall, given the starting point just a few weeks before and the scale and complexity of the task, this was a remarkable feat of airmanship, planning and logistics. It also proved to be a good start to the relationship between The Glider Pilot Regiment and the men of 38 Wing RAF, a partnership that would be put to the test over coming weeks, months and years and not be found wanting.

Notes

1. Mackenzie, Staff Sergeant, W., 1 Squadron, 1st Battalion GPR, correspondence with the author dated 26 May 2010.
2. Antonopoulos, Sergeant, S., 1 Squadron, 1st Battalion GPR By permission of *The Eagle*.
3. Antonopoulos, Sergeant, S., 1 Squadron, 1st Battalion GPR, *The Glider Gang*, Cassell, London, 1977, p. 65.
4. Wright papers, p. 15, by permission of the Museum of Army Flying.
5. Hall, Staff Sergeant, M., 1 Squadron, 1st Battalion GPR, Interview with the author 24 February 2009.

Chapter 7

A Race Against Time

Only Hoppy was full of confidence. 'If Italy spoils the show by packing in before the date,' he said – 'we'll do the operation as an exercise!'

All through May and June 1943, as the Turkey Buzzard crews continued to brave the numerous threats and hazards of their migration to North Africa, the 1st Airborne Division plan for their part in Operation HUSKY was steadily taking shape. Operation LADBROKE was the first ever large-scale Allied airborne operation and it was rapidly becoming evident to everybody involved that it was not going to be a straightforward task. Planning continued under the assumption that 1st Airlanding Brigade would be carried into battle in gliders flown by British pilots.

Even as the training of those pilots was in its earliest stages, the staffs at Major General Hopkinson's divisional headquarters and those of Brigadier General Ray Dunn's 51st Transport Wing were grappling with the complexities of producing the LADBROKE plan. The workload at Headquarters 1st Airlanding Brigade and 38 Wing RAF was also significant as these had the additional burden of coordinating the training of the glider pilots and their RAF and USAAF tug crews. Not only did the flying training programme have to prepare the Allied aircrew for the challenge of flying in the most demanding conditions, it also had to develop the techniques required to penetrate the formidable Axis defences on Sicily.

Allied intelligence had reported the presence of a capable early warning radar system that covered an extensive area of Italian airspace and posed a significant threat to any airborne operation mounted against Sicily. Early detection of the presence of a large formation of aircraft would alert anti-aircraft batteries and possibly fighters, either of which could wreak havoc among tightly packed transport aircraft carrying paratroops or a slow-moving stream of tugs and gliders. The loss of even a small percentage of these valuable transport aircraft or their aircrews was a cause for concern among USAAF planners as America had entered the war only eighteen months before and aircraft production had not yet reached its full industrial potential. Moreover, the Mediterranean theatre of operations was viewed as a secondary priority and as a consequence the USAAF Troop Carrier Wings not only remained desperately short of C-47 transports but also of the logistical support and personnel required to keep them in the air.

The Troop Carrier Wings employed the C-47 Skytrain as their main workhorse. Although they looked the part, painted in drab military colours, the airframes themselves were in fact early variants of the C-47 and therefore were far short of the technical specification required of a military transport aircraft of the day. Among the most significant of the missing modifications was the total absence of any armour plating to protect the aircrew and the lack of self-sealing fuel tanks.

In order to reduce the risk to these vulnerable aircraft and therefore minimise losses, Brigadier General Ray Dunn and his staff planned a combination of defensive countermeasures. Firstly, the approach to Sicily across the Mediterranean Sea was to be made at low altitude in order to avoid radar detection. Thus, the entire run across the 400 miles of open sea was to be made at extremely low-level requiring the USAAF pilots to fly at 100 feet. This approach height would be a challenge for experienced crews in daylight, let alone much less experienced pilots at night. While relatively safe from radar detection such an approach was, however, well below the minimum safe altitude for both parachute and assault glider operations. Therefore, any aircraft delivering parachutists or airlanding troops would have to climb and gain height, thus exposing itself to radar detection before completing its mission. In the case of a tug-glider combination, the tug had to climb at the last safe moment to an altitude of at least 800 feet to release its glider. This height was calculated as the minimum release height that would give the glider the range it would need after casting off to complete its glide to the nearest landing zones to the coast. Those gliders that were tasked to reach further inland would have to cast off at a higher altitude.

In addition to the hazards of a low-level approach, the USAAF tugs were also to avoid anti-aircraft fire on the approach to the release point. In order to minimise the risk, the release or 'cast off' of gliders was to be completed 3,000 yards off the coast of Sicily and thus well out of the effective range of enemy anti-aircraft guns. Thereafter, the tugs would be free to turn and run for safety across the Mediterranean at full throttle. Although not ideal, the distance of the release point from shore was not insurmountable. In normal conditions a well-handled WACO could fly a distance equivalent to fifteen times its height at the start of its glide approach. As long as the release height was adequate and weather conditions were good, the offshore release to an inland LZ was achievable.

Now fully aware of the planning constraints on the use of USAAF tug aircraft and the nature of the terrain that awaited his pilots in Sicily, Lieutenant Colonel George Chatterton analysed the problems he faced and identified the following objectives and capabilities required for the Sicily operation:

1. To give my pilots confidence enough in themselves to carry out the flight to Sicily and to land.
2. To land by moonlight on a rock-strewn beach, after being released at between 1,500 and 2,000 feet.
3. The gliders to be landed in groups of battalions, in order that the air landing brigade should be able to fight as a brigade group.
4. The loads in the gliders were to be infantry, jeeps and artillery.[1]

Before further training and preparation for the invasion could get underway, the glider pilots had to be grouped into the squadrons, flights and individual crews in which they would fly and fight. This was not a straightforward task, given that the bulk of the battalion had limited flying experience and most had undergone a similar amount of training. Advised by his squadron commanders, Chatterton set about dividing his pilots into groups of first and second pilots who were subsequently paired into a glider crew.

Staff Sergeant Harry Howard of No. 2 Squadron was selected to be a first pilot and then paired with Sergeant Jim Bennett who would act as his second pilot:

> At that time I was promoted to Staff Sergeant, as were half the flight and the others still as Sergeants were teamed up with a Staff Sergeant. None of us knew why some were favoured more than others unless it was based upon our glider course assessments. Jim was just as good a pilot as I was – I would have been quite happy from my experience with him to let him take off or land. In the air he probably handled the controls as much as, if not longer, than I did.[2]

Staff Sergeant Howard's upbeat view of the selection process is not uncommon among surviving veterans. This would suggest that, for reasons of sensitivity, the reasoning and criteria applied to pilot selection at battalion headquarters was kept within the headquarters staff. The view among those outside the battalion who knew the detail of the Operation LADBROKE plan and what was expected of 1st Airlanding Brigade was however far less optimistic. Squadron Leader Lawrence Wright was among those who had a good overview of the training of glider pilots in North Africa. After the war he recalled his concerns at the time:

> That gliders could be used in this way was contrary to all we had learned to date, and to the lesson of Crete, especially with glider pilots trained to the present low standard. About 500 of them had completed the Horsa course, but some with so few hours flying that Chatterton had to divide them into first and second pilots, none of the latter being fully experienced even by day. About 50 such crews were resuming their training in Algeria, and about 60 more were to follow, but in the past six months at home they had averaged only about eight hours in

> Horsas. None had done night landings, none had flown WACOs, but within six weeks they must fly these some 300 miles, mostly over water by night, and land by moonlight on a defended coast.[3]

In addition to the shortfalls in training and preparation mentioned by Wright, there was another critical area of weakness that hindered the training of glider pilots. The 1st Battalion GPR headquarters was significantly smaller than those of the other units in 1st Airborne Division. This reduced capacity to deal with the daily business of running the battalion, and dealing with all the issues that accompany a unit with such a specialist role, placed a great load on Lieutenant Colonel Chatterton and his tiny staff. The combination of the planning and execution of the training programme, together with the physical strain of living and working in North Africa, gradually took its toll.

At the beginning of June the Officer Commanding No. 3 Squadron, Major John Place, was unexpectedly summoned to Battalion Headquarters at Mascara. On arrival, the highly capable Dubliner was met by 1st Airborne Division's Assistant Director Medical Services (ADMS). Place learned that Lieutenant Colonel Chatterton was suffering from overwork and, as a result, had been ordered to bed for a rest. As the senior squadron commander, Place would now have to take on the mantle of command and the running of Battalion Headquarters in Mascara. The planning for Operation LADBROKE and the coordination of the battalion's work-up training was a complex and daunting task and the newly appointed Acting Commanding Officer desperately needed every ounce of staff horsepower he could muster. There were, however, few GPR officers with the correct training, experience and seniority to be found. In spite of these shortfalls, Place did have one advantage over his Commanding Officer: he knew Major General Hopkinson well and had a very different opinion of him:

> The headquarters staff struggled on under my willing but inadequate direction … the Adjutant had returned to his squadron and Peter Harding had taken over his job. The Froha squadron commander had returned to England because of ill health and Captain Tony Murray had assumed command.
>
> For a week I lived in Colonel Chatterton's flat in Mascara and spent most of my time running upstairs from my office to the General's and back again. Major General Hopkinson … 'Hoppy' as we called him was one of those men who, though small in stature, had the heart of a lion and a nature that endeared him to the whole division. He had insisted that the divisional commander must be qualified in every airborne discipline. Though well over forty years of age and a veteran of World War 1, he had learned to be a pilot of both gliders and both light powered aircraft, and had done several parachute jumps.

> To me he was not only the General but also a friend, for I had served under him in Northern Ireland from 1932 to 1937 and in Palestine in 1936 when he was my company commander in an infantry regiment. General Hoppy was a man of great charm and understanding and one of the most approachable of senior officers. His sense of humour was such that often his staff was not sure whether their legs were being pulled until they saw his eyes twinkle, and the pursing of his lips, a habit of his just before he burst out laughing.[4]

Place injected a significant amount of vigour and energy into Battalion Headquarters, and was later credited by many glider pilots with the success of the flying training programme under extremely difficult conditions.

The majority of the pilots were busy building and flying WACO gliders and thus remained unaware of the turmoil generated by the temporary absence of Chatterton. Sergeant Harold Lansdell and his comrades had quickly got to grips with flying the WACO at Relizane airstrip. As the training programme continued to gain momentum, he and his comrades in No. 2 Squadron had been split into groups of first and second pilots and thus now knew with whom they would fly on D-Day. Day by day, the tempo and complexity of their flying training increased, as did the availability of information on the general nature of the impending operation. It was obvious to Lansdell that the time available for training was dwindling and that in a few weeks time they would be taking off together for an, as yet, unknown destination. The training programme was designed to mould together as teams as well as building up flying hours and experience on the WACO as he recalled later:

> Topper Brown and I were teamed up with him as first and me as second pilot. Training time was short and only first pilots did the landings, eight of which were at night, and we learned later that Major General Hopkinson had witnessed the exercises, which were simulations for the Sicily landing and declared them successful. We had flown much too close for comfort over an American camp shortly before the night landing. Before knowing where it was, we were shown a model of the landing area in Sicily and told that 'On the orders of General Montgomery there will be no provision for the reception of prisoners.'[5]

Generally speaking, morale was good among the glider pilots as they progressed through the training programme. Lieutenant Michael Connell was one of the officers in No. 3 Squadron; his route into the cockpit of a glider was typical of many of the young officers in the 1st Battalion GPR. Originally commissioned into the Royal Irish Fusiliers as a second lieutenant in July 1939, he deployed to France in time to endure the frustrations of the Phoney War but subsequently gained combat experience during the final chaotic stages of the Blitzkrieg campaign of 1940. He survived the fighting and was eventually evacuated to England from Dunkirk in June.

With memories of the fighting in France fresh in his mind, he volunteered for training as a glider pilot and on completion of his flying training was awarded his wings, thereafter being posted as a lieutenant to the 1st Battalion GPR and North Africa where he found time to write home to his family on 9 June 1943. His brief letter has a timeless feel and could have been written by a soldier on operations today. It also gives a good insight into the morale, living conditions and the daily routine of the glider pilots assembled in North Africa that summer.

> Dear Mum,
>
> Thank you for your Airgraph dated 25th May, I also got my dressing gown and a letter from Joan thanking me for the 10/– I sent her, for which many thanks. An Air letter is the quickest way of writing Mum, I don't write more of them myself as they are rationed here; and don't forget to write on the page on the back. I have numbered this one two and will number them all including ordinary letters. The mail may go haywire again so don't worry if you don't have a letter for a few days or perhaps a week or so as they will soon sort it out, these hitches often happen. It's even hotter now and spend the greater part of the day absolutely dripping we don't work between 12 noon and 3 o'clock in the afternoon but start at 5.30 in the morning, what an hour. Am pretty busy and quite comfortable here. Write soon and often and don't forget the papers.
>
> Much love to all at home.
>
> Mike[6]

Less than a week after Connell wrote his letter home, he and the majority of the glider pilots were preparing for their first major test. The entry in the 1st Battalion GPR war diary for 13 June 1943 reads:

> Flying Training completed ... 116 crews were trained to full operational standard. 521 hours flown and 1,873 lifts were made.

The achievement of operational status had not come without cost to the battalion. Sergeants J. Cullen and E. Clarke were both listed as very seriously injured in a flying accident on 2 June 1943. Ten days later Staff Sergeant Frank Wheale, aged 23, and Sergeant Eric W. Hall, aged 25, were both killed when their glider crashed during a training flight. There was however little time for the battalion to mourn its dead.

With the basic WACO conversion syllabus complete and crews classified as ready to fly on operations, it was time to integrate the glider pilots with the other key component of Major General Hopkinson's plan: the men of the assault force. A series of airlanding exercises was planned to integrate the US 51st Troop Carrier Wing tug aircraft, the 1st Battalion GPR and the troops and equipment of 1st Airlanding Brigade. A series of work-up exercises were planned that would progress toward the end state outlined in Lieutenant Colonel George Chatterton's initial training objectives. With the basic handling skills in place, the combined force would now have to work collectively toward being able to deliver troops en masse onto their landing zones in Sicily.

In addition to bringing tugs, gliders and loads together, the programme would as far as possible rehearse every element of the LADBROKE plan. In spite of the shortage of time, the relative inexperience of all of the troops and aircrews taking part in the operation allowed for only the simplest of exercises. The training for LADBROKE was divided into three separate phases, with the first phase of the work-up training for 1st Airlanding Brigade being split into two separate exercises. The 2nd Battalion The South Staffordshire Regiment formed the main body for the first exercise, code-named Exercise Adam. The troops of the 1st Battalion The Border Regiment were meanwhile allotted the second exercise, codenamed Eve.

On 14 June 1943, less than a month before D-Day, the first of these airlanding exercises took place. Exercise Adam involved 56 WACO gliders and pilots from No. 2 Squadron flying from the strips at Matmore and Thiersville. The first gliders were due off the ground at 1845 hours, the bulk of their loads comprising the men, weapons and equipment of B and D Companies of the South Staffordshires. In addition, elements of Headquarters 1st Airlanding Brigade, a sub-section of sappers of 9th Field Company (Airborne) RE and a section of 181st Airlanding Field Ambulance would also be flying that day. The exercise was deliberately kept simple, its aim being to prove the loading and ground marshalling systems for the gliders and their tugs while also testing the preparation and co-ordination processes for the loading of the assault troops.

The aircraft were required to fly a relatively short and undemanding route in daylight. They had to follow a 70-mile triangular route with an estimated flight time of 20 minutes. At the end of the flight the glider pilots were to cast off and make their first landing in a fully laden glider on the airstrip at Froha. Although all of the gliders flew with live loads, none carried heavy items such as vehicles, guns or handcarts. The No. 2 Squadron crews carried the loads, or 'chalks' as they were called, that they were destined to carry on D-Day and the LZ was marked out to replicate the dimensions of LZ Able outside Syracuse.

The crews had trained to cast off from their tugs at a fixed release point with all aircraft making their approach from the same height. The exercise instruction directed that the formations should fly at an altitude of 800 feet and that, once released, the gliders were to make their descent at 70–20 mph in the manner developed during the Chatterton test flights.

The first serials of the South Staffordshires began rolling down their respective airstrips as planned at 1845 hours, leaving dense clouds of dust behind them. The glider-tug combinations climbed away from their home airstrips and thereafter successfully formatted into waves of four. The four gliders were then towed in echelon, separated by a two-minute launch interval.

The outline intent for the exercise was achieved; each formation completed the 70-mile transit flight successfully, building up flying hours and familiarity between tug and WACO crews, while the troops of 1st Airlanding Brigade gained valuable air experience and identified last minute pitfalls in their mounting instructions. On arrival at the designated release points, the pilots 'pulled off' from their tugs and thereafter each glider then flew its pre-designated course, turning onto new compass headings over pre-briefed points. Finally, it then made a fully laden training approach into landing lanes on Froha airfield at the designated landing speed. The exercise went relatively well, the last glider landed safely at Froha at 1945 hours. There were no casualties among the South Staffordshire chalks, although six of the No. 2 Squadron gliders crashed or made forced landings short of the destination airfield.

The next day, the 1st Battalion The Border Regiment carried out a dry run exercise named Vin Blanc. Using 3-ton trucks in place of gliders, the entire battalion went through a vehicle-borne rehearsal of the mounting and landing procedure for Exercise Eve. The glider pilots for each glider took part in the wheeled exercise, travelling with their respective infantry chalks. The exercise practised the battalion in marshalling, forming-up and landing of gliders in a pre-designated sequence across four lanes, the landing phase including nominated objectives for the rifle companies and support platoons after landing.

The glider pilots also practised their roles in the operation immediately after landing. The second pilot had to leave the cockpit and find a position from where he could look back across the LZ. He was to act as a sentry, warning the disembarking troops of the imminent approach of incoming gliders. The first pilot was given the task of leading the chalk away from the glider and off the LZ. Both pilots would be required to carry out these roles on the night of D-1.

However, the men of No. 3 Squadron and the Borderers would have to wait for their chance to go through their paces for the first time. Shortly after Exercise Adam, the training programme paused and consequently lost some of its momentum. The cumulative strain of the past few weeks was now beginning to tell on men and aircraft; by 16 June 1943 there was clear evidence of a dramatic increase in mechanical failures on the WACO fleet. The haste with which some of the aircraft had been assembled by inexperienced fitters, combined with a lack of well-organised maintenance, was now coming home to roost and the US North West African Air Force Command took the decision to ground most of the WACOs available for training. This drastic action was repeated again just ten days before D-Day to allow fitters to tend to battered and tired gliders.

A few days after Exercise Vin Blanc, with many gliders still grounded, Lieutenant Michael Connell of No. 3 Squadron found time again to write home. Aware of the censors reading his letter and of the need to avoid worrying his family, he left out any detailed description of life in North Africa or any concerns he may have had about the shortfalls in his training:

> Dear Mum,
>
> Just a line to let you know we have moved and are now once more under canvas having left our fairly comfortable barracks. It is pretty dusty here matter of fact the dust is being stirred up by a wind known as the Sirocco which is a hot wind, but otherwise we are pretty comfortable. The fruit is beginning to come in now and I have had a few peaches which are much smaller than the ones we get in England and some dates, figs, tomatoes and lemons but not in any quantity yet (A few days later) – I have had my photo taken by a press correspondent so look out in the papers a few days back it is a movie shot and shows me shepherding chaps into a glider. Think I had better stop there or there will be a gap in my letter …[7]

After a few short days of maintenance on 1st Battalion GPR's battered gliders, the flying training programme was resumed with vigour. It was now the turn of the Borderers to carry out a live exercise using gliders. Exercise Eve took place late on the afternoon of 20 June 1943. The mounting instruction and the loads for the exercise were identical to the plan that the Borderers would use for Operation LADBROKE. The training was designed to consolidate on the success of Exercise Adam and to be as close to a dress rehearsal for D-Day as possible. The exercise instruction states that the aim of the exercise was:

> To test out the flying organisation for the landing of 72 aircraft in one area.

The area that the exercise was chosen to replicate would later be revealed as LZ Baker, one of the 1st Airlanding Brigade's LZs outside Syracuse. Exercise Eve was larger in scale and more complex than Adam as this time the C-47 tugs of 51st Troop Carrier Wing would be augmented by Albemarle aircraft from 296 Squadron RAF. The combined formation was to tow 72 WACOs of No. 3 Squadron, carrying 632 officers and men of the 1st Battalion The Border Regiment.

The gliders lined up for take-off in their marshalling lanes on the strips at Thiersville, Matmore and Froha. Thereafter, the exercise course took the stream of four aircraft formations over a 100-mile route, the transit altitude and cast off height having been set at 1,100 feet. Each glider was in the air for about one-and-a-half hours before landing in lanes on the runway at Thiersville. The No. 3 Squadron crews under the command of Major John Place were allowed some flexibility in their cast-off heights. Those gliders with the longer approach to make would release at higher altitudes than those that were landing later and further back in the landing lanes. The exercise was declared successful in spite of the fact that fourteen gliders failed to reach the LZ. On completion of the exercise, one of the Borderer platoons reported that one of its gliders had looped-the-loop prior to landing.

A few hours later, under a bright full moon, Exercise Eve 2 took place. A smaller formation of twelve tugs and WACOs were scheduled to take off in darkness at 2345 hours, the glider crews being drawn from both Nos 2 and 3 Squadrons which provided six crews each. The exercise was intended to build on the success of the previous larger scale landings and in addition to carry out a fully laden night landing. Only eleven of the twelve WACOs got into the air, one aircraft failing to take off due to technical problems. They flew successfully at a transit height of 1,700 feet, carrying chalks formed by personnel from Headquarters 1st Airlanding Brigade and the Borderers' battalion headquarters. In a high risk move, Major General Hopkinson added his name to the manifest and flew on the exercise.

The night flying element of the exercise included a cast-off over an illuminated inverted 'L' navigation aid that marked the release point. All of the gliders reached the correct LZ, although three were damaged on landing. The exercise was reported as a success and the post-exercise report optimistically concluded that:

> A mass landing of gliders by moonlight had proved to be a practical proposition.[8]

The first phase of training had gone extremely well with no casualties and only minor damage to a handful of gliders. The mounting of the exercises had been successful, in particular the loading and marshalling of the gliders and tugs by the USAAF ground crews, while the take-offs, transit flight and landings had been executed well. However, the majority of the 1st Battalion GPR crews had still not completed a transit flight anywhere near the duration of that they would be expected to fly on D-1. Nor had they flown in formation at night or indeed over the open sea. The fact remained that landing in lanes on an open airfield in daylight was nowhere near the challenge that would have to be faced in darkness on the Sicily LZs.

In spite of the remaining shortfall in training and experience, 1st Airborne Division and its supporting USAAF aircraft and gliders now had to move to the forward airfields in Tunisia where, once in place, they would join Montgomery's Eighth Army. It would be from these airfields that 1st Airlanding Brigade would mount Britain's first large-scale airborne operation.

Phase 2 of the LADBROKE build-up began on Sunday 27 June 1943, with 1st Airborne Division leaving the training areas of Morocco and re-locating 550 miles to the group of forward airfields around Froha. Every available asset was used to move the division, the bulk of 1st Airlanding Brigade flying over the Atlas Mountains in USAAF C-47s or by glider while the remainder of the brigade and most of its vehicles moved overland in convoy.

The airlift used 84 WACO gliders, many of which were fresh from the assembly line and had yet to be test flown. In the case of these, a circuit of the airfield was completed immediately after take-off as an airworthiness test. Once this was completed and the pilots were satisfied their aircraft was fit for the 600-mile flight over the mountains, they informed their tug crews. The glider-tug combinations then left the circuit and began the flight to Tunisia. The operation was spread over a number of days, with a number of glider pilots making the journey over the Atlas Mountains more than once in order to ferry the full complement of WACOs to Tunisia.

Sergeant Norman Howes was a platoon sergeant in C Company of the South Staffordshires, and was among the infantrymen taking to the air as live glider loads for the transit flight to Tunisia. He was set to fly with his platoon on the first morning of the move but, as with every military plan, there were last minute changes. His memories of the events early on that morning were still vivid many years later:

> Company Sergeant Major Glynn was sick and I was designated to take his place in the C Company HQ glider. Lofty Wallcock would take over my platoon. When Company Sergeant Major Glynn got to hear of this, he told everybody to 'Go away' or something like that, and I was sent back to my own glider. 'Joey' Glynn staggered into his glider and off we went. Halfway over the mountains we ran into terrible turbulence and these WACO gliders were jumping about all over the place. I was told afterwards that a 1,000-foot drop was nothing. I was looking across at Joey's glider and suddenly the tail unit dropped off, it just seemed to split into two, the tail went up in the air, and, of course, the tug just released him, and down they went.[9]

There were no survivors of this tragic incident. The dead included both glider pilots, Sergeant James E. Harrison, aged 24, and his second pilot Sergeant Arthur Higgins aged 26.

Lance Corporal 'Reg' Brown was a member of A Company of the South Staffordshires. He was also flying out of Algeria that day:

> On Sunday 27 June 1943 we went by trucks to Thiersville Airfield. Gliders were awaiting us, Yankee WACOs (I hate them). We emplaned and took off for an 'unknown destination' that proved to be Sousse, some 600 miles away in Tunisia. It was a deadly trip; the gliders were thrown all over the sky, especially over the very mountainous parts that

> are such a prominent feature of the Algerian/Tunisian terrain. I was very pleased when, after some five-and-a-half hours flying, we landed at a landing strip near Sousse. On this trip, the tail came off one of the gliders in the air. All were killed including a friend of mine, Corporal Holmes of Birmington.[10]

A total of 81 WACOs reached Tunisia safely; five were slightly damaged in transit. In addition to the fatal crash, another two gliders made forced landings en route, fortunately with no further casualties.

Staff Sergeant Harry Howard and his second pilot, Sergeant Jim Bennett, were flying a WACO on the first day's lift. He hints at the problems faced by the crews of the heavily laden gliders after take off:

> ... it was daylight flight with take off at 6 am to avoid thermals over the Atlas Mountains but with the June sun full in our faces. Our tugs had to climb to 10,000 feet under difficult conditions especially with a full load attached to their tail. We were both glad when we reached our destination ... We had one major casualty during the flight. Arthur Higgins, with whom we were both friendly, lost his tail unit over the mountains and both pilots and their troops were killed in the inevitable crash two miles below. Parachutes were seldom if ever used and certainly never when carrying troops.[11]

The Atlas Mountains were a formidable and dangerous obstacle with summits that reached 7,000 feet. A tug-glider combination needed to reach an altitude of 9,000 feet to clear the peaks safely and avoid up draughts and turbulence. Gaining that altitude with a glider in tow took an average of 30 minutes laboured climbing for most of the C-47 aircraft. The trip was quite a test for the glider pilots, most of who had not flown for more than an hour of continuous flight prior to the airlift. The air currents and thermals over the mountains were as unpredictable as they were dangerous. One glider pilot reported that his combination had lost 3,000 feet in ten minutes while another plunged 1,000 feet after a single 'bump'. It was no fun being a passenger while all of this was going on; many of the passengers being airsick.

Staff Sergeant 'Jimmy' James was at the controls of one of the WACOs on the dramatic flight over the rugged mountain range:

> The flight over the Atlas mountains was awe inspiring. To look down at those formidable and sharp mountain peaks, the thought of an involuntary landing made me shudder. It was certainly a relief to see the plains and salt lakes coming into view.[12]

On the second day of the airlift operation, an incident occurred that gives an insight into the pressures that were building on all concerned. The second wave of six combinations was forming up over the Froha airfields watched by, among others, Major General Hopkinson; no doubt the tragedy of the tailless WACO crash and the deaths of all on board were on people's minds. Whether this was a factor in what happened next is not known. A glider cast off from its tug and landed back on the airfield. On landing, the pilot reported that the ailerons were not functioning properly and that he was concerned about his aircraft's airworthiness. On hearing this, Hopkinson insisted on flying the aircraft himself straight away and upon completion of his personal test flight pronounced the aircraft fit to fly. He then ordered the pilot grounded and sent home immediately. There were no further aborted test flights from the Froha airfields.

The relatively long transit flight further tested the procedures that would be used for Operation LADBROKE and any subsequent airborne operations on Sicily. These were valuable flying hours that were as much needed by the glider pilots as they were by the equally inexperienced tug crews of 51st Troop Carrier Wing. The post-operational report written by Lieutenant Colonel Chatterton in August 1943 summarised the build up training and the move of over 1,200 fully equipped men over the Atlas Mountains:

> This phase was truly significant. Never previously had such a large number of men been moved so quickly over such a distance. The credit should go to the pilots of 51st Wing for their excellent piloting. The outstanding point was that the Tug-Glider combination proved itself as a strategic weapon, with a range of a thousand miles. Moreover, this weapon could be used at night. Finally, this flight was invaluable experience for the Glider Pilots and was excellent practice for the operation.[13]

The move over the North African mountain range had been a success as both a strategic move and ferrying operation. However, although training had progressed well, there were still underlying concerns about the readiness of the glider pilots for a combat operation. At the conclusion of the move, the bulk of 1st Airborne Division left Mascara and travelled 600 miles to camps and airfields grouped around Kairouan, west of Sousse in Tunisia. The ground tail elements of the division began moving east on 19 June, the last troops arriving in Kairouan on 5 July 1943.

In spite of the epic flight over the Atlas Mountains, there were still concerns about the overall lack of flying experience among the glider pilots. Sergeant Wallace Mackenzie had two Turkey Buzzard runs behind him and two trips across the Atlas Mountains; by virtue of this he was now among the most experienced pilots in The Glider Pilot Regiment at that time. However, in spite of his total of amassed flying hours he was aware of a glaring gap in his experience and capabilities:

> Up to this time, I had just over 100 hours of powered flight, about half as solo pilot and of which only six hours were night flying. I also had

> 140 hours of glider flying behind me, half of which was as first pilot. However, of this total less than an hour had been at the controls of a heavy glider at night including two landings, both on wheels back in March ...[14]

At a higher level there were other doubts surfacing among those closely involved in the planning of LADBROKE and the formulation of plans for subsequent airborne operations. Squadron Leader Lawrence Wright had studied aerial photographs of the proposed glider LZs on the Maddalena Peninsula and had compared them to the parachute drop zones (DZ) for Operation FUSTIAN on the Catania Plain and those selected for Operation GLUTTON outside Augusta. After studying the stereo images, he was at first convinced that the photographs had been the subject of some form of clerical mix-up. To the experienced RAF officer, himself an accomplished glider pilot, the Catania Plain appeared to be ideal glider terrain while the Augusta DZ was less so.

The grainy images of the LADBROKE LZs raised numerous doubts and caused Wright serious concern. He felt that the entire Maddalena Peninsula represented an appalling prospect for an airlanding operation. His concerns began with the identification of the glider release point. How would the USAAF tug crews and glider pilots orientate themselves and then confirm their release points in darkness over water? Even if the gliders' cast-offs from their tugs went well and they began their glide inland, there would be no markers or navigation aids on the darkened coast or in place on the LZs to guide them. Each glider crew would have to fly through darkness searching for an unmarked LZ on a narrow neck of land bordered by the sea, rocks and high cliffs. Close scrutiny of the fields that had been designated as the LZs for LADBROKE revealed that they were all surrounded on all sides by potential hazards. The images of the terrain around the landing zones clearly showed a potentially deadly mix of low stone walls, rocky slopes, orchards and lemon groves. Any one of these obstacles could easily rip flimsy, aluminium framed, canvas-covered WACO gliders apart with disastrous consequences for all on board.

Convinced of the unsuitability of the LADBROKE LZs, Squadron Leader Wright challenged fellow RAF staff officers at Algiers and in Headquarters 38 Wing RAF. Wing Commander Wally Barton and Group Captain Tom Cooper both shared his concerns and argued to no avail against the suitability of the LZs. Group Captain Tom Cooper had little enthusiasm for the plan. From his post in Allied Force Headquarters in Algiers he had objected that:

> The release was over water, and involved judging distances from the shore, that the glider pilots were to make a straight glide in and would have no surplus height, that no marks were going to be put on the

> ground because the Americans said they would cause confusion, and the Army considered they would attract the enemy, and that the release run was made down moon.[15]

Determined to have his own say, Squadron Leader Wright went to the 1st Battalion GPR to raise his concerns with Lieutenant Colonel Chatterton himself:

> ... I found him upstairs in the bank, working out release heights, afraid to allow much excess in case the gliders overshot right across the peninsula, inclined to rely on American reassurances that their tug pilots could order off the gliders at the right spot for a straight glide in, landing to a set drill. He confided that Hoppy, having shown him the plan and sensed his immediate doubts, had given him half an hour in which to choose accepting it as it stood, or resigning his command ... Only Hoppy was full of confidence. – 'If Italy spoils the show by packing in before the date,' – he said 'we'll do the operation as an exercise!'

As a result of his continual questioning of the Operation LADBROKE plan, Wright was thereafter excluded from 1st Airborne Division planning sessions. This was an extraordinary step, given that he was one of the most experienced glider pilots in the RAF. He personally attributed the decision to exclude him to Major General Hopkinson. He firmly believed that the divisional commander was determined to carry out the LADBROKE plan at all costs.

The successful migration over the Atlas Mountains marked the conclusion of Phase 2 of the LADBROKE preparation plan. Phase 3, the final part, filled the week before D-Day with last-minute preparations, checks, briefings and rehearsals. The completion of the move over the mountains had also brought the Turkey Buzzard Horsa gliders of No. 1 Squadron together with the WACO gliders of Nos 2 and 3 Squadrons. There were, however, a number of issues to be resolved before the operation could be launched. This was certainly true for the RAF aircrews of 296 Squadron RAF who flew the twin-engined Albemarles, the squadron having been warned that it could expect to be given the task of towing Horsa gliders to Sicily. The Albemarle, however, was not the most powerful of tugs and 296 Squadron's pilots had little experience of towing Horsas in Mediterranean conditions. On 3 July 1943, less than a week before D-Day, Squadron Leader Peter Davis made a revealing entry about the preparedness of his squadron in his diary:

> An important test to be done this night – can our Albemarle tow Horsas in this climate the distance required? Fuel and temperatures critical, quite big issues depend on it. Given to me at last moment, crew tired

> but we set off in good spirits, though thirsty as usual. My observer Flight Sergeant Compton not quite on his usual good form, a pity since flying time etc, vital for necessary statistics on which might depend the lives of quite a few of my colleagues. All right in the end though, after two hours towing over the sea all figures obtained and engines did not blow up as the more pessimistic foretold. Landed at dusk with fifteen gallons left ... drank gallons after landing, all keen to learn results of the test.[16]

As the final week passed and D-Day approached, some of the underlying tensions that surrounded the LADBROKE plan surfaced. Lieutenant Colonel George Chatterton commented on one incident that gives some indication of the mood that surrounded the Froha airfields just prior to D-Day:

> One day I was passing the tent of one of the wing commanders, Peter May, who had been an instructor in the Royal Air Force for some years and whom I knew well. As I passed, the ground flaps were up and he could see my feet, on which I was wearing a very nice pair of Chukka suede boots.
>
> The Wing Commander asked me into his tent. 'I say George, I like those boots. May I have them if you don't come back?' I was somewhat stunned for a moment, but said, 'Oh, yes of course,' as casually as possible. 'Just ask my batman, Private Gaul, and he'll give them to you.' ... The odd thing was that when I did return from Sicily I found that my boots were missing, and my batman told me that Peter May had asked for them after I had gone. Perhaps the greater irony was that he put them on when he took off in his Albemarle, and was shot down and never seen again. Presumably, he went to the bottom of the sea wearing my boots.[17]

SUMMARY OF GLIDER PILOT TRAINING

No. 2 Squadron

Total no. of lifts by day	610
Total no. of lifts by night	205
Total flying hours by day	166 hrs 30 mins
Total flying hours by night	46 hrs 20 mins
No. of crews trained	57
Date started training	24.5.43
Date finished training	12.6.43

One officer injured, suffering from shock, abrasions etc.
1 sgt. pilot injured, broken leg.

No. 3 Squadron

Total no. of lifts by day	753
Total no. of lifts by night	305
Total flying hours by day	224 hrs 20 mins
Total flying hours by night	84 hrs 20 mins
No. of crews trained	59
Date started training	21.5.43
Date finished training	12.6.43

2 NCO Pilots killed. 2 NCO Pilots seriously injured

Totals for unit during the period 21.5.43 to 13.6.43

Lifts by day	1,363	Total 1,873 lifts
Lifts by night	510	
Flying hours by day	390 hours 50 mins	521 hrs 45 mins
Flying hours by night	130 hours 55 mins	
No. of crews trained	116	
Total casualties	2 deaths 4 injuries	

At the end of training Exercise Adam took place. 56 gliders took part and 54 landed successfully in the required landing area, taking 28 mins. One glider pulled off on take-off, and one successfully forced landed en route. No troops were injured during the exercise and only 5 gliders suffered minor damage.

From 8.5.43 to 18.5.43 60 sgt. pilots and 6 officers erected 52 gliders at LA SENIA.

Notes

1. Chatterton, Lieutenant Colonel, G., 1st Battalion GPR. *The Wings of Pegasus*, Battery Press, Nashville, 1962. p. 66.
2. Howard, Staff Sergeant, H., 2 Squadron, 1st Battalion GPR, Correspondence with the author dated 19 October 2010.
3. Wright, Squadron Leader, L., Headquarters 38 Wing RAF
4. Place, Major, J., OC 3 Company, 1st Battalion GPR, Diary Entry, by permission of *The Eagle*.
5. Lansdell, Sergeant, H., 2 Company, 1st Battalion GPR, by permission of *The Eagle*.
6. Connell, Lieutenant, M.B., 3 Squadron, 1st Battalion GPR, Letter to Mrs C.B. Connell dated 9 June 1943.
7. Connell, Lieutenant, M.B., 3 Squadron, 1st Battalion GPR, Letter to Mrs C.B. Connell dated 19 June 1943.
8. Airborne Division, Post Operational Report, Exercise Eve 2, dated 18 May 1943, ABFM.
9. Howes, Sergeant, N., C Company, 2nd Battalion, South Staffords, by permission of John Howes October 2010.
10. Brown, Lance Corporal, R., 7 Platoon, A Company, 2nd Battalion, South Staffords. By permission of South Staffords Museum.
11. Howard, Staff Sergeant, H., 2 Squadron, 1st Battalion GPR, Correspondence with the author dated 19 October 2010.
12. James, Staff Sergeant, J., 1st Battalion GPR, by permission of *The Eagle*.
13. Report by Commanding Officer The Glider Pilot Regiment, dated 2 August 1943, ABFM.
14. Mackenzie, Sergeant, W., 1 Company, 1st Battalion GPR, correspondence with the Author dated 26 May 2010.
15. Cooper, Group Captain, T., RAF, AFHQ staff, *The Army In The Air*, A. Sutton Publishing, Bath, p. 83.
16. Davis, Squadron Leader, P., 38 Wing RAF, Diary entry 3 July 1943.
17. Chatterton, Lieutenant Colonel, G., 1st Battalion GPR, *The Wings of Pegasus*, Battery Press, Nashville 1962, p. 69.

CHAPTER 8

Objective Waterloo

The men who wore the Red Beret were not the sort however, to meet their difficulties before they came to them. Difficulties were to be overcome and they would be!

The completion of the work-up training and relocation of both British and US airborne divisions over the Atlas Mountains was one of the indications that preparations for Operation HUSKY were now close to completion. The Kairouan airfields that the Allied airborne forces were now grouped around were across the Mediterranean from their objectives that were situated just beyond the rugged Sicilian coastline. The HUSKY plan had been under constant review and change since the decision to invade Sicily had been taken at the Symbol conference in Casablanca in January 1943. Detailed analysis of the island's geography and its defences had continued right through the spring and into the summer as 1st Airlanding Brigade trained for its first mission.

The ongoing intelligence analysis built up a detailed picture of Sicily, the largest island in the Mediterranean. It was immediately apparent that any landings attempted by an invading force by sea or by air would inevitably be channelled by the island's inhospitable and mountainous terrain. While surveying Sicily's 600-mile coastline, Allied planners could only identify a limited number of narrow strips of low land before rugged mountains climbed steeply away from the coast, and thus from the outset attention remained focused on the only significant area that would lend itself to any requirement for manoeuvre after landing. This was the relatively wide and inviting plain that ran along the east coast near Catania. This area, and much of the wider island, was dominated by the 10,000-foot volcanic peak of Mount Etna.

The ancient and medieval history of Sicily is dominated by war and invasion by foreign armies and analysis of the population distribution revealed that, as a result of this violent past, the majority of Sicilian towns and villages were built on steep hilltops in order to create natural fortresses. The road network linking these settlements was sparse and low grade and off-road movement by vehicles was assessed, in the main, to be impossible over the bulk of the island and, at best, difficult on foot.

As the HUSKY plan evolved, the Task Force 141 planning staff focused on the identification of viable landing sites that would be suitable for large-scale amphibious operations. The need for suitable locations at which to put the invading force ashore had been closely followed by a pressing requirement to secure ports and airfields as soon as practicable after assault troops were clear of the landing beaches. The need for ports was driven in particular by the predicted logistic demand for combat supplies.

The largest and most modern port on the island, and therefore the most suitable for the Allies' needs, was Messina. Located on the eastern tip of Sicily, just two miles from the coast of mainland Italy, it was, however, heavily defended by Axis forces and was also beyond the range of Allied fighters operating from airfields on Malta. A successful direct assault on it was thus considered impossible, and so it was discounted as a realistic objective during the initial phase of the invasion. The remaining ports identified as objectives after landing were: Palermo, Sicily's second major port to the North West; Syracuse; Catania; and Augusta on the south-east coast.

Axis airfields also figured prominently in Allied thinking, not only as their capture would deny them to the Luftwaffe and the Italian Regia Aeronautica but also because the possession of forward operating bases on Sicily would significantly extend the range of Allied aircraft as well as increasing their loiter time over the battlefield. Aerial reconnaissance over Sicily had identified three distinct clusters of airfields that the planners deemed to be priority objectives for the ground forces immediately they were ashore. One cluster was located on the Catania Plain directly in the path of the planned advance of the British Eighth Army, while a second was identified on the plain behind the town of Gela in the south, and a third grouped near Palermo to the north-west.

The difficult terrain of the island and the lobbying of the air and naval commanders for their requirements to secure airfields and ports created problems in the planning process. Others were posed by differences of opinion between British and US staff officers on the most effective strategy to be employed in mounting and executing the invasion. General Sir Bernard Montgomery and Lieutenant General George Patton, commanding the British Eighth and US Seventh Armies respectively, famously disagreed on how the invasion should be conducted and who should be in overall command on the ground.

Initially, the outline plans had envisaged simultaneous landings by an Eastern (British) Task Force and a Western (US) Task Force. The British were to land three widely dispersed divisions along the coastline between the port of Syracuse and the small coastal town of Gela. These landings would be followed on D + 3 by the arrival of a fourth British division making a direct amphibious assault on Catania. The Western Task Force, meanwhile, was to land a single division at Sciacca on D-Day; its task would be to move inland and capture Italian airfields on the western side of the island. It would be followed on D + 2 by a further two US divisions making a direct assault on the port of Palermo.

This was the plan to which Montgomery had objected so strongly. He anticipated strong Axis opposition in Sicily, particularly from the Italian garrison which, based on the performance of Italian units in the final battles in North Africa, he believed would fight tenaciously to defend home soil. He argued persistently for the cancellation of the British landing at Gela and the mounting of more concentrated and powerful landings further east toward Syracuse. However, his argument for concentration on Syracuse was opposed by Air Chief Marshal Sir Arthur Tedder, the RAF commander and senior Allied airman in the Mediterranean, who advocated the rapid occupation of the Gela airfields as soon possible after D-Day; in this he was supported by Admiral of the Fleet Sir Andrew Cunningham GCB, DSO** RN, the Commander-in-Chief Mediterranean Fleet and overall commander of Allied naval forces in the Mediterranean, who viewed the reduction in the number of invasion beaches and the subsequent concentration of ships en masse as an increased risk. In Cunningham's opinion, the large concentration of vessels would make life far simpler for Axis naval and air units to strike successfully at Allied shipping. He also supported the need for airfields on Sicily as quickly as practicable.

Arguments over the selection of invasion beaches rumbled on throughout the months of March and April with no hint of a mutually agreeable compromise in sight. Proposed amendments articulated by both General Alexander's and Montgomery's staffs were rebuffed by naval and air commanders. A proposal from Headquarters Task Force 141 to cancel the US landing at Sciacca and land that division at Gela, thus releasing the British division for use at Syracuse, was also opposed, this time by Patton. Frustrated by the lack of progress, General Dwight Eisenhower summoned all of the HUSKY commanders to a conference at Allied Force Headquarters in Algiers on 2 May 1943. Determined to resolve the impasse and produce a workable invasion plan, he exerted all of his influence as Supreme Allied Commander to forge a solution.

It was during this conference that one of the most amusing incidents in the history of the British/US relationship during the Second World War took place. The conference had broken up for a short respite during which General Montgomery had taken the opportunity to visit the lavatory. There he encountered Major General Walter Bedell Smith, Eisenhower's Chief of Staff. Never one to miss an opportunity, the astute Montgomery cornered Bedell Smith and convinced him that he alone had a viable plan that would ensure a successful Allied landing on Sicily. The plan advocated by Montgomery in his unique pithy style involved the axing of the Palermo wing of the landing altogether and the rebalancing of the task forces to the east. Essentially, this was a revised plan that involved parallel landings centred on Gela and Syracuse, offering mutual support between the British and US armies. The plan offered to Eisenhower was both robust and logical. The Supreme Allied Commander needed to resolve the crisis that so far had hindered the development of Operation HUSKY, and thus he accepted and formally approved Montgomery's proposed Syracuse-Gela amendment to the plan on 3 May 1943.

Following a directive from Eisenhower, the chain of command and the order of battle for the two Allied task forces was finalised for HUSKY. In overall command was Eisenhower, his deputy being Alexander, the commander of the 15th Army Group, who was given operational command of HUSKY and thus command of both task forces and their respective commanders.

The Eastern Task Force (Force 545) was formed around Montgomery's Eighth Army. Its naval component was commanded by Admiral Sir Bertram Ramsay KCB MVO RN and consisted of 795 ships and beaching craft with a further 715 ship-borne landing craft. These would have the task of delivering the 115,000 assault troops onto their objectives. In addition, the Royal Navy was also given the role of providing naval cover for both task forces. The Eastern Task Force air component was placed under the command of one of the RAF's most senior aviators, Air Vice-Marshal Harry Broadhurst.

The Eighth Army consisted of two formations: XIII Corps, under the command of Lieutenant General Miles Dempsey CB, DSO, MC, comprising the 5th and 50th Divisions and the 4th Armoured Brigade; and XXX Corps, commanded by Major General Oliver Leese CB, CBE, DSO, consisting of the 1st Canadian Division, 51st Highland Division, 231st (Malta) Infantry Brigade and 23rd Armoured Brigade.

The British amphibious capability for HUSKY comprised No. 3 Commando, Nos. 40 and 41 Commandos RM, and the Special Raiding Squadron, while 1st Airborne Division and 78th Armoured Division formed the mainstay of 15th Army Group's reserve available to the Eastern Task Force, but were held back in North Africa.

The core of Lieutenant General George Patton's Western Task Force (Task Force 343) was his US Seventh Army, which was organised into three separate task forces: The first, formed around US 45th Infantry Division, was designated Cent Force while the second, designated Dime Force, was formed around the US 1st Infantry Division and the 1st and 4th Ranger Battalions; both were placed under Headquarters US II Corps commanded by the venerable Lieutenant General Omar Bradley. The third element of Patton's command was 'Joss Force', based on the US 3rd Infantry Division and the 3rd Ranger Infantry Battalion.

The US floating reserve comprised the tanks of Combat Command A of the US 2nd Armoured Division and the 18th Infantry Regiment detached from US 1st Infantry Division. The American reserve located in North Africa comprised the US 82nd Airborne and 9th Infantry Divisions.

The US Navy provided a naval component commander for the Western Task Force in the form of Vice Admiral Kent Hewitt whose command consisted of 580 ships and beaching craft and 1,124 smaller shipborne landing craft. Hewitt's task was to deliver 66,000 troops ashore during the opening days of the invasion. The Western air component commander was another American, Major General Edwin J. House, who was the focal point for the 146 USAAF squadrons involved in the operation. When combined with those of the RAF's 113 squadrons taking part, the total number of Allied aircraft amassed for HUSKY was 4,300 of all types. This formidable air armada was kept extremely active establishing air supremacy during the weeks leading up to D-Day.

Throughout May and June, while the glider pilot squadrons were assembling and flying WACO gliders or braving the Bay of Biscay on Turkey Buzzard flights, the Allies steadily amassed their invasion force. Operation HUSKY required a huge amount of naval lift capacity to deliver the task force elements to Sicily, and thus a whole new class of amphibious assault vessels and landing craft was now employed by both Allied navies, including the Landing Craft Tank (LCT), Landing Craft Infantry (LCI), Landing Craft Vehicle or Personnel (LCVP) and the newly-developed DUKW six-wheeled amphibious truck. This array of vessels formed part of a huge naval armada assembled in the Mediterranean to carry and support the Allied forces. The naval planning staff identified a requirement for a total of 2,590 vessels to operate in direct support of the beach landings, the majority of which were assault vessels of the new types. The combined naval forces were expected to carry a staggering total of 181,000 troops, 14,000 vehicles, 600 tanks and 1,800 artillery pieces.

The majority of all elements of the HUSKY force were gathering within reach of their objectives by the first week in July, the co-ordination of their arrival off the coast of Sicily requiring careful planning. However, not all of the formations involved were assembled in North Africa. The US 45th Infantry Division was based in the United States from where it sailed to join the Western Task Force, making a brief landfall in Oran before landing in Sicily. Meanwhile, the 1st Canadian Division also had a long voyage ahead of it to join the Eastern Task Force, beginning its journey from Scotland. In the meantime, the Allies continued to devote a great deal of effort to masking the concentration of troops and shipping, maintaining the deception that Sardinia or Greece were their next objectives. A combination of dummy signals traffic, increased sabotage activity in Greece and the creation of decoy invasion forces were maintained right through to D-Day. This activity underpinned the success of Operation MINCEMEAT and consequently the German garrison on Sicily had still not been reinforced by the first week in July.

Unaware of the massive scale of the preparations elsewhere, 1st Airborne Division spent the final days leading up to D-Day settling into its new camps and bivouacs on the six Kairouan airfields. The US 82nd Airborne

Division also moved into the area and began its preparations for the coming operation. The majority of these airborne forming-up areas were on or close to the desert airstrips from which the airborne elements of HUSKY would be launched. There were very few permanent buildings available and any Nissen huts were allocated for use as briefing areas or command posts. The airfields themselves were little more than dust strips covered with metal panels and were so nondescript and austere that they did not have names. The airfields were widely dispersed around the 1st Airborne Division area as follows:

Strip A – Just north of Eldjem.
Strip B – Towards the sea.
Strip C – In the arid country to the west.
Strip D – Between the M'Saken and Eldjem road.
Strip E – North of the salt pan Sebkra de Hani (Horsa).
Strip F – M'Saken – Kairouan road (38 Wing RAF, Albemarle).

Lieutenant Tony Stafford, the Adjutant of the 1st Battalion The Border Regiment, described how 1st Airlanding Brigade troops made the most of their glider equipment as they settled into the olive groves around their bivouac site:

> With the arrival of all of the Battalion stores, equipment and tentage, the camp soon became highly organised. Great rivalry arose between the companies as to who could produce the most luxurious mess or the most efficient cookhouse. As a result many innovations were put to good use. Glider loading gear, which until now had been a great encumbrance, now took on a new lease of life in the more useful role of furniture. In the troops' mess tents the troughs were so arranged as to form tables and benches, while in the officers' messes an efficient sofa could be erected with the aid of sandbags and camouflage nets for upholstery. Electric light was supplied by lamps connected up to the battery of a 15 cwt truck. A No. 21 Wireless Transmitter fitted with a form of loud-speaker constructed from megaphones, served as a fairly efficient means for listening to the BBC 9 o'clock news from home and occasionally, programmes of dance music.[1]

The operation order for LADBROKE was issued on 6 July 1943, finally confirming that 1st Airlanding Brigade would have the privilege, together with all of the inherent risks, of being the first Allied troops to land in occupied Europe. Initial briefings to airborne commanders included a detailed overview of HUSKY with confirmation of Sicily as the invasion force objective finally ending months of speculation and rumour among the waiting Allied troops. The officers assembled for the briefings were given their first insight into the overwhelming size of the Allied invasion force that was about to launch an airborne and amphibious invasion of a size unprecedented in military history.

The 1st Battalion GPR briefing began at 1300 hours, the initial part of it devoted to outlining the planned British landings in some detail. It was essential for the success of the operation that the pilots understood the wider plan and 1st Airlanding Brigade's key role in it. As the briefing progressed, the assembled crews learned that XIII Corps was to assault the south-eastern coast of Sicily and that, once ashore and clear of the landing beaches, armoured columns would advance north-west as fast as possible with the mission of securing the ports of Syracuse and Augusta as quickly as possible. Their capture would then allow the Allies to land combat supplies and reinforcements quickly and efficiently. Without them, the landing of stores and personnel would be far more problematical as the campaign progressed with Allied supply lines becoming extended and increasingly constrained by difficult terrain and poor roads.

Intelligence predicted stiff and determined opposition from German and Italian troops principally along the line of the River Simeto. This would not only delay the Allied advance on Messina, but would also protect the Catania cluster of airfields that were vital to the Allied plan.

In order to ensure that the XIII Corps advance was not held up at the Simeto, the bridges across it had to be seized with lightning speed. The only way to effect this was by use of coup de main operations, and this critical task had been allotted to 1st Airlanding Brigade. The 1st Battalion GPR and its supporting USAAF and RAF tug squadrons had the weighty responsibility of carrying the brigade to its objectives, and their orders revealed that it was to be flown on to four separate LZs to the south of Syracuse.

The airlanding operation was set to take place under the cover of darkness on the night of D-1, 9 July 1943, and would be followed a few hours later on D-Day by a parachute operation carried out by the 'All Americans' of the 82nd Airborne Division carrying out their first combat drop. Shortly afterwards, in the half-light of dawn, the huge Allied naval fleets would appear off the Sicily coast and commence the seaborne landings delivering seven British, Canadian and US divisions on to the beaches of Sicily. On the east flank of the island, the British XIII Corps was scheduled to land two hours before twilight on 10 July 1943.

The briefing moved on to the air plan formulated by the 51st Troop Carrier Wing for LADBROKE. This element of the overall plan was inevitably affected by aircraft serviceability and glider pilot numbers. The USAAF had managed to assemble 109 C-47 Skytrain tugs from 60 and 62 Groups. These would be augmented by 35 tug aircraft from 38 Wing RAF, the ground crews of 295 and 296 Squadrons RAF having worked flat out to produce 28 Albermarles and seven Halifaxes for the operation. The combined total of 144 transport aircraft provided a tug fleet that could tow an assault force of 135 WACOs and eight Horsas. The maximum payload of the WACO was 3,700 lbs and thus the majority of the chalks flying in the American glider were limited to fourteen fully equipped men and a platoon handcart. The larger Horsa, on the other hand, could carry a payload of 6,900 lbs; its chalks were set at 32 men.

The take-off times for each of the six airfields were staggered to compensate for the varying distances and flight times to the objective. Due to the shortage of trained navigators among the USAAF tug squadrons, the WACOs being towed by USAAF tugs would fly in echelons of four, as they had in training, with the lead tug alone having one of the scarce navigators aboard. The WACOs and Horsas towed by RAF Albemarle and Halifax tugs, however, would fly as single combinations to allow for their varying types, modification states and engine performance. They had the luxury of a navigator in every tug crew and would thus fly as individual serials in a stream of aircraft. The air plan had been carefully calculated to synchronise the arrival of all 143 gliders on the Syracuse LZs between 2210 and 2230 hours.

1st Airlanding Brigade's plan was to land in advance of the seaborne forces and to execute a three-phase plan:

> Phase One, the capture of the Ponte Grande at 2315 hours 9th July by two companies of 2nd Battalion South Staffordshires to be landed in eight Horsas in the immediate vicinity.
>
> Phase Two, the landing of the main force and its advance to the bridge by 0115 hours, 10th July, except for one company to deal with the coastal defence battery en route.
>
> Phase Three, The 2nd Battalion South Staffordshires to hold the bridge while the 1st Battalion The Border Regiment passed through at 0145 hours to capture Syracuse by 0530 hours 10th July.[2]

Briefing on the plan for LADBROKE was given in detail to participating units on the day of its issue. During the preliminary briefing and orientation, commanding officers and their sub-unit commanders watched intently as a member of 1st Airlanding Brigade staff pointed out reference points on the maps and models around the briefing tent. The over-arching codename for the operation was 'BIGOT'. Familiar place names were given new codenames for the duration of the operation: Kairouan became 'Penarth'; Malta 'Finance'; Syracuse itself was 'Ladbroke'; and the Assembly Area was designated 'Andover'. The series of objectives allocated to airlanding infantry during Phase Three had another set of codenames: The Ponte Grande Bridge was called 'Waterloo'; the Syracuse railway bridge to the west of 'Waterloo' was codenamed 'Putney'; the seaplane depot became 'Calshot'; the Piazza Forro in Syracuse itself became 'Piccadilly'; the bridge linking the two halves of Syracuse was named 'Solent' while the railway station was 'Bulford'; the power station 'Battersea'; and finally the Palazzo Delgi Studi was designated 'Eton'.

The LADBROKE planners appeared to have left nothing to chance. Due to the absence of pathfinders or markers on the LZs, the intelligence staff of 38 Wing RAF had produced special black and white 'moonlight maps' for the operation. Every pilot was issued with one of these which were designed to help him identify the shoreline at night and navigate from his release point inland.

The preliminary phase of the operation was designed to create maximum confusion among enemy defences on the ground right up to the last possible moment, and to this end a novel new deception tactic would be employed for the first time in advance of the arrival of the first gliders on their LZs:

> A simulated air and amphibious drop on Catania would begin at 2200 hours on D minus 1 with the drop of three groups of 80 dummy paratroops each north west of Catania by bombers of North African Tactical Air Force (NATAF). This would be followed by the drop of two groups of 40 dummies each west of Augusta. If feasible, the bombers would then bomb Catania.[3]

Major John Place attended the Operation LADBROKE briefing. His comments hint at the underlying mood of excitement felt by soldiers as they anticipate an impending operation:

> In Airborne Forces, very often we have several briefings for one operation and the study of maps and aerial photographs takes several days. It must be borne in mind that every individual, and most especially unit and sub unit commanders, have to assimilate a mass of detail, none of which can be carried on them in the form of notes, marked maps or photographs in case the individual is captured on landing in enemy territory and by his notes and maps jeopardises the whole operation ... At last we all knew what the job was to be, the first invasion of Axis Europe, a great combined attack on the island of Sicily. As Glider Pilots our own particular task was the landing of an Airlanding Brigade together with anti-tank guns and Jeeps near Syracuse.[4]

The airlanding attack would be spearheaded by a coup de main operation on the Ponte Grande Bridge. This would comprise a gliderborne assault using eight Horsa gliders carrying A and C Companies of the 2nd Battalion The South Staffordshire Regiment reinforced with sappers from 9th Field Company (Airborne) RE. Overall command of the assault force, including the sixteen pilots flying the Horsa gliders, rested with Major Peter Ballinger of the South Staffordshires. He was well aware that the key to the success of the entire airborne phase of the invasion was the capture of the twin-span Ponte Grande Bridge objective codenamed 'Waterloo'. The entire coup de main force was to be flown in Horsa gliders, and not the smaller WACOs, in order to ensure that the assault platoons were delivered en masse and

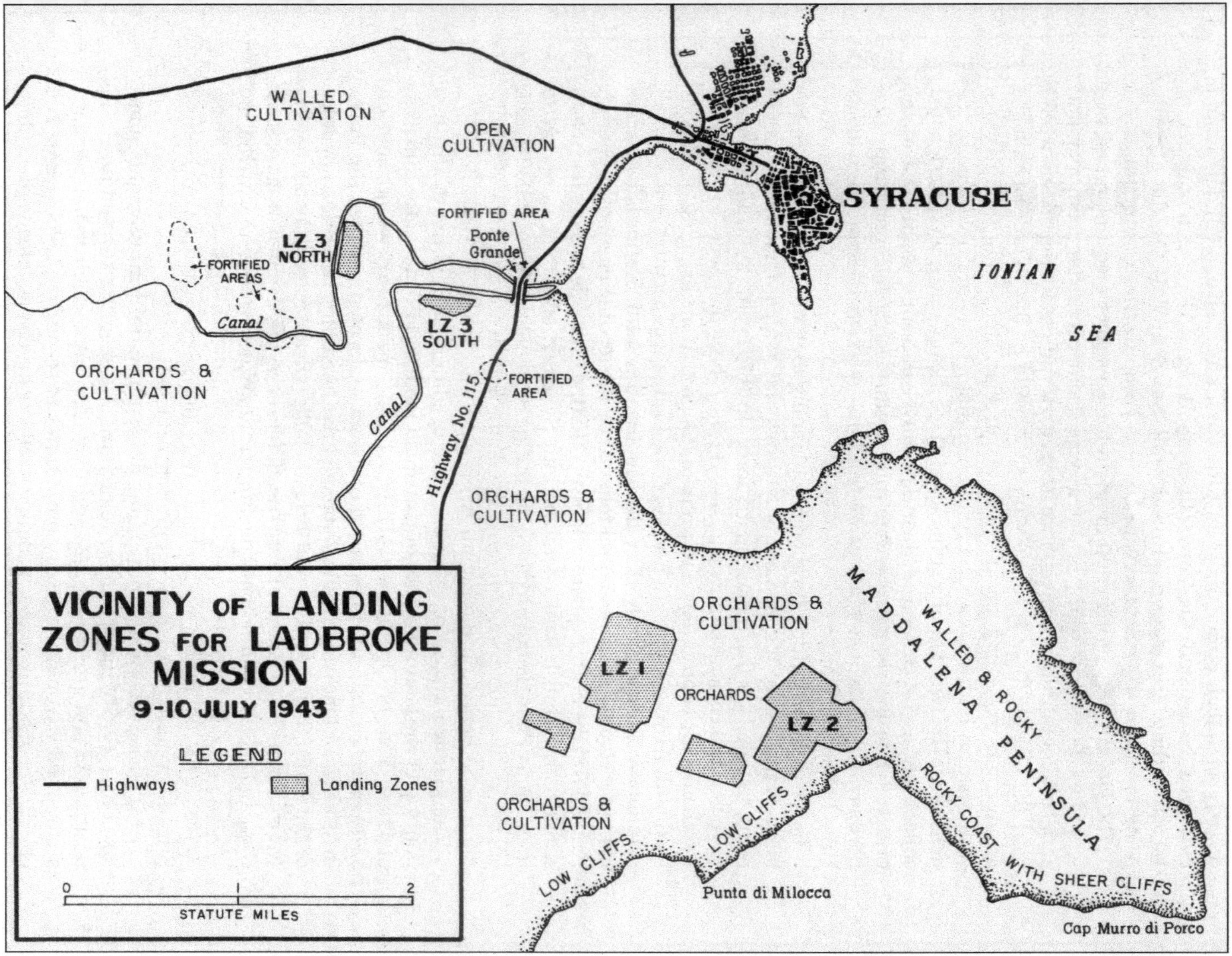
VICINITY OF LANDING ZONES FOR LADBROKE MISSION
9-10 JULY 1943
LEGEND
Highways
Landing Zones
0
1
2
STATUTE MILES
SYRACUSE
IONIAN
SEA
WALLED CULTIVATION
OPEN CULTIVATION
FORTIFIED AREA
Ponte Grande
LZ 3 NORTH
FORTIFIED AREAS
Canal
LZ 3 SOUTH
FORTIFIED AREA
ORCHARDS & CULTIVATION
Canal
Highway No. 115
ORCHARDS & CULTIVATION
ORCHARDS & CULTIVATION
LZ 1
ORCHARDS
LZ 2
MADDALENA PENINSULA
WALLED & ROCKY
ROCKY COAST WITH SHEER CLIFFS
ORCHARDS & CULTIVATION
LOW CLIFFS
LOW CLIFFS
Punta di Milocca
Cap Murro di Porco

directly on to their objective. As an added assurance, all eight gliders would be towed by trusted tug crews from 38 Wing RAF. The remainder of 1st Airlanding Brigade would meanwhile travel in WACOs, the majority being towed by C-47 Skytrains of US 51st Troop Carrier Command.

The Horsa pilots of the coup de main force were briefed to land on two separate LZs as close to the bridge as was deemed possible from map and aerial photographic reconnaissance imagery. If successful, the gliders would land the assault force accurately on either side of the river. Once on the ground and exploiting the element of surprise, the South Staffordshires would storm both ends of the bridge simultaneously and overwhelm the defenders. The twin landing strips selected for the operation were designated collectively as LZ 3. One of them lay only half-a-mile south-west of the bridge, while the second was one mile north-west of it. Significantly, the northern strip was just 1,500 yards from the outskirts of Syracuse with its large Italian garrison.

In the event of failure, contingency planning took into account the possibility of the loss of the element of surprise and bridge demolition charges being initiated by the Italian guard force. In this event, the coup de main force was tasked with securing a crossing site where they were to sweep the riverbanks for booby traps and prepare the ground for bridging operations by Eighth Army sappers. If, however, the bridge was secured intact and all demolition charges removed by the sappers, the South Staffordshires were to hold it against all comers until relieved by the leading elements of Eighth Army. With the bridge secure, Highway 115 (the Cassibile to Syracuse road), would carry British tanks straight into Syracuse and then north on to the Catania Plain. Failure to seize the bridge or prevent its demolition by the enemy would, however, severely impede the British advance inland, resulting in a bottleneck in the Eighth Army's advance north to Messina.

The planned arrival of the main force of gliders at 0115 hours, just two hours after the landing of the coup de main force, would signal the initiation of Phase Two of Operation LADBROKE. The main force would land on two separate LZs four miles south of Syracuse, located between the Punta di Milocca and the Maddalena Peninsula. The remaining two rifle companies of the South Staffordshires and Brigadier Pip Hick's brigade headquarters were earmarked to land on LZ 1. The gliders carrying the men of the assault companies of 1st Battalion The Border Regiment would meanwhile be landed on LZ 2, thereafter quickly rallying and preparing to execute Phase Three of the operation. Both phases were described in the 1st Airlanding Brigade operation order as 'Infiltration Attacks'[5].

As soon as practicable after landing, the South Staffordshires would undertake Phase Two of the operation, reinforcing and securing key buildings and positions in and around the LZs and 'Waterloo'. With their initial positions secured, they would then carry out a series of secondary tasks against key objectives outside Syracuse, including a railway bridge, an enemy gun battery codenamed 'Mosquito', two enemy defensive positions known as 'Bilston' and 'Walsall', and a coastal battery codenamed 'Gnat'. All these objectives had to be taken and subsequently held against counter-attack, successful completion of these tasks concluding Phase 2 of the operation.

Once the South Staffordshires were firm on their secondary objectives and the Waterloo bridgehead was secure, Phase Three of the airlanding operation was to be executed by The 1st Battalion The Border Regiment with a single company of the South Staffordshires attached to it. After landing, the Borderers would form up on LZ 2 and then advance into Syracuse. Their attack on the town would be supported by a bombing raid by Wellington bombers of 205 Squadron RAF on key points in the town between 0215–0245 hours, the aim being that the Borderers would then advance swiftly into the town on the heels of the confusion created by the bombing. This final phase was to be completed with all key buildings and likely enemy approach routes occupied or blocked by 0530 hours.

At this stage of the operation, the 1st Battalion GPR was expected to have rallied and regrouped at the Ponte Grande Bridge, its arrival there releasing a company of the South Staffordshires to move into Syracuse. Once in position, the glider pilots would act as the brigade reserve under the command of 1st Airlanding Brigade's deputy commander, Colonel Osmond Jones. They would, however, be relatively lightly equipped for their secondary task as 75 per cent of the pilots carried the standard British Lee Enfield No. 4 .303 rifle and 70 rounds of ammunition. The remaining 25 per cent were equipped with a 9mm Sten gun and six magazines. Every pilot was also to be issued with two No. 36 hand grenades.

After receiving his squadron's orders and being briefed on the detail and scale of the 1st Airlanding Brigade plan, Major John Place appears to have been in buoyant mood. His diary entry gives an indication of his own personal confidence in the plan and also implies similar confidence among his pilots under his command. His comments are confirmation that the hazards on the Syracuse LZs were known at least down to his level prior to take-off. In spite of the obvious risks, his overall view and that of his men appears to be that, although there were nagging doubts about the LZs, success in Operation LADBROKE was achievable:

> The more we saw of the plan, the more formidable it seemed. We were all completely confident and each man felt himself equal to half the Italian army. Our few doubts arose from the study of the Landing Zones. The largest was no more than 1,000 yards long by half that width ... and we were to land seventy gliders on it. But to complicate matters the area was criss-crossed by three foot high stone walls and in two places high tension cables crossed the area, to say nothing of the odd tree and enemy strongpoint which added their hazards!
>
> But our tails were up, and anyway we didn't have to fly the gliders back again. They were expendable equipment. We chaffed the crews of the leading gliders and requested them to ensure that the H.T. cables

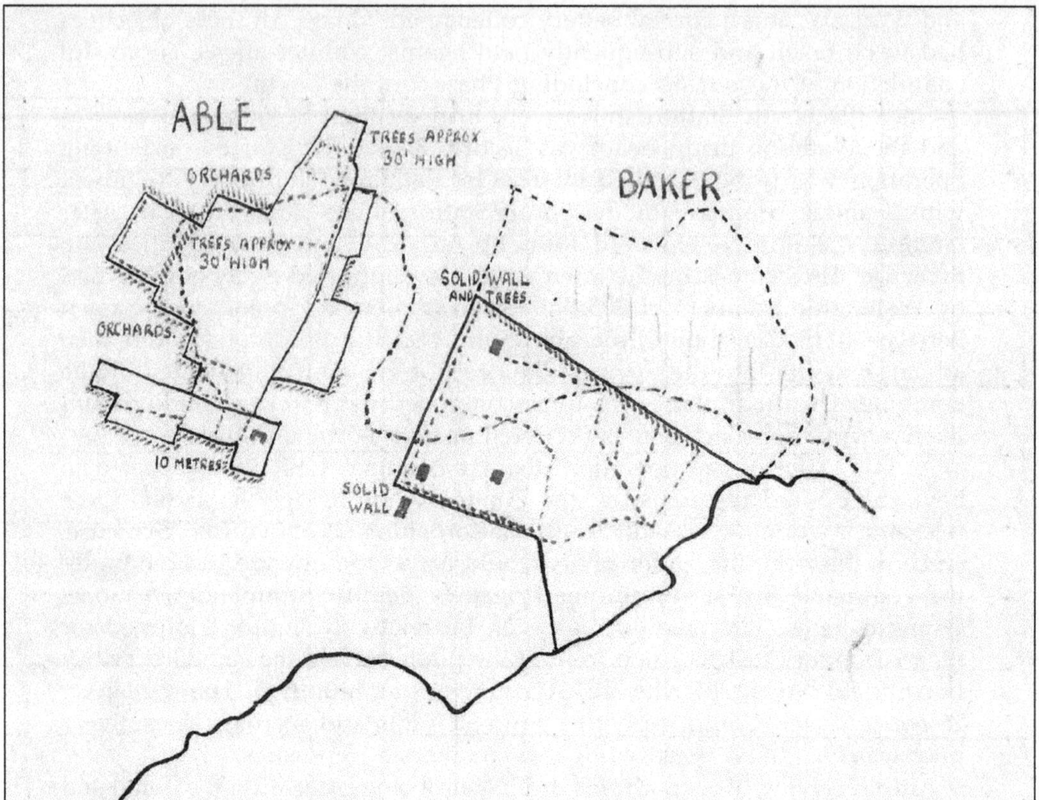

Sketch map from the orders for Operation LADBROKE – the low stone walls and orchards are clearly marked

> were removed and neat gaps left in the walls. We told them we didn't mind how they achieved the desired results but we had a fairish idea how they would be achieved! The men who wore the Red Beret were not the sort, however, to meet their difficulties before they came to them. Difficulties were to be overcome and they would be![6]

Over the few remaining days leading up to D-Day, the tempo of preparation increased noticeably. Following the delivery of the operation orders, the loading of every glider and every soldier on 1st Airlanding Brigade's airfields was subject to the closest scrutiny. The crews of 51st Troop Carrier Wing were also heavily involved in their own pre-mission preparations. Post-war historical analysis completed by the USAAF gives an overview of the effectiveness of them:

> Each group appears to have set its own schedule ... The 60th Group had to spend two hours each morning from 5 to 9 July studying maps and photographs, but the earliest formal briefing seems to have been on the 7th by the 64th Group. Most Groups began formal briefings of pilots after supper on the 8 July. Some protests were made later that some briefings ignored or underestimated high winds encountered on the mission. However, reasonably accurate weather reports were available and were transmitted to the flyers at least in most cases. Others claimed that early briefing and cramming had caused unnecessary strain and confusion. The 51st Wing complained that it had to call on its British airborne teammates to supplement its maps and photographic coverage. Nevertheless the briefing was considered to be satisfactory.[7]

1st Airlanding Brigade was also making best use of its remaining few days. Just prior to D-Day, the ration register of the 1st Battalion The Border Regiment listed a total of 43 officers and 753 other ranks fit to fly on the operation. Like his counterparts in the South Staffordshires, every single rifleman had a role to play in Operation LADBROKE. He also had his fair share of personal kit and equipment to carry. Beginning with his khaki drill 'KD' uniform, webbing, gaiters and boots, each man would parade for Operation LADBROKE wearing his maroon beret and Denison smock. He was then issued 120 rounds of .303-inch ammunition, of which 50 rounds was in a cotton bandolier. Those equipped with the Mk. 2 Sten Gun had eight 32-round magazines while those armed with .38 revolvers carried two Bren .303 light machine gun (LMG) magazines. Each section second-in-command also carried six Bren magazines in addition to those carried by the LMG Nos. 1 and 2. Each rifleman also carried one or two No. 36 grenades and two No. 77 white phosphorous grenades that were used to provide screening smoke.

In addition, each infantry platoon was equipped with a Bangalore torpedo, a specialised engineer charge designed to blast a path through minefields or barbed wire, along with a pole charge also for blowing obstacles and a Projector Infantry Anti-Tank (PIAT) with nine anti-tank bombs. In the anti-tank sections, each 6-pounder anti-tank gun had 24 armour piercing and nine high explosive rounds. Those in positions of command or responsibility carried even more accoutrements: officers, forward observation officers, sappers and NCOs added maps, compasses, binoculars and wire cutters to their respective kit lists. With all of this equipment stowed, every single soldier was also required to draw an individual lifebelt for use in the event of ditching.

With their operation orders issued, men began loading and rigging equipment while at the same time RAF and USAAF ground crew commenced fuelling and servicing tugs on all six of the Kairouan airfields. Meanwhile, 1st Airborne Division's camps were literally buzzing with activity. This continued through the afternoon of 6 July 1943 until it was suddenly and violently disrupted by a series of explosions and plumes of black smoke. Major John Place witnessed the resulting confusion from the 1st Battalion GPR camp:

> An ammunition dump situated about three-quarters of a mile from our camp had caught fire and we were told that a thousand tons of explosives had been blown sky high! What was worse was that the whole dump had not gone up at the same time. Parts of it were still exploding and showering mortar bombs and phosphorous grenades all over the landscape. As bad luck would have it our camp was down wind of the dump and we got more than our share of the bits and pieces. Had we not evacuated the area we would undoubtedly have had many casualties. As it was, several men were hurt by flying fragments.
>
> We felt rather miserable and silly later, when we saw squads of the Border and South Stafford Regiments marching into our area with shovels to clean up and put out the fires. We could do little to help as we had no tools left! In spite of our feelings we were very grateful to the infantry. They were lucky to have their camps out of range, as it were, of the dump.
>
> The catastrophe did nothing to help in the preparation for the forthcoming offensive. There was feverish activity required to assess the damage and get our indents in for the replacement of arms, ammunition and clothing, we were not the only unlucky unit.
>
> Had it not been for the stupendous work of the Lieutenant Quartermaster of the Airborne Recce Squadron (we had no Quartermaster of our own with us), we should never have achieved what then seemed almost to be the impossible. But then Quartermasters can usually do the impossible. They are wonderful people and the Recce 'Quarter Bloke' was no exception. He accomplished miracles and we are ever grateful to him.

> We were due to go to the 'take off' airfields the following day. Well we went but minus a big percentage of equipment and arms. We were assured, however, that we should go into action on the 9th with full kit, but we hardly believed it possible.[8]

The large stocks of ammunition around the airfields had been moved from Morocco to Tunisia by seemingly endless convoys of Eighth Army tank transporters. The ammunition and parachute supply containers had been dumped close to the Kairouan airfields and the airborne troops' bivouac areas because 1st Airborne Division had also been given the task of providing aerial resupply for the Eighth Army. The ammunition dump fire caused significant disruption but fortunately, in spite of the scale and ferocity of the explosions, casualties were light. There were, however, some repercussions. Sergeant Harold Lansdell of No. 3 Squadron witnessed the aftermath of the incident and had to change his crew and shift squadron as a direct result:

> I was not there when the nearby ammunition dump blew up and caused fires in much of the camp. Topper who was there had his vision affected by the fire, reported sick and was sent home. Being left spare after Topper went, I was transferred to No. 2 Squadron on the day of the Sicily operation. Flight Officer Kinney, a very experienced American glider pilot, was introduced to me to be my second pilot. He had ferried a CG-4A island hopping across the Atlantic, I had yet to land one.[9]

There was no obvious or logical explanation for the fire, and speculation as to its cause carried on long after the invasion was launched. Staff Sergeant Harry Howard of No. 2 Squadron witnessed the fire and the damage. He and many others had a good idea who the culprits may have been:

> We were encamped in olive groves near an Arab village called M'saken. I believe we were spied upon by German soldiers who had escaped from the Allies when Tunis fell and had taken refuge as Arabs in M'saken. Whether the division's ammunition dump caught fire and destroyed part of our site was due to German sabotage was anybody's guess. But . . .![10]

At this late stage, there were still a number of officers who remained unconvinced that 1st Battalion GPR and the USAAF tug force were ready for their mission on D-1. Squadron Leader Peter Davis of 38 Wing RAF shared his doubts with his diary, making this entry on 7 July 1943:

> Am very much concerned at the task of the Glider Pilots for this show, I think it is an almost impossible job for those pilots all of whom have few hours and little training. They do not know what they have undertaken, as they are going to land without lights of any kind, in a

> half moon. They have never done it before and in any case it requires the most skilful pilot to do it in moonlight, and this on top of a distant release, with very little margin. I am very pessimistic, but sometimes very bold attempts at this kind of thing seem to come off and in any case there is nothing I can do about it ... went swimming at the beach near Les Palmes, hundreds of 'Airbornes' there. Watched their brown bodies and wondered how many would be smashed up in the thing described above?[11]

No matter how detailed the briefings and well-rehearsed the troops, there was one single factor that the Allied commanders could not control: the Mediterranean weather. In the final days before D-Day the airfields and temporary camps of 1st Airlanding Brigade were subjected to increasingly strong winds that, along with the attendant dust storms, were a seasonal feature of the North African summer climate known as the Tramontana. This cold cutting wind was beginning to create problems for those already embarked aboard ships at sea and there was growing concern among some of the airborne planners preparing for LADBROKE. The strength of the Tramontana increased noticeably on a daily basis, gusting at speeds in excess of 30 mph and, after picking up the loose dust from the desert airstrips, creating huge rolling dust clouds. These conditions were not confined to the North African desert, and meteorological officers were forecasting exceptionally strong headwinds over Sicily on D-1.

In fact, the winds and dust clouds did not hinder the progress of the final preparations for LADBROKE. By dusk on D-2, the majority of the glider pilots had been moved by truck to the airstrips where they were detailed to attend final aircrew briefings and meet their respective chalks in the morning. Sergeant 'Dusty' Miller arrived at Airfield F, just north of M'Saken, in the company of his first pilot, Captain 'BG' Boucher-Giles. The dusty strip was home to the Albemarle squadrons of 38 Wing RAF. The WACO gliders and their tugs were prepared and lined up in sequence for take-off on the night of D-1. The two men were allocated a 6-pounder anti-tank gun and its crew as their load for the operation. Sergeant Miller described the scene as he and Captain Boucher-Giles searched for their WACO in the fading desert light:

> It took us nearly an hour to locate our glider but eventually found it down the end of the marshalled line. I carefully checked on the figure 110 scrawled on the nose in chalk. 'BG' and I laid our blankets down on the floor of the WACO and within a few minutes I was fast asleep.[13]

At first light on 9 July 1943 the pilots began to stir inside their gliders. It was D-1 and 1st Airlanding Brigade was still short of enough trained glider pilots to crew all of the gliders required for LADBROKE. In spite of the Herculean efforts of 1st Battalion GPR, 38 Wing RAF and 51st Troop Carrier Wing, the gliderborne force was still 24 pilots short with only 24 hours before take-off. There was only one other source of trained pilots available in North Africa, those of the USAAF. Lieutenant Colonel Chatterton went to Brigadier General Dunn and appealed for American reinforcements to fill the empty seats in the WACO cockpits. As always, the commander of the 51st Troop Carrier Wing was willing to help and agreed to find volunteer pilots to fly on Ladbroke. One of these was Flight Officer Bob Wilson:

> There was a notice on the squadron bulletin board, asking for five volunteers for detached service with the British. Nothing was said about flying into Sicily, just detached service . . . my name was fourth on the list.
>
> When we reached the British camp, we were greeted by a Colonel Chatterton, who was in command of that glider operation. He gathered us together and thanked us for volunteering for the invasion of Sicily. That's about as close to being scared to death as I have ever felt.
>
> We were issued red berets and Sten guns, which we had never fired before. One day, on our way to the firing range, we encountered a caravan of cars, so we got off the road and jumped under the wing of a glider to stay out of the way of the sun. It turned out to be General Montgomery coming to review the airborne troops. The general got out of the car and we could see him talking to Colonel Chatterton and the two of them looking in our direction. The colonel must have told Monty that we were Yanks who had volunteered to fly into Sicily, because suddenly the general fired a salute at us. That really made me feel good.[14]

The presence of pilots like Bob Wilson was unusual, all the more so when considering the route by which they had reached North Africa. In December 1942, having embarked on ships at Newport News in Virginia, they sailed for an unknown destination that later transpired to be Rio de Janeiro in Brazil. With their sea legs by now well established, they then left South America, rounded Africa and set course for Australia. Just a day's sailing from Sydney harbour, however, their course changed yet again and they now headed north-west to India, with rumours about action in Burma abounding. The ship then dropped anchor in the British harbour at Aden from where, after only a brief respite, it put to sea again and subsequently passed through the Suez Canal to Port Suez. It was here in Egypt, after 43 days at sea, that the by now well-travelled American pilots finally disembarked. Their saga was not yet over, however, as they next found themselves boarding trains and travelling north to Ismailia. Three months after beginning their journey, they finally arrived in Morocco to assist the British pilots with their conversion to the WACO glider. Many of them were now in Tunisia with 1st Airborne Division. Amongst them was Lieutenant Sam Fine:

> On the morning of 9 July 1943, Lieutenant Colonel Chatterton briefed us, that the American glider pilots were selected to go on this mission as co-pilots, to be observers of the operation and to report to our wing commander. Lieutenant Colonel Chatterton read off the American names and the stick we were to fly in. I was selected to fly in Glider No. 13 . . .[15]

The briefing for tug and glider crews took place on the afternoon of D-1 at 1300 hours. The Horsa crews that were taking the South Staffordshires' coup de main force confirmed their loads of 32 infantrymen with their platoon weapons. The load manifests also included Bangalore torpedoes; the presence of these or any other explosive devices within the confines of a glider troop carrying compartment was rarely popular among pilots or their passengers as the potential danger was obvious to all involved.

The loading of the more numerous WACO echelons was less straightforward than the Horsa combinations, the chalk loads varying from eighteen fully equipped infantrymen to a Jeep and four personnel. Not all of the available WACOs were fitted with lashing rings on their cabin floors. Those that were not had a much less effective hole in the cargo bay floor through which ropes could be passed and tied to secure the glider's load. The heavy loads were thus allocated to the fully modified WACOs and secured with full rigging sets, while the lighter loads and stores were tied down with rope.

WACOs would be carrying a full cross-section of Brigadier Pip Hicks's 1st Airlanding Brigade. Soldiers, vehicles and stores from the 1st Battalion The Border Regiment, the South Staffordshires, 9th Field Company (Airborne) RE and 181st Airborne Field Ambulance were all allocated chalk numbers and WACO gliders for the operation. The pilots of each glider were present to supervise the loading of their own aircraft, with chalk numbers and load manifests being checked and rechecked before the briefing. These checks were also carried out on an additional four reserve WACOs and their chalks which would join the attack should more tug aircraft become available.

The aircrew briefing for the operation took place after the overall briefing. The 400-mile course to be flown was given in detail, with tug and glider pilots plotting their respective routes and studying closely every turning point and bearing. After lifting from their respective airfields, the combinations were to make an initial rendezvous over the Kuriate Islands. They would then head toward the island of Malta where they were to make landfall passing over the Delimara point. From this point onwards all aircraft were dependent on the navigation skills of their crews. Tug navigators were briefed to turn at Delimara and take a new heading of 37 degrees magnetic. After flying for 71 minutes on this heading, the course changed to three degrees magnetic and pilots were ordered to hold this new northerly heading for eighteen minutes. This course and heading was planned to bring the combinations to their release point 3,000 yards off the Sicilian coast. The release heights given at the briefing were calculated to give each type of glider the reach to glide inland to the LZs. The operation order dictated the release heights: gliders were to release at 1,400, 1,800 and 4,000 feet for LZs 1, 2 and 3 respectively.

The final navigation leg and the last minutes before release would require the tugs and glider combinations to fly a parallel course to the coast and their LZs; at this point they would still be two-and-a-half miles short of landfall at Cape Murro Di Porco. After making the decision to cast off from the tug, each glider pilot was then responsible for making the critical turn inland. He had to ensure that this final turn was made at exactly the correct point and height to begin the final glide on to his allocated LZ. Meanwhile, the now redundant tug aircraft would be free to turn away from the Sicilian coast and its flak batteries. The tugs were ordered to make best speed back to their home airfields.

At this stage, if the air plan went well and the tug squadrons had navigated correctly, all gliders should then be in a position to make direct approaches to their LZs. Their primary task was to land safely at intervals in the well-ordered, four-glider sequences rehearsed during training. Immediately after coming to a halt in their allocated landing lane, the glider pilots were to assist in unloading their aircraft, with each crew carrying out its first and second pilot tasks as practised on exercise. They would then lead their airlanding troops away from the now abandoned glider and safely off the LZ.

Once clear of the LZs, the glider pilots were to make their way to a rendezvous point at the south-west corner of the Ponte Grande bridge where they were to be met by the pilots from the coup de main assault. The combined force was then earmarked to bolster the defences around the bridge and subsequently act as the 1st Airlanding Brigade reserve. From this point forward, operating as the equivalent of half a battalion of lightly equipped infantry, the pilots would come under the command of the brigade's deputy commander, Colonel Osmond Jones.

The operation now seemed to have acquired a life of its own as all the troops, airmen and aircraft moved into place in line with the timetable set by the operation order. However, many of the glider pilots affected by the ammunition dump fire remained deficient of weapons, ammunition, rations and other key equipment. In spite of these equipment problems and the increasing wind speeds, 1st Airlanding Brigade continued to prepare for the impending flight and the epic battle that would follow.

Notes

1. Stafford, Lieutenant, N.A., Adjutant, 1st Battalion Border Regt, *When Dragons Flew*, p. 59.
2. Otway, Lieutenant Colonel, T., Airborne Forces, London, Imperial War Museum, 1990, p. 119.
3. USAF Historical Study No. 74, Airborne Missions in the Mediterranean 1942–45, p. 25.

4. Place, Major, J., OC, 3 Squadron, 1st Battalion GPR, diary entry by permission of *The Eagle*.
5. 1 Airlanding Brigade Operation Order Number 1, dated 6 July 1943.
6. Place, Major, J., OC, 3 Squadron, 1st Battalion GPR, diary entry by permission of *The Eagle*.
7. USAF Historical Study No. 74, Airborne Missions in the Mediterranean 1942–45, p. 29.
8. Place, Major, J., OC 3 Company, 1st Battalion GPR, Diary Entry, by permission of *The Eagle*.
9. Lansdell, Sergeant, H., 2 Company, 1st Battalion GPR, by permission of *The Eagle*.
10. Howard, Staff Sergeant, H., 2 Squadron, 1st Battalion GPR, letter to the author dated 19 October 2010.
11. Davis, P., Squadron Leader, 38 Wing RAF, by permission of *The Eagle*.
12. Wright, L., Squadron Leader, 38 Wing RAF, *The Wooden Sword*, Elek Publishing, London, 1967, 128.
13. Miller, Sergeant, V., 3 Squadron, 1st Battalion GPR, *Nothing Is Impossible*, Spellmount Ltd, 1994.
14. Wilson, Flight Officer, R., USAAF, *The Glider Gang*, Cassell, London,1977, p. 73.
15. Fine, Lieutenant, S., USAAF, by permission of *The Eagle*.

Chapter 9

Operation LADBROKE

Stinging swirling dust clouds at each take-off run
Dust that slowly settled against the setting sun.
Wheeling and forming in the sky.
We wished them luck as they went by,
Lady of the olives, my own, 'Lily Marlene.'

There is no doubt that the days immediately following the release of the operation order for LADBROKE were unsettling for the men of 1st Battalion GPR. The fire at the ammunition dump disrupted what should have been a quiet period during which all participating troops should have been able to concentrate on their orders and allotted tasks. However, its aftermath was punctuated by a series of further incidents that interfered with 1st Airlanding Brigade preparations, these not boding well for the outcome of LADBROKE. Lieutenant Colonel George Chatterton recalled one particularly worrying episode that occurred during the final days before 9 July 1943. His presence on the flight line was requested by a junior officer who accompanied him out on to the airstrip to one of the WACOs being prepared for the operation. The urgency in his call was soon explained:

> 'Please look at the intercom, sir. The union seems to have been tampered with.' He pointed to the fitting and I saw black insulating tape around the wire.
>
> Well I said, 'What does that mean?'
>
> 'I will unwind the tape for you to see, sir.' He did, and then I realised that the wire had been cut.
>
> 'What on earth is this!' I exclaimed.
>
> 'Well, sir, I think you had better look at some of the others.'
>
> 'Let's get hold of an American officer first,' I said and we did.
>
> We then found that several aircraft had had the intercoms tampered with. After some investigations it was discovered that one of the fitters was an Italian-American who had taken action to prevent us attacking his country of origin.[1]

The American airman concerned was disciplined by the USAAF, although on the day this was of little concern. More precious time was expended checking and retesting as many glider intercom cables as possible. A number of other cables were found sabotaged and had to be repaired before take-off; it can only be speculated as to how many others failed due to sabotage or the failure of hasty repair work.

The fitting of intercom systems to allow communication between tug and glider is referred to in the 1st Battalion GPR war diary. It appears that intercom cables were still being rigged on the last aircraft right up until the final hours before take-off. The reality of what this key system comprised, and how it was fitted, warrants further scrutiny. Staff Sergeant H.N. 'Andy' Andrews later published detailed observations in his book *So, You Wanted to Fly Eh?* He and his USAAF co-pilot, Flight Officer Morris B. Kyle, who were introduced to each other on the morning of 9 July 1943, had been allocated Glider 10, which would carry senior passengers from Headquarters 1st Air-landing Brigade. The passenger manifest for the aircraft shows its chalk as including the brigade's deputy commander, Colonel Osmond Jones, and the Commander Royal Engineers (CRE) Headquarters 1st Airborne Division, Colonel Mark Henniker. Supplied with virtually no information, the two newly acquainted pilots set off on a walk around the airstrip to discover what they could about the impending operation. Staff Sergeant Andrews was concerned about a number of aspects of the LADBROKE plan, but one particular issue was prominent in his thoughts:

> My concerns for communication between the tug and the glider were top of the list. Morris said they were going to experiment with a telephone line between the tug and the glider, 'In fact they are fixing them up now. Let's go over and have a look.' I agreed it was a good idea. The troops could be left as they seemed to be in good spirits and appeared to be drawing lots for good seats . . . As we wandered across to the area where the American ground crews were fixing up the 'telephones' I began to wonder about the reliability of a system which hadn't been tested during a mass take-off. It became more of a worry when we got to the field where long rows of white nylon tow ropes were stretched out like enormous white snakes. A small group of American 'ground erks' (ground staff who looked after aircraft) were busy with marlin spikes, forcing a light field telephone cable between the nylon strands. At first I was puzzled by the large loops left dangling between the points of contact with the nylon rope. Of course, it was to allow for stretching of the nylon when it was put under tension – a good idea but there appeared to be little consistency between the loops each erk allowed. It was finished off with some tape for the initial security. I had a sinking feeling in my stomach and said to Morris, 'We had better try and get some visual signals as well. Could you contact the tug pilot and arrange something with a flashlight?' He thought it was a good idea.

> Worse was to come. I strode over to where the signals officer had a collection of field telephones – a common variety used by the British Army in small canvas containers about 12-inches long by 6-inches wide. The ends of the telephone cable were connected by two terminals in the normal way. What a 'Heath Robinson' affair I thought. It was made more comical when the signals officer said with a straight face 'You have to disconnect the cables before you cast off because the telephone won't go through the window of the glider – if you don't, it will pull the window out.'
>
> So here we were on the eve of the operation with a 'Mickey Mouse' system that could fail on several counts. The nylon could stretch and be greater than allowances made by the loops; the phone might not work; and you had to remember to disconnect the phone before releasing. Good luck I thought ...[2]

This account, and that of Lieutenant Colonel Chatterton, suggests that glider pilots, instead of focusing on the minutia of the LADBROKE plan, were being distracted by the pressing need for an inter-aircraft communication system, the integration of USAAF second pilots, and the need to replace vital stores and equipment lost or damaged in the ammunition dump fire. Moreover, there was increasing anxiety over an additional factor that was beyond the influence of even the most powerful and egotistical of the Allied senior commanders. As each day passed and D-1, 9 July 1943, drew nearer, the moon state improved as predicted. The close proximity of the moon influenced the tides and, more significantly for the glider pilots, the wind: the Tramontana was continuing to increase in speed and ferocity each day.

The problem of calculating release heights to compensate for the head-wind continued to vex Lieutenant Colonel George Chatterton. While his staff and that of Headquarters 1st Airborne Division grappled with the logistics of replacing the losses of the ammunition dump fire, he wrestled with his own critical dilemma:

> Two or three days before the date of the operation, a wind got up and blew at gale force. I was perplexed to know what height I should give for the gliders to cast off for landing, for to date we had been landing in dead calm, and now we were faced with conditions for which we were completely unprepared.
>
> I slept little those nights and waited for the wind to abate, but it didn't. I felt desperately alone in trying to make my decision and I left it to the very last moment. The difficulty was that I had no telephonic communications with the six strips on which the gliders were stationed. Somehow or other the height would have to be put round by word of mouth. I have to admit that I could not decide whether to instruct the pilots to go much higher or to keep to a lower height than 2,000 feet ... I was faced with the fact that we could not put the gliders too far inland

> because of olive groves and cliffs and I didn't want them to overshoot. Eventually I put the height up 500 feet, making a total of 1,900 feet above the sea.[3]

With time slipping away rapidly, 1st Airlanding Brigade's infantry, gunners, medics and sappers assembled as chalks, made final adjustments to their equipment and went through their own final pre-flight administration and checks. Meanwhile, the glider pilots had their own more immediate and significant concerns. Major John Place's diary encapsulates the situation on the glider strips during the final hours:

> We had camped out on the 'strips' for two days and on the morning of the ninth (we were due to take off at 1850 hours for Sicily), still no arms nor equipment had arrived! We began to look at each other. I almost expected to see some of our more inventive pilots fashioning stone axes and flint arrow heads, but no, they still had faith in the Quartermaster and he didn't let us down.
>
> At 1500 hours our equipment arrived, the Bren guns, Stens, rifles and grenades still with the grease packing on them! It took us an hour or two to clean them up but we had neither time nor 'spare' ammo to zero the arms. That, under the circumstances, was a small matter. The weapons would shoot and nobody except the fancy shots among us worried. Provided a 'Wop' was close enough, he'd 'go for a Burton' just the same, even if he wasn't hit plumb between the eyes.[4]

As the afternoon, and with it precious daylight, slipped away, the wind began to pick up. Groups of pilots sheltered from the heat in the shade of their aircraft wings as they set about frantically cleaning and preparing their new weapons. At the same time, away from the desert strips and oblivious to the frantic activity on the airstrips, the wheels of the LADBROKE plan continued to turn apace. At 1520 hours, convoys of Royal Army Service Corps 3-ton trucks began moving off from the 1st Airlanding Brigade bivouac sites, each with a chalk number on its front and side. Each driver was briefed to deliver his load to the glider bearing the same chalk number as his own. To insure against any confusion or errors, the commander of each chalk sat in the passenger seat of the truck's cab. All chalks were scheduled to be at their respective gliders approximately an hour before take-off.

On Airfield B at El Djem, Sergeant Jimmy James had carried out pre-flight checks on his WACO, Glider 51. While awaiting his passengers from E Company of the South Staffordshires, he watched the USAAF tug crew go through their own pre-flight checks. When the Americans had completed their walk-around inspection of their C-47, he walked forward from his glider to chat to the tug pilot:

> We followed our tow rope and introduced ourselves to the tug pilot and I suggested the partaking of a 'wee dram', as, tucked by the side of my seat, in the WACO was a half a bottle of John Haig whiskey, together with a bottle of water. His answer 'No thank you Sergeant, I don't imbibe in liquor prior to aviation'. The ground could have swallowed me up. However, it was arranged that following the ninety-degree turn across the Bay of Syracuse, he would give me a check every thirty seconds from the astro-dome for four minutes, for which I gave my second pilot, Sergeant Beard, my 21st Birthday watch to do the checking off.[5]

Close to Strip 'F' at M'saken, also known as Goubrine Strip 1, Lance Corporal Reg Brown waited with his comrades of 7 Platoon in A Company of the 2nd Battalion The South Staffordshire Regiment, part of the coup de main force tasked with seizing the Ponte Grande Bridge. They were waiting to be called forward from their battalion bivouac area to one of the eight Horsa gliders. His account gives a good insight into the pre-mission tensions experienced by the 1st Airlanding Brigade assault troops. They did not have the welcome distraction of busying themselves preparing a glider for flight:

> We had tea about 4pm, quite a good meal. A couple of sandwiches and a very rock-like rock cake were issued to each man to supplement his 48-hour ration. Then a little later we dressed, boarded trucks and left for a take-off strip (made solely for this 'op') on the edge of a salt lake near Kairouan. We had a mug of tea issued when we reached there – very welcome, for Africa can still turn on the heat! We were then taken up to our own particular glider – Number 128 was ours. We emplaned and were given our seating positions, also practised deplaning quickly. Next thing, we were told that the take-off had been put back one hour from 1750 to 1850 hours. So, with an hour to spare, the lads got busy, going around other members of the platoon getting signatures plastered all over 5, 10 or 50 franc bank notes and the British Military Authority notes we'd had issued to us the day before. That done, there commenced the maddest half hour of my life. The things that everybody said and did would have made the Crazy Gang blush. Singing, dancing, impersonating right up to the time we emplaned for the last time. It was the best that way, I guess. It doesn't give you time to think, if you keep doing things and saying things that have no meaning whatsoever.[6]

As 'H' hour and dusk approached, final preparations and checks carried on at all six of the glider airfields. The glider pilots used the last hours of full daylight to complete a final pre-flight walk-around check of their aircraft, their towropes, the telephone cables and the rigging of their loads. The men of the 1st Airborne Reconnaissance Squadron, meanwhile, had been allotted the task of receiving and marshalling incoming chalks of troops and ground handling gliders into take-off positions. They were working to a detailed staff table that listed the 144 available gliders and allocated load space between the 1st Airlanding Brigade units. On Airfields A and B, meanwhile, the South Staffordshires, 9th Field Company (Airborne) RE and some of the medical sections of 181st Airlanding Field Ambulance were allocated WACO gliders Nos 1–54. In addition, on Airfield E, the Horsa gliders of the coup de main force of the South Staffordshires were numbered 128–135. The 1st Battalion The Border Regiment and its support troops were at Airfields C, D and F, loading on to 72 WACO gliders numbered 55–127. The Borderers' load manifests give some insight into the scale and complexity of carrying an airlanding battalion into battle. Their strength numbered 43 officers and 753 other ranks, while their equipment comprised 58 folding bicycles, 55 platoon handcarts, four Jeeps, four 6-pounder anti-tank guns, thirteen No. 81 wireless sets, ten trolleys and four 3-inch mortars.

The 1st Airborne Reconnaissance Squadron completed its marshalling task by 1600 hours, well before last light. and thus 1st Airlanding Brigade had successfully met its deadline, with all 111 officers and 1,619 other ranks married up with their respective gliders and tugs.

The entire airlanding element of 1st Airborne Division, comprising eight Horsas and 135 WACOs, and its tug aircraft were now lined up and ready for take-off. Inside the gliders, some 30 minutes before the first combinations were due to take off, the chalks received a final brief from their pilots. Major John Place witnessed unusual scenes and the release of pre-mission tension around the gliders of No. 3 Squadron that evening:

> They arrived right on time and each glider captain put his 'live load' through a simple 'ditching drill' in the event of a forced landing in the sea. Each man was provided with a simple inflatable tube, we carried no dinghies. There weren't any and in any case we should have no room for them. Our ditching drill was carried out thoroughly, but I imagine that each strip had its own particular form as no standardised drill had been laid down!
>
> We all treated the matter in rather a hilarious spirit, even the 'live loads' whose shouts of 'I do like to be by the seaside', coupled with quite unprintable but trite observations on the efficacy of their 'water wings', caused howls of laughter and more unprintable retorts.[7]

Inevitably, as is the nature of every military operation, not everybody was busy all of the time, and this was particularly true of the USAAF glider pilots who had only joined 1st Airlanding Brigade that day. Among them was Flight Officer Bob Wilson who became bored and in turn curious about what his glider load comprised. He climbed into the WACO he was due to fly and examined the Jeep and trailer inside. He immediately regretted his curiosity when he lifted the canvas trailer cover and found a sobering sight:

> It really gave me a shock; it was material for marking graves – canvas bags, tags, and wooden crosses, somebody already knew that we would not all be coming back.[8]

At about 1500 hours, Lieutenant Ted Newport of the 1st Battalion The Border Regiment was supervising the loading of the men and equipment of his Anti-Tank Platoon on to their glider. He and his men witnessed a tragedy before take-off that darkened the mood of all who observed it:

> Having arrived at our airfield and, just as we were about to load our gliders, we witnessed an RAF Albemarle taking off at the same time as an American C-47 was about to land from the opposite direction. The RAF plane saw the American and though barely airborne banked steeply to avoid a collision, but stalled and crashed, exploding in flames ...[9]

Even as ground crews and rescuers attempted to extinguish the flames of the burning aircraft, the wind was gusting across the airstrips at speeds of up to 45 miles per hour. At all six of the launch airfields, the wind swirled around, picking up the gritty grey and red dust off the runways and the open desert. Many of the veterans' later accounts recall the turbulent conditions and the dust rattling against the canvas fuselages of the waiting gliders.

Finally, at 1848 hours, the first glider-tug combination began its take-off and lifted off the runway into the air. The air plan was now being put in motion and in spite of the rapidly worsening weather conditions, the glider-tug serials continued to take off at their designated times and sequence.

At Goubrine Strip 1, Lance Corporal Reg Brown and 7 Platoon of the South Staffordshires were now gathered around Glider 128. The Horsa was crewed by Lieutenant J.E. Lockett and Sergeant Granger, and was allocated an Albemarle tug from 295 Squadron RAF. The tug was in experienced hands; its pilot was Squadron Leader A.B. 'Wilkie' Wilkinson, one of the few survivors of Operation FRESHMAN, the ill-fated gliderborne operation mounted against the German heavy water plant at Vermork in Norway in November 1942. In addition to having taken part in FRESHMAN and subsequently Operation BEGGAR, Wilkinson was a pre-war civil glider pilot of some repute. Lance Corporal Reg Brown was probably unaware of the RAF pilot's considerable pedigree but in any case, as the time for take-off drew near, he had other more immediate concerns:

> At about 1940 hours, 8 Platoon took off; they had a slower tug plane and would take longer to do the trip. Theirs was a bumpy take-off. In fact, I thought once or twice that they wouldn't make it. It shook me a little. However, they eventually 'made it' and became airborne. Then, through the miniature sandstorm they'd made by their take-off run, I saw something drop from the glider. 'God!' I thought, 'someone's fallen out.' That

> shook me again, till I realised that 8 Platoon were making a skid landing. The pilot had jettisoned his landing wheels immediately he'd become airborne. That's what I'd seen drop. The lads around me had gone quiet and nobody spoke when, a few minutes later, we got the order to emplane. It was just as though someone had said 'Here goes, this is it'. We took up our positions, strapped ourselves in, waved a final 'cheers' to the cooks and those who were not coming on the 'op'. The doors were fastened in position; the pilots had a last minute check-up and we were nearly deafened when the engines of our Halifax tug roared into life.[10]

Meanwhile, glider-tug combinations were taxiing and taking off across all six of the desert strips, each doing so in the sequence specified in the LADBROKE operation order. At Airfield D, Staff Sergeants Ken 'Taff' Evans and Dick Martin were at the controls of their WACO, Glider 88, and were now ready to take off at Goubrine with elements of a platoon of B Company, 1st Battalion The Border Regiment on board. The Borderers, together with an airborne handcart loaded with PIAT bombs, was under the command of Sergeant Cherry. As first pilot, Staff Sergeant Taff Evans was concerned about the flying conditions that day and had decided to use all means available to improve his chances of reaching his LZ intact:

> Our destination was a landing zone west of the Maddalena Peninsula. From there we were to join up with the rest of the 1st Airlanding Brigade to take and hold the Ponte Grande – the vital bridge. As there was a 400-mile flight in gale force winds in front of Dick and me, we decided to take the benzedrine tablets which had been issued to us to boost our stamina, at the start. Just as well we did because it was a very hard and often hair-raising flight. This started from the take-off into the usual storm of dust and debris hurled at us by the slipstream of the tug. Owing to the stretching of the towrope as the load increased, the communication wire broke and we had no communication between tug and glider from then on.[11]

Elsewhere in among the ordered rows of gliders and tugs and the cacophony of noise and dust, other glider pilots waited for their turn to take off. Major John Place was strapped in and waiting in the cockpit of Glider 55, a WACO. He had an unusual second pilot:

> The General had once again decided to fly as my second pilot. I suppose really he had no business to be there at all, as our particular 'party' was a brigade job. The other shows were not in our area and anyway ... they were scheduled for a night or two later. But our 'Hoppy' wasn't going to be left out on any fun that was available. He was a man to whom fear

> was just a word in a dictionary. I honestly believe that he couldn't have spelt it if he had tried. This was for him, and for all of us, our first airborne action. He just couldn't miss it ... This was the real thing. I suppose everyone has much the same feeling when one sets off on a job from which one may not get back. It was for a lot of us our first action of the war. Perhaps I was fortunate, at least I had had my baptism of fire at Dunkirk, but that had been a long time ago, and my feelings no doubt were just the same as everyone else's.[12]

On Airfield E, Goubrine Strip 1, Lance Corporal Reg Brown and 7 Platoon of the South Staffords were finally on their way to the Ponte Grande bridge as Glider 128 taxied down the runway:

> We started to move down the strip, slowly at first. As our speed increased, the old Halifax's four engines roared louder than ever ... what a load we had on! Through the door leading to the pilot's cabin I could see the lieutenant glider pilot struggling with the controls as we raced along. We bumped and crashed, one moment, a few feet in the air, then crash – back to earth again. After what seemed minutes we became airborne and started to climb, and away we were, on a trip that was scheduled to take between two and a half and three hours. Away we were on our first airborne operation ...[13]

All the glider pilots had temporarily pushed their role in the landings to the back of their mind, their attention now focused solely on the immediate priority of getting off the ground safely. USAAF Lieutenant Sam Fine had to adapt and focus more quickly than most. He took his place in a WACO cockpit almost at the last minute as second pilot to Staff Sergeant Eric 'Lofty' Wikner in Glider 13 that carried men of B Company of the 2nd Battalion The South Staffordshire Regiment:

> I went to the field and got into the glider with a chalk marked '13'. It was already loaded with troops and my British pilot was already sitting in the left-hand seat. We acknowledged each other and I took my seat. We did not have any conversation whatsoever. The ground crew started to hook us up to the tow plane and after a short wait the dust started to blow all around us as the tow planes were revving up their engines. We could barely make out our tow plane when we started to roll and we were soon on our way. My pilot did a good job on take-off as we could not see our tow plane until we reached about one hundred feet. Soon we were over water and in a constant blank, as our tow plane began manoeuvring into the formation.[14]

The take-off times at each of the airfields had been staggered to compensate for the varying distances and the differing performances of their tug types, and this carefully planned sequence of aircraft take-offs worked well. Sergeants Ian Macleod and Peter Mansfield were the pilots in the cockpit of Glider 75, a WACO. They were lining up behind their tug at El Djem 2, their chalk comprising men and equipment from C Company, the 1st Battalion The Border Regiment:

> Just before dark we took off with twelve Border lads and a handcart on board, I was flying second pilot to Pete but he allowed me to take off, he would have the job getting us all down in one piece. On take-off one couldn't see the tug for red dust; one had to watch the small piece of rope for a fix. Airborne at last, but as usual the intercom had failed, we just had to keep position with the small blue lights on the tail of the Dakota. It was a difficult and bumpy ride and eventually we saw the lights of Malta …

Across at Airfield F, Gourbrine 2, a steady stream of combinations was also lifting into the air. Lieutenant W. 'Bunny' Carn was at the controls of Glider 125A behind an Albemarle from 296 Squadron RAF, with Sergeant David Richards, a Welshman from Barry Island, as his second pilot. The WACO was heavily laden with troops from the Mortar Platoon of the 1st Battalion The Border Regiment. Carn managed to look beyond the immediate vicinity of the cockpit as his glider lifted from the airstrip:

> I took off at about 2030 hours into a violent gusty wind about forty miles per hour, most unusual for Tunisia in July, well overloaded with twelve troops, a 3-inch mortar, Bren gun, ammunition and about 60 mortar bombs on the floor of the WACO. We did not have any trouble and did not return … but I saw two WACOs down on the salt marshes near to the sea, with their troops and pilots standing around them.
>
> I had a previous arrangement with Flying Officer Bazetta, our tug pilot, to give us at least another thousand feet over the target because of the strong wind. The Albemarle was faster than the Dakotas, and it was a very rough ride at under 1,000 feet for three hours or so, and the three small lights on the wing tips and the tail of the Albemarle all failed before Malta came up, so I was forced to fly on the red hot exhaust stubs, and the telephone along the rope also failed just after take-off. We slowly overtook several Dakotas and WACOs with our extra speed of about 140–150 mph. There was some flak and the odd searchlight off the Sicilian coast, but the flak was not accurate.[15]

Not all of the combinations cleared the North African coastline safely. Mechanical failures on tugs or snapped towropes forced eleven gliders to release their tows and make unexpected emergency landings in the Tunisian desert. Glider 125, piloted by Staff Sergeant John Braybrook and Sergeant

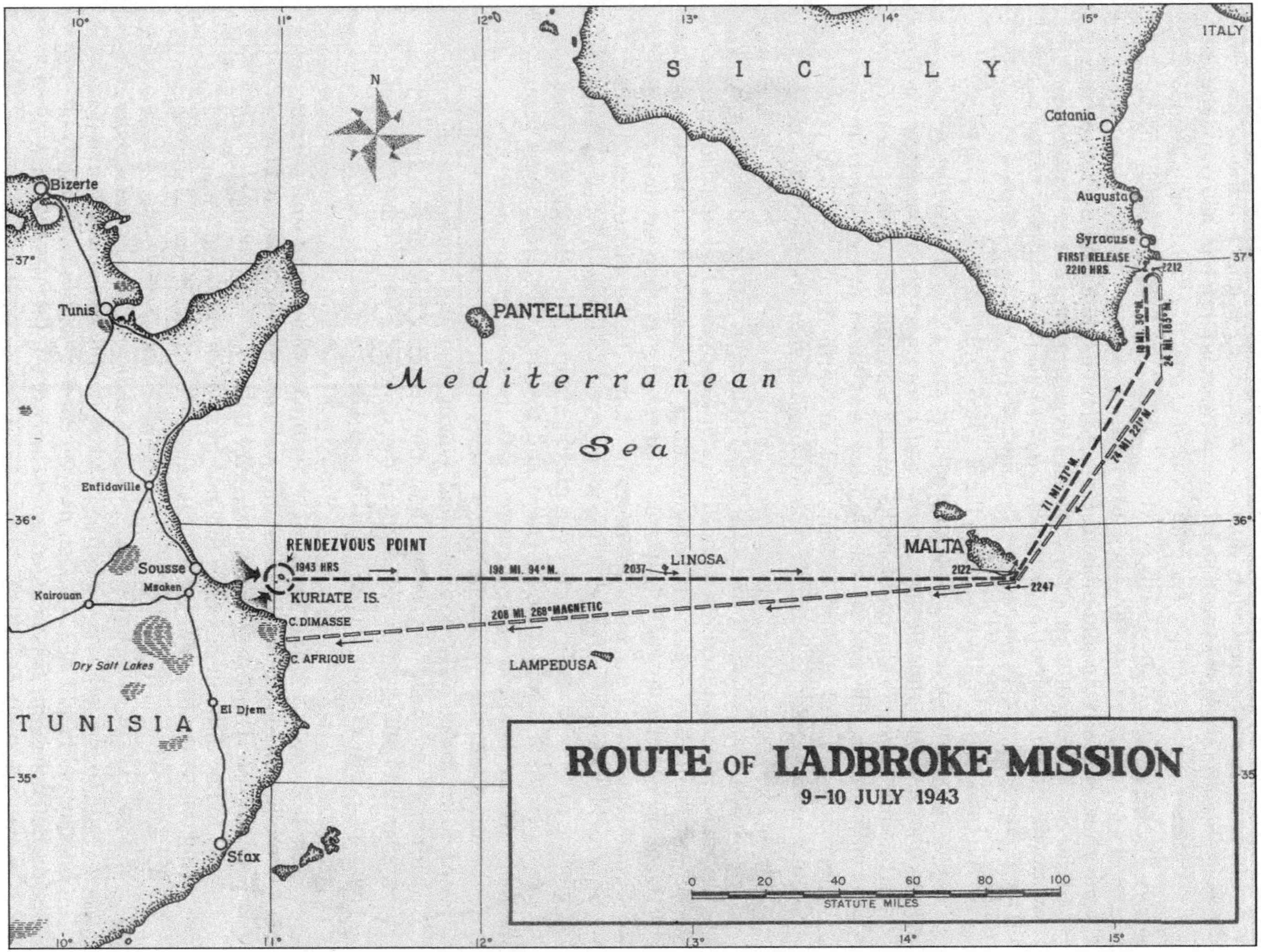

Official USAAF map of Operation LADBROKE route

Wynford Atkins, returned to its airfield as a result of an oil leak on their Albemarle tug. The two pilots managed to keep their glider in the air just long enough to scrape over the airfield's perimeter fence but they could not avoid a set of power cables. The glider, carrying men from the Mortar Platoon of the Borderers, came down so violently that its load of 3-inch mortar bombs came loose from stowage and rolled menacingly around the floor of the glider. Luckily for all on board they did not explode and the wayward glider came to a halt without any injuries to any of the crew or passengers.

Further out to sea Glider 120, carrying men of the Borderers' No. 14 Platoon and with Sergeants Phillip Read and William Gill at the controls, was clear of the coast and 20 minutes into its flight when problems began to develop. It was apparent soon after take-off that the glider and its load were out of balance. Even after the two pilots had rearranged their passengers in an attempt to rectify the problem, the glider was still dangerously close to becoming unflyable and so the decision was taken to cast off from its Albemarle tug and attempt to land back in North Africa. The two pilots continued to wrestle with the controls and managed to land safely two miles outside Msaken.

Staff Sergeants 'Taff' Evans and 'Dick' Martin in Glider 88 were more fortunate. Having taken off without incident and with the Tunisian coast behind them, they were now concentrating on keeping their WACO as stable as possible in the slipstream of their tug as they headed out in formation towards the friendly shores of Malta. As the streams of gliders approached the island, however, the wind speed increased further, at times gusting to 45 mph and placing even greater strain on the already stretched towropes. As a result, a single Horsa and two WACOs broke loose from their tugs in the darkness and crashed into the Mediterranean.

Meanwhile, other tug and glider crews were working exceptionally hard to maintain their positions and height over the wave tops of the Mediterranean; in steadily failing light, the stream of aircraft flew on with the gliders bobbing and weaving over the sea on the end of their 350 feet long towropes as Staff Sergeant Taff Evans later recalled:

> The tug-glider combinations were flying echelon starboard – four combinations to each echelon – and we were the end combination of our echelon. The flight to Sicily, skirting Malta was at 50–200 feet, which was rather difficult owing to the gale but which Dick and I managed well whilst the daylight lasted. It became very difficult when darkness fell and we were 'formating' on the three small lights on the tug's wings and tail. There were times when we lost sight of these in the squalls brought by the gale. As we approached Sicily, the formation rose to its operational height of 1,900 feet, thereby coming within radar range of the defence radar. This resulted in anti-aircraft gunfire. We flew steadily on for a short while until, suddenly, to our amazement and consternation, our tug aircraft turned fairly steeply to starboard and flew through

> the formation, weaving to port and starboard for several minutes. I had impressions of other aircraft flashing past us in the blackness and not very far away either! Dick and I were hard pressed to follow and the five or so minutes flying through the formation seemed more like five or so hours! It was an absolute miracle that the tow rope didn't snap.[16]

Elsewhere in the seemingly endless stream of yawing, pitching gliders and tugs, Glider 91 pressed on through the darkness toward Sicily. Staff Sergeant Jack Caslaw and Sergeant Andy Anderson were determined to reach their LZ, having promised to deliver their load of eight infantrymen from A Company, 1st Battalion The Border Regiment safely into battle. Jack Caslaw was in a relatively calm frame of mind:

> We were near the end of the pack, with a sky full of tugs ... and their 'matchboxes', skimming along at not more than one-hundred feet to evade radar or the equivalent. I said a little prayer to God and Saint Paul who had had problems in these waters, then sat back and enjoyed the trip, taking the wheel in half hour stints. We rounded Malta, and as it darkened, we climbed, and slid up the east coast of Sicily. Andy was flying and I sat back and remember thinking that the flak around the LZ wasn't a patch on that over Liverpool in late 1940.[17]

The great armada flew on, streaming steadily into the darkness as it headed further away from home airfields, leaving the light behind as it was engulfed in darkness. Somewhere amid the stream, in Glider 88, Staff Sergeants Taff Evans and Dick Martin were by now approaching the coast of Sicily. Their tug had climbed rapidly up to the pre-briefed release height. Evans now had to make the decision on when to cast off his tow from the tug aircraft. Everybody on board the WACO was aware that it carried a handcart packed with highly explosive PIAT bombs. This potentially deadly cargo was tied down in the centre of the glider's troop compartment and thus featured prominently in the minds of everyone on board, while also influencing the way Evans handled his glider:

> I recognised that we were now approaching our target area and released the glider. We were at 1,900 feet (approx) but still over the sea, when two searchlights from the peninsula came on and immediately picked us up. We were sitting ducks at that height and the light ack-ack guns fired a lot of shells at us. The balls of fire were whipping past the cockpit and I could see them going through the wings. I flung the WACO about as much as I dared; bearing in mind the load we were carrying. So dive, stall turn, dive again, steep turn etc, until I managed to shake off the searchlights. When we were free, Dick and I could see properly and

> we were still over the sea. However, I headed for where the land was and suddenly there was a great flash, a tremendous crash, pain and oblivion ...[18]

The ferocity of the Italian response surprised some of the tug and glider crews as they had expected at least to have some element of surprise during the early phases of Operation LADBROKE. In fact, the Italian and German defences had been placed on a high state of readiness since 4 July 1943, this being triggered by reports from Luftwaffe long-range reconnaissance aircraft monitoring Allied naval movements. A convoy of 25 troopships was reported off Cape Serrat and, most tellingly, Axis intelligence reported 100 ships entering the Mediterranean through the Straits of Gibraltar. Concern about impending Allied landings was further reinforced with additional intelligence reports of increased Allied naval activity in the central Mediterranean and a steadily increasing tempo of aerial activity over Sicily itself. Convinced that these reports were credible and indicated an impending attack on Sicily, General Guzzoni placed the Italian Sixth Army on the island on full alert. Although perhaps a few days premature in doing so, his deduction was nevertheless ultimately proved correct: the Allies were heading for Sicily. The gliders and tugs now approaching Capo di Murco were flying into pre-warned, highly alert air defences.

Consequently, Italian searchlights and anti-aircraft guns were enjoying some success against the slow-moving stream of transport aircraft and gliders. Trapped in the blinding glare of searchlights and attracting an increasing torrent of anti-aircraft fire, Staff Sergeants Evans and Martin had thrown their glider around the night sky as violently as they dared in a desperate effort to escape. As a result, however, they lost a great deal of precious height and became totally disorientated. Their rapid descent ended abruptly and disastrously:

> Afterwards we discovered we had just skimmed the cliff top, passing through a high tension electrical cable and smashing through a big stone wall. Three or four of the Border men had been injured and Sergeant Cherry put them in the shelter of part of the starboard wing. Dick had a 'greenstick' fracture of the left thigh bone, whilst my left foot was broken in half and I had injuries to my chest and throat where I had gone through the front of the glider. Dick and I were put in the port side of the wreckage. When the injured were settled, Sergeant Cherry took his half dozen fit men to try and link up with the main force of the 1st Airlanding Brigade, but after an hour or so they returned as they could not find anybody.[19]

Out to sea, more and more gliders were arriving at the offshore release point, casting off their tows and then running the gauntlet of flak and searchlights. In spite of the threat of the searchlights and the highly visible tracer streaking into the sky, to those gliders approaching the Capo di Purco the LADBROKE plan appeared to be playing out as intended. Lieutenant Bunny Carn was approaching his release point and, as he prepared to cast off, made a quick appreciation of the situation below. He was not allowed to loiter long however before the Italian defences acquired Glider 125A as a target:

> Over the Landing Zone at Capo di Porco there were one or two AA guns firing at us from inland and several heavy machine guns firing bright tracer, and one searchlight about a mile or so inland which latched onto us for sometime. We had about 3,000 feet over Capo di Porco, the sea was rough, and there was a large fire burning right near a small building on the tip of the landing area. The fire was so bright I could see eight or nine WACOs on the ground quite clearly, there was also some moonlight and I assumed the fire to be an aircraft, not a glider, because of its intensity and brightness it looked like a petrol fire. I was forced to dive out of the persistent searchlight in a 360 degree diving turn to lose height, and approached at about seventy-five miles per hour.[20]

Within sight of the coast, and still attached to their tug, was the crew of Glider 13: Flight Officer Sam Fine and Staff Sergeant Lofty Wikner. The American second pilot was handling the aircraft, carrying men from B Company, 2nd Battalion The South Staffordshire Regiment, as it glided onwards in the darkness. Just a few thousand yards off the coast, the two pilots were anxiously scanning the coastline looking for a reference point to initiate their turn inland:

> As we flew along the coast of Sicily it was lit up with searchlights and anti-aircraft fire ... I released and pulled the stick back ... made a left turn and headed to shore through the search-light and anti-aircraft fire ... I made a very nice touch down but was rolling too fast. As there was a stone wall ahead of me, I turned the glider to the left and hooked the left wing onto a tree. That stopped us very nicely ... A shot rang out (and) I was knocked out of my seat.[21]

Lieutenant Bunny Carn and Staff Sergeant David Richards had also made landfall on Sicily, Carn at the controls as they made their final approach in over the coastline:

> I landed quite well, put the brakes full on, and then we hit a low wall about two feet high which smashed the floor of the WACO and broke mine and Richards's ankles. Fortunately, all of our troops walked out all right, slightly airsick and one chap with a badly cut face from loose equipment flying about in the glider. Only one other glider came in after we landed, approaching very high and much too fast and crashing inland.[22]

Carn's account of his own solitary landing and the absence of other gliders in close proximity give an early indication that the 1st Airlanding Brigade plan was not going well. The scattered pattern of glider landings bore little resemblance to the neat well-ordered four-glider echelons landing in pre-designated landing lanes as practised on exercise in North Africa. The men emerging from gliders dispersed across the Maddalena Peninsular were in many cases shaken, injured or, at best, severely airsick and disorientated. As soon as officers and NCOs gathered their wits and gained their bearings, they soon realised that all was not as intended. Large numbers of gliders were unaccounted for and casualties on the LZs were high.

Staff Sergeant Jimmy James had a very different experience on the night. Following the polite and very professional rebuttal of his offer of a dram of whisky before take-off, the USAAF tug pilot further reinforced James's initial impression of him by his conduct in the air:

> The whole trip was immaculate and I was, to the best of my recollection, at the right height and at the right spot for release. From a tug pilot whose acquaintance I had only made for some five minutes, I could not have asked for more. In spite of the searchlights and flak, he continued on course perfectly, and hung on until I had released the glider from the rope. I have only praise and thanks to the American tug pilot to whom I was allotted to do the job.[23]

Not all of the 1st Battalion GPR was committed to flying on Operation LADBROKE. The final frenzy of activity and dramatic spectacle of the launching of the aerial armada was watched with an experienced eye by Major Philip 'Daddy' Cooper, the commander of No. 1 Squadron. He and a number of other pilots were held back on North African airfields in reserve, and were waiting impatiently to fly in support of the subsequent airborne operations planned for 1st Airborne Division's two parachute brigades. In fact, Cooper did not fly on Operation LADBROKE; in a spare moment he wrote a lighthearted song titled *Take off and Flight*, the words of which recalled the departure of the massed gliders of 1st Airlanding Brigade and their USAAF tugs on that night of 9 July 1943. Unaware of the success or failure of Operation LADBROKE and the fate of their friends and comrades on the other side of the Mediterranean Sea, the remaining glider pilots cheerfully sang the ditty to the tune of *Lily Marlene*:

> *Underneath the olive trees, where we used to wait*
> *Before we flew to Syracuse to open up the gate*
> *Slowly the days went drifting by.*
> *They kept us there, we wondered why.*
> *Lady of the olives, my own Lily Marlene.*

Rows and rows of WACOs, on each dusty strip,
Scores of big Dakotas, to take them on the trip.
Brigadier Hicks and all his men
And Colonel Chatterton with his new Sten.
Lady of the olives, my own Lily Marlene.

Stinging swirling dust clouds at each take-off run
Dust that slowly settled against the setting sun.
Wheeling and forming in the sky.
We wished them luck as they went by,
Lady of the olives, my own Lily Marlene.

The song contains no verses that tell the story of the landings on Sicily, nor does it tell the story of the night landing. It would be some days before news of what had befallen the gliders of 1st Airlanding Brigade finally reached those 1st Battalion GPR pilots who remained in North Africa. Exhausted after days of preparation and assisting in the loading and marshalling of the LADBROKE gliders, they repaired to their tents content with their efforts. They would wake, however, to a trickle of fragmented information and rumours about the events of the previous night over the Mediterranean and the Sicilian coast.

Notes

1. Chatterton, Lieutenant Colonel, G., 1st Battalion GPR, *The Wings of Pegasus*, Nashville, Battery Press, 1962, p. 68.
2. Andrews, Staff Sergeant, A., *So, You Needed to Fly Eh?* Burnaby, BC ISTE 1997, p. 66.
3. Chatterton, Lieutenant Colonel, G., 1st Battalion GPR, *The Wings of Pegasus*, Nashville, Battery Press, 1962, p. 69.
4. Place, Major, J., OC, 2 Squadron, 1st Battalion GPR, by permission of *The Eagle*.
5. James, Staff Sergeant, J., 1st Battalion GPR, by permission of *The Eagle*.
6. Brown, Lance Corporal, G.R., 2nd Battalion The South Staffordshire Regiment, by permission of Mrs D. Brown.
7. Place, Major, J., OC, 2 Squadron, 1st Battalion GPR, by permission of *The Eagle*.
8. Wilson, Flight Officer, R., USAAF, *The Glider Gang*, Cassell, London, 1977, p. 72.
9. Newport, Lieutenant, E., S Company, 1st Battalion Border, *When Dragons Flew*, p. 64.
10. Brown, Lance Corporal. G.R., 2nd Battalion The South Staffordshire Regiment, by permission of Mrs D. Brown.
11. Evans, Staff Sergeant, K., 1st Battalion GPR by permission of *The Eagle*.
12. Place, Major, J., OC, 2 Squadron, 1st Battalion GPR, by permission of *The Eagle*.
13. Brown, Lance Corporal, G.R., 2nd Battalion The South Staffordshire Regiment, by permission of Mrs D. Brown.
14. Fine, Lieutenant, S., USAAF, by permission of *The Eagle*.
15. Carn, Lieutenant, W.J., 1st Battalion GPR, by permission of *The Eagle*.
16. Evans, Staff Sergeant, K., 1st Battalion GPR by permission of *The Eagle*.

17. Caslaw, Staff Sergeant, J., 1 Squadron, 1st Battalion GPR, by permission of *The Eagle*.
18. Evans, Staff Sergeant K., 1st Battalion GPR by permission of *The Eagle*.
19. Evans, Staff Sergeant K., 1st Battalion GPR by permission of *The Eagle*.
20. Carn, Lieutenant W. J., 1st Battalion GPR, Letter Dated 15 September 1987, by permission MAF.
21. Fine, Lieutenant S., USAAF, by permission of *The Eagle*.
22. Carn, Lieutenant W. J., 1st Battalion GPR, Letter dated 15 September 1987, by permission MAF.
23. James, Staff Sergeant J., 3 Squadron, 1st Battalion GPR, by permission of *The Eagle*.

Chapter 10

Ill Met By Moonlight

In 38 Wing it was an unwritten law that the rope was never released at the tug end, except in dire emergency.

While the remaining glider pilots kicked their heels or slept on the now quiet, dust-blown North African airstrips, they speculated as to the outcome of the landing and the prospects for the success of Operation LADBROKE. It would be some days, however, before they would be apprised of the fate of their friends and comrades in Sicily. Little did they know that the gliders of 1st Battalion GPR were by now scattered across the Sicilian LZs and in many cases miles beyond them. A combination of inexperienced tug crews, enemy flak, searchlights, high winds and treacherous terrain had caused havoc among the glider formations, with many gliders ripped apart on landing in the darkness or, at best, scattered miles from their planned LZs. This disastrous series of events was far removed from the scenes envisaged in the LADBROKE plan.

On the LZs the missing gliders, their loads and the so far unseen casualties, created gaping holes in the ranks of 1st Airlanding Brigade. Remarkably, however, the operation retained its momentum. Those troops who had survived the turbulent flight and the hazards of landing set about moving off the LZs and carrying out their allotted tasks. In the darkness, however, most remained unaware of a tragic series of events that had resulted in a significant proportion of the airlanding force falling far short of making landfall on Sicily.

Amid the confusion, the number of missing gliders began to mount. Glider 83, flown by Staff Sergeant Stan Coates and Sergeant Vic Perry, was on that list. The WACO was carrying a chalk under the command of Captain Bill Hodgson of A Company, 1st Battalion The Border Regiment and consisting of a 3-inch mortar detachment, a Jeep, and members of A Company's headquarters. Some years later, Hodgson recounted the story of those on board Glider 83 on what was a dark and increasingly windy night over the Mediterranean:

> As the light faded there was a general dispersal until each tug with its glider was left to find its own way to the LZ. The small blue hooded lights on the trailing edge of the Dakota wings were the only things we would be likely to see before we reached Sicily. The main problem now was one of navigation. As part of the US Transport Command, the tug pilots were not experienced in towing gliders by night in unfamiliar areas ... The first landfall of Sicily should have been Cape Passero ... from this point the landing procedures set out during the briefing should have commenced ... The ETA for this point had passed and there had been no sign of land whatsoever. The tug pilot came over on the intercom and assured us that we would soon be in a position to cast off. After a further period of flying even he abandoned this theory and changed course to the west in search of Sicily. By this time ... somewhere off Syracuse the change of course brought them into Augusta, which was an Italian seaplane base. The Italians' reaction was to switch on searchlights and send flak up the beams in the direction of an intruder. Our tug pilot was taken aback by these sudden developments and put the Dakota in a steep turn in order to get back out to sea. When the change of plan was transmitted to our glider it was by means of a sharp tug on the tow rope which caused some minor aerobatics before both pilots could get it back under control. The only damage caused was to the wire in the rope which had snapped, by the force of the jerk. No communications were now possible between tug and glider. If the situation did little to reassure the glider pilots that all was well and going to plan, it must have been a good deal worse for the lieutenant and his section in the rear of the glider who had received no information since take-off ... From what he remembered from the briefing I came to the conclusion that the probable destination was now Malta.[1]

Naturally, after so many weeks and months of hard training, the men of Glider 83 were severely disappointed at not reaching their objective. Their frustration was further heightened by the thought that the rest of their company were now in Sicily carrying out their mission and taking the fight to the enemy. In fact, of the ten gliders that had taken off from North Africa carrying A Company's troops and equipment, only a solitary WACO had actually reached Sicily. Staff Sergeant Tom Stewart and Sergeant Martin Guinan, flying Glider 85, were carrying the bulk of a platoon of the Borderers. The field telephone link between the cockpit of the glider and their tug failed almost immediately after take-off. Unbeknown to those on board the glider, the tug crew were unable to navigate to the release point off Sicily and with no telephone link could not inform the glider pilots of this vital fact. Unsure of their exact position, the tug crew had turned back toward North Africa. Once across the North African coastline the tug released the WACO, which landed safely. In their ignorance, the two glider pilots and the platoon commander, although initially confused by the open sandy terrain, assumed that they were now in Sicily somewhere close to the LZ. The platoon commander was taking no chances:

> ... I formed an ambush on the straight featureless bit of road and waited for about two hours and then saw in the distance some headlights coming towards us. We had piled sand and a few stones on the road and the whole platoon stood ready. I thought it was strange that there were no signs of firing or bombing, but there it was. The troops had been commenting more and more on what a bloody awful place Sicily must be with this amount of sand, and not what they had expected.
>
> The vehicle approached and three of us got up. It was going quite slowly and I shone my torch. The vehicle drew up towards me. With my Sten ready, I approached. It was a 15-cwt open truck with two figures in front. A section ran up to the back. All was well. Then a voice from the driving seat said, 'What do you want cock ... a lift?'
>
> Good, I thought, better still, a British unit.
>
> 'Yes,' I said, 'but I have got about 20 men here.'
>
> 'That's alright,' said the cheerful driver. 'Get them all in – it will be a tight squeeze.'
>
> The platoon gathered round. 'What are you on, an exercise?'
>
> The driver replied, 'Oh we are from the mobile bath unit about eight miles down the road.'
>
> Amazing, I thought, the battle not really under way yet and a mobile bath unit already on shore from the sea-borne landings. All must be going well. I then asked if he had seen any airborne troops.
>
> 'No,' he said, 'Not down here', but there were some around Sousse.
>
> 'Yes,' I said. 'We were there before we left for the battle.'
>
> 'Really?' said the driver. 'Didn't you go off with them to the battle then or did you miss the way?'
>
> I then asked him where we were.
>
> 'About eight miles from the Mareth Line,' the driver replied.
>
> I was stunned. The Mareth Line in North Africa! We had landed back in North Africa and been rescued by a mobile bath unit![2]

In such circumstances, having endured a lengthy flight and survived enemy anti-aircraft fire, the two glider pilots and the members of the platoon had every right to be frustrated or angry with their lot, but were yet to find out how lucky they had been that night.

The vast majority of 1st Airlanding Brigade's glider lift had reached Malta safely, only five per cent of the formation failing to turn north at the crossed searchlights beacon. It was from that point on, however, as the glider stream turned on to the new northerly heading, that flying conditions deteriorated dramatically.

The speed and intensity of the headwinds worsened and the resulting turbulence made holding any semblance of a formation almost impossible. Pilots in both glider and tug cockpits struggled to keep their aircraft aligned with each other and to hold a steady course. Problems with the wind were further compounded by a steady increase in the density of cloud cover as the stream progressed northwards. Operation LADBROKE had been planned to coincide with a full moon period, the light levels being predicted to be sufficient for crews to see one another's aircraft and maintain formation and aid navigation. As the gliders and their tugs streamed further north, however, the clouds obscured more and more of the moon and consequently visibility diminished. The light level dropped so rapidly and so significantly that the glider pilots could not even see their own tug just 350 feet ahead of them at the other end of the towrope.

Regardless of the conditions, the glider crews fought to keep their aircraft intact, on station with their tugs and in the air. Battling on in the teeth of the headwinds, the lead echelons of combinations steadily approached enemy-controlled airspace. Sergeant Harry Lansdell was flying Glider 53A with an American co-pilot, Lieutenant Kinney, alongside him. The two of them suffered a fate that befell many of the incoming gliders:

> In the distance, the multi-coloured flak tracers were drifting lazily in great arcs and the natural tendency of the tug pilots was to drift off course away from the flak. The offshore breeze was not the only wind taking us away from the coast line that night. A telephone line had been lashed to the tow rope for communication between the tug and the glider. There were conversations between my co-pilot and the tug in scratchy American which I did not understand but Kinney seemed to, and bang, we were off! Being the last glider of all and subject to the most offshore drift, there was not the slightest hope for us to reach land only just to be made out in the distance. I gave the order to prepare for ditching.[3]

All along the coastline Lieutenant Colonel Chatterton's worst fears on release heights came home to roost with terrible consequences. Unbeknown to him, his decision to raise the release height for the glider force had not been fully circulated. In fact, the tug pilots of US 51st Troop Carrier Wing had been briefed to release all of the gliders, regardless of their intended LZ, at a height of 1,800 feet. The originator of this order has to date never been identified. As an individual factor it was serious enough, but combined with all of the other negative variables present that night, it was to have the gravest consequences.

The final operation order from the headquarters of 1st Battalion GPR stated that the gliders were to be cast off at a distance of 3,000 yards from the coast. In order to ensure that the gliders had the flight time and the reach to glide to their respective LZs, they were given specific release heights for each zone. The Horsa chalks were to be released at 5,000 feet, the WACOs for LZ 1 at 1,900 feet and finally the WACOs for LZ 2 were to cast off at 1,400 feet. The calculated glide range, even for the lowest gliders, was two miles. The confusion over release heights and the numerous and significant variables, not least the headwind, had not featured in the original calculation and consequently wrought havoc among the glider stream. The anti-aircraft batteries on the Sicily coast, those that had given Sergeant Harry Lansdsell and Lieutenant Kinney so much trouble, had been alerted to the presence of the incoming Allied aircraft by radar and the noise of the tug aircrafts' engines. The flashes from the muzzles of the heavy flak guns, tracer from the lighter calibre guns and the airbursts of high explosive shells at altitude caused even more confusion as the tug navigators tried desperately to identify landmarks on the darkened coastline. The flak was augmented by a number of Italian searchlight units that had survived earlier pre-emptive sweeps by RAF Hurricane fighter-bombers, a number of them succeeding in illuminating individual aircraft for the anti-aircraft gunners to engage. Although the anti-aircraft fire was actually some distance from the tug and glider stream, the noise and flashes of the flak created panic among some of the USAAF tug crews whose lack of combat experience soon became evident.

Tug crews reacted in varying ways to what was, in the majority of cases, quite distant fire. Some tugs were still well out to sea and miles from their designated cast off points for their gliders, yet they turned away from the flak and headed back out to sea with their gliders still in tow. Others cast off their gliders, abandoning those on board to their fate.

Out in the darkness and unaware of what was happening to the other gliders around them, Sergeant Geoffrey Fowell and Staff Sergeant Ken McConnell were wrestling with the controls of Glider 12 that had managed to take off from Airstrip A at Kairouan without serious incident. Behind them, anxiously willing them to get on to Sicily, was Lieutenant Davies who had under his command eleven men of the South Staffordshires' Mortar Platoon. Sergeant Fowell takes up the story of Glider 12:

> After leaving Malta we realised that we were on our own with no sign of the rest of the echelon. Communication with the tug aircraft failed on take-off and there was no other way of communicating with its crew. It was a question of hanging on and hoping for the best. After a while some light anti-aircraft fire was experienced ... presumably Sicily, which was a signal to the tug pilot to veer away to starboard and head north, apparently parallel to the coast, although this was not visible. Suddenly the towrope wrapped itself around the nose of the glider and the tug pulled away and headed back to Africa. We had been cast off at 1,200 feet, at God knows where and as it turned out, about six miles offshore. Assuming we were flying along the coast, we altered course, due east and flew hopefully toward land. With approximately 1,000 feet of height and into the teeth of a 30-knot wind, little progress was made

> and the chances of making land were to be charitable – slim! Ditching was therefore the only option. Ken instructed our passengers on the procedure while I concentrated on the business of ditching.[4]

The sudden release from tow with little or no prior warning was not an uncommon occurrence that night. Dozens of glider pilots found themselves in free flight with no idea of their position in relation to Sicily and the LZs. Those who were fortunate enough to find themselves at least in the vicinity of the release point attempted to correct their course, cross the coastline and make an approach on to the LZs. What was already a chaotic, and in some cases desperate, situation in the cockpit was worsened as wayward gliders and tugs loomed out of the darkness from all directions, altitudes and angles.

Heading into the chaos were Staff Sergeant Stan Coates and his second pilot Sergeant Vic Perry, the two men peering into the night trying to maintain their station in relation to their tug and to pick out pre-briefed reference points on the coast of what they hoped was Cape Passero. As they continually scanned the darkness ahead through the windscreen, they were increasingly aware of their responsibility for landing Glider 83 safely, and of the silent presence behind them of their chalk of twelve fully laden infantrymen from A Company of The Border Regiment. Staff Sergeant Coates later described the feeling of helplessness experienced by many glider pilots as they flew along at the end of their towrope at the mercy of their tug crews:

> ... We flew for some considerable time in the dark with no intercom between tug and glider. After a number of hours the pilot called out that we were approaching an island that looked like Sicily. Yes, he was sure it was Sicily, and the whole place was in darkness. The tug circled round and round and eventually our pilot said, 'Well, here it is.' and pushed the button freeing the glider. Down we came and landed most perfectly in the dark on a flat open piece of ground and came to a standstill. Out got the troops, guns at the ready, and pulled out the trailer. Suddenly there was the noise of an approaching vehicle. All the troops got down and waited. A Jeep with two men arrived, stopped, and the men got out. Up jumped the troops and dragged the trailer over to hook it on to the Jeep. The Jeep was pointing in the wrong direction and there was a certain amount of military confusion. No one seemed to be getting anywhere and least of all the Jeep and trailer.
>
> Eventually, I called out, 'Stop everyone, stay still – now where are the two men from the Jeep?' The two were produced and in a few short, sharp words I told them to get their Jeep fixed, so that the trailer could be hitched without further delay, and then all could move off to the battalion RV. The two protested greatly and said, 'Don't give us any more orders, we will now tell you what to do'. A certain amount of military back-chat went on between us and I kept saying, 'Come on, we

must get away from here and get to the battalion RV, and it doesn't matter what unit you are.' One of the two from the Jeep then said, 'Look here, old boy, there appears to have been a bit of nonsense. Where do you reckon you are, and what are you doing here anyway?'

By now my patience was exhausted, and I explained very tersely that I reckoned that I was very near the LZ just outside Syracuse and that I was now going to take the Jeep and move off with it, and if the two owners cared to follow they could do so.

Unabashed by this the two said, 'We are very sorry to inform you that you are not in Sicily, but on Malta, and what's more you are blocking one of the main runways, and the fighters cannot take off. So please take the Jeep and pull not only the trailer but also this bloody glider 200 yards in that direction.' This done, the fighters then took off. The glider party was then taken off to a canteen filled with wondering RAF. We were given food, drink and a lot of advice. We also thought that we were the only glider off course. We spent the remainder of the night listening to the fighters taking off and drinking ourselves into a depressed coma ...[5]

Overhead and beyond Malta, the incoming stream of gliders was by now widely dispersed and the carefully planned order of arrival had been thrown into disarray by a combination of headwinds, navigation errors and enemy flak. Sergeant Bob Boyce, the second pilot on Glider 17, and his first pilot, Sergeant Henry Dowds, had so far completed what they later recalled as an uneventful flight despite having lost communications with their USAAF tug almost immediately after their take-off from El Djem Airfield. The WACO passed over Malta and turned on to the heading for Sicily. On board was a chalk of infantrymen from B Company, 2nd Battalion The South Staffordshire Regiment. Sergeant Boyce remembered with great clarity the moment that he sighted the Sicilian coast and the events that followed:

We approached the coast of Sicily and some flak came up; we turned north and flew for some time. I could see a glow in the sky that I took to be Etna; we then turned back towards Syracuse and in to the shore; it was a pencil line on the horizon. Suddenly the tow rope smacked down across the Perspex cockpit. I landed the WACO on the sea and we got out quickly and clung on the wing, some of the men were unable to swim; the distance from and the direction of the shore were uncertain and I decided to wait for dawn. Five hours later it was getting light and the glider was beginning to break up. Fortunately, the seaborne assault was beginning and a landing craft passed within hailing distance. We were taken on board and it then took another hour before landing. We were wet, bedraggled, weaponless and not allowed to go ashore with the infantry. My feelings at the time were indescribable, and still are ...[6]

It was a tragic scene that was repeated off the Sicilian coast as, with appalling frequency, panicking USAAF tug crews, some without issuing any prior warning, cast off their gliders far short of their release points and turned south to head for the safety of North Africa. In their wake they left dozens of unfortunate glider crews and their passengers now adrift at the wrong height and on the wrong heading, most with little or no chance of making headway against the prevailing wind. At the moment of release, most glider pilots had no idea of their position in relation to the coast of Sicily and little or no time to orientate themselves before they simply ran out of height. In these circumstances they had to think quickly and take decisive action. Sergeants Ian Macleod and Peter Mansfield were the crew of Glider 75, a WACO flying amid the tail end of the stream of echelons that had lifted out of North Africa. They were carrying a chalk from the 1st Battalion The Border Regiment:

> We were among the last of the gliders, soon I spotted searchlights and flak and Capo di Murco, the lead into the LZ, the flak slowly curling up then whizzing by. Then suddenly we were on our own and looking down at a lot of sea. Pete made a first class ditch. We were both yelling out to break the sides out. It was fortunate that they had all been issued with small blow-up life jackets. Pete and I broke out from above the cockpit and scrambled out to see all the lads present. The Border Regiment lads had a fine sergeant, who was checking them for injury and to see that they were blowing up their rubber rings. One lad couldn't swim but was reassured by everybody that he would be taken care of. We dived back into the sinking aircraft and brought up ration tins and their two kapok seat cushions which floated. The instrument panel had sufficient light to see underwater. After a brief conference it was decided to swim to our immediate front, where our original LZ was located. We were both apologising for dropping in the sea. With the aid of a bandage from a first field dressing and bootlaces, we tied the kapok seat cushions together behind us. Loaded down with boots stuffed with ration tins, I took the boots off the non-swimmer, my own boots and anything else that could be tied on. Then once everybody was ready, we pushed off in a line from the wing.[7]

The pre-flight ditching briefs carried out prior to take-off paid valuable dividends for many glider crews and their passengers that night. Staff Sergeant Harry Howard, the first pilot on Glider 32, and his second pilot Sergeant Jim Bennett, a 26-year old Londoner from Catford, were also destined to ditch in the Mediterranean. Howard described the ditching drill carried out by both glider pilots as they descended rapidly toward the sea below, his detailed and emotive account also giving a sense of the burden of responsibility that he felt as captain of an aircraft in such a hopeless situation:

A war bonds campaign poster highlighting the role of airborne forces and their ability to land at night, a capability that was very much untried before Sicily.

Glider Pilots underwent elementary flying training at EFTS run by RAF Training Command. Staff Sergeant Wallace Mackenzie stands at the centre of the rear rank in front of the ever popular De Havilland Tiger Moth trainer at RAF Burnaston in 1942.

The two-seat Hotspur, was originally intended to be an assault glider, however, it never saw action. It proved to be an excellent training aircraft, Hotspurs equipped all of the Glider Training Schools throughout the war.

A Horsa Glider in the high tow position behind a Halifax tug aircraft of 38 Group RAF.

The steep dive capability of the Horsa, coupled with its load-carrying capacity was considered essential for the Sicily *Coup de Main* operations.

The early DC3 Skytrains operated by the USAAF lacked navigation aids, had no self-sealing fuel tanks, and lacked armour plate of any description, they were therefore highly vulnerable to anti-aircraft fire.'

The crews of 295 Squadron RAF flew the Handley Page Halifax on Operation Beggar and the Sicily lifts. The four engine tug had the range and the power required to tow a fully laden Horsa.

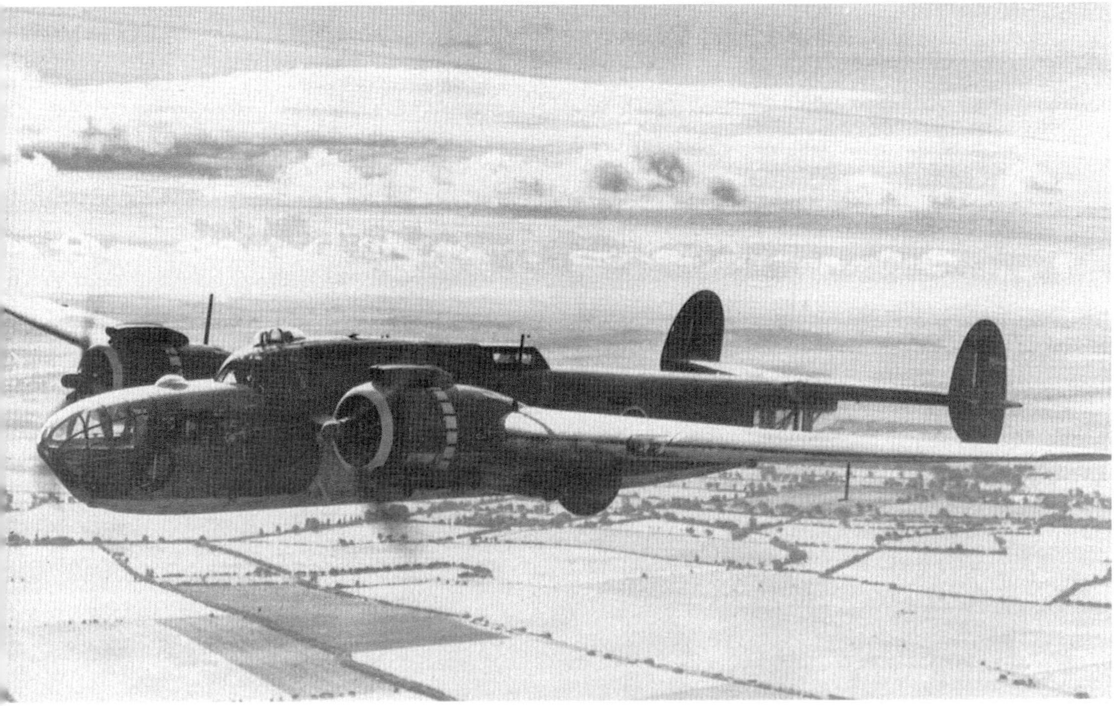

The Armstrong Whitworth Albemarle was originally designed as a medium bomber, it proved inferior to other RAF bombers and was therefore relegated to transport duties. The crews of 296 Squadron RAF did wonders with their aircraft, flying their Albermarles on both Sicily lifts.

Colonel George Chatterton DSO, Commander Glider Pilots, wearing RAF wings and the red tabs of a full colonel.

With space on merchant shipping at a premium in 1943 and time slipping away before the invasion, the shipping of crated Horsa gliders was ruled out. This led to the decision to mount Operation Beggar, later known as Operation Turkey-Buzzard.

The newly formed 2 Squadron GPR pose for a squadron photograph in January 1943, many would not survive the summer.

An element of 3 Squadron GPR pose for the camera before sailing to North Africa, only a few Glider Pilots are still wearing their hard earned wings. The majority have already removed them for the voyage as ordered.

The crew of Glider 32, SSgt Harry Howard and Sgt Jim Bennett in Mascara, Algeria. Sgt Bennett has modified his GPR wings to resemble those of the RAF. Sadly, he was killed during Operation Ladbroke, when their WACO ditched off Sicily.

One of the aerial photographs used to plan Operation Ladbroke. Syracuse and its port facilities can be seen at the top right, the bridge, the river, and the canal, are visible in the lower third of the picture.

Major General 'Hoppy' Hopkinson MC OBE, GOC 1st Airborne Division, wearing his AAC beret in North Africa before Operation Ladbroke. A qualified pilot and glider pilot, he was the architect of the British Airborne Division plan for the Sicily landings.

A WACO glider being prepared to accept an unusual load in the form of a mini bulldozer for use on Sicily by the Airborne Division's sappers. Note a trestle is positioned under the tail plane.

A Jeep being loaded into a WACO in Tunisia, the ingenious mechanism for raising the nose after landing would be fitted after loading was complete.

A Jeep and its all important airborne 6-pounder anti-tank gun being unloaded from a Horsa during a post-Sicily demonstration at RAF Brize Norton. Col George Chatterton can be seen watching (third from the right).

The *Coup de Main* on Ponte Grande as seen for propaganda purposes. This artists impression of the landing and Lt Wither's assault on the bridge was widely publicised in 1943.

Reality, daylight reveals Staff Sergeant Galpin's landing, a forlorn looking Horsa minus its nose wheel in the field close to the Ponte Grande Bridge – the little-known site of the Glider Pilot Regiment's first *Coup de Main*.

General H. 'Hap' Arnold (right), drafted the original requirement for a flying Jeep, this would ultimately lead to the development of the CG-4A WACO.

So close but so far, the wreckage of a WACO on the shoreline outside Syracuse bears witness to the tragedy of Operation Ladbroke.

An aerial view of Ponte Primosole Bridge taken in 1970. Sadly, the bridge has now been removed and the site bypassed by a new autostrada.

Major General Boy Browning with Churchill at Ringway in April 1942. Regarded as the father of Britain's Airborne forces, he could do little to influence Hopkinson's plans for 1st Airlanding Brigade.

Sergeant Tom Davidson of 2 Squadron GPR who survived the Sicily operations and went on to survive the war.

Sergeant Mike Hall, one of the handful of veterans of the hazardous Turkey-Buzzard missions, he was also among those selected to form the new glider force in India.

A banknote signed by members of C Company, 2nd Battalion South Staffs prior to Operation Ladbroke, written prophetically around the edge of the note is 'WACO No. 33, C 47, MISS CARRIAGE, GONE WITH THE WIND, WACO 33'. The names are Howes, Bull, Aston, Allsop, Wyatt and Holdsworth. Miss Carriage is thought to refer to the name of the USAAF tug aircraft that towed WACO 33.

10 November 1943, 5 Troop of 2 Squadron GPR pose for a photograph in Putignano, Italy.
Back: G. Pilcock, Perfect, A.H. Mills, J. Fairgreave, A.E. Richards, Saunders, W. May, H. Howard.
Centre: Wilson, S.J. East, L.E. Howard, J. Crook, S. Crook, S. Cook (Tow master).
Front Row: P. Weber, W. Mather, N. Meekin, T. Davidson, J. Lovett, Rednap.
Foreground: P. Coppack, Capt F.H. Barclay MC.

Lt Bernard Halsall epitomised Chatterton's 'total soldier'. After landing his WACO on Sicily, he led the infantrymen that he had carried into the battle for Ponte Grande. He was awarded the Military Cross for his leadership during the battle.

> As Captain and responsible for any other bodies on my aircraft, I have always been conscious of the fact that others have been lost when I was skipper. Ladbroke was the exception ... Perhaps one of the two incidents in the Sicily operation was excusable. All the South Staffs on board made a safe escape but I learned years later that two or three members of my load were presumed drowned when attempting to swim ashore from my ditched glider. As our weapons were lost, my advice was to stay put on the floating wing in the hope of rescue by the Navy a few hours later when the seaborne landings were due. The advice was ignored despite our being two miles offshore.
>
> The other is one which has been on, and never will be removed from, my mind. Although we both became sergeants upon completion of our flying course, Jim Bennett remained my co-pilot as a sergeant after I had been promoted to staff sergeant. I am sure that he was as proficient as me, but such differences are difficult to explain. Nevertheless we developed confidence in each other. When he was lost, after my tug cast loose from their end, a ditching was obvious in view of our distance from the Sicily shore. Jim fulfilled his duties and more in talking me down, reading speed and height and not least, removing his safety belt in order to warn our passengers in order to prepare for a speedy exit when we landed. Being a high wing aircraft, the WACO filled quickly with seawater and the troops had removed the side doors for escape. I had a fighting knife attached in a sheath to my leg and was able to slit the canvas top to the cockpit and escape on to the wing, but in the darkness could not see what my number two had done. He returned to his seat and had not re-fastened his belt for the landing. He would have been thrown through the windscreen – it's conjecture but remains a possibility. He was certainly not in the cockpit when, after the escape, I attempted to locate him. No body was ever recovered and his death is only recorded on the Cassino Memorial in Italy. Years later a letter from his brother only revived my sorrow. Although I did find some solace in the ensuing correspondence with his family.
>
> No other matters than this sad mishap are important to my memory of Sicily, except, of course, my rescue at dawn, after some six or seven hours clinging to the glider wreckage, by an assault landing craft returning to its mother ship.[8]

Unfortunately, Lieutenant Michael Connell of No. 3 Squadron was also among the fatalities of that night, as he flew Glider 58 with his second pilot Sergeant Herbert Hill who also drowned. Their WACO was among those doomed never to reach Sicily. Naturally after receiving news of the Operation LADBROKE losses; the Connell family were anxious to know what had happened to Michael. As a result of their enquiries after the war, they received a letter from Private H. Nolan of the 1st Battalion The Border Regiment who had been one of the passengers on board Glider 58 and had survived ditching that night. His letter is typical of the experiences of the men of 1st Airlanding Brigade who ditched:

> I only knew your son from the time we took off in Africa, until we came down off Sicily, but he was a grand chap and a fine pilot. We took off at about 6 pm in the evening and it was boiling hot, there was a dust storm at the time, and the pilots had to watch the sway of the tow rope for direction as it was the only thing that they could see.
>
> We got up without mishap and when we got a few thousand feet up the weather was grand, nice and cool and very clear. We circled around for a while to get into formation and then we were off. At about 8 o'clock we passed over the sea invasion force and it was a fine sight, one which made you proud to call yourself British. It would be nearly 10 o'clock when we saw the few lights of Sicily on the port side. Your son gave the order to get ready; we all donned our various articles of equipment and loaded our various weapons. We had previously had instructions from your son about what to do if we came down in water and we were ready for it.
>
> The lights of Sicily were now straight ahead of us and we could see the flames from the exhausts of the Dakota, which was towing us. There was a lot of flak and searchlights. We knew that we would cast off any minute now and crack we were off. I don't know what went wrong but in a few minutes we were in the water and your son had brought us down like a seagull alighting on the sea. We had the emergency doors off and were all out within a few seconds. We lost our Signals Sergeant – he was drowned in the first few minutes. The rest of us all climbed on to the wings and your son and my Major decided that the best thing to do was to swim for it. We were about a mile from the shore and I knew that I could never make it so along with four other chaps I stayed behind.
>
> The last time I saw your son was when he swam off with his sergeant pilot and Major, now Lieutenant Colonel, Haddon and about four other chaps. We that stayed behind were picked up by the Navy about eight hours after, and the glider was then completely under water. Later in the day I met Major Haddon and about three more swimmers, they had no idea what had happened to your son and his co-pilot, it seems that they were split up. Since then Major Haddon, Lieutenant Hope-Jones and myself, all members of your son's glider at Sicily, have been together and were all captured together at Arnhem after being shot down. I was wounded twice and am now in civilian life, working as a postman.
>
> Your son belonged to a grand corps and there is no praise too high for the boys of The Glider Pilot Regiment.[9]

The Connell family's investigation was further corroborated by the receipt of another letter, this one from another Glider 58 survivor. Lance Corporal

G.R. Thirlwell, another Border Regiment passenger who later recounted his experiences in some detail:

> I remember what a beautiful evening it was, the sky was as clear as could be. We were all sitting in the gliders waiting for the take-off. Suddenly, the singing was drowned out by the engines of aircraft bursting into life, about two minutes later we were off ... We had been airborne for about ten minutes when I became very ill with air-sickness. I don't remember anything of the journey.
>
> Somebody shook me and told me that we were nearing our target. At the thought of being on dry land again I pulled myself together. At that time the two glider pilots were having some trouble with the American pilots of the tug aircraft. I don't know exactly what was happening, but I gathered that the Americans wanted our pilots to cast off. We would be about five miles or more from our target. To cast off at that distance from the coast, would have been stupid ... our pilots would not cast off. After that I am not quite sure what happened, but I do know that the glider was doing a lot of swinging about as the tug was zigzagging. It was then that our pilots were forced to cast off. The senior pilot told us to prepare for crash landing.
>
> There was no one hurt when we crashed into the sea, thanks to two very good pilots. By the time the glider had settled in the water, everyone had climbed out and was sitting on the top. It was decided that we should all try to swim to the shore, the good swimmers helping those that were not so good. Not being able to swim at all, I stayed on the glider. The last time I seen your son, under the guidance of the senior pilot, he was swimming towards the shore, using a small wooden box to keep himself afloat ...

The fate of Glider 58 and the Connell family's campaign for information about its crew and passengers captured the interest of other service personnel involved in the Sicily landing. Not all were airmen. Petty Officer E. Mason of the Royal Navy witnessed the LADBROKE debacle from a different perspective. He took the time to write a letter giving an account of what he had seen from his position out at sea during the night and on the morning after the operation:

> I was there that night; I was a Petty Officer in the Royal Navy on board the troopship HMS *Dunera*. We had several thousand troops on board including a unit of commandos. As the ship got near to Syracuse, a number of planes towing gliders flew over, we were told they were going to land well beyond the coast line, while the commandos made their attack on the coastal defences. We had ten boats, each craft carried 22 commandos. As we went in at Avola Bay we saw several gliders in the sea, but we had to carry on to launch our commandos. After doing

> so we had to return to the ship to ferry out the rest of the troops in, but on returning I regret to say that there were no gliders to be seen, and nothing to pick up ... I have always wondered why they were in the sea, of course I can only speak of Avola Bay, but there were no aircraft about and flak was nothing to worry about. In fact it was well after daylight before they had a go at us.[10]

Not all of the USAAF Troop Carrier aircrews panicked and knowingly abandoned their gliders; some battled on resolutely against the headwind, ignoring flak and searchlights until they believed that they were at the correct release point and at the pre-briefed height. Staff Sergeant Jack Caslaw was in one of the few gliders that had communications with its attendant tug as it approached Sicily. His USAAF tug pilot and the other pilots in their echelon were still maintaining their four-ship formation to the best of their ability, in spite of the ever-worsening weather and the chaos around them. Undeterred, they had flown on regardless of distant enemy flak and were preparing to release their British gliders:

> A message came from our tug – 'This is it, good luck fellas.' The four Dakotas cast off their charges and I took over ... Then I saw we were going to ditch ... I held her off, and off, until the tail contacted a wave top, and she just swashed down into the water; no-one even lost their footing.[11]

Jack, his second pilot Sergeant Andy Anderson, and their passengers were picked up by a British destroyer early the next morning. Wind and fate show no respect for rank or position; this was particularly true on the night of Operation LADBROKE. Major John Place and his high-ranking second pilot, Major General Hopkinson, were among the gliders that had been forced to ditch in the darkness. They and their load of infantrymen from C Company, 1st Battalion The Border Regiment had been in the water for some time and were now little more than isolated spectators. They had no choice but to watch helplessly as the remainder of 1st Airlanding Brigade pressed on overhead toward their LZs. The commander of No. 2 Squadron and the commander of 1st Airborne Division were apparently out of the battle before it had even started, both men looking on in frustration and unable to influence the outcome of the plan that both had worked so hard to create. One can only imagine the thoughts running through Major General Hopkinson's mind as he witnessed the disaster that was unfolding around him. Major John Place, meanwhile, had other more immediate concerns:

> By now our waterlogged glider had made two efforts to sink, and each time all 17 of us found ourselves up to our armpits in the sea, and each time the wretched thing came to the surface again with a gurgle from its watery bowels as though it enjoyed taunting us. The aircraft's

> nose was a good deal lower 'in the drink' than its tail and I was afraid it might decide to plunge like a diving whale to Davey Jones, leaving us, unwilling Jonahs, floundering in the sea. If a man sat on the tail it might keep the nose up. I sat on the tail. If anyone has ever had the experience of trying to perch on the elongated fin of a WACO's rudder he will know what I mean when I say I was uncomfortable! The chop of the sea had gone, but there was now a rolling swell of only calm water. I rose and dipped with abandon, clutching the bracing wires each side of my razor-backed mount. The hour or more I spent on that tail was the longest in my life.[12]

As the darkness receded and the next day dawned, Place was still lodged in his unique and very uncomfortable vantage point. It was from that precarious perch that he witnessed the full scale of Operation HUSKY. In company with many other 1st Airlanding Brigade survivors, he saw the huge Allied naval armada loom into sight as it made its approach to the Sicilian coast. While this must surely have been an impressive spectacle, the prospect of rescue after a long and cold night must have also figured in his and everybody else's mind:

> Out to sea I saw the most tremendous sight in the world. Hundreds of great transports and dozen upon dozens of tiny assault craft, buzzing over the water like quaint water insects, as wave after wave of troops went ashore. Then, came a roar and a swirl of water alongside our glider as a returning assault boat drew up and took us off. He was going back for a second load of troops from his parent ship. Would he take us to the beach we asked? 'Not so and so likely' (this to the General!) 'We were survivors, we were, and the Navy don't land survivors on enemy beaches'. 'Not bloody likely it don't'. Turning to the General, a begrimed youth in shorts, tennis shoes and a tin hat held out a bottle. 'Ere y'are mate, it's a bit of orl right'. We all in turn, 'ad a bit of orl right'. Six and a half hours on a glider wing in the sea, even if it is the Mediterranean in the summer, makes one appreciate a tot of Navy rum.[13]

Closer into the shoreline, and also clinging to a sodden glider that was barely afloat, was Sergeant Tommy Gillies of No. 3 Squadron. He had taken off from Airfield D at Goubrine in a WACO carrying Chalk 103, a load made up of soldiers and equipment from A Company, 1st Battalion The Border Regiment. The Glaswegian ex-Highland Light Infantryman and his USAAF second pilot, Flight Officer Browning, had suffered an ignominious but ultimately lucky end to their flight as they were lifted out of the proverbial frying pan and into the fire:

> Released hopelessly short of the Sicilian coast, we successfully ditched but with the heavy load the glider began to sink almost immediately. It

> was soon almost totally submerged, leaving the crew to cling on to anything still above water. After some hours in the sea, I was able to swim to a marine commando landing craft spearheading the dawn landings. The commandos beached on some rocks only to be met by sustained machine gun fire. Me and several others were hit and were bundled into another landing craft and ferried to the *Winchester Castle*. Thankfully I had only sustained minor wounds and thus was able to enjoy a leisurely cruise to Malta ... I would not see what was left of a sadly depleted 3 Squadron for six weeks ...[14]

The night of 9/10 July 1943 was witness to many acts of bravery among the men of the 1st Battalion GPR and their passengers. Many of these individual acts of courage and sacrifice would go unobserved in the darkness out at sea, and consequently were never acknowledged. Some, however, were rightfully recognised and the citation for Sergeant William John Bayley's Distinguished Flying Medal typifies the courage shown by many glider pilots as they did what they could for their passengers at great risk to themselves:

> In July 1943, Sergeant Bayley was first pilot in a WACO glider detailed for a flight to Sicily; he was faced with very adverse weather. For five hours, he was unable to leave his position in the glider and owing to the strength of the wind; his hands were soon rubbed raw by the wheel of the glider. Eventually, he made an excellent descent into the sea and at once saw to the safety of his passengers. Assured of this, he dived into the interior of the submerged aircraft, salvaging arms and equipment, and afterwards he swam around encouraging the men on the wing of the glider until they were rescued. Throughout this trying experience, Sergeant Bayley showed great courage and fortitude, giving no indication of the pain or difficulties he was encountering and, by his cheerful confidence, set a magnificent example to all.[15]

Eventually, after the war, the full scale of the disaster would become known. However, in 1943 the losses on Operation LADBROKE were concealed under a blanket of operational security and a need to maintain morale and the spirit of Allied cooperation. Even for the men of 1st Airlanding Brigade who had survived the night and landed on Sicily, it would be some weeks before the full scale of the LADBROKE disaster would be realised.

The post-operation report accounted for all of the original 144 gliders that had taken off from North Africa. Apart from the handful that failed to get beyond Malta or ditched in the sea, it revealed that the remainder had been scattered or blown across Sicily over an area of more than 30 miles, with some even further adrift on the island. Only 56 gliders made landfall on Sicily and a meagre twelve successfully landed on or close to the Operation LADBROKE LZs. Eventually the grim account of the 73 ill-fated gliders that had been forced to ditch in the sea was pieced together. They had carried almost half of 1st Airlanding Brigade and the heavy casualty figures for LADBROKE reflect this. Initial reports estimated more than 500 casualties drowned at sea before landing. Included in that figure, were the 58 valuable pilots lost by the 1st Battalion GPR. This grim estimate of those lost at sea was however reduced to 252 personnel as a slow trickle of survivors who had been rescued by passing Allied ships and landing craft reported back from the distant ports that they had been transported to. Few military operations that have accumulated such significant numbers of casualties have succeeded; it is a testament to the men of 1st Airlanding Brigade and to their glider pilots that Operation LADBROKE did not fail before it had even started.

To this day, this facet of the first major British airborne operation and its associated cost in lives remains an emotive and controversial issue. There was considerable bad feeling between British and American aircrews resulting from the actions of the USAAF Troop Carrier Command aircrews, and the resulting horrific casualty figures, and a great deal of anger among glider pilots and their passengers. The arguments that flared up at the time are well documented and still resonate today. The general mood of the British airborne force is encapsulated in this statement made by Squadron Leader Lawrence Wright RAF:

> In 38 Wing it was an unwritten law (and it was observed on this operation) that the rope was never released at the tug end, except in dire emergency. Several glider pilots reported that on seeing distant flak, the Dakota pilots had turned away from the coast when three to five miles out, some switching off their formation lights without which the gliders could not keep station. One glider was thus jettisoned ten miles offshore. The most scathing reports were from the few American glider pilots.[16]

Those who survived the night and were rescued by ships were eventually returned to North Africa where they came under the care of Brigadier John 'Shan' Hackett and his 4th Parachute Brigade. As commander of the divisional reserve, the feisty cavalryman was given the task of administering the recuperation and regrouping of the LADBROKE survivors. Faced with a potentially volatile situation that he needed to contain, Hackett made a very quick and shrewd decision:

> Glider pilots who were recovered from the sea came back looking for tug pilots' throats to cut. I saw no option but to confine them to camp until after the American parade for the award of decorations for gallantry, by which time the admirable qualities always to be found in glider pilots had reasserted themselves and calm was restored.[17]

There are numerous occasions in military history where it can be said that those in senior command levels had little idea of the reality or the conditions that their subordinates were experiencing. This sentiment is certainly not true of 1st Airlanding Brigade's experience of LADBROKE. We left Major General Hopkinson, the overall commander of the operation, clinging on to Major John Place's WACO at the mercy of the elements. He was not, however, the only senior Airborne officer who shared the misfortunes of their troops that night. Lieutenant Colonel George Chatterton took off among the leading wave of gliders heading for Sicily; his second pilot was Lieutenant Peter Harding and among his passengers was the commander of 1st Airlanding Brigade, Brigadier Pip Hicks. Chatterton later wrote about his own experiences as he and Harding neared the release point:

> 'Can you see the release point, Peter?' I cried, trying to locate our position.
>
> 'Another five minutes or so sir,' he replied, looking at his watch. Then, 'There it is!' Peter shouted.
>
> 'I can't see a dammed thing,' I said, reaching for the release lever, and as I did I saw the tug starting to turn and dive. 'My god he's pushing off,' I shouted and heaved on the lever.
>
> The glider lifted up and after all that bucketing about seemed light and easy to handle. I turned toward towards the coast, and it was then that I received a jolt. As we lost height it seemed as if a great wall of blackness was rising up to meet us, and at that moment I realised that if this was happening to me, it was happening to the other pilots. What were we going to be able to do under these unforeseen conditions?
>
> Afterwards I discovered that the screen of blackness was a pall of dust created by the intensity and the length of the gale; it completely obliterated our target. The only thing that could be said in its favour was that it made the night so bad that the Italians could never have expected we would be such fools as to come. Descending into the darkness I had no idea where I was or what I was doing, but seeing a black object below, I turned my glider towards it and at that moment out of the darkness came a burst of tracer bullets. There was a jolt, and I saw the fabric tear open, and my port wing was hit as I began to turn. I straightened her out and down we came, the sea rushing up to meet us. Somehow I levelled out as, with a great splash, we ditched. The water came over my head as I fumbled with my strap, spitting out brine. Then two hands grasped my armpits and I was hauled out of the cockpit on to the fuselage.[18]

Chatterton had suffered the same fate as the majority of his pilots and was out of the battle. Indeed, as things stood just before dawn on 10 July 1943, at the most critical stage of Operation LADBROKE nearly all of 1st Airlanding Brigade's headquarters staff, including the brigade commander, together with the commander of 1st Airborne Division, had all failed to reach the LZs. All would be presumed missing. It was a far from promising, in fact disastrous, start to Britain's first major airborne operation. Meanwhile, to the men clinging on to the wings of their ditched gliders, the prospects for success must have appeared slim at best. However, against all odds, 51 WACOs and five Horsas had made it to Sicily, so all was not lost.

Notes

1. Coates, Staff Sergeant, S., 3 Squadron, 1st Battalion GPR, by permission of *The Eagle*.
2. *The Border Regiment Magazine* 1954, by permission of The Border Regiment Museum.
3. Lansdell, Sergeant, H., 2 Squadron, 1st Battalion GPR, by permission of *The Eagle*.
4. Fowell, Staff Sergeant, G., 3 Squadron, 1st Battalion GPR by permission of *The Eagle*.
5. Hodgson, Captain, W., 1 Border, *When Dragons Flew*, p. 65 by permission of The Border Regiment Museum.
6. Boyce, Sergeant, R., 2 Squadron, 1st Battalion GPR, by permission of *The Eagle*.
7. Macleod, Staff Sergeant, I., 1st Battalion GPR, by permission of *The Eagle*.
8. Howard, Staff Sergeant, H., 2 Squadron, 1st Battalion GPR, correspondence with the author dated, March 2010.
9. Nolan, Private, H., 1 Border, *When Dragons Flew*, p. 168 by permission of Border Regiment Museum.
10. Mason, Pilot Officer, E., Royal Navy, correspondence with Connell family 2010.
11. Caslaw, Staff Sergeant, J., 3 Squadron, 1st Battalion GPR, by permission of *The Eagle*.
12. Place, Major, J., OC, 3 Squadron, 1st Battalion, GPR, diary entry by permission of *The Eagle*.
13. Place, Major, J., OC, 3 Squadron, 1st Battalion, GPR, diary entry by permission of *The Eagle*.
14. Gillies, Sergeant, T., 3 Squadron, 1st Battalion GPR, by permission of *The Eagle*.
15. Bayley, Sergeant, W., 1st Battalion GPR, published in The London Gazette 27 January 1944.
16. Wright, Squadron Leader, L., 38 Wing RAF, *The Wooden Sword*, Elek Publishing, London, 1967, p. 158.
17. Hackett, Lieutenant General, J., Foreword, *One Night in June*, Shannon & Wright, Airlife Publishing, 1994.
18. Chatterton, Lieutenant Colonel, G., CO 1st Battalion GPR. By permission of *The Eagle*.

Chapter 11

One Way Ticket

On the landing zone below I could see several aircraft in flames and the criss-cross of tracer bullets. It seemed no safe place to land as obviously quite a battle was raging down there.

The 56 gliders that successfully ran the gauntlet of wind and flak suffered mixed fortunes on finally reaching Sicilian soil. Inevitably, as a result of the chaos out over the sea and the mayhem of the final run-in to the release point, they were widely scattered all across the south-eastern corner of the island. Several chalks landed miles away from their LZs and spent the whole of the first day of the operation, or longer, searching for the main bodies of their respective units. These isolated groups linked up with other stragglers as they headed towards Syracuse and the Ponte Grande bridge. They had, however, negotiated the first and most dramatic hurdle: that of surviving their landing.

One of the critical variables in the glider survival equation that night was the performance of tug aircraft and their pilots. Aircraft serviceability aside, the conduct and bravery of each individual tug crew ultimately determined the survival of those on board the glider that they towed. Lieutenant Arthur F. Boucher-Giles and Staff Sergeant Dusty Miller were delivered to the correct release point by their 296 Squadron RAF Albemarle tug flown by Squadron Leader Bartram. The tug crew had done all that was required of them and shortly the fate of all on board the WACO would rest firmly with the two men seated in its canvas and perspex cockpit. Boucher-Giles described the scene that he observed over the enemy coast:

> The Border Regiment boys in the back of the glider were very calm and extremely happy, and someone produced a bottle of whiskey which cheered us up all round. At 2230 hours we sighted Cape Passero, which was the signal for the turning-in run. Gaining height to cast off, we flew in. As I was sitting on the left of the cockpit as first pilot, I got Staff Sergeant Miller to fly the glider for this run-up while I looked out

> for the cast-off point which was some two and a half miles short of Capo Murro di Porco. We were subject to spasmodic firing from heavy ack-ack guns during the run-up, and as we approached the cast off point at 2245 hours there seemed to be a good deal going on in the way of flak and searchlights. Indeed, it was like Blackpool on illuminations night, the fireworks party being at our expense. We got caught in a searchlight shortly after casting off at 1,800 feet and had the utmost difficulty in getting the glider out. Subsequently I found out that my tug pilot had flown down and shot the searchlight out for me. However, both Miller and I were far too busy to worry about anything but getting the glider down safely.
>
> On the landing zone itself below I could see several aircraft in flames and the criss-cross of tracer bullets. It seemed no safe place to land as obviously quite a battle was raging down there, so I simply kept my lift spoilers up and landed a few hundred yards farther on in a field west of the landing zone.[1]

Other glider pilots were forced to intervene directly in the decision-making process on board their attendant tug. Staff Sergeant Jack Barnwell was flying Glider 52A, assisted by an American second pilot, Flight Officer Russell Parks. To their credit the two men eventually managed to land their WACO less than five miles from the Ponte Grande bridge. This achievement is even more remarkable when the events leading up to the release of Glider 52A are taken into account. If it had not been for what can only be described as a heated or fraught exchange over the field telephone between the two aircraft commanders, the glider would never have reached Sicily. The incident began while the combination was still five miles off the enemy coastline flying at an altitude of 3,000 feet. It was at that distance from shore, and not the designated 3,000 yards, that the USAAF major flying the C-47 tug wanted to release the glider and return to North Africa. Years later, we can only speculate as to why the tug captain wanted to release the glider so far out. Perhaps he believed that the additional altitude would compensate for the longer glide? Those on board the glider had their own views and were not happy at the prospect of beginning their glide from so far out to sea. The terse exchange that took place between the pilots in the two darkened cockpits was later encapsulated thus:

> Tug Pilot: 'Pull off!'
>
> Glider Pilot: 'I can't reach land from here, you'll have to turn round and take me back.'
>
> Tug Pilot: 'Pull Off!'
>
> Glider Pilot: 'If you don't turn around and take me back, I'll have you court martialled for cowardice in the face of the enemy – now turn around and take me back!'[2]

Who knows what fate might have befallen Glider 52A if Staff Sergeant Barnwell and Flight Officer Parks had not intervened so forcefully, or if the telephone cable had been severed preventing communication between the two aircraft. In the event, the tug turned back on to the correct heading toward Sicily. The release of Glider 52A finally took place in a far more dangerous place than the point where the tug had initially shied away from the threat of flak, the two aircraft parting company at an altitude of 5,000 feet above Syracuse harbour where they both attracted the collective attention of the anti-aircraft batteries.

Further back in the glider stream, Sergeants Tom Davidson and Victor Langton were at the controls of Glider 33, which was also being towed by a USAAF C-47. On board were Sergeant Norman Howes and his comrades from C Company, 2nd Battalion The South Staffordshire Regiment. The appearance of flak bursting in the darkness rattled a number of the C-47 crews, and this was certainly the case with Glider 33's tug crew. The combination was making its run in toward the coast, the glider dipping and bucking in the slipstream of their tug, when Sergeant Howes witnessed the shock of abandonment:

> ... the weather began to close in rapidly. It began to get very dark and very, very, windy. You could feel the gliders being thrown about; there was just one pinpoint of light from the glider, from the tug in front. My seat was almost directly behind the two pilots so we were in conversation throughout, and they were keeping me filled in as to where we were and where we were going and without them I wouldn't know ... exactly our heading. It got darker and darker and stormier and stormier, the wind was really throwing us about no end and men were beginning to be sick.
>
> Immediately ahead of us, just to the right of our heading I saw a cone of anti aircraft fire coming up and the Pilot said, 'There's Syracuse', so thank God we were on target when we arrived and I gave the order to the plane 'Stand to'. That is, on that order, men put their feet across the seats, their feet in between each other across the seats, they wrap arms around each other and brace themselves into one congealed unit as it were, and then I was with the pilots and slowly we saw this ... cone of fire disappearing to our left so obviously we were veering, we were veering south away from the island, which obviously was a wrong heading and I heard the pilot saying on the intercom 'Get us inland, get us inland'
>
> The American, it was an American Dakota that was pulling us, said 'Are you going or aren't you? You're right by your target now'. Our pilot said 'We're way off, we're way off! Get us inland, get us inland!' And the American came back and said, and I will remember these words, (pause) I will remember these words, he said 'F*** you! I've got

to get this kite back to Africa, you're going!' and then I heard our pilot shout out, 'Christ! He's cut us off!' and while we still had weight on the rope he let go our rope and we were free, we were adrift.

From that moment on I couldn't see Syracuse or this cone of fire again. It disappeared somewhere on my right and I could see nothing whatsoever; we could just hear the wind, the wind and silence of the glider. All the men were very, very quiet, deathly quiet, just praying I suppose. I could see nothing in front except a black mass. And suddenly I saw a glimpse of light above the black mass and that must have been the cliff top because immediately after that we hit the ground, and we hit the ground like the clappers, we must have been doing 100 to 120 miles an hour. Just, as we hit, the glider just began to disintegrate as we went forward. Bits were dropping off all the way across. I remember in my report, when I got back, I said, 'When the glider stopped we stood up and shook it off of us'.

Well, we eventually did stop and don't forget, under our feet we've got about two or three hundredweight of high explosive packed in cast iron pipes and I heard one glider pilot shout to his mate , 'Christ, those Bangalore torpedoes!' And that is the last that I saw of them. I never spoke to them again after that; I never saw them again after that. I'm not criticising them, they'd done their job, they'd got us there and I could understand their anxiety at these two Bangalore torpedoes.[3]

The dubious honour of being the furthest off-track was later attributed to Glider 24, a lone WACO flown by Sergeant Jim Wallwork and Sergeant Dickey Richards and carrying a chalk commanded by Lieutenant Broadbridge of the South Staffordshires. He and the men of 22 Platoon of D Company emerged from their glider to find themselves three miles north of Potopalo, 56 miles west of LZ 1. Sergeant Wallwork helped his passengers unload their platoon handcart from his WACO and then headed north as part of the platoon:

Almost as soon as we had left the glider we were machine-gunned, apparently from a nearby Italian position. We returned the fire and the Bren gunner cleared off the whole lot. The Italians came from an Italian barracks close by and it was apparently guarded. Far too many for us, so we went back to the glider to get a few things, and when we returned the barracks seemed to be deserted. Later a British mortar pinned us down as we moved north and still later, we made our first real attack on a field gun, a 6-inch howitzer. It was exposed and we were uphill from it, so it was easy to pop in on it. By daylight, we estimated that we had moved north about ten miles. We went cross-country for the most part, and it was still a long way from the bridge. On our right, we could see the sea about half a mile away. Soon after we heard a tank

> firing, and then three tanks came along the road and one of them fired on us. They were the first seaborne troops we had seen. It was about 0700 hours. We hitched a ride on the tank ...[4]

Credit is due to Lieutenant Broadbridge for his sound leadership and the quality of his men; in spite of several more skirmishes with the enemy, he and his tired platoon eventually linked up with elements of the 51st Highland Division, finally rejoining 1st Airlanding Brigade at dusk on 12 July 1943. They had sustained no casualties and in addition had managed to retain all of their weapons, equipment and their platoon handcart. It is ironic that Sergeant Jim Wallwork should find himself so far off target and yet, less than a year later, be credited with what is still described as the greatest feat of airmanship of the Second World War: landing the leading glider of the Pegasus Bridge coup de main force within 40 yards of the bridge at night. Such were the fortunes of war, and the importance of a good tug pilot and crew to every glider pilot.

Among those that were lucky enough to avoid ditching was Glider 88 flown by Sergeants Dick Martin and Ken Evans. At about two miles from the coast, they were still under tow when their combination came under accurate anti-aircraft fire. Immediately, the tug took violent evasive action and in the process released the glider to fend for itself. Descending through the bursts of flak and lines of tracer, the WACO successfully crossed the coastline although the two pilots had very little height left to play with and even less margin for error. They hurriedly identified an LZ but, as the heavily laden glider approached the ground, things quickly began to go wrong. They were now, in fact, 200 yards inland with the coastal cliffs receding out of vision behind them, the ground rushing up out of the darkness to meet them, and the nose of the glider ploughing through low-hanging telephone wires. Seconds later, after a sickening crash and an eruption of dust, the WACO crashed into a low stone wall and came to a sudden halt. Inevitably it was the two pilots in the cockpit who bore the full force of the impact, but surprisingly they both survived the crash. Sergeant Martin sustained numerous wounds and later lost his sight, while Sergeant Evans suffered two broken legs and was thus immobilised.

Eventually, after the dust had settled, there was some movement in the crumpled troop compartment of the wrecked glider. The chalk was mainly drawn from No. 11 Platoon of B Company, 1st Battalion The Border Regiment, under command of Sergeant F. Terry. Another passenger was Corporal John Waring of the Signals Platoon, while the load included a handcart packed with signals equipment. Emerging from the shattered glider, the shaken infantrymen assessed their situation. All had suffered cuts and bruises and some were clearly in shock. Corporal Coates, Privates Lathan, Davison, Jones and Miller were seriously hurt and, like the two injured pilots, could not be moved. The injured Borderers and the two pilots were given first aid and then placed under the care of one of the relatively unscathed members of the platoon. With their injured treated and aware that time was slipping away, the remainder of the chalk set off as a patrol with the intention of locating the LZ and linking up with the rest of their battalion.

The patrol did not find the LZ but did join up with a group from the Mortar Platoon of the South Staffordshires, whereupon the combined force returned to the wreck of Glider 88 and gave further aid to the casualties.

First light revealed another crashed WACO about 150 yards away across the field. This was glider 125A, flown by Lieutenant Bunny Carn and Sergeant David Richards, both of whom had been seriously injured when the glider hit a low stone wall on landing. Lieutenant Carn's legs were both broken and Sergeant Richards was also in great pain with a matching pair of broken ankles and a greenstick fracture to his left leg. The men of the Mortar Platoon of 1st Battalion The Border Regiment had assumed that both pilots were dead and, aware that time was of the essence, had moved off from the glider to find their RV point. Lieutenant Carn eventually extracted himself from the wreck with two broken legs; this cannot have been easy, but his matter of fact account gives no hint of the excruciating pain that he was surely enduring at the time:

> Sergeant Richards and I had to cut ourselves out of the mess and damage to the front of the glider. I managed to crawl into a large thorn bush to get some cover, where I lay all night and had a good view of the Wellington bombers bombing Syracuse at about 0200 hours. They dropped their chandelier flares first of all, then, came in quite low on their bombing runs.[5]

Other glider pilots had also fallen foul of the hazard presented by the numerous low stone walls that surrounded the tomato, lemon and olive plantations and groves that bordered the LZs. Unfortunately for them, in most cases it was the nose and therefore the cockpit that bore the violent brunt of the impact on landing, the aluminium framed, canvas covered gliders offering no protection against the unforgiving solid walls that blocked their landing runs. Some were killed while others at best sustained horrific lower limb injuries. Thus it was that a large number of pilots were incapacitated and were effectively out of the battle before it had started. Other more fortunate and uninjured pilots, who had by luck or design avoided the plantations and their walls, made off with their chalks at best speed from their widely scattered LZs toward Syracuse.

One of those who landed his glider intact was the recently married Staff Sergeant Les Howard whom one could forgive for being happily distracted. He probably felt that all was good in the world and that his luck was ascendant after his wedding. He was right, because his luck held that night over the Mediterranean. He was at the controls of Glider 35, one of the dozen or so that landed anywhere near the LZs. He and Sergeant Jimmy Tigar had survived the trials of the flight from Airfield B and delivered their load of South Staffordshire infantrymen as planned. It is however, a well-known military maxim that even well made plans rarely survive the first few minutes of their execution, and it is even rarer that any plan survives exposure to enemy action. The men of Glider 35 were about to learn that this was certainly true in their case:

> We landed safely on the island two miles south of our target. We all set out to the bridge at Syracuse. We were fired at several times on the way and eventually got off the main road and went a little further inland. We saw in the distance what appeared to be a large house and went forward towards it, when we were fired at from the house. We returned fire and then heard a lot of screaming and shouting, the noise going further and further away. We edged up to the building to discover it was a barracks of some kind. The occupants had evidently got out of bed and vanished, leaving most of their arms and weapons there. We decided to stay on in case they came back so we hid behind the stone walls around the lemon trees growing in the grounds of the building. At about 0700 hours we were relieved by The Green Howards who informed us that we had taken their first objective. Their CO ordered us to stay put and he would organise our relief. We were there for two days before we were driven to Syracuse.[6]

Staff Sergeant Howard and the men of Glider 35 were lucky that they landed relatively close to their intended LZ. Others did not fare so well that night, the airborne plan literally being blown to the four winds and taking gliders with it. However, regardless of their setbacks, in indomitable Airborne style wherever they landed, the airlanding troops set out at best speed in darkness across the rugged volcanic terrain to rejoin their brigade. Those that emerged from their gliders closer to the Ponte Grande bridge and Syracuse carried on with their allotted tasks. As these determined groups moved through the countryside toward their objectives, they came across Italian positions or patrols. These encounters sparked numerous skirmishes and exchanges of fire, triggering a whole series of separate and unco-ordinated attacks that erupted in the darkness; many were initiated by one half of No. 11 Platoon of B Company, of the South Staffordshires. The men of the platoon had glided in under anti-aircraft fire with one wing ablaze but thankfully survived the landing and extracted themselves and their equipment from their glider. After fighting off an Italian counter-attack and orientating themselves to the ground around them, the South Staffordshires waited for some time for the other three and a half platoons. After a while, however, it became apparent that the remainder of B Company were nowhere nearby.

With precious time and any remaining element of surprise slipping away, and with no prospect of reinforcement, the men of No. 11 Platoon set off into the night to carry out B Company's mission. Led by Captain R.S. Foot, the company second-in-command, this small force moved toward the Ponte

Grande bridge. En route, it grew in size as it collected stragglers from the 1st Battalion The Border Regiment. The B Company objective was a sizeable strongpoint codenamed 'Bilston', after the West Midlands foundry town. Captain Foot pressed on with his composite force and launched an improvised plan of attack. In spite of great bravery and aggression, however, the strongpoint proved to be too heavily defended and the attack was repulsed by the Italians. During the confusion of the action, the men of The Border Regiment became separated from Captain Foot and his South Staffordshires. There was then a lull while No. 11 Platoon reorganised and prepared for another attack. Although the assault force was by this time reinforced by a handful of sappers of 9th Field Company (Airborne) RE, this second attack was also beaten off.

Having failed to destroy or capture 'Bilston', the resourceful Captain Foot decided to push one mile further north and try his luck against a similar strongpoint that had been allocated to E Company and codenamed 'Walsall'. In spite of the great courage and élan shown by the South Staffordshires, however, this attack suffered the same fate as that on 'Bilston'. Realising that his small force lacked the firepower and punch to tackle the Italian positions on its own, Captain Foot thus decided to push on and link up with the main force at the Ponte Grande bridge.

While No. 11 Platoon progressed from one objective to another, there were other numerous small groups of 1st Airlanding Brigade survivors roaming the Sicilian countryside that night; among them were a number of senior commanders and staff officers who had not expected to catch a whiff of cordite that night. The experience of Colonel Osmond Jones, the Brigade's deputy commander, was a notable case in point. He had survived what was described at the time as a 'hairy landing'. In fact, Glider 10 had barely made landfall, coming to a precarious halt on the very edge of a cliff, tangled in barbed wire with its tail hanging precariously above the crashing waves below. Almost immediately after the glider settled into its final resting place, ensnared helplessly in the barbed wire like a trapped animal, its shaken occupants came under fire from a searchlight position sited just 100 yards away. Returning fire, the chalk quickly evacuated the exposed glider; unfortunately, in the rush to escape, two passengers, Father Hourigan, a Roman Catholic chaplain, and a signaller, were captured by the Italians.

Glider 10 was flown by Staff Sergeant Andy Andrews and Flight Officer Morris Kyle, the American second pilot, who provided a first-hand account of the landing during his post-operation debriefing:

> We came in low over the beach. I could see that we were going to land in a barbed wire emplacement. I looked at my watch ... it was exactly ten minutes off twelve o'clock. I got out on the right side of the ship with eight men including Colonel Jones who was first out. Together we made our way to the vineyard 100 yards distant. We joined our men

> and waited for the others. Some bits of conversation floated to us and we gathered from it that the men we were waiting for had fallen into the hands of the Italians from the gun emplacement. Colonel Jones decided to make an attempt to release them. He shouted directions to them three times. His plan was that he would throw a phosphorous bomb to divert the Italians and the men would slip away while their attention was distracted. Our luck hadn't hit its stride yet for the bomb fell short of its mark and landed on top of the glider, setting it on fire and exposing us completely.[7]

Forced to withdraw from their now over-exposed rescue attempt, the small group headed inland where it encountered No. 2 Section of the 1st Battalion The Border Regiment's reconnaissance platoon. After a hasty exchange of ad-hoc recognition signals, culminating in a whistled rendition of *The Lincolnshire Poacher*, the two small forces quickly combined. Colonel Jones now had a composite force totalling fourteen men. After a sharp but brief skirmish with what appeared to be an Italian patrol, the group halted in the vicinity of a railway station. Wary of inadvertently wandering into an Italian ambush or strongpoint in the dark, the group lay up in some deserted farm buildings at about 0400 hours and waited for daylight. After a few short hours, any semblance of peace and quiet was rudely disturbed when an unseen inland Italian gun battery opened fire on the Allied landing beaches from close by. The calm was then even further shattered by the response from the Royal Navy warships now assembled purposefully offshore. At 0700 hours a real storm of noise erupted as salvoes of heavy naval shells began to roar over the farmhouse as the Royal Navy probed inland, trying to locate and silence the troublesome battery and other targets.

Just over an hour later, the bombardment subsided and Colonel Jones sent the reconnaissance platoon section out to locate and observe the battery. It returned unscathed and undetected from the patrol, reporting that it had located the battery, which consisted of five guns sited a quarter-of-a-mile to the south of the railway station. The section commander described a compact and well organised position with gun positions, dugouts and a number of sandbagged weapon pits and tents. Colonel Jones and the patrol cross-referenced their information with a 17th Infantry Brigade map that they had with them and found that the battery was designated on the map as Objective P4. Undeterred by the apparent size of the battery and the depth of its defences, Colonel Jones decided to attack the guns with his small and lightly armed force. The plan of attack was simple; it depended on a combination of surprise, momentum, violence and aggression.

At about 1100 hours the attack was initiated using phosphorous grenades to set light to the long grass around the battery. The resulting smokescreen gave the assault group cover as it advanced to a jump-off point just 40 yards from the gun line. As the grenade party moved forward, a pair of Bren LMGs poured machine gun fire into the battery to keep the gunners' heads down.

The first wave of the assault was led by Lieutenant Budgeon, supported by Staff Sergeant Andrews and Flight Officer Kyle, all armed with Sten guns. Close behind the pilots followed a second assault wave comprising Colonel Jones, Major Tomkins and four reconnaissance platoon riflemen. With no glider to fly, and as he was the sole owner of a pair of wire-cutters tucked into his web belt, Staff Sergeant Andrews was in the forefront of the hastily planned attack:

> I felt a rush of adrenaline, a few anxious moments waiting for the Bren to start, and then as if from a starter's gun in an athletic event I took off for the wire. I was conscious of our chaps giving covering fire as I knelt down and started to clumsily fumble with the cutters at the strands of barbed wire. My Sten got in the way so I dropped it. Just at that moment Colonel Jones dashed up and said, 'Follow me.' He had spotted that the wire I was so busily trying to cut was a movable knife rest barrier. Colonel Jones threw it open and we trooped in after him shouting 'Whoa Mohammed,' the traditional war cry adopted by the Airborne after North Africa.[8]

As the first wave broke cover, it was followed closely by the second. The assault force charged into the Italian position, firing and throwing grenades in all directions. The startled garrison was quickly overwhelmed, stunned by the handful of determined airlanding troops and the sheer violence and shock of their attack. Six Italian gunners were killed in the short bloody battle on the battery. The small British force did what it could to disable the guns and blow up ready-use ammunition stocks. Finally, they set tents alight before moving off from the now dormant battery with 45 Italian prisoners. As luck would have it, the attack on the battery resulted in the rescue of two glider pilots who had been captured by the Italians the night before. As Colonel Jones and his force entered the gun position, the two pilots were being interrogated by an Italian officer in the nearest dugout. Staff Sergeant Andy Andrews describes the fighting:

> The prisoners happened to be in the first dugout we came to. The grenades exploding inside wounded one of the glider pilots in the leg. The Italians were firing back now and a gunfight took place. I knelt on one knee with the rifleman beside me and fired carefully at the sandbags less than 50 yards away where a few heads could be seen. I soon found that my Sten gun was of little use, the rounds kept sticking. I cursed and swore in frustration, but had to be content with firing single shots by a process of removing the magazine, ejecting the fired round with my fingers and then reloading. The Sten isn't noted for its accuracy anyway and I am not the world's best shot. Still I must have given some moral support to the rifleman beside me. The firing soon

> stopped and I could see a lone Italian running like a rabbit for the far end of the compound. All this action reminded me of a Western shoot-out which was frequently seen on the screen in those days.[9]

The glider pilot wounded in the bunker was most probably Sergeant Geoffrey 'Pop' Dawkins of No. 2 Squadron who later reported a similar incident when explaining his wounds to medics.

By midday, the battle for the gun battery was over and the guns firmly in Airborne hands. Colonel Jones and his by now 100-strong column then started to move away from the battery. As he and his men began to shake their Italian prisoners out into an untidy column, however, they saw a welcome sight approaching in the distance: the distinctive steel helmets and bayonets of British infantry approaching from the direction of the landing beaches. They belonged to the lead elements of 17th Infantry Brigade led by an advance company of the 2nd Battalion The Northamptonshire Regiment that was heading determinedly for its initial objective, none other than the P4 Battery. Pleased to see the Northamptonshires, Colonel Jones handed over his gaggle of prisoners and wounded to them, and then watched as they set about destroying all of the remaining ammunition stocks on the enemy position.

The first night of the invasion was extremely fluid and the pendulum of battle swung freely back and forth between invader and defender. Amid the confusion of the night landing Staff Sergeant Jimmy James was one of many glider pilots wounded and taken prisoner, he gives a vivid description of the ruthlessness and realities of the battle in Sicily:

> I remember the horror I experienced as a wounded prisoner of the Italians after landing. I believe I was lying on the straw in a farm stable at dawn when the Marine Commandos came in. A wizened Italian guard was on his knees in the doorway, his hands up crying 'Mercy'. He received a bullet through his head. An Italian on a stretcher, having lost a leg above the knee, also received a bullet. He was then tipped on to the floor of the stable. I was then placed on this stretcher and taken to the Forward Dressing Station. This, of course was the action of elite forward troops with no time for ceremony or sympathy but a job to be done in war, but it is something that is difficult to dismiss from my mind.[10]

While the stragglers from the gliders who were scattered across the island worked through the night to regroup and carry out their respective tasks, those out at sea continued to battle for survival against the elements. For many the struggle against the sea was an unequal one and they succumbed to the overwhelming power of the waves. Others continued to fight and cling on desperately through the night. Not all had the misfortune of ditching miles out to sea; a number of gliders had come extremely close to reaching land but ultimately had been defeated by the simple lack of a few feet in altitude and the cumulative effect of the headwind at what was seemingly the last possible moment. To their intense frustration they had been forced to ditch within sight of the coast. Prominent among this number was Lieutenant Colonel George Chatterton. He and his passengers very soon realised how close they were to the Cap Murro di Porco and its now alerted Italian defenders. Any initial feeling of relief at surviving the drama of ditching was soon transformed into frustration after making out the silhouette of the coastline and the potential sanctuary of dry land:

> 'Are you all right, George?' I heard Pip Hicks call.
>
> 'Yes, sir, I think so,' I answered, still in a daze. Then as the mists cleared, I saw the forms of my passengers in the sea, on the wings and on the fuselage.
>
> 'Everybody keep down on the wings,' Hicks ordered, and we lay flat looking at the coast, the glider floating like a boat and giving us something substantial to hang on to.
>
> A searchlight suddenly shone from the shore, swung across the sea, rested on us for a moment, and then swung out again. 'Keep still, dead still' hissed Hicks. We did. The light swung out again and this time lingered on us. A brief moment, and then a hail of tracer bullets streamed from the shore, and I remember sinking in the sea, sick and terrified with an awful helpless feeling, for there was no cover. The hail of bullets continued in bursts but by some mercy none hit us; they were just too high and hit the sea behind us. 'It's no good staying here' I said to Pip Hicks. 'Shall we swim for it?'
>
> 'OK, George,' he replied 'I think under these circumstances it would be best. Quietly as possible ... come on everybody ...' Pip Hicks looked huge, like a Spanish Galleon, as he ploughed through the water, and I told him to keep down, but he said he couldn't because his Mae West was blown up too high. Soon we reached the shore, soaking and shaking with cold, and without weapons for they had gone to the bottom. We felt quite helpless.[11]

The brigade commander and his chalk had survived the ditching, as had a number of other glider loads. Those that had reached the shoreline did so with little equipment and the majority emerged from the water with no weapons. They were at this point extremely vulnerable to capture. Those that were uninjured did their utmost to find weapons and rejoin the fight. In some cases these troops took great hauls of Italian prisoners, many of whom were quite eager to surrender.

Lieutenant Joe Hardy, the Regimental Signals Officer of the 1st Battalion The Border Regiment landed in the sea but was close enough to the shore to reach it. In company with his Commanding Officer, Lieutenant Colonel George Britten, he escaped from Glider 57 as it sank. At first light, he swam to the shore and scaled a cliff in shorts and stockinged feet. Armed with only a .38 revolver, he clambered over the clifftop only to find himself staring directly into an Italian machine-gun position whose occupants were every bit as startled to see the two bedraggled British officers clambering over the clifftop. Hardy seized the initiative and told them, in his worst pigeon Italian, '*La guerra finito, Mussolini kaput.*' The Italians surrendered immediately and with indecent haste handed over their weapons; with a little prompting from their British captors, they even dutifully instructed the two officers on how to use the newly captured weapons. It quickly became apparent to Hardy and Britten that it was quite impossible for them to consider moving across occupied country with dozens of prisoners-of-war in tow. So they, like many others that night, were forced to leave their Italian prisoners to their own devices while they pushed on towards the Ponte Grande bridge. They later ran into a much larger mixed group of 60 Italian soldiers and civilians, whereupon Hardy repeated his earlier Mussolini bluff to the crowd with similar success, the Italians again being very happy to surrender. Having given the captive Italians orders to destroy their own weapons, which they duly did, the two British officers departed to the friendly cheers of those they left behind.

The use of bluff to undermine fragile Italian morale was fairly prevalent among the airlanding troops on the night of 9 July 1943. Even 'men of the cloth' were not averse to using their powers of persuasion in a just cause, especially when caught in a tight spot with the Italian Army. Captain Alan Buchanan, the Chaplain of the 2nd Battalion The South Staffordshire Regiment, had the misfortune to be captured with another soldier almost immediately after landing on Cape Murro di Porco. Unperturbed by this sudden reversal of fortune, Padre Buchanan quickly struck up conversation with the English-speaking officer in charge of the Italians guarding him and his fellow prisoners. He explained in detail that thousands of Allied troops had landed all around them and that they were now hopelessly outnumbered and totally surrounded. Therefore, he suggested, it would be better if they became his prisoners instead. The now rattled Italian officer discussed this worrying news with his men who readily agreed to surrender. Padre Buchanan and the handful of now freed British prisoners then disarmed their captors and marched them off in the direction of Syracuse and, hopefully, the rest of 1st Airlanding Brigade.

The record for the single biggest haul of prisoners on the night must be held by Private Ron Etherington, a soldier in the intelligence section of Headquarter Company of the 2nd Battalion The South Staffordshire Regiment:

> All the time flares were being dropped and coastal guns were firing tracer out to sea. The three of us dived over a wall and then cut across very rocky country. We could hear machine guns firing from some distance away. We moved cautiously through the countryside, we could see because it was lit up at times by the searchlights and flares.

> After a time, we met up with some of our chaps who like us, had been dropped well away from the landing zones. In retrospect, I would imagine we must have landed at least six or seven miles from our landing zone number 3, our target area ... During the night, we dodged an enemy column by seeing it first, and managed to hide up until it had passed. Our aim was to get to the bridge as quickly as possible without too much delay and trouble. Dawn was breaking and by now we were tired, having been on the move all night and having to be watchful at the same time.
>
> We came to a small field and rested ourselves behind one of the small walls that ran across it. One of the lads then pointed and said: 'There's a whole lot of Italians over there.' About 200 yards in front of us we could all see the Italian soldiers dug in near a cave, which was let in to a small hill. At this, we immediately came to, and our small group lined up at the wall peering at them and awaiting the outcome of the confrontation. It was then that they saw us, and one of the Italians waved a white cloth and started to approach us. The officer with us told us to be careful and not to leave the cover of the wall until the Italian officer came up to us. After some difficulty in establishing communication between him and us, he informed us that he and his men wished to surrender. Our officer said that some of our chaps would go back with him to disarm his troops. He designated three of us to go with the Italian and told us that we would be covered all of the way. When we arrived at their position, I thought the whole Italian Army was there and, without any exaggeration we counted about 120 men, they were all complete with their rifles, there were two machine gun and ... suitcases! They really were ready to surrender. The smiles on their faces said it all, so very pleased and overjoyed to think for them, the war really was over.[12]

The abundance of suitcases among Italian troops was commented on by many Allied veterans of the Sicily campaign. In fact the bulk of the Sicily garrison was made up of low-grade regional troops who were little more than local militia pressed into service. They were not fully-equipped and lacked much of the ancillary equipment issued to regular troops. Most had just a rifle and a uniform, and carried what possessions they had in their personal suitcase. Many were Sicilians who lived on the island and had little love and even less loyalty to Mussolini and his fascist regime. The coastal units were very much second-line formations, their ranks mainly filled with men in their forties and fifties, and originally intended to perform labouring or other second line administrative duties. The bulk of the coastal division officers were mostly men who had long retired and had been called up again. Morale among these troops was low, not least because of the second-rate equipment and weapons with which they had been issued. An attempt had been made to improve their armaments with weapons seized from the recently disbanded Vichy French army. However, by the time the promised arms arrived in Sicily, they had often been rendered inoperable and were supplied with the wrong type of ammunition or none at all.

These formations were not the battle hardened, well-motivated Italian formations whom Montgomery and the Eighth Army had faced at the end of the campaign in North Africa, but consisted of low grade static units with fragile morale. The appearance of an overwhelming Allied invasion force, followed in many cases by the swift departure of their fascist officers, was all that was required for the average Italian soldier on Sicily to throw down his rifle, abandon his post, reach for his suitcase and set off for home.

Lieutenant Colonel W. Derek McCardie, the Commanding Officer of the South Staffordshires, also employed unorthodox methods in an attempt to deceive the Italians. He had been a passenger on board Glider 3 flown by the Officer Commanding No. 2 Squadron, Major Tony Murray. The two men escaped their WACO when it ditched in the sea two miles off shore and managed to swim to a beach. Lieutenant Colonel McCardie recorded his memories of the night:

> Major Murray and I rested until about 0400 hours and then made our way barefooted along the beach defences, pretending that we had a strong force moving behind and giving various hand signals to preserve the illusion. Eventually we joined a commando raid which was going in on the south coast. We got our feet bandaged up, commandeered a motorcycle and moved up to the battalion RV, taking three Italians prisoner on the way.[13]

As the night of 9 July slowly turned into the morning of a new day, the fragmented elements of 1st Airlanding Brigade did their utmost to combine into a coherent force. Their commander meanwhile was encountering much the same difficulties as his men. Alongside Lieutenant Colonel George Chatterton, Brigadier Pip Hicks had managed to swim ashore in his Mae West and was now trying to get his bearings. Lieutenant Colonel Chatterton:

> We had been lying underneath the cliff, wondering what to do next, when we heard a boat approaching ... Out of it leapt a number of armed men of the Special Air Service (SAS) who were following up our attack by a sea landing. By some miraculous chance they had missed the point where they should have landed and hit just where we were, under the rocks. Thankfully we joined in with them and advanced up the cliff. During the night we had various adventures while engaging strongpoints and pillboxes, I acting as an ordinary trooper, and by dawn we had captured 100 to 150 prisoners.
>
> The Italians in Sicily had all manner of queer ways of fighting, some of which had to be dealt with quite ruthlessly, as the following incident illustrates:

> I was acting as an escort for some prisoners and was dressed in my sea-soaked battledress, with an Italian topee on my head, and armed with a British rifle. Winding down a narrow lane, the guards out in the front of the column and a dozen or so of us on either side of it, we were brought to an abrupt halt by the crack of a rifle, one of the guards in front falling mortally wounded. Momentarily we were stunned, then, seemingly without reason, one of the SAS guards in front of me, whose head had been half turned towards the prisoners, turned right round and pushed his way into the column. Without a word, he stopped in front of one of the men, lifted his rifle barrel, and without warning, swung it up and brought it down with a crack on the man's head. The Italian sank to the ground without uttering a sound, his skull crushed in.
>
> 'Why on earth did you do that?' I asked incredulously.
>
> 'Didn't you see the bastard?' he replied.
>
> 'No,' I answered. 'Why?'
>
> 'Well,' he continued, wiping the butt of his rifle, 'He was up the tree. He shot my chum in the back and then dropped into the column. I happened to turn round just as he dropped.'[14]

The hours following the launch of Operation LADBROKE were certainly littered with incident and tragedy. It is difficult to understand how, in spite of all of the setbacks and errors that disastrous night, the men of 1st Airlanding Brigade managed to rally themselves and, in spite of their losses, prosecute their orders as well as they did. The 1st Battalion GPR, taking part in its first major operation, acquitted itself well in the air and in battle, many of its pilots later receiving recognition for their actions during and after the landings. Staff Sergeant John Alfred Ainsworth was recommended for the Military Medal, his citation encapsulating the spirit of all of the glider pilots who flew that night:

> This Staff Sergeant was forced to land his aircraft far out in the sea when attacking Sicily. Having seen that his crew were provided with life saving jackets and that all had been extricated from the waterlogged part of the glider, he swam ashore three miles distant. With nothing but a fighting knife, he killed two sentries and with the rifle of the second continued fighting throughout the battle. The leadership and courage of this Staff Sergeant Pilot was in the best traditions of the service.[15]

Staff Sergeant John Ainsworth and many others certainly lived up to the Chatterton's concept of the glider pilot as a 'Total Soldier'. He deservedly received the Military Medal for his bravery and leadership on Operation LADBROKE. Less than a year later he would sit alongside Staff Sergeant Jim Wallwork as second pilot in the cockpit of the leading Horsa glider on the Pegasus Bridge coup de main mission. However, the dramatic seizure of the crossings over the River Orne and the Caen Canal, and the part that Wallwork and Ainsworth and their comrades would play in it, were still an entire campaign away. All that mattered that night in July 1943 was a different bridge: Objective 'Waterloo' – the Ponte Grande. In spite of the casualties suffered out at sea and the terrible attrition on land, a few of the airlanding force gliders succeeded in reaching the LZs and pressing home their mission with vigour.

Notes

1. Boucher-Giles, Lieutenant, A.F., OC, 9 Troop, 3 Squadron, 1st Battalion GPR, by permission of *The Eagle*.
2. Barnwell, Staff Sergeant, J., Squadron, 1st Battalion GPR, by permission of *The Eagle*.
3. Howes, Sergeant, N., C Company, 2nd Battalion, South Staffordshire Regiment, by permission of John Howes.
4. Wallwork, Sergeant, J., 1st Battalion GPR. By permission of *The Eagle*.
5. Carn, Lieutenant, W.J., 1st Battalion GPR. By permission of *The Eagle*.
6. Howard, Staff Sergeant, L., 5 Flight, 2 Squadron, 1st Battalion GPR, Interview with the author March 1993.
7. Kyle, Flight Officer,. K., USAAF, by permission of *The Eagle*.
8. Andrews, Staff Sergeant, A., *So you wanted to fly Eh?* Burnaby, B.C. ISTE 1997, p. 95.
9. Andrews, Staff Sergeant, A., *So you wanted to fly Eh?* Burnaby, B.C. ISTE 1997, p. 96.
10. James, Sergeant, J., 2 Squadron, 1st Battalion GPR, by permission of *The Eagle*.
11. Chatterton, Lieutenant Colonel, 1st Battalion GPR, *The Wings of Pegasus*, Nashville, Battery Press,1962, p. 74.
12. Etherington, Private, R., HQ Company, 2nd Battalion the South Staffordshire Regiment, by permission of family.
13. McCardie, Lieutenant Colonel, W., CO, 2nd Battalion the South Staffordshire Regiment, by permission of *The Eagle*.
14. Chatterton, Lieutenant Colonel, G., 1st Battalion GPR, *The Wings of Pegasus*, Nashville, Battery Press, 1962, p. 92.
15. Ainsworth, Staff Sergeant, J.A., 1st Battalion GPR, Military Medal Citation, National Archives.

Chapter 12

The Battle for The Ponte Grande

There was a gauntlet of sniping and fairly heavy machine gun fire to run before we could get through, but we made it to the bridge ...

The successful seizure of the Ponte Grande twin-span bridge over the River Simeto and Mammaiabica Canal by a gliderborne coup de main operation was the lynch-pin of Operation LADBROKE. Intelligence reports stated that the bridge was located just outside the area of responsibility of the Italian 206th Coastal Division whose primary role was to counter any allied sea-borne landing in its area. This formation was considered to pose the main threat to any airlanding assault.

The division was commanded by General Achille d'Havet, but was under the overall control of the commander of the Augusta-Syracuse Fortress Area, Rear Admiral Primo Leonardi. On paper, the forces arrayed against any landing appeared formidable with the fortress assessed as being one of the strongest enemy-held areas in southern Europe. In addition to the 206th Coastal Division, the two key ports were protected by six medium and six heavy coastal artillery batteries. Their heavy guns were augmented with eleven additional dual-purpose coastal and anti-aircraft batteries and another six batteries of anti-aircraft guns, while a mobile reserve of artillery existed in the form of an armoured train with four 120 mm guns. The area within the fortress itself was garrisoned by the four infantry battalions of the 120th Coastal Defence Regiment under the command of Colonel Mario Damiani. The garrison could also mobilise reinforcements from battalions made up of local naval and air force personnel. Significantly, the well trained and relatively well equipped 54th Infantry Division Napoli was ordered to be prepared to send reinforcements to the area if requested.

The mission of flying into the midst of this potential hornets nest and seizing the Ponte Grande Bridge by coup de main was given to A and C Companies, 2nd Battalion The South Staffordshire Regiment. The operation was allocated eight of the 27 precious Horsa gliders delivered by the Turkey Buzzard crews, the choice of the larger glider over that of the WACO being based on the requirement to deliver the maximum possible number of assault troops on to the objective in a single lift. This, coupled with the British glider's superior handling characteristics in a confined space, made the Horsa a better option.

In an attempt to apply an aviation 'belt and braces' to the Ponte Grande glider force, each Horsa was allotted a 38 Wing RAF tug aircraft rather than a USAAF C-47 Skytrain, with Headquarters 38 Wing RAF allocating seven Halifaxes from 295 Squadron RAF and a single Albemarle from 296 Squadron. The twin-engined Albemarle could reach Sicily with a Horsa in tow, but it would struggle to return to North Africa. This aircraft, coded 'PM', was flown by Wing Commander Peter May, the Officer Commanding 296 Squadron RAF, while its Horsa, numbered Glider 129 and carrying the men of 8 Platoon of A Company of the South Staffordshires, was flown by Sergeants Len Guthrie and Stan Pearson.

The slower airspeed of the Albemarle necessitated an earlier take-off, 30 minutes in advance of the other Halifax-towed combinations. In addition, in order to extend the range of the tug by reducing drag, Glider 129 jettisoned its undercarriage immediately after taking off.

Although post-operation analysis does show that RAF-towed gliders were delivered on target with more accuracy than those towed by their American counterparts in the 51st Troop Carrier Wing of XII Troop Carrier Command USAAF, this was not reflected in what befell A Company en route to the Ponte Grande. Three of the four A Company Horsas came down in the sea; 9 Platoon in Glider 130 had fourteen men drowned on ditching, while nine clung desperately on to the glider and waited for rescue. They were eventually lifted out of the sea and straight into captivity by an Italian patrol boat; the remaining seven of the platoon escaped the wreck and swam ashore where they encountered British troops.

Meanwhile, on what was fast becoming a terrible night for A Company, the whole of 10 Platoon on board Glider 131 was lost at sea. The men of No. 7 Platoon in Glider 128 had slightly better fortune, albeit having lost two of their number drowned, when rescued from their ditched glider by the Royal Navy. The fourth A Company aircraft, Glider 129 carrying No. 8 Platoon, reached Sicily but landed some distance from LZ 3. Immediately after disembarking, the platoon moved off from the glider and marched through the night toward its objective, a piece of important high ground overlooking the southern approach to the bridge.

The C Company landing was more successful, with all its four gliders reaching Sicily and two landing on LZ 3.

Glider 134, carrying No. 16 Platoon, landed intact but ten miles south-west of LZ 3; unfortunately, however, it came to a halt within range of an already alerted Italian machine gun position. Almost instantly the Italians opened fire on the glider, which burst into flames; fifteen of the 31 men on board, including the platoon commander, were killed. The remainder, however, succeeded in escaping from the burning aircraft and made for Syracuse; although they played no part in the Ponte Grande action, they eventually managed to link up with advancing troops of the Eighth Army.

Glider 135, with No. 18 Platoon on board, fared a little better than No. 16 Platoon and landed six miles to the east of LZ 3. Disembarking from the Horsa, the platoon and its two glider pilots quickly headed towards the Ponte Grande. After successfully fighting their way through to Syracuse, they reached the bridge shortly after Eighth Army troops had arrived to secure the crossing.

The first of two C Company Horsa gliders to reach LZ 3 was Glider 133 carrying Lieutenant Lennard Withers and his men of No. 15 Platoon. It was towed by a Halifax of 295 Squadron RAF flown by Flight Lieutenant Tommy Grant who had a considerable amount of flying experience, having joined 38 Wing RAF directly from the Royal Aircraft Establishment at Farnborough where he had been a test pilot. That night, however, he had to call on all his experience as he encountered more than his fair share of problems. Until now, he had never flown a Halifax-glider combination at night, let alone handled one on an operational mission over the sea and enemy-occupied territory. To make matters worse, the Halifax's compass proved faulty and its auto-pilot unserviceable.

Almost immediately after take-off, the aircraft developed engine problems and Grant was forced to make the decision to abort the mission and turn the tug and glider back toward North Africa. As the aircraft limped back and rejoined the circuit at Airfield E, however, the problems with the engines inexplicably rectified themselves and Grant managed to attain full power. With four good engines to call on again, he took the brave decision to head back out to sea and attempt to rejoin the glider stream en route for Sicily.

The crew of Glider 133 was made up of Staff Sergeant Dennis 'Galp' Galpin and Sergeant Nigel Brown. Staff Sergeant Galpin takes up the story from his seat in the cockpit:

> This delay however, put my glider well behind the others, but we did not mind, realizing how near we had been to being out of the show completely. As we left the coast of Africa it was beginning to get dark. We couldn't see any Horsas in front of us but there were a few WACOs in sight ... Leaving Malta we began to climb and by the time we had reached Cape Passero we were at six thousand feet. Through the intercom I heard the navigator giving the courses and landmarks to the pilot, and this was a great help, as I knew exactly where we were and how long it would take to reach the objective. Flying up the coast of Sicily, heading for Syracuse, I could see that someone was getting a reception, but so far we had not been detected.[1]

The hostile reception was also about to be extended to the Halifax-Horsa combination as it flew within range of the Sicilian coastal defences. The

Halifax was picked out by Italian searchlights and then bracketed by repeated bursts of anti-aircraft fire; one of which hit the wing of the aircraft and set it alight. Despite the wing being on fire and with flak bursting around them the aircraft, Flight Lieutenant Grant and his crew nevertheless pushed doggedly towards the release point. Staff Sergeant Galpin continues:

> Just short of our casting off point the skipper said he would take us a little nearer to the objective because of the increased wind strength, thus making sure that we had enough height ... The outline of Cap Murro di Porco was just in front and below us, when the tug turned to the right and I was given the signal to cast off.
>
> Once I had cast off it was impossible for either my co-pilot or myself to see anything except the dim outline of Cap di Porco below us, so my co-pilot set the pre-determined course on the compass and we set off hoping for the best. We had been flying for what seemed a few minutes when I at last recognized where I was. I had flown too far north and was over Syracuse itself, so I turned towards where I imagined the objective lay. Very soon I recognized our landing zone, just as depicted on the night map. We were then flying at about 2,000 feet. I was just congratulating myself on having aimed right when a searchlight caught us in its beam and quite a few guns gave us their undivided attention. I took violent evasive action, but failed to shake off the searchlight, and by so doing I was back out at sea again, so I decided to come down low and approach the bridge with a little speed in hand, flying parallel with the canal and river, knowing I would come to the field sooner or later.
>
> The searchlight followed my glider right down to the deck level and as I was crossing the coast it very kindly showed me exactly where the field lay, lighting up the bridge at the same time. As soon as I saw this I pulled the nose of the glider up to reduce speed, put on full flap and flew the aircraft right down to the ground.[2]

After completing what was an extraordinary piece of flying, the two glider pilots managed to get their Horsa and its passengers down on to the ground. Prior to the final turn of their run in, the pilots shouted back into the darkened troop compartment behind them and ordered the troops to brace themselves and prepare for landing. These precautions were intended to prevent the infantrymen from being thrown out of their seats or losing their legs if the floor of the gliders' troop compartment was ripped out on landing. Lieutenant Withers and his men reacted as trained, linking their arms with the man on either side, and raising their boots off the floor and on to the bench opposite. Fortunately, on this occasion the floor of the Horsa was not torn out, but the landing did not pass without incident. Staff Sergeant Galpin made good use of all of the 116 square feet of the Horsa's huge barn-door size flaps and its air-assisted wheel brakes in his attempts to slow the glider down, with the result that it came to a noisy halt on LZ 3 but not before the nose wheel of its undercarriage had been ripped off in a ditch.

As the dust cloud generated by the landing began to settle, the relieved men of No. 15 Platoon emerged from their damaged glider with all their equipment and a few cuts and bruises. Lieutenant Lennard Withers climbed down gingerly from the glider's troop door nursing a sprained ankle. Keeping a watchful eye on the LZ for the rest of the C Company gliders, and a sharp lookout for the enemy, he began to organize his platoon. It is difficult to pin down the exact time of landing for Glider 133 due to the delay over North Africa; a rough estimate would put it on the ground at around 2245 hours. Once on the ground, Staff Sergeant Galpin and Sergeant Brown celebrated their mutual survival with a swift tot of whiskey each before assisting Lieutenant Withers in orientating the platoon position in relation to the bridge. All three men knew that, due to their tug's engine problems, they were in all probability one of the last, if not the last, glider to have arrived over the LZ. With that in mind, the absence of any other gliders or even a sighting of other airlanding troops was a cause for immediate concern. Where were the rest of the coup de main gliders? Where had they landed? Indeed, with no obvious sign of the other gliders, were they even at the correct bridge?

It must have been a relief for all concerned when some minutes later the unmistakable dark silhouette of another Horsa glider loomed into sight out of the night sky. This was Glider 132, flown by Captain John N.C. Denholm with Sergeant Ron Knott as second pilot. On board were No. 17 Platoon, a small group of sappers and, most importantly, the officer leading the coup de main raid, C Company's commander, Major Edwin Ballinger. Staff Sergeant Galpin and Sergeant Brown looked on as the Horsa made its approach to the LZ. At this stage the onlookers were not sure as to which of the other gliders they were observing or who was on board.

Any jubilation among No. 15 Platoon at the sight of another glider carry-ingreinforcements evaporated in an instant when a burst of concentrated machine gun fire ripped through the darkness and into Glider 132. A stream of trace rounds poured into the canvas-covered wooden fuselage just as the Horsa seemed to momentarily hover above the ground under full flap, while waiting for the undercarriage to touch down on the ground. With fire riddling its side and passing straight through its packed fuselage the stricken glider appeared to halt about 300 yards from the Ponte Grande Bridge; with a muffled crump, followed by an intense flash, it then exploded and burst into flames before settling on to the canal bank.

There was little time for Lieutenant Withers and his platoon to comprehend the disaster that confronted them. The only logical conclusion as to the cause of the explosion was that a tracer round had ignited one of the types of explosive ordnance stowed on board, possibly one of the Bangalore torpedoes carried by the sappers for use against barbed wire and other obstacles. It was obvious to all who had witnessed the explosion, and now solemnly surveyed the burning glider, that there could be little chance of survival. Nevertheless, Staff Sergeant Galpin and Sergeant Brown approached the wreckage to offer what aid they could and were confronted with a scene of sickening carnage, finding one terribly injured survivor to whom they administered a shot of morphia to numb his pain. In fact, a total of three survivors were found. Sadly, however, exploding phosphorous bombs and Bangalore torpedoes had ensured that any others of those on board Glider 132 were beyond aid.

With his company commander dead and no other gliders in sight, Lieutenant Withers was no doubt experiencing at first hand the oft-quoted loneliness of command. He now realised that his glider was in all probability one of the last to have cast off from its tug, and thus there was little prospect of any reinforcement from C Company. Perhaps the A Company gliders had landed on the north side of the canal and river and were moving toward their pre-briefed objectives, or perhaps No. 15 Platoon, with its handful of sappers and two glider pilots, was on its own? It very quickly became apparent that there were no other gliders and that no other troops would appear. Withers and No. 15 Platoon were indeed on their own and so an assault originally planned around a force of 254 men would now have to be executed by a single platoon totalling no more than 30.

Acting decisively, the 21-year old lieutenant adapted his plan and issued a set of quick battle orders to his men. Aware of the military maxim that a bridge must be taken both ends at once, he divided his force into two groups. He decided to lead from the front and take a small five-man section across the canal and river to the north to mount a diversionary attack on one of the pillboxes protecting the crossing. It was his intention that this attack would draw the Italian garrison away from positions on and around the bridge. With the fire fight in full swing on the north bank and the Italians distracted, the remainder of No. 15 Platoon would then storm the southern end of the bridge and overrun its defenders.

As soon as the platoon was briefed and organised, the two sections set off toward the bridge. Withers led the northern section stealthily across the canal, up and over its banks, down into the river and up and out over the far riverbank. Once the six men had regrouped, they moved toward the pillbox and its still unsuspecting occupants. Satisfied that he and his men were in a suitable jump-off position for an assault, he initiated the attack by opening fire on the concrete pillbox. Almost immediately his section followed suit, pouring in a hail of small arms fire and a blizzard of grenades. The sudden ferocity of the attack stunned the defenders on the north bank; taken completely by surprise, they were overwhelmed after managing to loose off only a few badly aimed shots. The simultaneous assault from the south bank was prosecuted with equal vigour and was also successful; neither assault group suffered any casualties. The bridge's garrison laid down its weapons and surrendered to Lieutenant Withers and No. 15 Platoon. By his courage and quick thinking, the young officer had just gained the 2nd Battalion The South Staffordshire Regiment a new battle honour.

The South Staffordshires' platoon had undoubtedly achieved an audacious victory, but now it had to secure the objective and hold on to it until relieved. Well aware of this, Withers sited his men in defensive positions and waited for the inevitable counter-attack. The sappers, assisted by the platoon's medical orderly who was set to work cutting any wire that even remotely resembled a detonator cable, meanwhile commenced the critical task of removing detonators from the demolition charges that they found positioned around the bridge. Withers knew that his isolated platoon would be hard-pressed to hold onto their gains against a well organized counter-attack and was also well aware that it was only a matter of time before reinforcements from 1st Airlanding Brigade or the Eighth Army reached the bridge. He and his men just had to hold on to their positions, no matter what.

Unfortunately for Withers and his small force, the Italians had already been fully alerted to the invasion, the alarm having been raised by an Italian Army radio station at Cape Murro di Porco. In an effort to prevent this happening, the station had been attacked by a force of 150 airlanding troops but, in spite of the threat of being overrun, the Italian signallers had shown great bravery and held out long enough for them to transmit the alert signal to their headquarters. The element of surprise was lost and those elements of the Italian communications network that remained intact soon relayed the alarm signal to garrisons throughout Sicily.

The commander of the Italian XVI Corps, General di Corpo Carlo Rossi, reacted immediately by issuing orders for four of his mobile formations to converge on Syracuse and the Ponte Grande bridge. These, however, were never received. Ironically, the scattering of gliders had worked in favour of the British; on leaving their gliders, the airlanding troops had carried out orders to disrupt the Sicilian telephone network by cutting telephone lines wherever they found them. Had the landings gone to plan and gliders landed on their allotted LZs, the effect of these orders would have been localised to the Syracuse area; as it was, the wide dispersal of landing sites magnified the impact of this ad-hoc sabotage and paralysed the island's telephone system.

The first test of No. 15 Platoon's hastily sited defences arrived at 2345 hours in the form of a lone truck carrying twelve Italian soldiers. Driving straight up to the bridge, they were not given the chance to disembark and close with the bridge defences before Lance Corporal George Pratt and his section unleashed a withering torrent of small arms fire into the tightly packed troop compartment of the truck, killing many of its occupants. The actions of Private W.H. Charlesworth, a Bren gunner at the bridge, are recorded in the South Staffordshires' battalion war diary and give an indication of the nature of the fighting that night. During the initial action, he personally accounted for five Italians and then, having expended all his ammunition, used his Bren gun as a club in hand-to-hand fighting with the remaining Italians. The hours after the truck attack passed anxiously for the bridge's defenders as there was still no sign of reinforcements from either A or C Company, and there was the ever-present threat of larger and more determined counter-attacks from the Syracuse garrison or one of the better trained Italian mobile formations. Worse still, there was the possibility of an appearance by German armour.

Meanwhile, prior to No. 15 Platoon seizing the Ponte Grande, other gliders were landing in the darkness by the light of a quarter-moon. Most of their pilots had little idea where they were when their aircraft finally came to rest. Flight Officer Samuel Fine USAAF had an eventful landing in Glider 13 flown by Staff Sergeant Lofty Wikner; it would appear that all on board their WACO were lucky to survive:

> We released over water at 2,500 feet and glided down toward Sicily with streams of tracer bullets zipping by on both sides of us. It was one hairy night, believe me!
>
> I spotted a large field by the light of the quarter moon and landed safely, although we did a double ground loop when both wings hooked into trees. I had thirteen British troops aboard and before we could get out of the glider, Fascist troops behind a stone wall started firing at us. I was hit in the right shoulder and one of the first troopers out of the glider was hit too. The rest of the British troops returned fire with a vengeance and the Fascists took off. But before this happened I was hit again in the same shoulder. We headed for the Ponte Grande bridge, which was our objective and which we were to keep intact for tanks from the British Eighth Army.[3]

Lieutenant Arthur Boucher-Giles and Sergeant Dusty Miller in Glider 110 were also now down on the ground. They were about to experience one of the same problems with the WACO that had concerned Lieutenant Colonel Chatterton in the weeks leading up to the operation: that of the tactical limitations imposed by the glider's small lift capacity. One of these was that the airlanding infantry battalions' 6-pounder anti-tank guns and their attendant Jeeps had to be split from each other and flown in separate gliders:

> It was rather a heavy landing due to the dazzling effects of the searchlight and the fact that there was only a quarter-moon, and a wind of some considerable strength. We were all a little bruised and shaken, but the only serious injury was to Sergeant Hodge of The Border Regiment. The gun had worked loose in its mooring during the bumpy crossing and when we landed had slipped forward and dealt him a frightful blow in the back.
>
> We came under pretty heavy fire from small arms, as we lay still under the wings of the glider for about a quarter-of-an-hour, hoping that

> a jeep would connect up with us so that we could get the six-pounder away. As nobody, either friend or foe came to us, we made Staff Sergeant Hodge as comfortable as possible, left one man to guard him, and setting my compass for a night march, in the best Officer Training Unit tradition, Miller and I and the two other Border Regiment boys marched off in the direction of the bridge ...[4]

Meanwhile, Lieutenant Withers and his small force around the bridgehead were unaware of the mixed fortunes of the other LADBROKE gliders. At 0430 hours there was some cause for optimism when the first elements of 1st Airlanding Brigade began to trickle into the Ponte Grande bridgehead. The new arrivals, however, were few in number and therefore of more psychological, rather than military, value. Seven men led by their platoon commander, Lieutenant William Gordon Welch of the brigade headquarters defence platoon, entered the South Staffordshires' small perimeter. Having landed in Glider 6, they had beaten off an Italian patrol and taken nine prisoners while on their way into the bridgehead. Although few in number, they nevertheless were still a very welcome addition to Lieutenant Withers's small force. Moreover, the information they brought about the situation around the LZs and the bridge was just as important to Withers as the increase in weapons and numbers.

Shortly after Lieutenant Welch's section arrived, a second Italian counter-attack using a troop of three armoured cars was launched from the north. An attack by armoured vehicles posed a significant problem for the lightly armed South Staffordshires; nevertheless they were unfazed and threw everything they had at the armoured cars. The Italians returned fire and swept the South Staffordshires' positions with a lethal hail of cannon and co-axial machine gun fire until the commander of the leading car was hit by British fire and slumped down into his cupola. The loss of their troop leader had an immediate effect on the resolve of the Italians who broke off the attack and withdrew. As soon as the armoured cars receded from sight, more airlanding troops took the opportunity to move forward out of the darkness and enter the perimeter. At about 0500 hours Major Basil S. Beasley, the Officer Commanding 9th Field Company (Airborne) RE, reached the bridge with fifteen of his sappers.

At the same time, Staff Sergeant 'Kay' Cawood was also making his way toward the bridgehead, having flown in with Staff Sergeant Bert Holt as his second pilot in Glider 106; the two men had become separated in the darkness and were making their way separately to the bridge. Staff Sergeant Cawood managed to locate and join a group of glider pilots and other airlanding troops led by Lieutenant Boucher-Giles and, as the group neared the bridge, heard the sound of a vehicle horn being blown repeatedly. After a few seconds, Cawood realised that the horn blasts were in fact a message being transmitted in morse code. Listening intently, he decoded the message: W-A-T-E-R-L-O-O-T-A-K-E-N. The bridge was in British hands! The news was passed around the troops with him, boosting their morale noticeably. Their advance picked up speed as they pushed on along the road, passing Staff Sergeant Galpin's abandoned Horsa. Lieutenant Boucher-Giles, assisted by Sergeant Miller, continued to lead the way, stopping only to knock out a machine gun in a pillbox en route:

> As dawn approached we joined up, in an orchard a mile or so south of the bridge, with another party of troops who had made their way from the landing zone. Lieutenant Colonel Walch took command as the senior officer present, and we found after a little recce that the bridge itself had already been taken and was in the hands of the South Staffordshires. There was a gauntlet of sniping and fairly heavy machine gun fire to run before we could get through, but we made it to the bridge in two waves, with only one or two casualties.[5]

The arrival of two more senior officers lifted the unexpected burden of command of the bridgehead from the shoulders of Lieutenant Withers. Lieutenant Colonel Arthur G. Walch OBE, originally an infantryman of The Loyal Regiment, assumed command, releasing Withers to return to command his own men. The young platoon commander was later wounded in the hand but survived the battle; he was subsequently awarded the Military Cross in recognition of his courage and leadership throughout the Ponte Grande battle. Staff Sergeant Dennis Galpin was also rightly singled out for his flying skills and bravery in the air; he was awarded the Distinguished Flying Medal – one of the first of many awarded to officers and men of the 1st Battalion GPR.

The bridge defenders were now reorganised to hold both north and south ramps of the bridge using the banks of the canal and river for cover. They also had to ensure that any approach overland from the west along the canal and river banks was covered by what few Bren guns they had available. In the wake of the armoured car attack, Italian mortar batteries now harassed the bridge's defenders with intermittent mortar shoots, these increasing in frequency and improving in accuracy as the morning went on. It was in one of the very early gaps in between the mortar 'stonks' that Flight Officer Sam Fine and his comrades also reached the bridge:

> When we got to the bridge at sunrise, we found that Lieutenant Lennard Withers and a platoon of South Staffordshire infantrymen had captured it with a daring night-time raid from the front and rear. Seven gliders that were carrying additional troops for the bridge assault never appeared.[6]

The trickle of reinforcements increased in volume as the level of daylight improved and by 0700 hours the defenders numbered seven officers and 80 men, a significant increase in numbers and firepower but still too weak a force to beat off a well organized counter-attack by determined troops. The lack of heavy weapons and ammunition was a major cause for concern because, other than their rifles and Sten guns, the positions around the bridge were being held by just four Bren guns. The only indirect fire weapons available were one 2-inch light mortar and a single 3-inch medium mortar. The crew of the 2-inch mortar could offer little in the way of punch as they possessed just a handful of smoke rounds. The 3-inch mortar had been put to effective use against an Italian mortar position that was shelling the British positions from the south-east but, after this successful counter-mortar, had just three high-explosive rounds remaining and these were being held back for emergency use.

Following the mortar exchange, the Italians mounted another attack by two companies of Italian naval infantry from the Syracuse garrison. These, however, lacked skill and determination, and were thrown back with heavy casualties.

The situation away from the Ponte Grande remained confused following the airborne landing. The scattering of gliders across Sicily and the resulting reports generated overnight by Italian outposts and strongpoints prevented the Italian commanders from identifying a main landing or the Allied objectives. This confusion was later heightened further by the appearance of the Allied naval armada off the coast and the subsequent British, Canadian and American amphibious landings. The confusion was further heightened further among Italian and German headquarters by large numbers of reports of American parachute landings spreading all over the island.

In direct contrast to the British airborne landing, the American operation had no glider component and, in spite of the totally unsuitable weather conditions, the US 82nd Airborne Division had pressed on and dropped 3,400 paratroops on the western flank of the Allied landings. The objective of the US airborne operation was to capture the high ground overlooking the industrial port of Gela. If successful, the 'All Americans' would secure the flank of General Patton's Seventh Army as it came ashore. Taking place at the same time as the landings by 1st Airlanding Brigade, the American drop was plagued by exactly the same problems caused by high winds and navigation errors.

The drop was carried out by paratroopers of the 505th Parachute Infantry Regimental Combat Team, a new airborne formation commanded by Colonel James 'Jumpin Jim' Gavin. The tall New Yorker and his men approached the coast in a formation dispersed and fragmented by flak and high winds. Unlike the British glider formations, the USAAF transports carrying Gavin's men had to cross the coastline in order to deliver their sticks of paratroopers on to their DZs. It was at this critical point that those C-47s that had pressed on were exposed to well-directed flak that brought down a number of aircraft, killing the crews and the helpless paratroopers on board. The flak caused panic among some of the C-47 crews, resulting in the formation scattering further. The mid-air chaos resulted in a drop that spread the 505th Regimental Combat Team over an area of 25 miles. Horrifically, many paratroopers were killed when they were dropped at below safe operational altitude and their parachutes failed to open, while even more were seriously injured as a result of their parachute canopies deploying only partially.

Against all odds, however, some elements of the 505th Regimental Combat Team were dropped in the correct place and carried out their mission. Notably, 250 men of the 3rd Battalion 505th Parachute Infantry Regiment captured the high ground near Ponte Olivo airfield to the north-east of Gela. The battle that followed around Gela and the surrounding high ground was a real baptism of fire for Colonel James Gavin and his men. In addition to the expected Italian troops that they had been prepared to face, the Americans were surprised to encounter German armour and troops from the Hermann Göring Division who mounted aggressive counter-attacks against the Gela beachhead and the ridge line held by the paratroopers. The Germans spearheaded a number of their attacks with formidable Tiger tanks, against which there was little that the lightly armed paratroops could do, albeit they did succeed in knocking one out using a captured 75mm pack howitzer. Fortunately, contact was established with the US 45th Infantry Division which broke up the German attacks with heavy artillery and naval gunfire from US Navy vessels offshore.

Those paratroops who landed much further afield followed their Airborne training and did everything possible to join the battle. Isolated groups independently set about doing what they could to inflict damage on the Italian defences, cutting telephone wires, laying ambushes and, in the case of larger groups, attacking strongpoints and barracks that they stumbled across. Together with the British glider landings and bombing raids, these widespread incidents and many false alarms flooded the Axis command network with hundreds of seemingly unrelated reports of Allied troop landings. Consequently, during the first hours of the landings, confusion reigned on Sicily, in particular around Syracuse and the Ponte Grande bridgehead.

One group of Italian soldiers had obviously not been made aware of the capture of the Ponte Grande by the British. At 0700 hours on 10 July 1943 the troops on the north side of the bridge heard the sound of a vehicle approaching from the north, along the N115 highway, toward their positions. Oblivious to the danger that lay ahead of them, a truck carrying Italian troops drove straight up to the bridge. Sergeant Dusty Miller watched intently as the vehicle got nearer and nearer to the bridgehead:

> To my amazement a speeding object caught my eye coming down the road out of the cutting on the hillside. It was a lorry and I knew that it was not one of ours, for we had brought in only Jeeps. I pushed my Sten forward and carefully sighted on the lorry. It was still half a mile away and was slowing down as it approached the bridge ... The lorry drew nearer and nearer and then, when it was 200 yards from the bridge,

> I saw at least one of the men was a civilian and old at that. Two others by his side were wearing the familiar Italian Army soft caps. I could not see through the windscreen to identify the man in the cab, but I had seen enough.
>
> The lorry had almost stopped at the bridge and the men were peering inquiringly over the sides of the lorry. I held my fire, for I was under the impression that our men, who were dug in right by the roadside on the river bank, had signalled them to stop and had them covered.
>
> There came a shattering roar of firing from the end of the bridge and the lorry swerved off the road, the windscreen dissolving into fragments. The engine roared for a moment then died and the lorry jerked to a halt on a grass verge. Again came the crash of rifle fire, screams rent the air and I saw one of the soft-capped men topple over. The old man stood swaying on his feet, his two arms thrust skyward, while cries of fear poured from his lips.
>
> Another short burst and he spun around, his old battered hat flying off as he fell. The firing stopped for a moment I felt sickened by this wanton killing of what seemed to be an old, harmless civilian, who probably had hitch-hiked a lift on the lorry.[7]

Soon after the firing ceased, British medics moved forward to the bullet-ridden lorry. Very few of the unfortunate Italians on board the truck survived the ambush.

However, in spite of apparent chaos, not all of the Italian troops in the area were disorganised as pressure on the bridgehead continued to mount. At 1130 hours, a battalion of the Italian 75th Infantry Regiment from the 54th Napoli Infantry Division arrived with a battery of artillery attached. Thereafter, the volume of artillery and mortar fire falling on the British positions increased steadily throughout the day. During a particularly heavy artillery attack, a number of Italian prisoners being sheltered in one of the captured pillboxes were killed by a direct hit from their own guns.

Lieutenant Boucher-Giles was by now in command of the sixteen glider pilots who were holding thinly-defended positions on the south bank of the river:

> I was myself given command of the glider pilots and some four or five others, amounting to some twenty men, to hold the south bank of the southernmost canal. This canal led straight into the sea, and the only cover was actually on the bank. This was fortunate in a way because the Italians so outnumbered us that if they had the courage to come in, as good German infantry would undoubtedly have done, they would have overrun us by sheer weight of numbers alone.
>
> The greatest difficulty was to keep the men from expending all their ammunition, as we did not know how many hours we should have to hold the bridge until Monty's forces came up. However, early direct

> hits wiped out both Bren guns and annihilated the crews. The second in command, Major Beazley, Royal Engineers, came over to my side of the canal, and was unfortunately killed by a burst of machine-gun fire, which also killed one of my Staff Sergeants, and incidentally put a bullet through my back pack and knocked my rifle out of my hand. Things were getting pretty grim and we were by now suffering quite a lot of casualties.
>
> We had no machine-guns and very small supplies of ammunition, so we could not easily put in a counter-attack. Had we been able to do so, I feel sure that the Italians would have melted away with shrieks of terror. As it was, all we could do was occasionally knock off one or two of the bolder ones when they showed themselves within reasonable range; but as they were in excellent cover and extremely cautious this was not easy.[8]

Other witnesses state that Lieutenant Boucher-Giles had numerous close shaves during the battle, with Staff Sergeant Andy Andrews recounting how a sniper's round knocked a mug of tea out of the lieutenant's hand. Providence was obviously smiling on the Boucher-Giles name that day; he also escaped death when in separate incidents Italian rounds struck his rifle, small pack, and closest of all, only just missed his cheek.

Not all of the glider pilots inside the bridgehead were defending the south bank, another ten were spread out around the position – a total of 26 in all.

Later in the morning the rate of incoming fire from the Italian guns began to fall off and then suddenly at 1220 hours all shelling ceased. The emphasis of the attack shifted to lighter, infantry support weapons. With the rate of mortar and machine gun fire raining down on to the British positions increasing noticeably, it was obvious to those with combat experience that this change in the rhythm of the battle could only mean one thing – an imminent infantry attack.

The defenders were now at a real disadvantage; with the majority of their positions surrounded by open terrain offering little cover or protection from incoming fire, and little ammunition remaining to return fire, there was not much the British could do to counter the enemy mortars and prevent them from inflicting further casualties. Cover was almost non-existent, so any movement outside trenches was immediately exposed to machine gun fire or the blast of high explosive mortar bombs. Emboldened by the lack of British fire, Italian infantry began to edge forward purposefully in the wake of their increasingly heavy mortar barrage. All that the British could do now was to fire a few single shots to deter the Italian advance. By 1230 hours there was still no sign of reinforcement from the main body of 1st Airlanding Brigade or immediate relief by Eighth Army tanks, and thus the prospect of being overrun and losing the bridge was rapidly becoming reality.

Pressure continued to mount until finally at 1245 hours, in an attempt to put some desperately needed time and space between the defenders and the oncoming Italian infantry, Lieutenant Colonel Walch ordered a withdrawal to a more tenable position to the east of the bridge. This was a last ditch attempt to gain a few more hours of breathing space for the beleaguered airlanding troops and the advancing seaborne forces. The lack of radio communications between the bridgehead and the powerful Allied naval forces arrayed offshore was frustrating as the firepower of just one of the many destroyers whose guns were in reach of the Sicilian coast would almost certainly have kept the Italians at bay. The same can of course be said of air power and the Eighth Army's artillery batteries that landed that day. Just a single Royal Artillery forward observation officer, forward air controller or naval gunfire officer equipped with a serviceable radio would have given the airlanding troops the firepower they so desperately needed to strengthen their precarious grip on the bridge and beat off the Italian attacks. There was, however, no such radio link, and the vacuum created by the withdrawal was quickly filled by the advancing Italians.

In falling back, however, the defenders did gain a little more precious time. Sergeant Dusty Miller was among the glider pilots clinging on to their position on the south bank when news of the withdrawal was passed to him and his comrades by word of mouth:

> The enemy firing seemed to be increasing and the whine of bullets became almost continuous. Our firing appeared to be decreasing somewhat and I began to feel a little anxious, and longed to hear a report of some sort on the position. I did not have long to wait. My attention turned towards the hills behind was suddenly diverted by the sound of splashing in the river just behind me. Swiftly I turned and crawled up the bank almost to the summit while I trained my Sten in the direction of the noise. Sergeant Cawood did the same. A dripping figure carrying a rifle appeared over the crest and instantly I recognised him as one of our men. I relaxed my finger on the trigger. Another man followed closely on the heels of the first. Together they slipped swiftly over the brink while the bullets snapped past. They dropped down alongside and I noticed that the first man was a sergeant from one of the regiments we had carried in. He seemed rather agitated and was panting with his exertions.
>
> Alarmed, I asked him what was wrong. He struggled for breath and then replied that he had been ordered over this side as the front could not be held much longer. He also stated that the rest of the men were following him over at intervals. We were to move off under the bridge and then back up alongside the road until we reached the crest of the hill where we would take up new positions ...[9]

The withdrawal to the east reduced the British perimeter as intended but, combined with the absence of mortar support for the troops airlanding and the ever-diminishing rate of small arms fire, this encouraged the Italians to become more aggressive in their tactics. The number of mortars and machine guns brought to bear on the beleaguered British positions increased through the afternoon as did their effectiveness of their fire. Meanwhile, casualties among the airlanding troops continued to mount. Behind an increasing weight of fire, Italian Infantry worked their way steadily closer to the bridge. Simultaneously, Italian machine guns, some of them as close as 40 yards were pouring enfilade fire on to the area of both the northern and southern ramps of the bridge. Elsewhere their infantry were close enough to bombard isolated British outposts with grenades until the defenders were forced to withdraw further. It was a hopeless battle and by 1515 hours only 20 of the defending troops remained unwounded and capable of returning any fire.

Ammunition levels were by now below the critical level and, after just another fifteen minutes, all remaining ammunition had been expended. The final option of a last ditch bayonet charge was ruled out as a pointless sacrifice. With no heavy machine guns or mortars to support such a desperate action, charging across open terrain against numerous machine guns would have been certain suicide for no apparent reason. Therefore, with no prospect of reinforcement or relief, there was little more that could be done. Thus, with huge reluctance, the order to surrender was given.

The surrender was accepted by the forward company of Colonel Francesco Ronco's 75th Infantry Regiment. Not all of the survivors of the battle, however, were prepared to allow themselves to be taken into captivity. Lieutenant Gordon Welch and seven of his men managed to slip away along the canal bank to the east and hide themselves from Italian eyes while the remainder of the Ponte Grande force reluctantly waited for the Italians to come forward and take them into captivity. Flight Officer Sam Fine was among the handful that still offered resistance:

> There were 72 British Officers and troopers on that bridge and one American (me) when the fascists counter-attacked. We held out as long as we could but when we got to fifteen defenders, and our ammunition ran out, we had to surrender. They were using heavy machine guns and a howitzer. Just before we surrendered, I was wounded in the neck.[10]

Flight Officer Fine was down to the last two rounds of ammunition in his pistol when he surrendered. He had already been wounded twice in the right shoulder shortly after landing; his third wound, this time to his neck, gives some indication of the ferocity of the fighting around the bridge. His excellent account is, however, inaccurate in one respect; there were in fact two other Americans at the bridge. Roderick MacDonald, a US Army war correspondent, who achieved notoriety for his part in the defence of the bridge during which he had used his own Colt .45 pistol to good effect. The other was another USAAF glider pilot, Flight Officer Russell Parks, who had acted as second pilot to Sergeant Jack Barnwell, the two men bringing in Glider 52A to land three miles from the bridge. Both had found their way to the bridgehead where they played an active part in the defence of the perimeter.

Historically, the initial moments immediately following surrender are tense and dangerous for the vanquished, as both sides attempt to make an almost instant transition from full-blown combat. Sergeant David Baker had landed Glider 38 with his second pilot, Lieutenant Dale, and after a hard fight they were now between the canal and the river, hemmed in on all sides. Casualties had mounted throughout the afternoon until their position became untenable. Sergeant Baker and six others were thus forced to abandon their position and withdraw across the canal, wading through neck-deep water as enemy fire passed overhead. The group was now isolated and pinned down in a water-filled dyke. Surrounded on all sides the situation was desperate when the sudden explosion of a hand grenade, close to the lip of the dyke, indicated that the enemy was closing in and that a final assault was imminent. Sergeant Baker:

> A quick conference followed and the officer in charge decided that our position was now hopeless and he took the action to surrender. He tied a white handkerchief to a rifle and stepped out of cover. The rest of us waited, not too optimistically, expecting that he would be shot down. But the firing stopped and we followed with our hands above our heads. The Italians surrounded us and pointed to their dead comrades at the same time speaking excitedly. I felt the point of a bayonet prodding into my back. A young Italian officer saved the day and persuaded his men to march the prisoners off. We moved about half a mile, down a lane into a hollow, on one side of which were some more despondent airborne types who were already under guard.[11]

The order to surrender slowly took effect across the remaining British positions; the Italians in jubilant mood surged forward and overran the now impotent British defences. Lieutenant Boucher-Giles and his tiny force of glider pilots held on to their positions on the riverbank until 1600 hours before they were forced eventually to surrender. At this point many of the British survivors were concerned that this sense of overwhelming triumph might turn into a desire among their captors to avenge the losses that the airlanding troops had inflicted on them during the battle. Initial fears of summary execution proved to be unfounded, however, and the British were treated properly as prisoners-of-war. All, including the walking wounded, were herded into a column alongside a smaller group of Eighth Army prisoners by Italian guards. It seemed that a dramatic reversal of fortunes was now complete: the operation had failed and a spell in a prisoner-of-war camp awaited the captors of Ponte Grande Bridge. Flight Officer Sam Fine was among the walking wounded in the column, and witnessed a remarkable incident that would swing the pendulum of battle back in favour of the British again:

> As the enemy was marching us away along a dirt road through some woods, a British officer suddenly appeared from behind a tree right in front of us – he was at least 150 feet away – and took a shot with a pistol at the fascist guard on point, smacking him right between the eyes. The other guards didn't know where the shot came from and while they were scurrying around among us, I grabbed two rifles from a couple of them. I tossed one to a trooper near me and the two of us shot every fascist we could see. The rest of our captors were huddling in the woods behind trees and bushes and meekly surrendered. Later in the afternoon we managed to link up with some troops of the British 5th Infantry Division.[12]

Finally, at 1615 hours, the leading elements of the Eighth Army reached the bridge. Lieutenant Gordon Welch and his party of evaders emerged from cover as a patrol of the 2nd Battalion The Royal Scots Fusiliers came into view. The Lowland battalion was at the head of the 17th Infantry Brigade drive from the landing beaches toward Syracuse. Welch quickly briefed the Scots on the situation at the bridge and then guided them forward to launch a new attack. The Italians, having no stomach for a renewed battle, either surrendered or fled. The timely arrival of the Eighth Army turned the tables on the Italians and the Ponte Grande pendulum swung back again in favour of the airlanding troops. All around the bridgehead prisoners under Italian escort were unwittingly being marched into the path of oncoming Eighth Army troops. As a result the majority of those who went into captivity only stayed under Italian guard for an average of an hour-and-a-half.

The collapse of the bridgehead was inevitably fragmented and each group of British troops left to act independently. Sergeant Jimmy Fairgreave, a Scot from Edinburgh, and his second pilot, Sergeant Taffy Lovett, avoided capture and did their best to stay out of enemy hands; Sergeant Fairgreave's account paints a vivid picture of how fluid and dangerous the situation was for them immediately after the order to surrender was given:

> How on earth we weren't picked off there and then I'll never know; it was a good job there were no Germans in opposition ... at a later stage we were pulled back when the bridge came under mortar fire. This meant we had to cross two waterways and in so doing I slipped on the bank of the canal and plunged right in losing my weapon in the act. I can still remember Taffy Lovett's anxious look as I struggled in the water. Once over, we dashed for cover in some bushes just beyond and must have lost contact at this point. Whilst I lay shivering in cover for some time, I heard spasmodic firing and then a chorus of surrenders

> followed by silence. I had no idea that this action had taken place in a dry ditch that I later found behind me. When I found the ditch there was a small group of Airborne sitting dispiritedly, including two glider pilots. One was an officer and another chap called Chandler who was from No. 4 Troop of the old 2 Squadron ... I imagine that these survivors had run back along the ditch when the others were about to be taken. Time passed by and I thought that we would be captured very soon, when quite suddenly I was amazed to see columns of troops coming down the road toward the bridge; they were unmistakably ours and must have been the advance party from the Eighth Army. We ran along the dry ditch and met them at the bridge. It was casual and we stood chatting when the mortars started up again, so we jumped into the ditch once more. The 'Jocks' did not react quickly enough and the shell was well aimed, resulting in a number being hit. We jumped out, meaning to pull them back into shelter if possible, when a second shell landed near us and we all fell in a heap. Quickly an armoured car scuttled up the road to deal with the mortar crew and as if by magic an ambulance appeared and took the wounded men off.[13]

17th Infantry Brigade wasted little time before advancing across the recaptured Ponte Grande Bridge and on toward Syracuse. Initially resistance was stiff on the outskirts of the port but there was little that the garrison could do to hold the British advance. After two hours of fighting, Syracuse was in the hands of the Eighth Army. While the fighting in Syracuse was in full swing, an increasing number of 1st Airlanding Brigade troops were arriving at Ponte Grande. That night at 2100 hours, responsibility for the bridge was formally handed from 17th Infantry Brigade to 1st Airlanding Brigade. The next day, 11 July 1943, the brigade gathered sufficient strength to be able to deploy the 1st Battalion The Border Regiment to occupy Syracuse. While the Borderers were establishing themselves there, the remainder of the brigade were busy regrouping, rearming, recovering its wounded and burying the dead.

Notes

1. Galpin, Staff Sergeant, D., 1st Battalion GPR. By permission of *The Eagle*.
2. Galpin, Staff Sergeant, D., 1st Battalion GPR. By permission of *The Eagle*.
3. Fine, Flight Officer, S., USAAF, by permission of *The Eagle*.
4. Boucher-Giles, Lieutenant, A.F., OC, 9 Troop, 3 Squadron, 1st Battalion GPR, by permission of *The Eagle*.
5. Boucher-Giles, Lieutenant, A.F., OC, 9 Troop, 3 Squadron, 1st Battalion GPR, by permission of *The Eagle*.
6. Fine, Flight Officer, S., USAAF, by permission of *The Eagle*.
7. Miller, Staff Sergeant, V., 9 Troop, 3 Squadron, 1st Battalion GPR, *Nothing is Impossible*, p. 48.

8. Boucher-Giles, Lieutenant, A.F., OC, 9 Troop, 3 Squadron, 1st Battalion GPR, by permission of *The Eagle*.
9. Miller, Staff Sergeant, V., 9 Troop, 3 Squadron, 1st Battalion GPR, *Nothing is Impossible*, p. 52.
10. Fine, Flight Officer, S., USAAF, by permission of *The Eagle*.
11. Baker, Sergeant, D., 1st Battalion GPR. By permission of *The Eagle*.
12. Fine, Flight Officer, S., USAAF, by permission of *The Eagle*.
13. Fairgreave, Sergeant, J., 2 Squadron, 1st Battalion GPR by permission of *The Eagle*.

Chapter 13

Pyrrhic Victory

Although a few more glider pilots turned up at the garden I actually came to accept that there were many of my friends missing ...

Those embroiled in the fighting around the Syracuse LZs and the Ponte Grande inevitably were unaware of the wider progress of Operation HUSKY. While the fighting raged around the Syracuse bridgehead, further afield the complex amphibious phase of the invasion was well underway. The landings were mounted on a previously unseen scale, and were in fact at that point in time the largest amphibious operation in history. The combined Allied invasion fleet supporting the landing comprised 2,590 vessels drawn principally from the Royal Navy and US Navy.

The seaborne armada, divided between the East and West Task Forces, approached the coast of Sicily to land a huge Allied army that would, after just a few weeks, total more than half a million troops. Like their airborne comrades the night before, the soldiers and sailors making the run-in to the Sicilian coast were at the mercy of the weather. They endured the elements while the landing craft were loaded with troops, marshalled into formation and then finally released to head for their objectives. It was an exceptionally rough passage, the sea conditions deteriorating due to the high winds of up to 40 miles per hour (mph) that earlier had disrupted the glider stream; now they whipped up the sea, creating high waves. Consequently, many of the Allied assault troops, packed into flat-bottomed shallow draught landing craft, suffered from seasickness during the long journey from their transport ships to shore. A number of the smaller craft involved in the landings were overwhelmed by the huge waves, several sinking without trace and taking their heavily laden passengers with them.

In spite of the adverse weather, delays and all of the technical difficulties encountered by the Allied naval forces, the amphibious landings were generally well executed with the majority of the seaborne forces landing on Sicily. The overwhelming air and naval superiority of the Allies proved a decisive factor from the first minutes of D-Day, with naval bombardments ranging along the coastline, picking out and shattering shore batteries and strongpoints that had been identified as pre-designated targets. In the face of such a maelstrom of fire, the Italian gunners rarely remained to man their batteries, the majority electing not to take part in what could only be an unequal duel with the flotillas of warships arrayed offshore. The bombardments also proved effective in driving the forward units of Italian troops, dug in around the landing beaches, out of their trenches and bunkers. Meanwhile, the landing craft battled through the waves and on to the beaches. Luck that night was fortunately on the side of the sodden and cold troops who came ashore in the wake of naval gunfire and air support, as there was little in the way of organised or aggressive Italian resistance.

Throughout the first hours of D-Day, the formidable combination of strong tides and gale force winds continued unabated. The British Eastern Task Force reported problems with the handling of its tank landing craft and for much of the day landing armour and other vehicles on the beach remained difficult. British tactics required tanks to be landed in among the leading waves of assault infantry, and this required skill and practice even in ideal sea conditions. One troop of British Sherman tanks had been scheduled to spearhead the first beach landing but its tanks and their seasick crews failed to get ashore until more than six hours after their designated H-Hour. This was typical of the experiences of the majority of British and Canadian tank crews that day.

Fortunately, any resistance offered by Italian troops on the shoreline was at best half-hearted and soon melted away under fire. As the leading units of the Eighth Army moved inland off the beaches they encountered little to slow their advance, albeit there were isolated areas of resistance in spite of the overwhelming Allied naval gunfire. A few of the more resolute Italian batteries did manage to engage the oncoming Allied forces, some inflicting casualties and causing some disruption. Any such success, however, was short-lived; by opening fire the Italian gunners exposed themselves to overwhelming counter-battery fire from the ships massed offshore.

As a result of the Allied superiority in firepower and weight of numbers, the British beachheads expanded rapidly behind the advancing waves of troops, the beaches and surrounding areas soon being filled by the flood of incoming troops, vehicles, fuel, equipment, rations and much-needed ammunition. The volume of incoming combat supplies increased significantly once the port facilities at Syracuse were captured intact and opened up to Allied shipping. Indeed, the docks were receiving ships and unloading supplies by late on 10 July.

Meanwhile, off the west coast of Sicily, the US Western Task Force landings had also encountered problems, US Navy landing craft were battered by high wind and waves, while also struggling to navigate around unmarked sandbanks. The situation was further confused when a number of them delivered their loads to the wrong beach, while others arrived hours late and well adrift of their planned landing sequence. The already poor situation was not helped by poor inter-service coordination that resulted in sporadic USAAF air cover over the beachhead, the absence of which was effectively exploited by the Luftwaffe as Stuka dive bombers, unmolested, sank a number of ships and landing craft while German fighters roamed over the beaches downing a number of US Navy observation aircraft and thus for a while effectively blinding the naval gunners offshore. In spite of these difficulties, however, as increasing numbers of troops and armour finally struggled ashore, the American beachhead began to consolidate.

However, in the centre of the US Seventh Army area, troops met with serious resistance and a series of potent counter-attacks. Mercifully for the Americans on the beaches, however, the first enemy counter-attack was fragmented and lacked its intended punch. The first strike against Gela was intended to be a well co-ordinated and decisive thrust mounted by heavy Tiger tanks of the Hermann Göring Division, supported by regular troops from the Italian 4th Livrono Mountain Infantry Division. Fortunately the latter did not arrive on time, forcing the German panzers to attack without infantry and artillery support from their allies.

Poor communication and co-ordination also undermined an aggressive Italian counter-attack along Highways 115 and 117. This separate thrust into the Gela beachhead was mounted by a group of mobile columns released from the Italian reserve before the American beachhead had been established. The core of the attacking force was formed around the tanks of the Niscemi Armoured Combat Group and infantry of the Livorno Division. These relatively well trained formations pressed home their attack with some vigour and came close to reaching the beachhead. Fortunately for the Allies, the Italian counter-attacks, although individually well executed and potentially decisive, lacked close co-ordination between tanks and infantry. Critically, they had also failed to co-ordinate their actions with the German counter-attacks. What had been a threatening and potentially decisive counter-attack was eventually beaten off.

The failed Italian counter-attack was followed up later in the day by a second determined German armoured thrust into the centre of the Gela beachhead, again mounted by the Hermann Göring Division. Using the same axis as the Italian attack, this was a more powerful assault spearheaded by panzer grenadiers and Tiger tanks and came dramatically close to penetrating the still vulnerable American beachhead. In spite of dogged American resistance and suffering heavy casualties, the German infantry advanced behind their huge Tiger tanks, the oncoming column advancing to within 2,000 yards of the sea and overrunning elements of the hard-pressed US 45th Division that stood in their path. The proximity and momentum of the German threat forced even the fiery Lieutenant General George Patton to accept the reality of the situation and endure the ignominy of re-embarking his headquarters back aboard his command ship.

With their backs to the sea, the Americans fought the oncoming columns with great bravery and determination, and eventually the combination of sheer grit on their part and heavy casualties inflicted on the Germans finally slowed the advance to a standstill. It was at this critical point, just as the latter were regrouping, that the full weight of US Navy gunfire was brought to bear. The destroyer USS *Shubrick* and the cruiser USS *Boise* fired a devastating barrage of shells that finally shattered the German attack. By last light on 10 July 1943, the immediate threat had receded and the US Seventh Army welcomed the onset of the cover of darkness while it replenished supplies and evacuated its wounded while also reorganising and reinforcing its battered defensive perimeter around the port of Gela.

The next day on D+1, 11 July 1943, the armour and infantry of the Hermann Göring Division reappeared to attack the US beachhead again. A combination of confined space, difficult terrain and general congestion made it difficult for the Americans to manoeuvre in response to this new threat. During the course of a hectic battle, the US 1st and 45th Infantry Divisions bore the brunt of repeated attacks that saw German tanks again almost break through the American lines and advance on to the beaches. Once again it was the overwhelming weight of US naval gunfire and artillery that broke up the German armour and prevented the Gela beachhead from being overrun. The US beachhead was now secure and Lieutenant General Patton and his headquarters, now ashore once more, set about injecting new vigour and momentum into the Seventh Army landings.

While the US Seventh Army battled to hold Gela on D-Day, in North Africa the troops of 2nd Parachute Brigade, under Brigadier Eric Down, had begun their final preparations for Operation GLUTTON: the capture of the town and harbour of Augusta. The prospects for the drop looked good, the low number of USAAF transport aircraft lost on the Operation LADBROKE lift resulting in a complete complement of C-47s being available to support the 2nd Parachute Brigade lift.

The final preparations for GLUTTON began at 1100 hours with the loading of the parachute supply containers aboard the 102 transport aircraft allotted for the operation. While this activity was underway on the desert airstrips, final orders and briefings were in progress. In addition to the parachute aircraft, the brigade's heavy equipment had already been loaded and rigged on board twelve WACO and six Horsa gliders, the latter being loaded with the 6-pounder anti-tank guns and Jeeps of 2nd Airlanding Anti-Tank Battery RA.

The take-off time for GLUTTON was set for 1845 hours on 10 July 1943. With all of the transports, tugs and gliders loaded, fuelled and lined up on their desert airstrips, the paratroopers of 2nd Parachute Brigade and their attached airlanding troops assembled and waited in the heat of the North African sun for the order to board their aircraft. Unaware of the scale of the disaster that had befallen the majority of the men of 1st Airlanding Brigade, or of the ferocity of the fighting now raging around the Ponte Grande, they rested in tents or in the shade under the wings of their transports and gliders.

The process of loading waves of troops on to the aircraft would of course take time, as would the final pre-flight checks and the starting of aircraft engines. A lead time of 45 minutes was required for this activity. More importantly, the arrival of such a large formation of aircraft over Sicily and the appearance of a parachute brigade on the battlefield required careful planning and detailed coordination with the air, naval and ground forces already deployed on and around Sicily.

Operation GLUTTON was intended to deliver 2nd Parachute Brigade ahead of the Eighth Army: once on the ground the paratroopers were to capture Augusta, adding further impetus to the Eighth Army's advance from Syracuse, north across the Catania Plain. The decision to issue the executive order that would initiate the launch of the airborne operation rested with the Headquarters XIII Corps. If the drop was to be made on 10 July, the XIII Corps initiation order was expected at Headquarters 1st Airborne Division by no later than 1800 hours. In fact, no order from XIII Corps was received at the divisional headquarters until 1945 hours, and that, to the frustration of all involved, was for a postponement of the drop of 24 hours.

This delay inevitably led to speculation as to how the glider landings had gone the night before. Accurate casualty figures were unavailable, and information on the situation in Sicily was non-existent. Rumours and wild stories had begun to circulate around the airfields almost immediately after the return of the RAF and USAAF tug squadrons. Those airlanding troops who had suffered the ignominy of being towed back to North Africa were understandably very angry and forthright in their condemnation of the USAAF tug crews. Accusations of cowardice were levelled at them, and survivors of the LADBROKE lift accused the C-47 crews of refusing to fly in harm's way. The Americans were also accused of deliberately releasing their comrades' gliders at unsafe altitudes and too far out to sea in order to avoid enemy anti-aircraft fire and thereby save their own lives. The survivors were in many cases incandescent with rage, describing their allies as murderers who had abandoned hundreds of airborne troops to drown in the darkness miles from land. As mentioned earlier, Brigadier Shan Hackett the commander of 4th Parachute Brigade was sufficiently concerned for the morale of his own troops and the safety of USAAF crews that he confined all 1st Airborne Division troops in North Africa to their tented camps.

Frustrated by the postponement of their first major operation, Brigadier Eric Down's men remained confined to their camps while awaiting the order that would launch Operation GLUTTON. Unbeknown to most of the paratroopers, senior officers in the brigade staff were already concerned about the viability of some of the DZs allocated around the port of Augusta and the highway bridge that they had been ordered to capture. In addition, they were also convinced that the DZs were too small and poorly defined, and they considered they would be exceptionally difficult for tug pilots and their inexperienced navigators to locate from the air.

Once confirmed, the news of the disastrous events that had befallen 1st Airlanding Brigade inevitably dealt a significant blow to the morale of 1st Airborne Division, not least among the ranks of 2nd Parachute Brigade, and inevitably created a feeling of doubt in some minds about the impending operation and its prospects for success. It was not unreasonable to expect, given the anticipated difficulty of locating the DZs and the absence of the element of surprise now that the invasion was underway, that 2nd Parachute Brigade might well suffer a similar, or even worse, fate than that suffered by 1st Airlanding Brigade.

Luckily for the men of 2nd Parachute Brigade, the tanks and infantry of XIII Corps had by this time broken out of the beachhead and were advancing north with momentum. They had cut through the Italian defences and overrun and captured Augusta's port facilities and its main highway bridge. The brigade drop was thus no longer required, and so Operation GLUTTON was cancelled and the brigade stood down.

In the immediate aftermath of Operation LADBROKE, the men of 1st Airlanding Brigade were literally scattered all over North Africa and Sicily, not to mention those that had been rescued from the sea by ships and were now spread right across the Mediterranean. As a result of the LADBROKE debacle, the 1st Battalion GPR was now a shadow of its former self, as only the gliders and crews kept back for Operations GLUTTON and FUSTIAN could be considered to be an effective force. The majority of the battalion had been committed to the Syracuse landing, and most of those who survived had suffered very mixed fortunes. 500 men had set out to capture the Ponte Grande, but only 85 had actually taken part in the battle and they had suffered heavy casualties.

Once the highway bridge was safely in Eighth Army hands, those glider pilots who were still fit to fight were retained as part of the bridge garrison and given the role of a close-in defence platoon. It was at this point that the ferocity and cost of the fighting that they had survived around the bridge became apparent. Eventually, as the Allied front line had moved north beyond Syracuse, they were able to move out of their trenches and explore the bridgehead that they had fought so hard to hold. Staff Sergeant Andy Andrews gives a candid description of the situation around the bridge, and the realities of war:

> The infantry types were getting organised and soon had everyone in fire positions as a close bridge force and we had to look forward to a long cold night. The reaction was beginning to set in and I alternated periods of severe shaking with tramping up and down to keep awake. I still had my army sweater and even this didn't keep me warm. The roll call was very humbling and brought a touch of realism to the situation when you learned of those who had been killed for certain and the missing believed dead; and this didn't account for those picked up by the invasion fleet or the wounded who had been evacuated to hospital

> to Malta or North Africa. I kept thinking of the stories that could be told when we all get together again.
>
> Morning was a welcome relief. A watermelon and some large tomatoes were scrounged from a nearby field. Later Major Tony Murray called an 'O' Group and we learned that we were to move to the other side of the bridge to some high ground. The march across the bridge started off with everyone's morale high but the talk and the chatter soon died to a pregnant silence as we passed the bodies of friend and foe. I thought that there, but for the grace of God, go I. Some of the bodies were frozen as if in a waxworks, their last earthly actions in nightmarish attitudes that I cannot forget. And I expect that they will stay forever in the minds of those who passed that way.[1]

At the same time as Staff Sergeant Andrews and the Ponte Grande defenders were regrouping and moving to their new positions, the more widely scattered elements of 1st Battalion GPR were also on the move, regrouping and moving toward the bridge and into Syracuse itself. Many of them headed into the Italian port to scour the Eighth Army's medical facilities for their wounded co-pilots and comrades. Lieutenant Bunny Carn was among the wounded:

> I got to the Casualty Clearing Station in Syracuse and saw a large number of troops with leg injuries. There was no penicillin in 1943, with the result that many wounds and injuries resulted in amputations. Lieutenant Tommy Breach lost his leg and my own prospects were not very bright. But I was lucky; all of the wounded were taken to the Syracuse Hospital. The corridors were full and we were moved into the hospital in turn on stretchers. The surgeon was an Airborne doctor and the rest of the team Italian. Later we were all taken down to the docks in an elderly Italian ambulance and deposited on the quayside waiting to be taken out to the *Amra*, a South African ship with accommodation for about 450 wounded. She was very comfortable, almost luxurious with operating theatres etc, but I remember some anxiety because the previous hospital ship had been sunk by aircraft ... fortunately without loss of life. The hospital moved off to Alexandra with a brief stop in Tobruk en route.[2]

Lieutenant Colonel George Chatterton and his small group of glider pilots and airborne troops had by now separated from Major Paddy Mayne's Special Raiding Squadron. As he made his way in from the coast toward Syracuse and the Ponte Grande in daylight, he very soon began to realise just how badly the operation had gone for his battalion. Later in life, long after the war, he would compare the LADBROKE landing to the infamous, and equally costly, charge of the Light Brigade at Balaclava in 1854. Perhaps it was the scenes that he witnessed along his route into Syracuse, and subsequent years of hindsight, that led him to make that comparison:

> As the day drew on I found gliders everywhere, many in the fantastic positions they had crashed in the night. I remember one which had obviously hit the top of a tree and tipped up, the load – a Jeep – remaining in the glider, the cockpit having pitched forward to the ground. The amazing thing was that the dead driver of the Jeep was still in the seat at the wheel. He had been killed outright.
>
> Later I found another glider, carrying a 6-pounder anti-tank gun. This time the gun had burst through the cockpit, crushing the pilot who was dead underneath. Another I discovered fixed in the side of a cliff. Obviously the pilots had been killed on impact, but the load of troops had survived ... Later the the next day we came to the bridge, Ponte Grande, where we found the aftermath of the battle. Galpin's glider was still in the field, a memorial to an epic piece of glider piloting ... On the other side of the canal I could see the tail of Captain Denholm's glider. I crossed over and the sight that met my eyes was indeed terrible. The glider had hit the bank, and the effects of the explosion inside the glider could clearly be seen. The crew and passengers had been blown forward as if down a funnel, but of the pilot there was no sign. As I stood looking at this macabre and tragic pile of bodies I thought back to gay Denholm. I remembered that as I was briefing the pilots he had appeared at the door, his beret at a jaunty angle and his long fair hair showed beneath. He had just arrived, after being towed 1,500 miles across the sea and the desert in one of the Horsa gliders. As he leaned on the door, he said in his typical drawl, 'I say, I've come to see a man about an operation' ... I walked back to the bridge deeply affected and somewhat overwhelmed.[3]

Around the bridge, the glider pilot defence platoon was now confident that the advance of the Eighth Army had pushed the Italian Army well away to the north. It was also immediately obvious that there was no appetite among the civilian population for any form of armed resistance against the Allied invasion. With no obvious threat to the bridge, some of the garrison were allowed to explore their surroundings, Staff Sergeant Andy Andrews took the opportunity to leave the platoon bivouac area in the garden of the barracks close to the bridge and ventured away from the bridgehead's inner perimeter. Following the unwritten tradition of soldiers through the ages, he and his comrades set out to explore the foreign land that they had landed in, and to forage for exotic souvenirs of their victory:

> I went to Syracuse. My companion was Squadron Sergeant Major Masson. We walked into some deserted apartment blocks and found that they had been looted. In one bedroom contents of a bedside table

had been spilled on the floor and among the mess were a hypodermic syringe and various drugs. In the next room I found an admiral's dress uniform complete with dress sword. I wish now I had taken the sword but my inclination was not to participate in this type of 'liberating' from civilians. Once with Lieutenant Boucher-Giles, I went to the barracks by the bridge. Again we were far from the first to visit; each camp bed had been ransacked. During the inspection I found a 9mm Breda automatic which I gave to Boucher-Giles. I picked up some picture postcards of the city, a regimental postcard of the Alpini Regiment fighting in Greece, a medal ribbon and an identity card. I felt that the previous military owners would not miss them. In a short time the eeriness of the place sent me back to our garden.

Although a few more glider pilots turned up at the garden I actually came to accept that there were many of my friends missing; it was a feeling that was to be experienced three more times, although I didn't anticipate that at the time.[4]

At the same time, making his own way inland toward Syracuse was Private Ron Etherington of the 2nd Battalion The South Staffordshire Regiment. He and his friend, Ron Andrews, approached the Ponte Grande bridgehead:

> ... Eventually we arrived at the Ponte Grande road bridge, the main objective. It was the first time that I had seen a dead body and there were many, both British and Italian. While we were greeting other members of the battalion, a buzz went round, and coming down the road towards the bridge, standing in his Jeep with the famous black beret and salute, was MONTY! I can still see him after all these years and still think he was a good General. We now started to move towards Syracuse, our part of the operation now finished. There was only one small panic when nearing the city; our group had stopped and we had dismounted from the trucks, when in the distance we saw two fighter planes, which we didn't recognise, coming straight for us. Everyone dived into the trees that bordered the road and some like Ron Andrews and myself dived under the trucks as the planes machine-gunned the road, luckily without any casualties. The planes were Italian Fiat G50 fighters, it was a complete surprise as we had not seen any Italian planes before. We eventually resumed our journey and entered Syracuse.[5]

The mood among those glider pilots who had survived their landings and made it to Syracuse alive was not entirely sombre. Many were relieved to find friends whom they had believed to be killed on landing, in battle, or missing at sea, were in fact alive and well.

One of the most notable meetings, and what must have been an exceptionally colourful exchange of stories, took place when Lieutenant Colonel George Chatterton met up with the deputy commander of 1st Airlanding

Brigade, Colonel Osmond Jones. The two of them had much to talk about, not least the latter's account of the role played by the handful of Chatterton's glider pilots that had taken part in Jones's heroic assault on the Italian coastal gun battery. The two men compared their experiences and then did some exploring of their own. In company with a number of glider pilots, they set out aboard somewhat unusual transport to keep, given their location and circumstances, an unlikely appointment. Lieutenant Colonel Chatterton described Colonel Jones as a brave, amusing man with an eye for the girls. He recalled their first conversation on meeting at the bridge in detail:

> 'I say George', he said on meeting me, 'I've got an invitation to lunch.'
>
> 'Don't be silly,' I answered, 'What do you mean?'
>
> 'Well,' he replied, smiling, 'after I had captured the guns, I saw a villa, so I decided to capture that too. Lo and behold, there emerged a lovely American girl. Her husband was in the cellar, but he was an Italian and didn't like the sound of the battle raging around the villa. She was tickled that we were British, and I got on so well with her that she asked me to lunch today. I said I would come as soon as I finished fighting, and I also asked if I could bring a friend. I thought that you might like to come too. Will you?'[6]

The two men gathered a group of glider pilots and a staff officer from the vicinity of the bridge and clambered aboard Colonel Jones's transport, a commandeered Italian fire engine of 1900 vintage, towing behind it a 6-pounder anti-tank gun, and off they set for their lunch party.

If Allied senior commanders thought that the weather was to blame for the LADBROKE debacle and the poor execution of Operation HUSKY 1, they would soon receive further confirmation that they and their planning staffs had still to grasp the doctrinal and technical intricacies of co-ordinating the large-scale use of airborne forces. A few nights later they were made uncomfortably aware of a critical shortfall in staff experience, planning mechanisms and technical judgement. Three nights into the invasion, on 11 July 1943, the US 82nd Airborne Division carried out a second, reinforcement lift into Sicily, codenamed Operation HUSKY 2. The plan for the operation involved dropping 2,000 paratroopers of the 504th Regimental Combat Team unopposed on to undefended and cleared DZs. Simple in theory, the plan was that the 504th would be dropped under cover of darkness on to the DZs previously used by the 505th Regimental Combat Team during Operation HUSKY 1.

Notwithstanding the fate suffered by their sister combat team on the first drop, the men of the 504th were told that HUSKY 2 would go ahead regardless. They woke to find that the high winds had dropped and morale thus took an immediate and corresponding rise. They busied themselves with the detailed planning and preparations for what would be their first combat drop since the 504th's formation. The pre-operation omens were good: in addition to the benign assessment of the DZs, the terrible weather had abated and conditions were now considered ideal for flying and, most importantly, for parachuting.

HUSKY 2 was launched as planned on the night of 11 July, but soon those involved were faring little better than their predecessors 48 hours earlier. The transit from North Africa on board USAAF XII Troop Carrier Command C-47 transports was plagued with problems, not least of which was the recurrence of the navigational errors of HUSKY 1. Furthermore, the incoming formations of aircraft encountered an additional hazard as they approached the coast of Sicily and passed overhead the ships of the US Navy's Eastern Task Force. Unbeknown to the USAAF C-47 crews and the paratroopers packed into their aircraft, the ships below them had endured constant Luftwaffe attacks. Having just beaten off another German air raid, the US Navy gunners were in no mood to lose what could be vital minutes confirming the nationality and intent of the approaching formation. The first ships opened fire and were quickly joined by the rest of the anchored fleet, blazing away with every available anti-aircraft gun. This apparent lack of fire discipline was not unprecedented. Historically, naval forces had assumed all aircraft to be hostile and in the interests of self-preservation opened fire on potential raiders without hesitation. After three years of German air superiority in North Africa and the Mediterranean, the Royal Navy was equally wary and had a similar attitude to unknown aircraft approaching their ships.

The fears of the sailors below were of little concern, however, to the aircrews and paratroopers on the receiving end of the anti-aircraft barrage. The slow-moving C47s in their tight vic formations were an easy target at their jump altitude of 700 feet, and even the most panic-stricken gunner found it hard not to get a shell in close proximity to the unarmoured transports. The USAAF crews nevertheless pressed on with determination towards what they hoped would be the relative safety of the coastline and their inland DZs. As they neared the coastline, however, the situation took another dramatic turn. Alerted by the naval gunfire, the US Army gunners ashore also believed that a German air attack was approaching from the sea and, having manned their guns, opened fire on the incoming waves of C-47s. The 504th were literally trapped between the devil and the deep blue sea and the USAAF crews had no alternative but to push on through the flak.

As they headed for the DZs, the C-47 pilots were bravely attempting to fly straight and level at the jump altitude of 700 feet, but the anti-aircraft fire created havoc amongst the helpless mass of aircraft. Tragically a fifth of the formation, 23 C-47s, was shot down while the remainder flew on through the barrage to the DZs. It is a measure of the ferocity of this friendly fire that almost every aircraft on the mission was damaged, half of them subsequently being declared non-airworthy and scrapped after limping back to North Africa.

The 504th Regimental Combat Team fared no better, suffering ten per cent casualties during what must be remembered was the regiment's first combat jump. The carnage in the air had a direct effect on the ability of the paratroopers to rally and execute their mission. The 2,000-strong regiment that had taken off from North Africa had been decimated and was now totally scattered. Twenty-four hours after the drop, the 504th's commanders could only account for 25 per cent of its strength.

Two days after the near failure of Operation HUSKY 2, during the afternoon of 13 July 1943, orders were received for the withdrawal of 1st Airlanding Brigade from Sicily and its return to Sousse in North Africa.

Although it was obvious to every member of the brigade that the landing had not gone to plan, the full scale of the losses incurred during the first night of Operation LADBROKE still remained unclear. It was only when the brigade began to concentrate for the sea transit back to North Africa that gaps in the ranks became starkly apparent. Accurately quantifying the full extent of Operation LADBROKE casualties was still, however, almost impossible as survivors of the ditchings and the scattered landings remained missing or unaccounted for in Egypt, Algiers and Malta. Many other survivors were still on board the ships that had rescued them from the sea and would therefore be unable to rejoin their units for some weeks. The four LCTs that were tasked to carry the brigade back across the Mediterranean carried just 800 of the 1,730 men that had flown in the opposite direction only four days before.

Notes

1. Andrews, Staff Sergeant, A., *So, You Wanted to fly Eh?* Burnaby, B.C. ISTE 1997, p. 111.
2. Carn, Lieutenant, W.J., 1st Battalion GPR. By permission of *The Eagle*.
3. Chatterton, Lieutenant Colonel, G., 1st Battalion GPR, *The Wings of Pegasus*, Nashville, Battery Press, 1962, p. 94.
4. Andrews, Staff Sergeant, A., *So, You Wanted to Fly Eh?* Burnaby, B.C. ISTE 1997, p. 112.
5. Etherington, Private, R., HQ Company, 2nd Battalion the South Staffordshire Regiment, by permission of family.
6. Chatterton, Lieutenant Colonel, G., 1st Battalion GPR, *The Wings of Pegasus*, Battery Press, Nashville, 1962, p. 95.

Chapter 14

Operation FUSTIAN

The only previous glider landing of any size had been the German capture of Crete a couple of years earlier which, eventually captured the island after very heavy German casualties.

All through the preparations for Operation GLUTTON, the staff at Headquarters 1st Airborne Division had remained focused on marshalling resources to ensure that 2nd Parachute Brigade was delivered to its objectives. However, the speedy progress made by the leading elements of XIII Corps through Augusta and further north on to the Catania Plain negated the need for the drop and brought Brigadier Gerald Lathbury's veteran 1st Parachute Brigade to the fore. The two brigades exchanged places, with 2nd Parachute Brigade unloading its equipment from its aircraft and moving into reserve while the recently reconstituted 1st Parachute Brigade began final preparations for Operation FUSTIAN.

Brigadier Lathbury was a veteran parachutist, an early pioneer of parachuting and well-known among the leading exponents of the use of airborne forces in the British Army. He and his Red Devils were ordered to drop on the coastal plain ahead of Eighth Army's advancing formations with the mission of seizing a vital crossing over the River Simeto, a road bridge known as the Ponte Primosole. The intended axis for the British drive north ran along the main road between Augusta to Catania. The British armour spearheading the thrust from Augusta up the road toward Catania would have to cross the 30-yard width of the Simeto six miles to the south of Catania. The river was correctly assessed to be a wide and fast-flowing waterway that would present a significant obstacle for Eighth Army's Royal Engineer bridging units if the Ponte Primosole was not captured.

The bridge was the only existing crossing on the axis and thus its capture intact was seen as vital to the maintenance of momentum of the British and Canadian advance on Messina. Codenamed 'Marston', the Ponte Primosole was far from an architectural gem, consisting of a functional lattice-work design of steel construction protected by concrete pillboxes at either end. Its appearance, however, was of little interest to the staff of XIII Corps who were more concerned with its characteristics and dimensions and, above all else, whether it could take the weight of the 33-ton Sherman tanks that were leading the advance north. Failure to secure the bridge would result in unacceptable delays to General Montgomery's drive on Messina. In short, the Italian Army could not be allowed to destroy the crossing; the Ponte Primosole had to be captured intact, a classic task for airborne troops.

The plan to seize the bridge had been conceived in North Africa in early May. Envisaged as the third of the series of three airborne operations to be mounted in Sicily, it was always intended to be a combined parachute and glider operation to be carried out just hours ahead of rapidly advancing British armour. While Montgomery had always considered the bridge to be the lynch pin in any plan to cross and capture Catania and its surrounding plain, the Italian and German high command also appreciated its importance in their plans and thus intended to hold on to it.

Once the landings finally were underway and Montgomery and his headquarters were ashore, the HUSKY plan seemed to be evolving even better than expected. During the first 48 hours, a mood of optimism began to take hold in the Eighth Army headquarters; indeed, Montgomery was so confident in the ability of his troops to smash through to Messina that he launched a second thrust inland in addition to the long-planned drive across the Catania coastal plain, with Harpoon Force being ordered to thrust inland and advance on an axis through Vizzini, Caltagirone, Enna and Leonforte. In spite of now supporting two separate thrusts divided by mountains, Montgomery still remained confident. He sent the following brief telegram to General Alexander on 12 July 1943: 'Hope to capture Catania and its airfields by about 14 July.'

Unfortunately, however, Harpoon Force ran into elements of the Hermann Göring Division at Vizzini where resistance was stiff and the terrain favoured defence. The advance to the north thus came to an immediate halt. With the Vizzini thrust blocked, British attention shifted back onto the coastal plain and the capture of the bridge at Ponte Primosole once again became all important.

The bridge would be a tough nut to crack. The 1st Parachute Brigade drop on the bridge was originally planned for the night of 12/13 July 1943 and would require very careful timing and co-ordination, the progress of the leading elements of Eighth Army being the controlling factor in cueing the launch of the brigade from its North African airstrips. By now, however, there were problems with the Eighth Army's rate of advance north from Augusta, which was beginning to slow. The tanks and infantry of XIII Corps were not gaining ground at the rate anticipated and thus were behind schedule. Meanwhile back in North Africa, Lathbury's paratroopers were enduring a long and frustrating wait for the order to take-off; at the last minute Operation FUSTIAN was postponed for 24 hours and would now take place on the night of 13 July 1943. This would give XIII Corps another full day to fight its way to within striking distance of the Ponte Primosole.

Although frustrating for those keyed up and ready for battle, the additional hours on the ground in North Africa was a valuable opportunity to recheck equipment, parachutes, and review orders and plans. The delay to the drop also created extra time and space for the hard-pressed USAAF transport crews of XII Troop Carrier Command. With Operations HUSKY 1 and 2 now complete, some of the aircraft and crews that had until now been dedicated to supporting the US 82nd Airborne Division were now made available to reinforce 51st Troop Carrier Wing USAAF and 38 Wing RAF on FUSTIAN. By the afternoon of 13 July 1943, 1st Parachute Brigade had direct call on 116 transport aircraft, eight WACOs and eleven Horsas.

The loading of a parachute brigade aboard transport aircraft and gliders was still a relatively new science requiring very detailed planning. The brigade headquarters staff had to decide on the desired order of arrival of units on the DZs, and in many instances that of individuals. The paratroopers, supplies and equipment were then divided into aircraft loads and given stick or chalk numbers. Each stick or chalk could then be loaded on to aircraft and gliders in compliance with the brigade air staff table that allocated every single soldier, vehicle, gun and piece of equipment to a C-47 or glider. This was a complex task subject to a multitude of variables and, more often than not, numerous changes of plan.

Sergeant Wallace Mackenzie, of No. 1 Squadron of 1st Battalion GPR, was earmarked to fly Glider 128 alongside Lieutenant Robin Wachli, the two of them being among 38 glider pilots selected to fly on Operation FUSTIAN who also included four USAAF glider pilots in their number. Sergeant Mackenzie remembered the run-up to the lift, and his account hints at the changes to the plan:

> A few days before, we had met the anti-tank crew whom we were to carry along with their gun and a jeep. We went out into the desert and fired a few shots at oil drums in the distance. This was our only meeting with that crew, and in the event, this was not the crew allocated to our glider when the day came and we only had the briefest greeting with the new crew before take-off.[1]

The 1st Parachute Brigade that Sergeant Wallace Mackenzie and the other FUSTIAN glider pilots encountered prior to the operation had undergone significant transformation since its return from the Tunisian campaign. The remnants of the original brigade, although without doubt battle-hardened, had required substantial reinforcement and re-equipping before it could be considered fit for combat again. The parachute battalions had borne the brunt of the brigade's fighting in Tunisia and, their casualty figures reflected this. Following the arrival of reinforcements from England and an infusion of men from 2nd Parachute Brigade, however, the brigade was now close to full strength. Its core consisted of the 1st, 2nd and 3rd Parachute Battalions, to be supported on FUSTIAN by 1st Airlanding Anti-Tank Battery RA less one troop of its 6-pounders. In addition, it possessed its own organic engineer and medical support in the form of 1st Parachute Squadron RE, less one troop, and 16th Parachute Field Ambulance.

In addition, there were a number of smaller units attached to the brigade for the operation, including detachments from the divisional pathfinder unit, 21st Independent Parachute Company, 38 pilots from 1st Battalion GPR, and the 4th Army Film and Photographic Section. Finally, and of major importance to the success of the operation, two parachute-trained naval bombardment teams and a forward observation party from 1st Airlanding Light Regiment RA would also accompany the brigade. These small, highly trained forward observer teams would provide the vital communication links for calling down artillery support from the guns of XIII Corps and, if also required, naval gunfire from a Royal Navy cruiser positioned off-shore. The total number of airborne troops dedicated to seizing the Ponte Primosole was close to 1,900 men.

A review of the detail of Operation FUSTIAN revealed that although apparently simple in concept, with less objectives and tasks than those allocated to 1st Airlanding Brigade for LADBROKE, in reality it was no less complicated. Although both plans centred on the primary objective of seizing river crossings, LADBROKE also called for the two gliderborne battalions to capture and hold a range of secondary objectives. After landing, the infantrymen of the South Staffordshires and the Borderers were required to disperse over a wide area in and around Syracuse in order to secure their objectives. Even if the landings had gone exceptionally well, this was a potentially risky plan that diluted the fighting power of 1st Airlanding Brigade and left the Ponte Grande bridgehead potentially vulnerable to a determined counter-attack.

In direct contrast to LADBROKE, the plan for FUSTIAN intended to keep the landing force concentrated on the primary objective once on the ground. Brigadier Lathbury's orders focused exclusively on taking a single objective by use of a mix of surprise, aggression and overwhelming force. This was exactly the type of task that had been envisaged for The Parachute Regiment on its formation less than a year earlier.

In order to reduce any risk of confusion and to prevent the overlap of DZs and LZs, 1st Parachute Brigade was allocated a total of six, the parachute element being spread across four separate DZs north and south of the river. The parachute drop would be followed by eight WACO and eleven Horsa gliders, the glider lift being allotted two LZs on to which the gliders would deliver the brigade's heavy equipment including the 6-pounder anti-tank guns of 1st Airlanding Anti-Tank Battery RA. The plan split the LZs and DZs evenly, three to the north of the bridge and three to the south.

The division of tasks dictated the allocation of DZs to each of the units. The key task of capturing and seizing the bridge, and holding it against counter-attack, was given to 1st Parachute Battalion under command of the redoubtable Lieutenant Colonel Alastair Pearson. In line with well-established military doctrine, the battalion was ordered to seize both ends of the bridge and thus was allocated DZs close to its objective on either side of the river. The northern DZ, located less than a mile to the north-west, was designated DZ 1, while the second was situated one-and-a-half-miles to the south-west and designated DZ 2.

The first, and therefore most critical phase, of the coup de main operation was entrusted by Lieutenant Colonel Pearson to T Company, reinforced by a platoon from R Company. The plan was well thought out, logical and designed to ensure that minimum time was wasted on the ground before assaulting the bridge.

The drop was planned for 2000 hours. Immediately after landing on DZ 1, while the majority of the men of T Company were gathering in their supply containers, a single rifle platoon and a section of sappers were to race straight for the northern end of the Ponte Primosole. At the same time, on the southern side of the river, the R Company platoon was to regroup as quickly as possible and move at speed from DZ 2 to seize the southern end of the bridge. If all went as planned, both platoons would overwhelm the defences immediately, disable and remove any demolition charges prepared by the Italians, and await reinforcement by the main body of T Company.

At the same time as 1st Parachute Battalion was carrying out its task, two platoons from Lieutenant Colonel E.C. Yeldham's, 3rd Parachute Battalion would be jumping on to DZ 4, three miles north-west of the bridge. Its task was to attack an Italian anti-aircraft battery, assessed by Allied intelligence to consist of four guns, which posed a threat to the main parachute drop and the subsequent glider lift. The two platoons were ordered to knock out the guns before the second waves of parachute aircraft carrying the main force arrived over the DZs.

While the two platoons from 3rd Parachute Battalion were tackling the battery, the attack on the bridge by 1st Parachute Battalion should be close to completion. With the bridge captured, T Company was to establish defensive positions and await the arrival of the remainder of 1st Parachute Battalion. Within minutes of the bridge's capture and the silencing of the anti-aircraft guns, the second wave of parachutists was due to arrive over their DZs. Twenty minutes after the first drop, the balance of 1st Parachute Battalion were due to jump on to DZ 2, south-west of the bridge. Pearson's orders from Brigadier Lathbury were clear: immediately after rallying the battalion on DZ 2, he was to make straight for the bridge and quickly deploy his entire battalion in defence around it.

Ten minutes after the arrival of 1st Parachute Battalion, a third formation of USAAF transports would appear overhead, bringing the remainder of 3rd Parachute Battalion, which would join its two platoons that by then should have neutralised the anti-aircraft battery to the north of the bridge. Thereafter, the battalion was to establish a defensive screen a mile to the north of the bridge and hold off any enemy counter-attacks from the Catania garrison to the north.

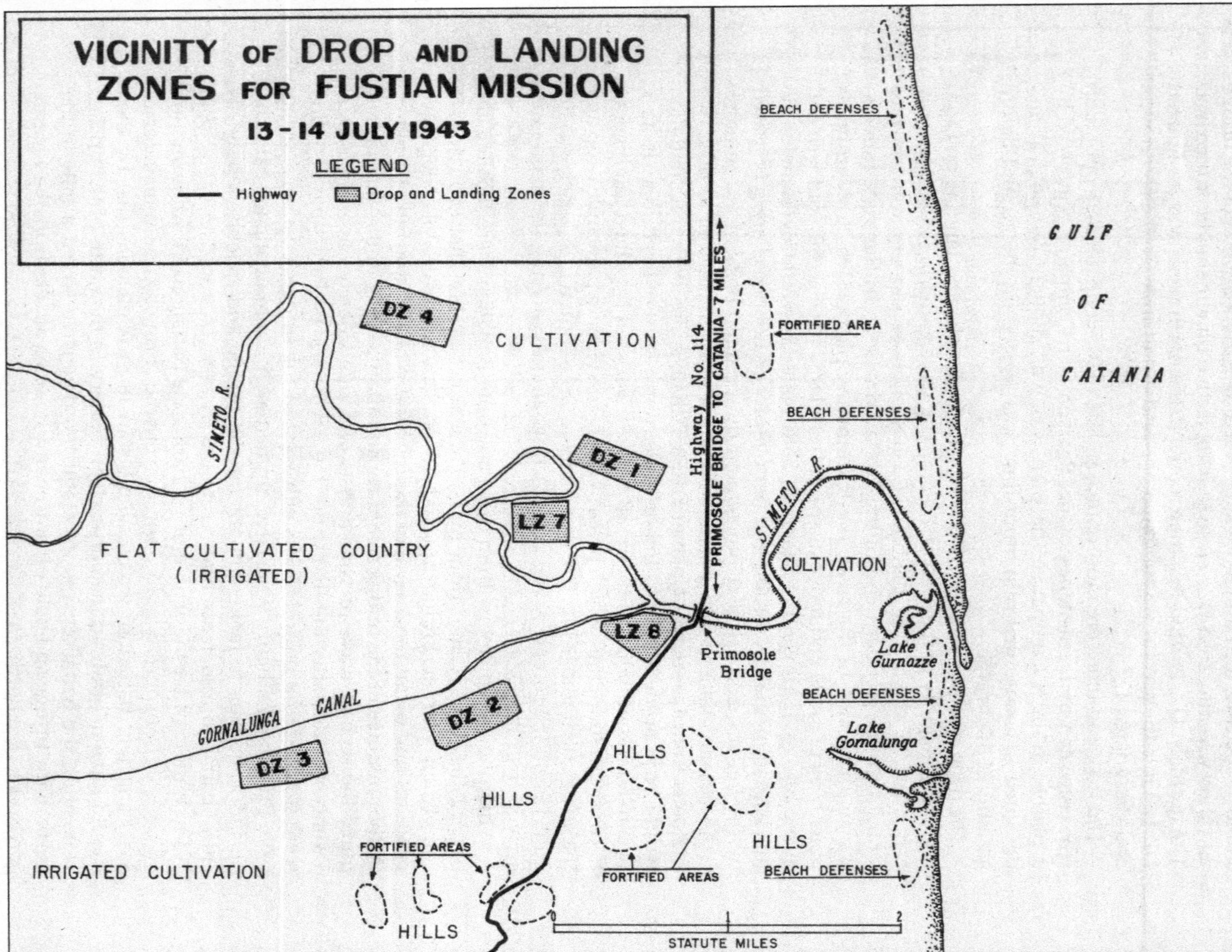
VICINITY OF DROP AND LANDING ZONES FOR FUSTIAN MISSION
13 - 14 JULY 1943
LEGEND
Highway
Drop and Landing Zones
GULF OF CATANIA
BEACH DEFENSES
FORTIFIED AREA
BEACH DEFENSES
Highway No. 114
PRIMOSOLE BRIDGE TO CATANIA - 7 MILES
CULTIVATION
DZ 4
DZ 1
LZ 7
LZ 8
DZ 2
DZ 3
SIMETO R.
SIMETO R.
CULTIVATION
FLAT CULTIVATED COUNTRY
(IRRIGATED)
Primosole Bridge
Lake Gurnazze
BEACH DEFENSES
Lake Gornalunga
GORNALUNGA CANAL
HILLS
HILLS
HILLS
HILLS
FORTIFIED AREAS
FORTIFIED AREAS
BEACH DEFENSES
IRRIGATED CULTIVATION
0
1
2
STATUTE MILES

The equally important task of defending the southern approach to the bridgehead was given to Lieutenant Colonel Johnny Frost and his 2nd Parachute Battalion. Frost's unit also included a core of experienced paratroopers who had not only fought in North Africa but had also played a central role in Operation BITING, the first-ever British coup de main raid in February 1942 in which, as mentioned earlier, the battalion's C Company, commanded by Frost at the time, attacked a German radar station at Bruneval, on the coast of northern France.

The FUSTIAN plan was very different to anything that Frost and his men had experienced previously. The 2nd Parachute Battalion task was similar in outline to that of 3rd Parachute Battalion to the north: having dropped on to DZ 3 three miles to the south-west of the bridge, it was to establish and maintain a robust defensive screen to the south of the bridgehead. There, however, any perceived similarity in execution and function ended; as Frost and his officers soon realised, they had been given a challenging task to complete over difficult terrain.

Analysis of maps and aerial reconnaissance photographs revealed that the area to south of the bridge was relatively hilly and that three areas of prominent high ground were occupied by Italian troops, allowing them to dominate the area to the south of the bridge. Further intelligence reports indicated that each of the three Italian positions was held by dug-in infantry of at least platoon strength, each believed to be supported with a mix of platoon and heavy weapons. Additional reports speculated that the objectives could also have been further reinforced with artillery batteries manned by a complement of some 200 gunners each.

The three hilltop positions were 2nd Parachute Battalion's objectives, and were codenamed Johnny I, II, and III. Whatever strength in which the Italians held the three hills, Frost knew that it was critical to the success of the operation that he and his battalion must clear the enemy out of every single position and drive them off the high ground. The mood in the battalion and amongst the rest of 1st Parachute Brigade remained generally optimistic, a feeling that was further reinforced by briefings on the poor quality of the Italian garrisons on their respective objectives. The anticipated advantages of initial surprise, the cover of darkness, superior training and raw Airborne aggression, imbued a confident spirit among them all.

In hindsight, this underlying optimism may well have coloured the judgement of those planning the Ponte Primosole drop. It has been argued that the allocation of just 30 minutes from P-Hour, the time when the first parachutist would exit the door of his aircraft, to the brigade being in possession of the bridge and pushing out into the approaches was completely unrealistic. However, this was intended to be a coup de main operation mounted by veteran airborne troops against what was expected to be poorly trained and low-grade enemy. In the initial minutes and first hours of what was intended to be a well-executed surprise attack, the initiative should rest with the aggressive attacking force. These were the assumptions under which Operation FUSTIAN was mounted.

Although confidence for the prospects for the success of the coup de main phase of the operation was high, the longer term predictions were less optimistic. Intelligence reports from Sicily indicated that in spite of losses, the Italian Army still retained a mobile counter-attack capability and, of even more concern, that there was German armour deployed on the island. It was the threat of the latter that had created the requirement in the FUSTIAN plan for the follow-up wave of gliders. The anti-tank capability of 1st Parachute Brigade was light and extremely limited, and in order to hold on to the bridgehead until the tanks of XIII Corps arrived, a heavier punch than the extremely short-range PIAT carried by the parachute battalions was required. The only way of delivering a heavier anti-tank capability into the bridgehead before the arrival of British Armour was by glider. Three four-gun troops of 6-pounder anti-tank guns from 1st Airlanding Anti-Tank Battery RA were thus included in the operation.

The glider lift was expected to deliver the guns and their crews on to two separate LZs inside the brigade perimeter. The areas for the gliders were identified as LZ 7, which was situated 2,000 yards west of the bridge, and LZ 8 that was situated just 500 yards to the south. The plan called for the gliders to release from their tugs at 500 feet from which they would make their approach to their respective LZs, each of which was to be marked out by pathfinders from 21st Independent Parachute Company using a green lamp for LZ 7 and an orange one for LZ 8.

Once on the ground, the 6-pounders were to be integrated into the brigade defence plan and deployed to create an in-depth anti-tank screen that would hopefully defeat any Italian or German counter-attack. The guns were dispersed between the parachute battalions, four being attached to 2nd Parachute Battalion to the south while six would be sited to the north with 3rd Parachute Battalion. The remaining two guns were to be held with their Jeeps and gunners at the brigade headquarters as a mobile reserve.

The Eighth Army plan predicted the arrival of XIII Corps at the bridge by midday on 14 July 1943, only twelve hours after the 1st Parachute Brigade drop. The presence of the twelve 6-pounders was believed to be a potent enough anti-tank force to shield the bridgehead for the critical time lapse between the drop and the arrival of XIII Corps from the south along the Augusta road. It was anticipated that, once on the ground, 1st Parachute Brigade would have to hold the bridge for a maximum period of twelve hours before British tanks arrived to relieve the bridgehead. If the plan was to succeed, and the men of 1st Parachute Brigade were not to be overrun by enemy tanks, it was crucial that 1st Battalion GPR delivered the 6-pounders successfully.

Sergeant Wallace Mackenzie was earmarked to fly Horsa No. 128 into LZ 8, and recalled the joint crew briefings held with the RAF tug crews from 295 and 296 Squadrons:

> We had a briefing attended probably by about three-dozen of us, some Air Force, some Glider Pilots. Our objective was to land as close to the bridge as possible and to the south of it. Our guns were to provide protection against enemy armour for the paratroops and Airlanding troops. There was a simple model of the river and the bridge and an indication of where we were expected to land. Somebody had been taken on a flight over the area and reported that they had not been able to get a good look at the actual terrain, but they did not think that there were any obstacles placed there to interfere with glider landings. There was some discussion as to the wisdom of using the floodlight on the glider for landing and the general consensus was that it would make us sitting targets for small arms fire when we were close to the ground and effectively helpless. The general conclusion was that we should not use the lights. This was the only specific discussion about tactics that I recall. In retrospect I suppose that there was no discussion because nobody had ideas about the questions that we should ask. The only previous glider landing of any size had been the German capture of Crete a couple of years earlier which eventually captured the island after very heavy German casualties.[2]

The relative small scale of the Operation FUSTIAN glider lift was just within the lift capacity of 38 Wing RAF. Each of the nineteen gliders involved would have a RAF tug aircraft for the mission; in the aftermath of the Operation LADBROKE debacle, the glider crews and their passengers were in no mood to willingly take their chances with a USAAF tow. The decision to employ RAF tugs, although popular, however created a number of technical headaches for the tug crews and the pilots of the gliders that they would tow to Sicily.

Once again, the mixture of aircraft types employed by 38 Wing RAF had an effect with regard to operational range and, therefore, ability to deliver gliders to Sicily. There were not enough of the powerful four-engined Halifax bombers of 295 Squadron RAF available to tow all eleven of the FUSTIAN Horsa gliders, each of which, when fully laden, weighed in at a hefty 6,900 lbs. The shortfall in Halifax availability for the mission would thus have to be made up with Albemarles from 296 Squadron RAF.

The necessity of using the Albemarle created its own specific set of technical constraints over and above those already experienced on previous sorties to Sicily. The weight of a fully laden Horsa glider placed significant strain on the much less powerful twin-engined Albemarle. The only way to lighten the weight of the glider, and yet retain its full load carrying capacity, was to jettison the undercarriage. The decision was thus taken that the four Horsa gliders being towed by Albemarles would be modified before flight by removing the wire-locking that normally secured the undercarriage assembly to the fuselage. The crews of each of these Horsas were briefed that they had the option to jettison their undercarriage if they ran into problems at any point during the flight. If they elected to do so, thus reducing weight and drag, they would then land the aircraft as its designers had originally intended: using its heavily reinforced central skid.

The intricacies and hazards of landing a glider in occupied territory at night undoubtedly weighed on the minds of the crews selected for Operation FUSTIAN, as did the fate of their comrades on LADBROKE and the losses inflicted on the US 82nd Airborne Division by flak from Allied shipping and US anti-aircraft defences ashore. In light of the previous losses, the route for the operation was planned with extra care. The glider force would assemble with its 38 Wing RAF tugs at Strips 'E' and 'F' before taking off on its 400-mile flight to Ponte di Primosole. The first leg took the stream of glider-tug combinations to a rendezvous point over the Kuriate Islands east of Sousse. Thereafter, the route passed over the south-east corner of Malta and then across to the south-east corner of Sicily itself. Five miles offshore, each combination was to turn north and follow the coastline, passing Syracuse and Augusta on the port side. The final turning point before the run-in to the release point was at the mouth of the River Simeto. Here the tugs were required to turn inland and track along the river, using its bends and the reflection of the moon on the water for reference and guidance to the release point. Once the tugs had released their gliders, each was then free to turn out south and east, climbing away from the release point, from 500 feet up to a band of height between 1,000 and 3,000 feet for the homeward journey.

Throughout D-1, great efforts were made to remove the risk of any repetition of the costly fratricide that had so tragically disrupted Operation HUSKY 2. Determined efforts were made to ensure that the Allied navies were aware of the airborne forces' approach route to Sicily, and of their planned exit route. Instructions were transmitted, warning all shipping of the presence of large numbers of friendly aircraft transiting through the naval aircraft exclusion zone, their planned altitude, and the timings of Operation FUSTIAN were circulated to all Allied naval commanders at sea. Both USAAF and RAF aircrews were also briefed on the boundaries of the ten-mile aircraft exclusion zone that was in place around the Allied fleet.

The delay in the launching of 1st Parachute Brigade allowed for the gathering of further intelligence, analysis of which revealed that the Italian anti-aircraft defences had been reinforced in the vicinity of the objective. A pre-mission bombing raid to suppress flak positions in and around the bridge was considered but then ruled out on the grounds that a pre-emptive raid would alert the Italians to the possibility of an imminent airborne assault. Diversionary bombing raids or attacks by ground attack aircraft were also ruled out due to a lack of available aircraft. There was an overriding concern that any pre-emptive strike would remove the element of surprise and therefore compromise the parachute drop. Intelligence reports from Sicily also speculated further as to the potential presence of Italian and German armour lurking within striking distance of Catania and the Ponte Primosole.

After several days of fighting, the enemy were well aware of the Allied lines of advance on both sides of the island. The Eighth Army's intention of continuing its drive north along the eastern coast through Catania and on to Messina was now obvious. Moreover, the coastal plain along which the British were advancing was overlooked and dominated by high ground, while also divided by a series of rivers that made ideal obstacles and ready-made lines of defence for the defenders. By 13 July, in spite of some dogged defence on the part of the Germans and Italians, the lead elements of XIII Corps were still moving relentlessly closer to Catania and it appeared to Allied and Axis planners to be only a matter of time before British tanks would be entering the city. Meanwhile, Italian commanders estimated that XIII Corps was just 24 hours from the Ponte Primosole. If the bridge was captured, thousands of withdrawing Italian and German troops would be cut off and captured in the south. The Italian assessment of the imminent British threat triggered the reinforcement by German troops of the thinly spread Italian forces in the area of the River Simeto.

Unknown to the Allies, enemy strategy for the defence of the island would only depend on the island's existing German forces for a few more hours, as the Oberkommando Wehrmacht (OKW) was about to intervene dramatically in Sicily. While Allied attention was focused on the advance inland from the landing beaches, far from view German strategic reserves were preparing to come to the aid of the island's beleaguered garrison.

On airfields in the south of France, German airborne forces in the form of Fliegerkorps IX were held as a potent mobile reserve. This was a formation built around two divisions of veteran Fallschirmjäger, many of whom had extensive combat experience of the blitzkrieg campaigns of 1940, the airborne assault on Crete and, most recently, of the Eastern Front.

Since its arrival in France, the 30,000 strong Fliegerkorps IX had been undergoing a programme of refit and reinforcement, steadily absorbing drafts of replacements from Germany. Its commander, Generalleutnant Kurt Student, was desperate to regain favour with Adolf Hitler and revitalise the fortunes of the Luftwaffe's airborne forces. Once ranked among the favoured elite of the German military by Hitler, the reputation of the Fallschirmjäger had waned dramatically following the heavy losses incurred during the German invasion of Crete. Hitler no longer saw any future in the large-scale use of airborne forces, a view contradictory to that held by Allied commanders and General Student himself.

Dismissed from Hitler's inner circle, Student had languished in reserve with his troops in France, kicking his heels while trying to find a way back into favour in Berlin. News of the Allied landings on Sicily seemed just the opportunity for glory and redemption that he was seeking. Pushing hard for an immediate airborne counter-attack, he argued forcefully for a parachute drop of 3,000 Fallschirmjäger on Sicily just 24 hours after Operation LADBROKE. Much to his frustration, however, his proposal was ruled out as both too hasty and dangerous by the OKW.

The Fallschirmjäger would, however, have their day on Sicily. At midnight, on the same evening as the rejection of Student's hasty plan, Generalmajor Richard Heidrich, a veteran of Crete and the siege of Leningrad, and the commander of 1. Fallschirmjäger-Division, was summoned to his headquarters near Avignon where he was ordered to report directly to Feldmarschall Albert Kesselring in Rome. On arrival in the Italian capital, he received verbal orders directly from the senior German commander in Italy that he and his division were to deploy to Sicily. The next morning, if any further indication of the gravity of the situation was needed, further orders came to Heidrich, this time from Berlin and from Reichsmarschall Hermann Göring himself. Desperate to gain favour with Hitler, and also to ensure that his Luftwaffe formations regained a prominent position in the Führer's thinking, Göring intervened directly in the developing Sicily situation and ordered the immediate despatch of one Fallschirmjäger regiment to reinforce the hard-pressed Luftwaffe division in Sicily that bore his name.

The German plan for the immediate reinforcement of Sicily involved the bulk of 1. Fallschirmjäger-Division, the operation being spearheaded by Fallschirmjäger-Regiment 3, a recently reinforced formation commanded by one of the most colourful of the German airborne commanders: the bulldog-faced, cigar smoking Oberstleutnant 'King Ludwig' Heilmann. Once the first wave of Heilmann's Fallschirmjäger was established on the ground, they were to be followed on to the DZ by a machine gun battalion and a signal company. A third wave consisting of combat engineers and anti-tank gunners would then arrive, providing Heilmann with a powerful force with which to hold the German bridgehead. Finally, the balance of 1. Fallschirmjäger-Division, in the shape of Fallschirmjäger-Regiments 1 and 4, would be dropped. Heilmann issued his warning orders quickly, and on Luftwaffe airfields across southern France, Fallschirmjäger units and Luftwaffe aircrews busied themselves preparing for a drop on a still unknown DZ somewhere in Sicily.

Close to midnight on 11 July 1943, the night originally planned for Operation FUSTIAN, Oberstleutnant Heilmann was summoned to a telephone to receive a call from Lieutenant General Heidrich. The conversation between the two veterans was short and business like:

> You will personally reconnoitre the landing zone. The Field Marshal will provide you with a swift combat aircraft, start at 0500 hours in the morning. Conduct yourself according to the situation. We ourselves don't know what is going on over there. Good Luck![3]

Before first light on the morning of 12 July 1943 a small reconnaissance party led by Heilmann took off from Avignon on a non-stop flight to Sicily. The regimental commander chose just two officers to accompany him on the flight: Hauptmann Franz Stangenberg and his logistics officer, Hauptmann Sprecht. The flight from France passed uneventfully until Heilmann's aircraft approached Catania. Close in to the island, he saw that the city was under Allied air attack with thick columns of black smoke rising above it. More worrying though for Heilmann and his companions, however, was the sight of RAF Spitfires circling menacingly like predatory hawks overhead. Their Luftwaffe pilot was, however, aware of the lurking threat and, employing great skill and a considerable amount of courage, flew his aircraft into Sicily at low-level. Oberstleutnant Heilmann later described the pilot's skill and use of terrain as almost infantryman-like. By following contours and using the valleys around Mount Etna to avoid interception, the lone German aircraft avoided interception and landed safely at Catania airfield.

Almost immediately after disembarking from their aircraft, the reconnaissance group set about their business. Time was short as Heilmann and Hauptmann Stangenberg set off to identify DZs and LZs to the south of Catania while Hauptmann Sprecht was despatched into Catania to commandeer whatever transport he could to move the Fallschirmjäger off their LZs and up to the town of Lentini where Oberstleutnant Heilmann stated that they would be required. With just hours before the drop was due in later that day, all three men were pressed for time and set about their respective tasks with urgency.

While Hauptmann Sprecht scoured Catania for vehicles, the two-man DZ reconnaissance party took its chances moving across Catania amid Allied air raids. Eventually, after being forced to take cover more than once, they were finally clear of the airfield and the town. With time slipping away and the take-off time for the German lift looming, they settled on an open area to the east of Route 114. The DZ they selected was thought to be easy to identify from the air as it was bounded on each side by the Gornalunga and Simeto water courses. This ideal DZ was in fact, just a few hundred metres north of the equally ideal DZ selected for Lieutenant Colonel Johnny Frost and his 2nd Parachute Battalion. History would suggest that both men had a similar eye for a good drop zone. With the DZ identified, Stangenberg had little time to transmit map co-ordinates and approach details to the transport crews on the airfields in Southern France. The German drop had been carefully timed to slip through Allied air defences in the half-light of early evening, before darkness settled, as observers on Sicily had noticed that the majority of Allied fighters returned to their bases in North Africa and Malta before last light. There was thus a fleeting window of opportunity for the Luftwaffe to deliver Fallschirmjäger-Regiment 3 on to Sicily if it could take off on time.

Stangenberg made his telephone call to France with just minutes to spare, passing on the vital DZ information. The reinforcement drop was now on. The run-in to Sicily did not pass without incident, however, and for a few moments it must have appeared that disaster was imminent. As the German formation approached the port of Messina, it was intercepted by 20 USAAF P-38 Lightning fighters. Luckily for the Germans in their very vulnerable Ju-52 transport aircraft, the American fighters were heading for home after a long patrol and therefore had little fuel left in their tanks. They were thus forced to break off their attack and allow the Germans to press on southwards.

The arrival of 1. Fallschirmjäger-Division on Sicily passed unnoticed by the Allied air forces and the Eighth Army. At 1800 hours on 12 July 1943, Oberstleutnant Heilmann and his two companions lit bonfires to mark out their hastily selected DZ. Almost miraculously the seemingly ever-present Allied fighters, that they had observed loitering overhead for the entire day, disappeared as they returned to their home airfields and thus the skies over Catania were clear. Shortly afterwards, the first wave of the German lift appeared on the horizon to the north. Unescorted by Luftwaffe fighters, the Heinkel 111s and Junkers Ju 52s carrying the 1,400 men of Fallschirmjäger-Regiment 3 made a textbook run-in to the DZ. The German gamble had paid off. Aside from a few injuries caused by the rocky surface of the DZ, there were no casualties among the Fallschirmjäger and none of the transport aircraft were lost. Within 45 minutes of the drop, the newly arrived reinforcements were married up with the vehicles requisitioned by Hauptmann Sprecht and on their way to Lentini and Vizzini to join the hard-pressed Hermann Göring Division in the frontline.

On the following day, the Luftwaffe gambled again and attempted to airland 1. Fallschirmjäger-Division's machine gun battalion, along with its signals and anti-tank companies, at the airfield at Catania. This time, however, luck deserted the Fallschirmjäger as from the outset the operation was plagued with bad luck. This second lift included a number of massive Messerschmitt Me 321 Gigant transports. While still in southern France, a number of Me 321s carrying anti-tank weapons and their crews crashed on take-off, killing all on board. As the mission progressed toward Sicily, more of them crashed en route, reducing the anti-tank company's strength further. On arrival at Catania, the German formation flew into the middle of an Allied bombing raid and incurred yet more losses. Having finally landed safely, two of the huge aircraft, still loaded with anti-tank guns, were then destroyed by Allied bombs on the ground.

Fallschirm-Maschinengewehr-Bataillon 1 meanwhile had much better luck, its aircraft arriving on the airfield without losses and landing safely. Once on the ground, the battalion's commanding officer, Major Schmidt, set off immediately by vehicle to find Oberstleutnant Heilmann's command post in Carlentini. Meanwhile, the battalion moved off the airfield led by its second in-command, Hauptmann Laun, whose orders were to move the battalion to a holding position 2,000 metres south of the Primosole Bridge where he was to prepare for battle and await orders. On reaching the Fallschirmjäger-Regiment 3 command post near Carlentini, Schmidt received his orders from Oberstleutnant Heilmann. At the conclusion of the briefing, the latter made the following comment to his subordinate:

> Something is bound to happen tonight. The enemy will try to sneak through to the Catania Plain, and to do so he'll send in more troops –

> either by sea or by air. If he manages to land them in our rear and to dig in, then we're cut off for sure. So your battalion will remain south of Catania. Hold the bridge over the Simeto and put one company between there and the sea.[4]

Heilmann had made a sound appreciation of the situation on Sicily, his insight and experience telling him that the Ponte Primosole Bridge was vitally important to the German position on the island. He was determined to do all that he could to hold on to it, and the positioning of such a powerful unit as his machine gun battalion was an indication of his intentions. The presence of such formidable opposition so close to the Ponte Primosole would be an unexpected and extremely unpleasant surprise for Brigadier Gerald Lathbury and 1st Parachute Brigade.

Notes

1. Mackenzie, Sergeant, W., 1 Squadron, 1st Battalion GPR, correspondence with the Author dated 26 May 2010.
2. Mackenzie, Sergeant, W., 1 Squadron, 1st Battalion GPR, correspondence with the Author dated 26 May 2010.
3. Heilmann, Major General, L., Commander 1 FJR, *Fallschirmjäger auf Sizilien*, 1959
4. *British Army Review*, April 1985.

Chapter 15

Red Devils Over Etna

The odd glider came in almost silently. One caught in a searchlight was riddled with machine-gun fire and crashed against the bund.

At 1935 hours on the 13 July 1943, ten minutes earlier than planned, and just a few short hours after the last of Major Schmidt's Fallschirmjäger machine gunners had marched away from the Catania airfield, the first wave of the 51st Troop Carrier Wing transports carrying 1st Parachute Brigade began taking off from their North African airstrips. The follow-up glider lift was planned to take off at 2200 hours later that night.

Operation FUSTIAN got off to a good start. On the airfields, the USAAF ground crews were well organised and efficient, and the loading and marshalling of the parachute battalions' C-47s went without any incident worthy of note. The brigade was spread between a fleet of dedicated parachute transports: 105 C-47s provided by 51st Troop Carrier Wing, the 60th and 62nd Troop Carrier Groups each providing 51 aircraft while another three came from the 64th Group. This impressive force was further augmented with seven Halifaxes from 295 Squadron RAF and twelve Albemarles from 296 Squadron RAF. Lieutenant Colonel Johnny Frost later gave a personal account on the final hours before the operation from a 2nd Parachute Battalion point of view:

> On the 13th we again embussed and drove to the airfield. There were no hitches, delays or troubles. We had such excellent relations with the Americans that one felt that nothing could go wrong. The weather was perfect and at 7.30 pm the battalion began to take off. A Company and part of Battalion Headquarters were being flown by one of the best squadrons. This squadron had always managed to drop us accurately on the exercises we had done before, and their commander was confident that he could do likewise in Sicily.[1]

The air-assembly phase of the operation also went relatively well. Steadily, one by one, the USAAF and RAF squadrons lifted from their airstrips, circled and formed up into their holding formations.

While the parachute lift assembled in the air, the glider force was going through its final pre-flight checks on the ground. The eight WACOs and eleven Horsas were now loaded with a total of ten 6-pounder anti-tank guns, eighteen Jeeps, and 77 gunners of 1st Airlanding Anti-Tank Battery RA, the number of guns less than planned originally.

There were a small number of aircraft serviceability problems spread between the parachute and glider waves. A C-47 returned to the ground immediately after take-off and was replaced with a reserve aircraft. More seriously, a Halifax tug became unserviceable before take-off and had to be replaced on the runway with a stand-by Albemarle. In addition, the glider fleet also suffered some problems, with take-off accidents and a control failure on one glider removing two WACOs and a single Horsa from the lift plan. Nevertheless, these incidents did not affect the flow of aircraft from the mounting airfields, and each serial was airborne within 45 minutes.

Echelons of aircraft formated on each other below 1,000 feet, then climbed and turned on to the initial heading, setting out as planned across the Mediterranean on the same heading as used in Operation LADBROKE. Each aircraft type cruised at different speeds across the sea, the C-47s flying at 140 mph, the Albemarle tugs at 125 mph and, finally, the heavier Halifaxes at 145 mph. The lift was exactly on schedule as it headed out to sea toward Malta in good weather. As planned, the sun set before the lead aircraft reached Malta so the remaining legs of the flight would be made through what was a hazy night illuminated by the light of a bright half-moon. Navigation conditions were far better than they had been for LADBROKE but many of the very inexperienced USAAF navigators struggled to maintain an accurate fix on their position.

Only two aircraft, one C-47 and a lone Albemarle, turned back before Malta, both with engine trouble. As the remainder of the formation flew on, untroubled by weather and holding good formation, the crews and the sticks of paratroopers they carried must have begun to feel that the initial good omens on the airstrips were holding true. Surely this was not going to be a repetition of the disastrous Syracuse landing that they had all heard so much about.

It was as each formation approached Malta that the navigators on board each aircraft were forced to concentrate on fixing their positions. From a location five miles south-east of Delimara Point, each echelon had to follow an overly complex five-point course designed to maintain a ten-mile safety buffer between the aerial armada and the enemy defences on the Sicilian coast. All formation leaders were ordered to follow this course until they reached a turning point opposite the mouth of the River Simeto.

Any feeling of optimism present in the darkness was soon dashed as the 1st Parachute Brigade lift slowly turned and began a 40-mile approach to the Sicilian coast at Cap Passero. Elements of the USAAF formation drifted off course and strayed into the naval aircraft exclusion zone; tragically this occurred shortly after the ships below had received a warning of an

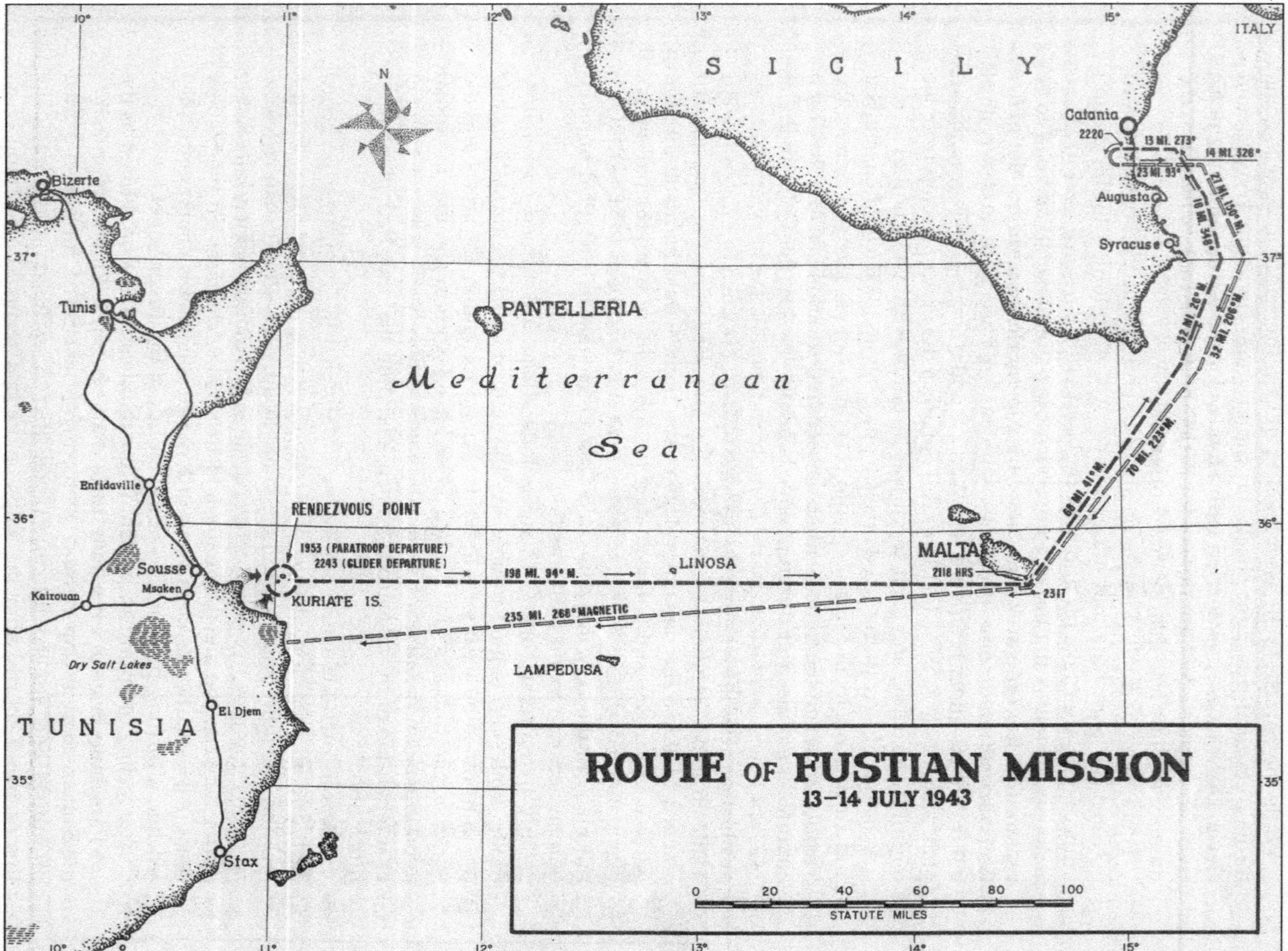
ROUTE OF FUSTIAN MISSION
13–14 JULY 1943
SICILY
ITALY
Catania
2220
13 MI. 273°
14 MI. 326°
23 MI. 93°
27 MI. 150° M.
18 MI. 348°
Augusta
Syracuse
32 MI. 26° M.
32 MI. 206° M.
70 MI. 225° M.
68 MI. 41° M.
MALTA
2118 HRS
2317
LINOSA
LAMPEDUSA
PANTELLERIA
Mediterranean
Sea
RENDEZVOUS POINT
1953 (PARATROOP DEPARTURE)
2243 (GLIDER DEPARTURE)
198 MI. 94° M.
235 MI. 268° MAGNETIC
KURIATE IS.
Bizerte
Tunis
Enfidaville
Sousse
Msaken
Kairouan
Dry Salt Lakes
El Djem
Sfax
TUNISIA
N
0
20
40
60
80
100
STATUTE MILES

incoming German air attack. Almost predictably, in a tragic repeat of the episode that had engulfed Operation HUSKY 2, anti-aircraft gunners among the naval fleet below opened fire on the slow-moving C-47s packed with helpless paratroopers. What began initially as a flurry of isolated fire spread rapidly and developed into another ferocious and seemingly uncontrollable fleet-wide barrage of flak.

The anti-aircraft fire hit two C-47s that plunged into the sea in flames, killing all on board. Another nine aircraft were so badly damaged that they were forced to break formation and turn back toward Malta or North Africa; in addition to damage to their airframes, they were carrying wounded aircrew and paratroopers hit by the flak. An additional six C-47s also turned back, claiming that they had heard their squadron commander give the order to abort the lift and return to base, a claim that was never substantiated. The losses mounted further when another two aircraft took evasive action and crashed into each other in mid-air before falling into the sea with no survivors.

The anti-aircraft fire out to sea again gave the Italian batteries on Sicily advanced warning of the approaching aircraft. As soon as the remainder flew into range, the Italians opened fire with every available gun. Committed to the final leg of the flight, the C-47s were forced to run another gauntlet of fire.

The barrage of flak punched yet more holes in the already depleted formation carrying 1st Parachute Brigade. Nine more C-47s were hit, falling out of formation and plunged earthwards in flames. The tight formations preferred by the USAAF for parachuting were now beginning to break up and disintegrate as individual pilots attempted to avoid flak and other wayward aircraft. The forced dependence of 51st Troop Carrier Wing on just a handful of experienced navigators was once again proving its undoing. Individual pilots, separated from their flight leaders, found themselves isolated and disorientated in enemy airspace. Each aircraft had its own story to tell, with one of the most remarkable accounts involving one of 1st Parachute Brigade's senior officers.

Lieutenant Colonel Alastair Pearson, the Commanding Officer of 1st Parachute Battalion, had managed to doze off in the rear of his C-47 during the flight across the Mediterranean. His aircraft had been untroubled by naval anti-aircraft fire but he was woken by a distinctive change in the note of the aircraft's engines; on looking out of the rear cabin window he was immediately aware that something was drastically wrong. The red volcanic glow of Mount Etna was clearly visible in the darkness out on the port side. Having studied the geography of Sicily in great detail for days before the mission, he realised that he and his men were well to the north of their DZ. Furthermore, the aircraft's position and heading indicated that it was flying even deeper into enemy territory than planned. He quickly surmised that this could mean only one thing: the two pilots flying the C-47 had either turned away from the DZ deliberately or were lost. Pearson got out of his seat, unbuckled his parachute and struggled quickly out of his equipment before heading purposefully towards the cockpit.

As the burly Scot went forward in the darkness, he stopped and asked one of his men, whom he knew to be a court-martialled ex-RAF pilot, whether he could fly a C-47. Having confirmed that the latter thought that he could do so, Pearson forged on to the cockpit where he was confronted with a scenario far worse than the simple navigational error he had initially anticipated. A few seconds passed during which he wasted no time in assessing the situation that confronted him in the half-light of the cockpit instruments. The Commanding Officer of 1st Parachute Battalion already had a well-earned reputation for being a no-nonsense, decisive commander who did not suffer fools lightly. True to his reputation, he took just a few seconds to arrive at a robust albeit, unorthodox solution. He later recounted the fraught minutes following his arrival in the cockpit and the reaction of the USAAF aircrew to his presence:

> His co-pilot was sitting with his hands over his face, crying, 'We can't, we can't!'
>
> 'Can't do what?' I said.
>
> 'We can't go in there!'
>
> I could see quite clearly blobs of fire. I knew what was going through his mind, it was going through mine as well, because on the ground were what I thought were burning Dakotas. I said to the pilot 'There's nothing for it old boy, we've got to do it. If your co-pilot's no good, I've no hesitation in shooting him.' I pulled out my revolver.
>
> The pilot continued with his protests, so I said, 'Don't worry about that, I've got a bloke in the back who can fly this.'
>
> He replied, 'Yeah, but he won't know how to land it!'
>
> I said, 'No one has asked him to land the bloody thing – you don't think he's going to hang about to land it, do you? He'll be stepping out very sharp!'[2]

Faced with Pearson's uncompromising ultimatum and a loaded revolver, and realizing that the irate lieutenant colonel meant every word of what he said, the two pilots realised that their chances of survival were greater flying through the flak that surrounded the DZ than if they refused to do so.

The C-47 changed heading and began a flak-buffeted run inland toward the Ponte Primosole DZ. Pearson had just enough time to refit his parachute and equipment before the order to stand up was given. The tunnel-like darkness inside the aircraft was now dimly lit by the crew chief's red warning light next to the door, the intermittent flashes of flak, and the longer burning glow of parachute flares fired by the Italians below. In a scene replicated in every C-47 over the DZ, paratroopers went through their well-practised and almost instinctive drill of checking each other's equipment.

Once satisfied, each soldier hooked his static line to the cable running down the central spine of the cabin, and made one final check before fixing his eyes on the open door and the all important glow of the red light by the door.

At this point Lieutenant Colonel Pearson was looking out of the open door checking the position and track of the C-47. He was only reassured that both were correct when he recognised the distinctive loop of the River Simeto and his battalion's objective, the Ponte Primosole. However, he and his fellow stick members were by no means home and dry yet, as they still had to survive the drop. Just before the green jump light was switched on by the pilot, giving the signal for Pearson and his men to exit the aircraft, the C-47 began a nose-down approach towards the DZ. This was deliberate and expected by the paratroops as the nose-down attitude raised the tail of the aircraft, giving them a clear path as they fell away from it.

As during Operation LADBROKE, the execution of this critical delivery phase of the 1st Parachute Brigade drop varied dramatically between squadrons, flights and even individual aircraft. The 1st Parachute Battalion drop was particularly badly disrupted, and the fate of Lieutenant Colonel Pearson's stick was typical on the night. As soon as the eagerly anticipated green light flashed on, he and his men instantly began exiting the aircraft as quickly as possible, exactly as they had been trained. Unfortunately, the pilot of their aircraft had miscalculated his height on his approach to the DZ with the result that the drop had been made at too low an altitude. Most of the parachutes had barely deployed and their canopies filled with air before the paratroops hit the ground at perilous speed. A number were injured or at best winded and bruised. Tragically, by the time that the last member of the stick had exited the aircraft, it was well below the recognised safe jumping altitude and consequently his parachute had barely deployed. Tragically, he was killed outright on landing.

The scattering of elements of the formation by flak and navigation problems inevitably squandered any prospect of a concentrated drop with even the slightest element of surprise. Aircraft arrived from all directions, at varying heights and at different times. Before the first parachutes opened, the Italian and German defences were alerted and their gunners stood to their weapons. Those paratroops who did jump on to Ponte Primosole were greeted by prolonged bursts of machine gun fire marked out in the darkness by menacing arcs of tracer racing up from the ground toward them as they hung helplessly below the canopies of their parachutes. With the whole sorry scene illuminated by flares, casualties were heavy and many of Brigadier Gerald Lathbury's veterans were dead before they touched the ground.

The chaos and confusion in the air and in the cockpits of the C-47s was transmitted to the paratroops themselves, with many of the sticks in turn scattered on the ground because they had been prevented from exiting the door of the aircraft swiftly with the minimal interval between individuals. Any violent manoeuvre carried out by the pilot in an attempt to avoid flak or another aircraft resulted in additional chaos in the rear of his aircraft.

Heavily laden paratroops standing up in line and ready to jump could do little to prevent themselves from falling over and even less to right themselves and regain their position in their stick. Consequently, individuals struggled to get to their feet and jumped from their aircraft whenever they could, resulting in single paratroopers or fragmented groups, rather than formed sticks, being scattered far and wide. Some members of 1st Parachute Brigade landed as far afield as the slopes of Mount Etna itself.

Analysis after the operation would reveal that less than 20 per cent of the 1,856 paratroops that began Operation FUSTIAN were actually dropped on their correct DZ. Closer scrutiny revealed that the percentage was made up of twelve officers and 283 soldiers. Much of that total was drawn from 2nd Parachute Battalion, where it would seem that Lieutenant Colonel Johnny Frost's faith in his favoured USAAF transport squadron had been well placed:

> Our flight went exactly to plan. Later I learned that some of the other squadrons had flown over the Navy and had been fired upon. This had caused considerable confusion so that several aircraft became dispersed and a number were actually shot down. We, however, saw none of this. At the expected time we turned westwards towards Sicily and headed to what was obviously a fully alerted defence. From the door and the windows of the aircraft we could see streams of tracer moving upwards. A number of fires were burning on the ground and smoke was rising from several other places. I could glimpse the mouth of the river and the high ground to the south of it. Our aircraft flew steadily on. Our gum chewing crew chief ordered us to our various stages of readiness, the aircraft throttled back to the recognised best parachuting speed, and despite distractions from the ground we were all duly dispatched to our duties down below.[3]

The 1st Parachute Brigade plan included one additional new safeguard that had been omitted from that of Operation LADBROKE. It made provision for pathfinders to mark the glider LZs and thus saw the first ever use in action of specially trained and equipped pathfinder troops by British airborne forces. In among the sticks of paratroopers set to jump into the darkness were six members of Major John Lander's 21st Independent Parachute Company. Their orders were to make their way to the southern glider LZ and on arrival set up a Eureka beacon that would guide the 38 Wing RAF tugs to a release point within sight of the bridge and the LZ. The FUSTIAN plan allowed the parachute force two hours on the ground before the glider stream was due to appear overhead. During this time, elements of the parachute battalions were to ensure that the LZs were secure while the pathfinders set up their Eureka. Once cast off from its tug, each glider would lose the course corrections provided by the Eureka via the tug aircraft's Rebecca receiver. In order to keep the gliders on track for the LZ, the pathfinders would mark the LZ using flares to create a rudimentary flare path for the incoming aircraft. However, the pathfinder plan depended on one critical factor: the pathfinders themselves had to be dropped on, or close to, the objective to stand a chance of carrying out their task.

The six-man pathfinder team was in the same position as everyone else to be dropped that night: entirely at the mercy of the aircrew that delivered them to its designated DZ. It suffered a similar fate, being scattered far and wide. The two-man team tasked with operating the Eureka was dropped more than eight miles from its intended DZ but this, however, was the least of their concerns. Both men had been ordered to jump at a height of 200 feet and this resulted in both being knocked unconscious on landing and, critically, their Eureka being wrecked. Even if they had been uninjured and had been able to reach the glider LZ, the beacon was useless. After regaining consciousness, the two pathfinders joined up with stragglers from 3rd Parachute Battalion and made their way toward the bridgehead, attacking and ambushing Italian troops at every opportunity en route.

The remainder of the pathfinder team, carrying the flares to mark the LZ, were dropped on the correct DZ but, due to navigational errors, 90 minutes late and thus well after the bulk of the brigade. The team decided that there was now no point in setting up the flare beacons and thus also joined up with the main force heading for the bridge. The failure to deliver the pathfinders either on time or on to the correct DZ left the incoming tug and glider crews to find their own way to the LZ. This was not the start that the men of 21st Independent Parachute Company wanted for their newly formed unit. Disappointment at the failure to mark the Simeto LZ was further heightened by the loss of the company commander on the operation. Major John Lander had flown as a passenger on one of the RAF tugs to see for himself how well his men marked the LZs. Tragically, the aircraft in which he was travelling was shot down and he was killed.

Meanwhile, unaware of the chaos ahead of them in the air, and below them on the ground, the glider lift was airborne and heading for what would now be an unmarked LZ. Sergeant Wallace Mackenzie's flight in Glider 128 had gone well so far:

> We had an easy flight to Sicily, after a hectic take-off through the dust, flying almost directly over Malta at the halfway point. There were some bright patches of moonlight on the journey and our tug pilots took us into exactly the spot where we needed to be. We could at this stage see the bridge and the shape of the river.[4]

Squadron Sergeant Major Walter 'Wally' Atkinson and Staff Sergeant Terence Montague were also in the glider stream, flying a WACO numbered 118B and towed by an Albemarle from 296 Squadron RAF. Their load comprised a Jeep and crew from the headquarters of 1st Airlanding Anti-Tank Battery

RA and an Army Film Unit cameraman. Sergeant Major Atkinson survived the war to tell the tale, while 21-year old Staff Sergeant Montague was later killed on Sicily. This account, given post-war by Sergeant Major Atkinson, gives some idea of conditions on the night and what the glider pilots had been briefed to expect to see from the pathfinders deployed on the glider LZ:

> At last we were ready to begin the run in to the landing zone. We climbed to 1,000 feet and began the run in, losing height again until we were at 500 feet. We had been told at the briefing that a pathfinder force of the 21st Independent Parachute Company would have dropped flares to lay out a skeleton flare path for us, but the lights on the landing zone were much too brilliant for flares; they included several searchlights and the odd machine gun, with light ack-ack for good measure. By this time we were over the area and could see numerous fires which seemed to be placed at uniform intervals. Having seen photographs of our particular landing zone, which showed the field to be corn or hay, and as our intelligence had assured us that the only opposition we were likely to encounter would be from the local Home Guard, we were perhaps just a little doubtful whether we were in the right area, or even in the right country! The air around us was getting quite warm; one burst of small arms fire had passed between the cockpit and the passengers and, as we later discovered, made rather a mess of the undercarriage and fuselage and the left front wheel of the Jeep.[5]

The ferocity of the anti-aircraft fire thrown up on the night by the Italians is commented on in almost every account recorded by FUSTIAN survivors. Squadron Leader Peter Davis of 296 Squadron RAF towed Lieutenant Bill Barrie and his second pilot, Sergeant Ivor Williams, in Glider 120 over to Sicily. On his return and after safely landing his Albemarle back in North Africa, he made the following entry in his personal diary:

> Target area one raging battle, never seen such a sight, fires, flares, flak of all sorts, searchlights – only needed Mount Etna to blow off to make it complete. Felt sorry for Bill Barrie. We escaped with a lot of loud bangs and one small hole under the wing. Do not like being fired at on tow.[6]

The post-mission report filed by Lieutenant Bill Barrie for Glider 120 gives an account of the sortie from the other end of the tow rope. His report reads:

> Good tow. Tow rope broke when circling and looking for LZ 7 at 0107 hours at 1,600 feet. Glider made successful landing 2,000 feet west of LZ 8. Landed on skid. Gun and Jeep OK, unloaded in three hours. Intercom OK up to coast, but very weak after that.[7]

The length of time taken to release the tail unit off the Horsa and extract a Jeep and gun is notable. Three hours of hard physical effort before a battle-winning asset like a 6-pounder anti-tank gun can be brought into play is far from ideal in any scenario; it is even less so on a coup de main operation. Nevertheless, after a great deal of sweat, brute force and colourful language, Lieutenant Barrie's load was eventually extracted from Glider 120 and brought into action that night.

The problems and delays encountered in unloading Jeeps and guns from the Horsa gliders used on both Sicily operations were attributed to a combination of factors of which twisting and crumpling of glider fuselages during rough landings was certainly the most significant. Crumpling could be aggravated further by choosing to land on the glider's skid rather than the undercarriage. If, after coming to a halt, the glider came to rest at an odd angle, leaning on one wing tip or the other, in the case of a skid landing; or, as in the case of Staff Sergeant Dennis Galpin's Horsa, when the nose wheel has broken off on landing and the aircraft has adopted a nose down-tail up attitude, removing the tail unit and unloading guns and Jeeps was problematical. Many glider pilots also commented on the lack of practice that they were given in this drill and on the fact that training aircraft used for practice were well worn and had easily removable bolts and tail units. Examination of the post-operational reports reveals a wide spectrum of time taken to unload gliders on both operations. The reports for Operation FUSTIAN record times between 30 minutes to unload a Jeep and its 6-pounder gun, to nine-hours to extract a single Jeep. In most cases there was judicious use of the axe provided for use by passengers to create emergency exits in the glider fuselage when ditching at sea.

Not every glider-tug combination was blessed with the same good luck that Squadron Leader Peter Davis experienced with Glider 120. Flight Lieutenant Geoffrey 'Buster' Briggs was the second-in-command of the twelve Halifaxes that formed A Flight of 295 Squadron RAF. He flew on Operation FUSTIAN at the controls of Halifax 'R for Robert', towing Glider 124. Already a highly experienced pilot, he was also a veteran of Operation Turkey Buzzard. He and his crew were towing a Horsa glider flown by 27-year old Squadron Sergeant Major John Preston from Slough in Buckinghamshire, whose second pilot was 26-year old Sergeant John M. Broadhead from Sheffield in Yorkshire. The load for the Horsa was made up of a 6-pounder gun and Jeep with six gunners from D Troop of 1st Airlanding Anti-Tank Battery RA.

Halifax R for Robert had taken off late, at the second attempt, from Airfield E at Goubrine No. 1. The first take-off had failed when the towrope snapped shortly after the combination began its take-off run. Having replaced it, Buster Briggs was eventually successful in getting the heavily laden pair of aircraft off the ground. Having finally climbed out of its self-generated dust storm, the combination joined the tail end of the stream of tugs and gliders heading for Sicily. The two glider pilots had been briefed to put their glider down on LZ 8 on the Catania Plain. Buster Briggs takes up the story of Glider 124:

> The flight to Sicily took about three hours. We were briefed to fly at about 1,500 feet, but owing to the barrage balloons flying from ships at sea, we climbed to about 2,500 feet for safety. It was a clear night and the lights and flak were visible several miles away. Over to the starboard as we approached Catania Mount Etna glowed red, all very wonderful. Of course there were many aircraft around all invisible in the darkness.
>
> My navigator, Bob Seyman, was very experienced and took us straight towards the Landing Zone near Catania ... As we approached the enemy coast there was heavy flak and my Halifax shook several times. Suddenly the glider pilot, Sergeant Major Preston, called me down the tow rope telephone cable to say that they had been badly hit, that the Horsa was 'like a sieve' and that they had lots of wounded. I offered to tow them back to Tunisia as I had plenty of fuel for the journey. The glider pilot declined and asked me to tow them out to sea for half an hour so that they could dress their wounded. I said OK but I had better climb to 4,000 feet to avoid collisions with other aircraft. This I proceeded to do so in gentle circles. The night was pitch black and the whole coast several miles away seemed almost on fire, with houses, haystacks etc, all burning. With Mount Etna in the distance it was an extraordinary sight. I saw several aircraft blow up due to flak. After about half an hour Sergeant Major Preston called me again on the telephone and said that they were ready to go 'into battle'.
>
> Again I offered to take him back to Tunisia but he declined. We set a straight course for the landing zone, but the fires and chaos on the ground made this impossible to identify. However my navigator said we were over the site (the glider pilot naturally overheard the conversation) and said 'Right I'm going now then.' I felt the rope go slack, and so set off back to my airfield.[8]

This particular account given by Briggs modestly omits the detail that by circling for 30 minutes he and his crew significantly increased the risk to themselves. That half hour of orbiting in the darkness must have seemed like an eternity for the Halifax crew members, each of whom was well aware that they were sitting ducks for any roaming German night fighter. On board the Horsa, however, time must have rushed by as the two glider pilots and the gunners accompanying their load attempted to treat their wounded comrades. This was not a simple task, being dressed in full equipment and webbing, clambering over the gun and Jeep together with the lashings that held both in place, and all of this accomplished within the confines of the tightly packed and darkened fuselage of the glider.

The circling continued until Sergeant Major Preston indicated that all was now well on board his battered Horsa. Fully aware of the flak that awaited him and his load before they reached the ground, regardless of the wounded and the flak, he made the decision to press on into the battle and deliver his vital load to the bridgehead, releasing the Horsa from its tow at 700 feet and making a good landing. The 6-pounder gun and its crew thereafter played their part in the battle to the full. Sadly, however, Squadron Sergeant Major John Preston and Sergeant John Broadhead were killed in action after landing, and both are buried in the Commonwealth War Graves Commission cemetery near Catania's airport.

Meanwhile, somewhere to the south, another 1st Battalion GPR warrant officer was also looking to deliver his load on to the LZ and join the battle. Sergeant Major Wally Atkinson was about to cast off his tow and attempt to bring his WACO glider into land. He remembered clearly the combination's final minutes as it approached the release point and the eventful landing that he and his second pilot made:

> We were now circling the area and did so twice before the tug crew, who had played their part wonderfully, said that we must depart down to the ground. We realised now that we really were over the target. We released, and dived to avoid the small arms fire. The enemy must have thought that we were finished because the fire suddenly ceased, so we attempted to carry out a landing between the fires still blazing in a building and the fields. All went well for a time. We could see that the fires had been started by haystacks set alight by ack-ack fire. Unfortunately, one stack had not been set on fire, so we didn't see it until we hit it with the port main-plane. In the end this turned out to be an advantage, as it afforded perfect cover from the fire of the enemy and gave us time to unload the glider and move for cover.[9]

The dispersal of the incoming transports and glider tugs, coupled with the absence of LZ markers and navigational aids, had played a part in wrecking the FUSTIAN plan. Almost immediately after landing, the fragmented elements of the brigade attempted to rally in the darkness. Those commanders present quickly realised that all was not well but in the confusion they had no way of knowing just how bad the situation was, nor could they know that less than 300 of the 1,856 men who had clambered aboard aircraft in North Africa were now in a position to play their part in striking out from their DZs to seize the Ponte Primosole bridge. Small parties of paratroops did exactly as they had been trained and began to group together and move toward their designated rendezvous points. These stumbled into enemy posts and patrols, and exchanges of fire began to break out in the darkness. Although some resistance had been expected, the accuracy of the incoming fire and the night discipline of the enemy did not tally with what would reasonably be expected from Italian Home Guard units. Soon after the first skirmishes, the realisation spread that there were well trained German troops in the area and their unforeseen presence added a new dimension to the already difficult task ahead.

Each of the parachute battalions suffered varying degrees of bad fortune during the drop. The worst affected was 3rd Parachute Battalion. Although the Commanding Officer, Lieutenant Colonel Yeldham, dropped well away from DZ 4, he managed to make his way to his battalion rally point. On arrival, he was shocked to find that he could muster just five men from his entire battalion. Deciding that he was in no position to establish the defensive screen to the north as he had been ordered, he set off with his meagre force to join the 1st Parachute Battalion at the bridge.

1st Parachute Battalion had fared little better on the night. As mentioned previously, Lieutenant Colonel Alastair Pearson's plan had opened with the dropping of a platoon on DZs 1 and 2 on either side of the river in order to assault both ends of the bridge simultaneously. In the event, neither platoon dropped on to its designated DZ and no coup de main was mounted.

At DZ 1, Captain J. Rann had managed to muster a force of around 50 men. Realising that the original plan was in tatters, and that time was against him, he set out to take the bridge, reaching it at 0200 hours. At this point, a seven-man patrol led by the battalion's Regimental Signals Officer, Lieutenant James Lasenby, went forward and completed a hasty close reconnaissance of the Italian defences, returning fifteen minutes later to report on the Italian dispositions. Within minutes, Captain Rann gave a set of very quick battle orders and the 1st Parachute Battalion assault on its objective 'Marston' was launched. Surprise was complete, resistance was minimal, and the 50-strong Italian guard force threw down its weapons and surrendered. In spite of all of the setbacks encountered en route to Sicily and the chaos on the DZs, 'Marston' was finally in British hands!

Away from the action at the bridge, Brigadier Gerald Lathbury had landed to the south of the river on the slope of the Johnny III feature. Like many of his men he had been dropped at 200 feet, well below the recommended safety altitude for his parachute. Luckily for him, he had landed on soft soil and so walked away from his landing without injury. An hour after landing, unaware of Captain Rann's success at the bridge and having gained his bearings and gathered whatever troops he could find, Lathbury advanced with his own ad-hoc force on the bridge from the south. As he approached the bridgehead, he sent forward scouts to observe the bridge. These soon reported back with the news that elements of 1st Parachute Battalion were holding the Ponte Primosole and so he moved up to the bridge and took stock of what troops he had to hold the bridgehead. While he was doing so, however, he was wounded when a lone Italian soldier, who had avoided capture during the fight for the bridge, broke cover and threw a hand grenade into the British position. This exploded close to Lathbury who was hit by shrapnel that lodged in his back and thighs.

In spite of his wounds, however, he refused to step down and remained in command of his brigade.

As the few remaining hours of darkness passed by, individual paratroopers and small groups continued to arrive at the bridge. Before first light Lieutenant Colonel Alastair Pearson arrived with the members of 1st Parachute Battalion he had managed to gather on DZs 1 and 2. He assumed command of the bridge itself and set about organising what men he had to receive any potential counter-attack. The bridge force was further reinforced, albeit on a tiny scale, when Lieutenant Colonel Yeldham and his 3rd Parachute Battalion survivors joined the defence, bringing it to a total of 164, a figure that was never exceeded. The 3rd Parachute Battalion's drop had been so badly scattered that by midday on 14 July the battalion strength peaked at four officers and 35 other ranks, with Lieutenant Colonel Yeldham placing himself and his men under the command of Lieutenant Colonel Pearson.

South of the river, meanwhile, Lieutenant Colonel Johnny Frost and 2nd Parachute Battalion were also experiencing a night of mixed fortunes. The majority of the aircraft carrying the battalion had been pushed along by a stiff tail wind that had boosted airspeed significantly. In fact, the 2nd Parachute Battalion C-47 echelons arrived over Sicily a good 20 minutes ahead of the remainder of the brigade. To some degree, this premature arrival gave the first waves of aircraft an initial element of surprise. The Italian anti-aircraft defences were slow to react to the approaching formation and the lead echelons received only erratic fire from the ground, this unexpected window of opportunity allowing the C-47 crews to concentrate on delivering their sticks of paratroops on to their DZs below. The sticks that jumped from these lead aircraft included Lieutenant Colonel Frost, his battalion headquarters and the lead elements of A Company, commanded by Major Dickie Lonsdale. The majority of these sticks were dropped relatively accurately on or around DZ 3.

The apparent paralysis of the Italian air defence system was, however, short-lived. Before any of the remaining echelons could begin dropping their sticks, the guns below opened up, the ferocity of the flak barrage scattering the incoming waves of transports and consequently the remainder of the 2nd Parachute Battalion drop. Lieutenant Colonel Frost was making slow progress from DZ 3 to his battalion rendezvous point. He had made an awkward landing and injured his leg but nevertheless continued pushing on toward the rendezvous, rallying those of his troops he met on the way. As he limped across the DZ, he witnessed the chaotic scene overhead:

> My stick and I were quite close to our pre-arranged rendezvous. We could see the bund and the high ground comprising the 'Johnny' features. Most of the fires we had seen from the air were stooks of corn burning and not crashed aircraft, as we had feared. However the streams of tracer were there and enemy weapons of various calibres were being

> fired at all approaching aircraft. Enemy artillery were firing air bursts in our general direction. The effect of this was alarming and annoying rather than dangerous, for whenever I tried to say something important to my entourage, my words were blotted out by a peremptory 'crack' from above.
>
> Meanwhile, although the entourage was growing, it soon became obvious that all was not well. Long after the time had passed when we should have assembled, only a handful of my headquarters had arrived. Most of Dickie Lonsdale's A Company were present, but otherwise just odd bits and pieces of the battalion. There could be no doubt that few of the other squadrons had flown in as staunchly as ours had done. In fact we saw no other aircraft flying in formation anywhere. Some Dakotas flew over the general area at varying heights. Most of these were going flat out and some were weaving through the air in desperate evasive action. On one occasion two of them approached each other from opposite ends of the dropping zone. We watched with bated breath, for a really sickening crash seemed inevitable. However, they tore past each other, perhaps not even knowing how near they had been to disaster.
>
> Some aircraft had static lines streaming behind them from the door, showing that they had unleashed their sticks somewhere. In the doorway of others one could just see the shape of a man. The odd glider came in almost silently. One caught in a searchlight was riddled with machine-gun fire and crashed against the bund.[10]

By the time Frost reached his destination, he had gathered in about 50 men, the bulk of which were from A Company. Over the next 30 minutes his tiny force was joined by a steady trickle of individuals and small groups who in the main were men from C Company. By 0200 hours, just as Captain Rann and his ad-hoc 1st Parachute Battalion force were closing in on the bridge, Lieutenant Colonel Frost had only managed to scrape together a force of just 112 men. With no obvious prospect of any further reinforcement, and time slipping away, his options were limited. He decided that he could wait no longer, and gave orders to move off from the battalion rendezvous. 2nd Parachute Battalion was going to press on and attack regardless of the night's many setbacks.

Notes

1. Frost, Lieutenant Colonel, J., *A Drop Too Many*, Barnsley, Pen & Sword Ltd, 2008, p. 177.
2. *Forgotten Voices of the Second World War*, London, Ebury Press, 2004, p. 231.
3. Frost, Lieutenant Colonel, J., *A Drop Too Many*, Barnsley, Pen & Sword Ltd, 2008, p. 178.
4. Mackenzie, Sergeant, W., 1 Squadron, 1st Battalion GPR, correspondence with the Author dated 26 May 2010.

5. Atkinson, Warrant Officer 2, W., 1st Battalion GPR by permission of *The Eagle*.
6. Davis, Squadron Leader, P., 38 Wing RAF, diary extract 14 July 1943.
7. CAB 106/689 App D Report on Gliders operating on 1 Para Brigade Operation – Fustian.
8. Briggs, Flight Lieutenant, G.H., OC A Flight, 295 Squadron RAF, by permission of *The Eagle*.
9. Atkinson, Warrant Officer 2, W., 1st Battalion GPR, by permission of *The Eagle*.
10. Frost, Lieutenant Colonel, J., *A Drop Too Many*,Barnsley, Pen & Sword Ltd, 2008, p. 179.

Chapter 16

The Battle for the Ponte di Primosole

Despite the fact that they were first and foremost pilots, they showed remarkable adaptability, courage and self-discipline which, augured well for the future.

Led by the limping figure of the Commanding Officer, the depleted 2nd Parachute Battalion headed away from its DZ. With no second-in-command or adjutant to assist him, Lieutenant Colonel Frost had to think fast and adapt his original plan to seize his objectives. Alongside him was Major Dickie Lonsdale who was confident that he and A Company had adequate numbers and the required firepower to take Johnny 1.

As they headed for their objectives, Frost and his men encountered Brigadier Gerald Lathbury and the handful of his headquarters staff; in spite of everything that was going on around him, and the problems with which he was grappling, Frost remembered that it was the brigade commander's birthday and wished him many happy returns as they met.

Lathbury, however, had more important things on his mind. He and those accompanying him had been dropped in the wrong place, he had no communications with his battalions, and he could hear the sound of battle emanating from the direction of the bridge. He urged Frost to push on to his objectives without further delay. Lathbury later summed up his situation:

> ... It was obvious that things had gone wrong. Only a very small part of the Brigade Headquarters had arrived and most of the wireless sets had gone astray; one having fallen in the river. There were no communications with any of the battalions and on-one knew what had happened.[1]

The confused situation was further heightened by groups of Italian troops who suddenly appeared; in the darkness, it was difficult to detect whether these were looking to fight or surrender.

The night, however, also yielded reinforcements. As 2nd Parachute Battalion approached the base of the Johnny 1 hill, it was met by a small group led by Lieutenant Tony Frank who informed Frost that he and his men had already been to the summit of Johnny 2 where they found that the Italian hilltop positions had been abandoned. Pressing on to Johnny 1, they encountered minimal resistance and now occupied the key hilltop where they were holding 130 Italian prisoners.

After a very brief discussion, Frost ordered Major Dickie Lonsdale and A Company up on to the hill where they were to dig in and reinforce Lieutenant Frank and his group. By 0530 hours the force holding Johnny 1 numbered more than 140 men, but it possessed no support weapons or radios.

As the parachute battalions went about their respective tasks on the ground, the air plan continued overhead. The airlanding component of the operation was about to come into play, with the glider lift by now approaching the mouth of the River Simeto.

The gliders however were also encountering problems; by the time that the leading combinations made landfall on Sicily, a third of their total had been lost. In addition to those that had been left behind in North Africa, one had been released accidentally out to sea while a further four were missing, believed to have been brought down by anti-aircraft fire, and a further three made disastrous crash landings miles away from the two LZs. Four gliders made better landings, but were cast off far too soon by their tugs; to add insult to injury, their occupants emerged only to find themselves in the midst of Italian or German positions. Most were taken prisoner without firing a shot.

The fateful positioning of Major Schmidt's Fallschirm-Maschinengewehr-Bataillon 1 close to the bridge also played a significant role in further heightening the chaos around the bridge, both in the air and on the ground. During that first night it captured 82 members of 1st Parachute Brigade, while its machine guns accounted for three transport aircraft and two gliders.

A handful of gliders did, however, succeed in avoiding the ground fire and made it through to the area of the River Simeto. Glider 126 was a Horsa carrying a 6-pounder anti-tank gun, Jeep and crew from A Troop of 1st Airlanding Anti-Tank Battery RA, being flown by Staff Sergeant H.G. Protheroe with Sergeant Jock Kerr as his second pilot. The two pilots knew that they had a good tug crew looking after them as the Halifax ahead of them in the darkness was being flown by Flight Lieutenant Tommy Grant, one of the most experienced pilots in 38 Wing RAF, who three nights earlier had towed the Horsa flown by Staff Sergeant Galpin and Sergeant Brown to the Ponte Grande. Staff Sergeant Protheroe was by this stage an experienced pilot himself, having flown a Turkey Buzzard mission from Cornwall to Morocco as well as flying over the Atlas Mountains at the end of the build-up training programme. He later summarised his memories of the briefing before the operation:

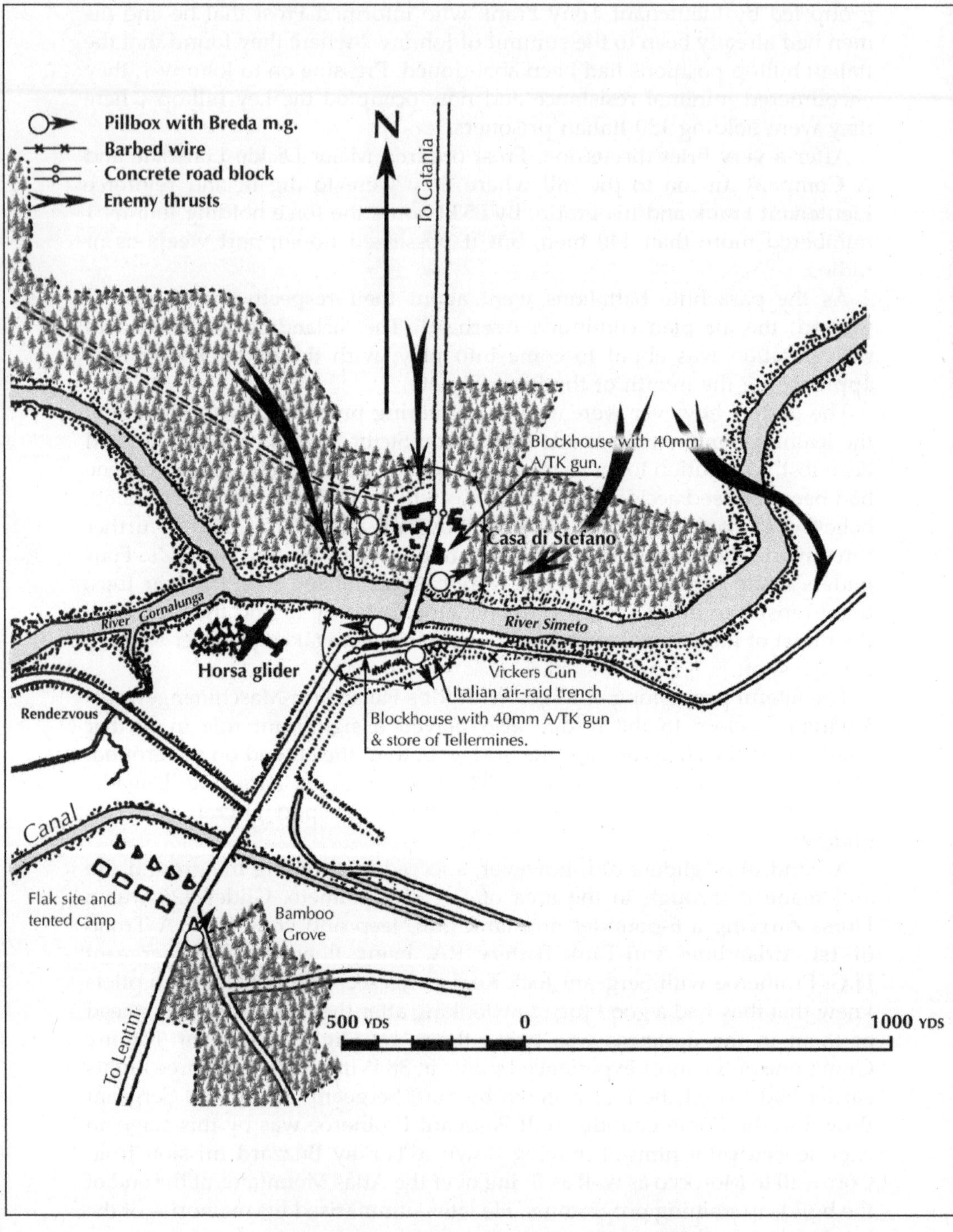

Map of the assault on the Ponte di Primosole

> The day came when we were briefed for the operation on the Primosole bridge. We were to carry an anti-tank gun team (this consisted of an anti-tank gun, a Jeep, and gun team with two other members of the battery) and we were to land in a field south-west of the bridge and adjacent to it. There were a number of WACO gliders taking part in the operation, and their landing zone was further west of the bridge and the north side of the River Simeto. During the briefing I met our tug pilot Flight Lieutenant Grant who was flying a Halifax. I recognised him from the days when he gave me instruction in Hotspurs.
>
> At the briefing we were told we would approach the landing zone at about 2,000 feet from the coast south of the Simeto river. As we approached the LZ we would see a flare path laid out by the independent parachute company.[2]

The confidence that Staff Sergeant Protheroe had in Flight Lieutenant Grant and his Halifax crew turned out to be well placed. The combination had a relatively untroubled transit to Malta and turned inland from the Sicilian coastline exactly as briefed in North Africa.

> As time went on you could see the outline of land on the port side of the glider in the moonlight. In the distance we could see the lights of a town which was obviously Catania. A strange sight bearing in mind that an invasion had taken place not many miles to the south. We turned inland and soon tracers could be seen, some between us and the tug. We could hear what sounded like small arms rattling on the gun or the Jeep. There was no sign of a landing strip marked by a flare path, all I could see was fire and smoke.
>
> The tug pilot said 'Here we are' or words to that effect. I replied that I had no idea where we were. The tug pilot then came back and said that he could make another run in and this he did. On the second approach I could see the reflection of the moon in the river, and later the bend in it, and a silhouette of the superstructure of the bridge. After pull-off I approached the road south of the bridge and put on full flap so that I could land as close to the road as possible and avoid running into the river. Sergeant Kerr said, 'Don't forget the electrical pylons,' to which I replied, 'We are OK; we are almost over the road; the pylons are behind us.' No sooner was this remark made than there was a crash and sparks flew in all directions.[3]

Hours later, in daylight on the following day, the two men would discover that they had managed to hit a telephone pole and cables. However, at this exact moment in time the cause of the crash was of little interest as they had far more pressing concerns:

> The impact had practically destroyed the Horsa cockpit and we had been thrown from our seats and were travelling along the ground at a

> fair speed. The contact of our heads with the ground let us know that we were travelling at a fair speed. I was praying that I did not contact anything before we came to a stop.
>
> As we extracted ourselves from the damaged glider a few bursts of machine gun fire came from a pillbox on the south-west corner of the bridge. We made for the bank of the Simeto to take cover until the reception was more cordial. The firing soon stopped and I realised Sergeant Kerr wasn't with us, I went back to the glider and Sergeant Kerr had injured his leg and was still there. Seeing he was as safe there as anywhere else I rejoined the gun crew. [4]

Not all of the gliders were so fortunate. It is believed that Glider 127, flown by Major Astley Cooper, originally of the Cheshire Regiment, and Sergeant Cyril Morgan, crashed after their Halifax tug was shot down while taking them around for a second pass over the bridge. At a height of 500 feet, the Halifax tug presented an easy target and was hit by flak, exploding in flames almost instantly. Blinded by the flash of the explosion, and gliding at a low altitude, the Horsa's two pilots had very little time to make a decision on where to land and attempted to do so in a river bed to the north-east of Lentini. Unfortunately they were unsuccessful, and both were killed along with two of the passengers from the headquarters of 1st Airlanding Anti-Tank Battery RA, while a further three were badly injured.

Glider 128 fared little better. Sergeant Wallace Mackenzie and Lieutenant Robin Walchli were under tow by a Halifax of 295 Squadron RAF flown by Flying Officer Jerry Norman. Lieutenant Walchli had a personal interest in getting his load delivered on to the LZ. Originally a gunner himself, he had served alongside the anti-tank gunners he was carrying, as their battery reconnaissance officer. He later described the tow and release as 'perfect', but the final stage of the flight proved far from being so. As they made their approach to the LZ, the two pilots handled their Horsa well, successfully avoiding the high tension cables on their run-in and staying clear of the bridge superstructure as they made their final turn before landing. At this critical point, however, fate intervened. With little or no height left to play with, the glider's undercarriage struck the lip of the canal bank with disastrous results. The Horsa crashed on to the bank, catapulting both pilots out of their seats and through the perspex front of the cockpit. The aircraft was wrecked and consequently, much to Lieutenant Walchli's frustration, use of the vital 6-pounder anti-tank gun and its attendant Jeep was denied to the gunners of 1st Airlanding Anti-Tank Battery RA.

Meanwhile in the darkness, Brigadier Gerald Lathbury looked on helplessly as the German machine gunners threw up a torrent of fire at the incoming glider lift:

> . . . One Horsa glider came over our heads at about one-hundred feet; it was clearly visible in the light of the fires and every German machine

> gun and light flak gun turned onto it. We could see about five streams of tracer going through the fuselage, then it disappeared into the darkness and a moment later we heard it hit the ground with a crash.[5]

Later than planned, Staff Sergeant D. White cast off Glider 129 from its tow at 1,500 feet and immediately turned his Horsa into a rapidly descending circuit. Sitting alongside him in the second pilot's seat was Staff Sergeant Henry Webb; behind them, braced for landing, was a gun crew of 1st Airlanding Anti-Tank Battery RA along with its 6-pounder gun and Jeep. As the glider descended, the two pilots were constantly scanning LZ 8 whilst well aware that they were 27 minutes late and that the enemy below was all too plainly on full alert.

As it circled over the 500-yard triangular-shaped LZ, the Horsa attracted multiple streams of anti-aircraft fire arcing up from all directions, each delineated by red balls of tracer. The glow of burning haystacks and flashes of flak ensured that the LZ and the glider were almost fully illuminated and thus clearly visible. Nevertheless, Staff Sergeant White and Sergeant Webb were determined to fly on regardless through the flak and deliver the gun and its crew at the spot where one point of the LZ touched the bridge. Watching from the darkness below was Staff Sergeant Protheroe:

> I saw the outline of another glider a few hundred feet above us and warned other people around me to keep clear of the landing zone. Soon afterwards a glider came over the superstructure of the bridge . . . I later learned that this was Staff Sergeant White's glider.[6]

Glider 129 was hit by flak and small arms fire but Staff Sergeants White and Webb succeeded in flying through the maelstrom of anti-aircraft fire and made a rough landing on LZ 8, bringing the Horsa and its load to rest just 100 yards south of the Ponte di Primosole. Although the glider was close to where it needed to be, the landing had damaged it and shifted its load inside the fuselage. The two pilots and the gun crew now had to remove the tail but it would take four hours to extract the 6-pounder gun and a further five hours to remove the Jeep from the Horsa's twisted and splintered fuselage.

While the glider crews on the ground struggled to unload, the surviving tug crews turned their aircraft and headed for home, their part in the operation complete. Squadron Leader Peter Davis had successfully towed Glider 120 to within sight of the Ponte Primosole. Back in the safe environment of Airfield E, he made the following entry in his diary that night, his words hinting at his post-mission excitement and the adrenalin still coursing through him:

> At last it has come off, and my aircraft has stayed serviceable <u>and</u> I towed a Horsa with umpteen guns etc to near Catania. All this very

> thrilling, and no longer feel the frustration of a few days ago ... very tired but now but mightily pleased I have pulled my guns to battle – Glider Pilot was Bill Barrie – a good type who used to drink with us in the Kings Arms. If he kept his head he should be down safely, but, as we approached release point, got caught in a couple of searchlights, he was blinded and therefore tow rope broke, but he was in easy distance of the field and knew where he was and only had to follow the river. 'Jock' my tail gunner, saw him evade the searchlight as we did. Wonder what his fate was and if I shall ever see him again.[7]

Even after Davis had made the flight back, debriefed and returned to his tent, it is likely that the gun he had delivered was still not in action. The majority of the gliders that had landed close enough for their crews and loads to feature in the operation were badly crumpled or damaged. This was making unloading the Jeeps and guns much more difficult than anticipated. Helmut Wilhelmsmeyer, a German historian and Fallschirmjäger veteran, included the following account based on interviews with veterans in an article he wrote for the *British Army Review*:

> Whilst the Brigadier and the group of men with him were approaching the bank of the River Simeto, they heard a sound of cracking and splintering very close to them. It was if wood were being chopped with an axe. They saw that a glider had landed at the edge of a pine clearing, having just cleared the upper edge of the bridge. A second glider landed in shallow water close to the river bank with one wing broken and the other pointing skyward. The nose was stove in and the framework of the fuselage could be seen through the torn skin. Both pilots had been thrown through the plastic windows of the cockpit. The survivors were crawling from the wreckage and some were dragging out the anti-tank gun that they had brought with them. Despite the black face camouflage they wore, the pallor caused by the shock of the crash could be clearly seen.[8]

While Staff Sergeants White and Webb, together with the anti-tank gun crew, hacked furiously at Glider 129's fuselage and then wrestled free the 6-pounder, the rest of the bridge's defenders were racing to establish a defensive perimeter before first light and the inevitable enemy counterattack. The sappers of 1st Parachute Squadron RE had worked swiftly, successfully disarming and removing the demolition charges placed on the bridge by the Italians. Meanwhile 1st Parachute Battalion made best use of existing irrigation ditches, hastily abandoned Italian trenches, and whatever sandbagged positions and dugouts that were positioned around the bridge itself. There was also a group of concrete pill boxes sited to protect the southern approaches to the bridge; these and a number of Italian machine guns were pressed into service by Lieutenant Colonel Alastair Pearson's men.

The remaining hours of darkness passed quickly, but dawn did not bring the expected eruption of incoming artillery and mortar fire, as Staff Sergeant Protheroe observed:

> When dawn broke after many hours of silence the first thing to strike me was Mount Etna, straight in front of us towering above the country with a wisp of smoke coming from it. The first sign of action after this was the appearance of a spotter plane making observations in the area of the bridge. We took a few pot shots at it, and it eventually flew off. Next, we were visited by a fighter plane and he took pleasure in subjecting us to a few sorties of machine gun fire.[9]

The first ground activity recorded in unit war diaries and personal accounts appears in the form of a probing reconnaissance made by an Italian armoured car. This lone vehicle was swiftly dealt with by one of the 1st Parachute Battalion outposts using a Gammon bomb. Thereafter, a mood of relative calm settled around the bridge. While sentries maintained a keen vigil over the approach routes from the north and south, the remainder of the force at the bridge continued to dig in and improve its defensive positions.

In due course, another vehicle also approached the bridgehead. On hearing from a German motorcycle despatch rider that the Simeto crossing was in British hands, Hauptmann Stangenberg had left Fallschirmjäger-Regiment 3's headquarters to confirm this intelligence for himself; withdrawing on coming under fire, he sped back to his headquarters to organise a counter-attack. His immediate options were, however, limited. Knowing that the Fallschirmjäger battalions were already heavily committed elsewhere, and thus unlikely to mount an assault on the Ponte di Primosole, his only option was to form an ad hoc counter-attack force from the divisional troops around the headquarters.

Stangenberg contacted Generalleutnant Richard Heidrich at Feldmarschall Kesselring's headquarters in Rome. Desperate for manpower, he needed Heidrich's permission to utilise Kompanie 1 of Fallschirm-Kommunikation-Bataillon 1, the divisional signals unit, as part of his counter-attack force. Permission to use the company in the infantry role was granted as there were no other German troops available and many of the Italian units were considered unreliable.

Kompanie 1, under the command of Hauptmann Erich Fassl, would form the core of Hauptmann Stangenberg's ad hoc force, the latter having also tasked a group of NCOs with gathering up from elsewhere every available man who could carry a rifle. During the ensuing hours, it was steadily reinforced with Luftwaffe ground crew, administrative personnel from the Hermann Göring Division and 1. Fallschirmjäger-Division, its strength eventually reaching over 200 men. Stangenberg also ordered the laying of a field telephone line between the headquarters and a battery of 88mm guns sited south of Catania Airfield, this allowing him to call for supporting fire from the battery once he was ready to mount his counter-attack.

While the signallers of Fallschirm-Kommunikation-Bataillon 1 were busy setting up their telephone link, their counterparts in 1st Parachute Brigade were also dealing with a pressing communication task, one deemed vital to the success of Operation FUSTIAN: the establishment of radio communications with the Eighth Army. The brigade's link to the advancing British armour to the south was provided by its No. 22 radio sets. These, along with the batteries that powered them, had been packed in parachute containers and dropped separately as they were too heavy to be carried by individual paratroopers. They were, however, scattered, over a wide area and a number of sets were damaged beyond repair or simply not recovered in the darkness. The result was that Brigadier Lathbury was dependent on just two No. 22 sets for establishing and maintaining radio communications with the Eighth Army and the Royal Navy offshore. Furthermore, they were also to provide him with a vital link to a unit that was tasked with clearing a path for General Montgomery's thrust to Messina.

During the latter stages of planning for Operation FUSTIAN, the bridge across the River Lentini, the Ponte di Malati, situated ten miles south of the Ponte di Primosole, was identified as a potential bottleneck that could slow the momentum of the British advance. In order to avoid this, Montgomery's staff came up with a plan to secure the bridge in advance of the arrival of British armour. It was an audacious one, relying on surprise and speed of movement, and involved an amphibious landing close to Malati at the same time as 1st Parachute Brigade began dropping on to its DZs. The capture of the two bridges by commando and airborne forces was critical to the success of Montgomery's plans.

Just 24 hours before FUSTIAN was due to be launched, the task of taking the Ponte di Malati intact was given to Lieutenant Colonel John Durnford-Slater DSO and his No. 3 Commando which would hold the bridge until the arrival of 4th Armoured Brigade, under Brigadier John Currie DSO, MC, the spearhead of 50th (Northumbrian) Infantry Division commanded by Major General Sydney Kirkman CBE, MC. With both bridges secured, Montgomery intended that Kirkman's division would advance at speed north toward Catania, punching through any opposition it encountered and advancing over 30 miles in 24 hours. At a final orders group on 13 July 1943, Montgomery stressed that Kirkman was to get forward with 'all possible speed'.

Brigadier Lathbury had been briefed to expect radio communication from No. 3 Commando, updating him on the progress of 4th Armoured Brigade to his south, and to expect commando patrols that were to link up with the two brigade bridgeheads during the night. By first light, however, no communication had been received from No. 3 Commando, nor had any commando patrols made an appearance.

At the Ponte di Malati, meanwhile, No. 3 Commando had succeeded in capturing its objective but subsequently had been surprised to encounter Fallschirmjäger and panzers rather than the second-rate Italian units that they had anticipated. Once the Germans had become aware of Lieutenant Colonel Durnford-Slater's force at Malati, they threw a steadily increasing number of units into action against the lightly armed commandos. The latter held on grimly, awaiting the arrival of 50th Division, but hour-by-hour the pressure mounted with the commandos suffering heavy casualties.

50th Division meanwhile was well behind schedule, being embroiled in fierce fighting in and around Lentini, and thus the Sherman tanks of 4th Armoured Brigade were still miles away from the beleaguered commandos, and even further from 1st Parachute Brigade. Eventually, with little ammunition remaining and casualties mounting, the men of No. 3 Commando were forced to abandon their objective and withdraw, attempting to evade capture as they headed back for the Allied lines.

In the meantime at the Ponte di Primosole, oblivious to the dramatic events unfolding at Malati, Brigadier Lathbury and the remnants of his brigade fought on throughout 14 July, hanging on in the vain hope that they would soon hear the distinctive sound of Sherman tanks approaching.

At 0630 hours, there were indications that 2nd Parachute Battalion was not having an easy time south of the river from where the sounds of battle could be distinctly heard by those at the bridge. Indeed, Lieutenant Colonel Johnny Frost and his men had their hands very full as Fallschirmjäger, supported by machine guns and heavy mortars, pressed home a determined counter-attack from the west.

This early morning opening battle went on for an hour before the German attack was suddenly broken up by a salvo of naval gunfire. Captain Francis Vere Hodge, the Royal Artillery naval gunfire forward observation officer attached to the brigade, had succeeded in making radio contact with the cruiser HMS *Mauritius* on station offshore. Using one of the brigade's remaining two No. 22 radio sets, he had tuned in to the naval gunfire support net and called for support. The cruiser's 6-inch guns delivered salvo after salvo of devastating fire into the midst of the German counter-attack close to the Johnny 1 feature. By the time she had finished firing, there were very few Fallschirmjäger still on their feet; those that were able to walk abandoned their attack and withdrew very shaken to the west. This timely and decisive intervention by HMS *Mauritius* went some way to making amends for the casualties among the transport aircraft and gliders caused by the naval 'friendly fire' fratricide of the previous night.

In the meantime, the second No. 22 set was being used by the 1st Parachute Battalion command post to try and establish communications with the advancing Eighth Army and with No. 3 Commando. At 0930 hours the battalion's signallers finally managed to contact the leading troops of 4th Armoured Brigade. The codeword 'Marston One' was passed over the radio net, indicating that Operation FUSTIAN had been successful and that the

Ponte di Primosole had been seized intact by the airborne troops. The radio link was however fragile and an hour later radio communications between the two brigades were lost and, despite continual efforts thereafter, was never re-established.

At 1000 hours, German attention switched from the perimeter to the bridge itself. A flight of Messerschmitt 109 fighters appeared and executed a series of attacks, strafing the trenches around the bridge and forcing the defenders to take cover, thus disrupting the work on improving the defences. This was the first of what was to be a regular pattern of air attacks throughout the day, with fighters roaming at will over the bridge and the surrounding valley, strafing anything that moved. Thereafter they returned to the airfield at Catania, which could be observed from the British positions from where Brigadier Lathbury and his men watched the Luftwaffe ground crews swarming over the Messerschmitts, rearming and refuelling them. Thereafter, the aircraft took to the air again to begin another round of low-level attacks on the bridgehead.

As the morning progressed, a slow trickle of stragglers succeeded in dodging the air attacks and finding their way into the bridgehead from the surrounding countryside. Their arrival, however, did little to reinforce the force around the bridge as a combination of air attacks, artillery and increasingly accurate mortar fire was taking a steady toll on the defenders around the bridgehead.

At midday the intensity of the German pressure increased with an hour-long artillery barrage that began to rain down on the area. At the same time, Hauptmann Stangenberg gave the order for his hastily assembled counter-attack force to move off. He organised it into two separate columns, personally taking command of the main force and setting off on the most direct route along Highway 115. The signallers of Kompanie 1, led by Hauptmann Fassl, were instructed to march on a parallel route to the east of the highway before being ordered to attack the British right flank. The two columns were reinforced with an 88mm self-propelled gun and several anti-tank guns.

At 1310 hours the German counter-attack was in position. The barrage lightened and then ceased to allow two Messerschmitt 109s to make strafing runs on the bridge. The artillery and air attacks were then followed up by Hauptmann's Stangenberg's assault, which was well executed, falling on all three sides of the British position on the north bank manned by Lieutenant Colonel Yeldham and the five officers and 35 men who comprised 3rd Parachute Battalion at the Ponte di Primosole. In spite of the heavy weight of fire thrown at them, they succeeded in holding the north end of the bridge and beating off two attacks.

While the fighting was in full swing to the north, the Germans also began to test 1st Parachute Brigade's southern defences. At 1410 hours, a pair of Messerschmitt fighters made a series of strafing attacks on 1st Parachute Battalion's positions around the southern end of the bridge. This was followed up two separate attacks on the ground, each made under cover of smoke with one attempting a left-flanking move, and the other a move to the right, but Lieutenant Colonel Alastair Pearson and his men held their ground and inflicted heavy casualties on their attackers. Casualties were mounting to the north and south of the bridge, but it was the shortage of ammunition that was causing the most concern as stocks were running very low. Meanwhile, enemy strength was estimated to be at least at battalion level, supported by German artillery that was now engaging the bridge with direct fire. With no further news of 4th Armoured Brigade or from No. 3 Commando, the situation appeared far from promising. Staff Sergeant Protheroe was manning the 6-pounder anti-tank gun that he and Sergeant Jock Kerr had carried in their glider:

> During the day a fair amount of action developed away to our right. We could hear machine gun fire and mortars. At the same time, I noticed our glider, or the remains of it, had been set on fire, probably by a mortar shell or something similar.[10]

The defenders had barely recovered from the consecutive attacks on the north and south of the perimeter before the noise of incoming shells signalled another concerted assault. The artillery was recorded in the 1st Parachute Brigade war diary as being heavy and accurate, with yet more casualties being taken to the makeshift field dressing station established on the southern end of the bridge by Lieutenant Colonel Wheatley and a handful of his men of 16th Parachute Field Ambulance. Beginning at 1500 hours, the shelling continued unabated for an hour, keeping the defenders' heads down while German and Italian troops moved up closer to the British positions. At 1600 hours the barrage stopped and the enemy infantry emerged from cover to launch another determined assault. Once more the defences held, but they came very close to caving in under almost overwhelming pressure.

Sensing that the level of fire from the British positions was diminishing, the Germans continued to pound the bridgehead remorselessly. By this time, Brigadier Gerald Lathbury was seriously concerned that his brigade was about to be overrun. Ammunition levels were dangerously low and his small force could not hope to sustain the rate of attrition that the artillery fire and repeated attacks were inflicting on his force. At 1705 hours, with German infantry probing forward again, he made the decision to abandon his foothold on the northern end of the bridge and concentrate what was left of his force on the southern bank of the river. He hoped that by withdrawing to the south he could still hold the bridge, concentrate what remaining firepower he possessed, and be able to link up with the relief force from the south.

On receiving the order to withdraw, Lieutenant Colonel Yeldham and the survivors of 3rd Parachute Battalion withdrew under fire across the bridge without incurring casualties. They were followed by those of 1st Parachute Battalion, headed by Lieutenant Colonel Pearson. Although 1st Parachute Brigade no longer held the bridge itself, and despite running increasingly low on ammunition, at this point it was still able to dominate it with fire from captured machine guns. Realising that frontal assaults were not going to dislocate the airborne troops, the Germans changed their tactics and began to look for a way to outflank them instead. Using their artillery to keep the British pinned down, they began to move across the river to the east.

The German artillery was still creating significant disruption in the British positions. While it made absolute sense in military terms to move to the south, the ground was far from ideal for defence. Apart from a few concrete pillboxes built by the Italians to guard the bridge against attack from the south, there was little other cover available. The terrain was open and exposed, the only protection other than the pillboxes being provided by great beds of reeds close to the riverbank, but these offered cover from view rather than protection against incoming fire. With the pillboxes occupied by brigade headquarters and the wounded, the majority had to take their chances in the open.

German artillery and mortar fire continued to pour into the British perimeter, making movement almost impossible. The little cover provided by the reed beds and corn in adjacent fields soon disappeared as they were set alight and burnt to stubble. German anti-tank guns were now sited close to the brigade's defensive positions and began systematically to blast the concrete pillboxes with high-explosive shells. At 1845 hours, the situation worsened further as by then the Germans had crossed the river 400 yards to the east of the bridge and were advancing in force. Moreover, all communication with 2nd Parachute Battalion to the south was lost.

At 1915 hours, enemy infantry could be observed preparing to launch a new attack from the east. Finally, at 1935 hours, Brigadier Lathbury was forced to accept that the brigade's position at Ponte di Primosole was untenable and reluctantly gave the order for his men to withdraw to the south and attempt to link up with 2nd Parachute Battalion. Under cover of darkness, the bridge's surviving defenders broke into small groups and slipped away.

Along with the majority of his men, Lathbury succeeded in evading capture and arrived at 0600 hours on 14 July in Lieutenant Colonel Johnny Frost's position on Johnny 1. There, to his frustration, he discovered that Sherman tanks of 44th Royal Tank Regiment, the leading element of 4th Armoured Brigade, had arrived in 2nd Parachute Battalion's position at 1945 hours on the night before. It was, however, only a small force and it was not until midnight on 14 July that it was reinforced by elements of 151st Infantry Brigade, consisting of the 8th and 9th Battalions of The Durham Light Infantry, which linked up with the remnants of the 1st Parachute Brigade. Even then, however, both of the Durhams' battalions had been on the march for 24 hours and were exhausted after covering 20 miles in the blazing heat of the Sicily sun. Consequently, they were not in a sufficiently fit state to mount an immediate attack across the river against stiff opposition.

Having briefed Brigadier John Currie, 4th Armoured Brigade's commander, on the situation at the bridge, Lathbury was finally able to talk to Frost face-to-face. Naturally, he wanted to hear first-hand what had been happening to the 2nd Parachute Battalion while the remainder of the brigade had been holding on grimly to the bridge. The fighting around Johnny 1 had certainly been hard fought, the intervention of HMS *Mauritius* breaking up the German attack in the nick of time. Frost explained that he had not been able to spare any of his men to reinforce the bridge and that even if he could have done so, he was not certain that they would have been able to get through. The battalion had also taken over 100 Italian prisoners while managing to hold the high ground against a series of enemy attacks. He was also able to report that he had been reinforced during the night by a company of the 9th Battalion, The Durham Light Infantry.

Meanwhile the leading elements of 151st Infantry Brigade, commanded by Brigadier Ronald Senior DSO, were advancing on the Ponte di Primosole, the task of retaking the bridge having been allotted to the Durhams' 9th Battalion.

The attack began at 0800 hours on 15 July. There was, however, no finesse to the plan that called for a frontal assault supported by the artillery of two field regiments as well as by mortars, machine guns and the tanks of 44th Royal Tank Regiment. This seemingly overwhelming weight of fire, however, failed to blast a path through to the bridge and the Durhams paid a heavy price, suffering heavy casualties and being thrown back to a line somewhere between the river and the Johnny 1 feature. Later that day, the battalion was moved on to Johnny 1 to relieve 2nd Parachute Battalion. Unable to advance and locked in an artillery duel with German and Italian batteries to the north, the leading elements of 50th Division were thus brought to a halt.

Later that morning, Brigadier Lathbury was admitted to a field dressing station to have his wounds treated, following which he and Lieutenant Colonel Alastair Pearson attended an orders group held at the headquarters of 151st Infantry Brigade. Both knew the terrain around the bridge well and thus had expected to be asked to advise on how best to recapture it. To their disbelief and horror, however, the plan presented was an exact re-run of the first disastrous attack of the previous day, using the 8th Battalion of the Durhams in another Great War style frontal assault. At this point Lieutenant Colonel Alastair Pearson, unable to contain his disbelief and anger any longer, blurted out, 'Well if you want to lose another bloody battalion, that's the right way to do it!'

Following this outburst, and having managed to calm down his irate battalion commander, Lathbury persuaded Brigadier Senior to consider an alternative plan of attack, proposed by Lieutenant Colonel Pearson, involving a river crossing upstream from the bridge, as executed earlier by the Germans against 1st Parachute Brigade. Pearson suggested that the crossing and subsequent attack should be made at night, and offered to guide the lead companies of the assaulting battalion down to the crossing point. Such a crossing, if successful, would enable the Durhams to mount a surprise attack on the German flank. His suggestion and offer were accepted by Brigadier Senior, and the attack took place that night. It proved to be a complete success and the Ponte di Primosole was back in British hands at 0600 hours on the morning of 16 July.

Meanwhile, as preparations were underway to retake the bridge, some of those who had held it so resolutely for so long and then, when ordered to do so, succeeded in slipping away from the bridgehead, were heading south towards Syracuse and the British lines. Staff Sergeant Protheroe was among them as they evaded capture:

> A British officer called us together and advised us to make our way back towards Syracuse, going along the high ground between the coast and Lentini. The gun was taken to the foot of the hills and after removing the striking pin it was abandoned too … During our journey south, darkness fell and we slipped past a farmhouse which was occupied by troops and on the road you could see the outline of a convoy. At this stage we had no desire to be dead heroes and continued our journey. Later we were again subjected to a burst of machine gun fire but it was well off target. Before daybreak we took shelter amongst some rocks as we felt we had earned a rest. The next we knew it was daylight and someone said we were in our own lines. We were given a drink of water by our own troops. It tasted like champagne, as our supply had run out the previous day.[11]

In the meantime on Johnny 1, while the night river crossing and attack was in progress, the survivors of 1st Parachute Brigade were gathered in from their positions. An hour after the bridge had been retaken, a convoy of trucks arrived to take the brigade back to Syracuse harbour for embarkation for North Africa. The cost of taking and holding the Ponte di Primosole had been heavy, the post-battle casualty figures making stark reading for Brigadier Lathbury who had begun the operation with 1,856 men. The force that had taken and the bridge and the Johnny features had totalled only 295 officers and men. At the end of the battle, 27 had been killed in action, and a further 75 were listed as wounded. Following 1st Parachute Brigade's return to North Africa, a further 313 men were listed as missing. It would take weeks to account for the numerous stragglers who had been scattered during the drop, those taken prisoner and those later found to be dead. Weeks later, the total figure for those killed on Operation FUSTIAN had settled at 295.

The cost to The Glider Pilot Regiment, when added to the losses incurred on Operation LADBROKE, was thought by many at the time to be unsustainable. Even after the landings were over, the list of casualties continued to increase. Some had been captured during the fighting or had landed too far behind enemy lines to stand any chance of escape. Sergeant Major Wally Atkinson and his second pilot, Staff Sergeant Montague, were attempting to avoid capture and get back to Allied lines:

> Knowing that our troops were to the south, we decided to try to get through to them. The only way across the river was by a narrow bridge, about a mile along the bank and guarded by a single sentry. We were prevented from reaching the bridge, however, by concentrated small arms fire from the south bank of the river and had to take cover in the riverbed returning their fire. Very soon we suffered our first casualty, the Royal Artillery gunner, who was fatally wounded, and within a short time we were surrounded and made prisoners. Our captors turned out to be not Italian Home Guard units but German paratroopers who had been dropped the previous night to await our arrival.
>
> Later that day we were forced to march with the retreating German forces, and at one stage I began to doubt whether the Germans intended to continue to be burdened with us. We were herded together into a small hole, the sentries fingering grenades with obvious intentions, but something or someone must have made them change their minds. The next day we were constantly shelled by our own artillery and strafed by the American Air Force which was responsible for several casualties, one of them being my co-pilot, Staff Sergeant Montague, who was fatally wounded.[12]

Nine days later, Sergeant Major Atkinson reached Stalag VIIA, a prisoner of war camp outside Munich. He was to remain there until Soviet troops liberated the camp in May 1945.

The bravery shown by the men of The Glider Pilot Regiment in their cockpits and on the ground was recognised after the battle. Those who reached the LZs and delivered troops into battle featured prominently in the list of honours and awards following Operation FUSTIAN. Staff Sergeants Protheroe and White were both awarded the Distinguished Flying Medal, while Lieutenant Bill Barrie was also recognised for his bravery at the Ponte di Primosole, being one of the first members of The Glider Pilot Regiment to be awarded the Distinguished Flying Cross. His citation is testament to his personal skill and courage during FUSTIAN. Sadly he was killed just over a year later while leading a patrol during the battle of Arnhem in September 1944:

> This officer was a pilot of a Horsa Glider carrying a Jeep and a six-pounder anti-tank gun.

> He showed great courage and skill in piloting his glider for five hours in very rough weather. On arriving in the battle area, he had to face flak and searchlights. It was through his skill and coolness that he landed his glider successfully and that his load went into action on the ground.
>
> Lieutenant Barrie was an example and inspiration to all throughout the operation.[13]

In spite of the recognition and praise that his men had rightfully earned for their actions at the Ponte di Primosole, Lieutenant Colonel George Chatterton made the following candid assessment of the FUSTIAN glider landings:

> Only four Horsas on Operation FUSTIAN had landed their 6-pounder guns close to the Primosole Bridge, and only two of those landed on the correct Landing Zone south-west of the bridge. The first pilots of those two were Staff Sergeants Protheroe and White ... The one redeeming factor in the almost catastrophic glider participation in the landing was that the members of the Regiment proved their undoubted ability to take on the role of 'total soldier' once on the ground. Some operated anti-tank guns and others made good use of a captured German 88mm gun during the defence of the captured Primosole Bridge. Despite the fact that they were first and foremost pilots, they showed remarkable adaptability, courage and self-discipline which augured well for the future.[14]

In the wake of the near failure and heavy losses associated with Operations LADBROKE, HUSKY 1 and 2, and FUSTIAN, Allied commanders openly expressed serious doubts as to the continued viability of the use of airborne forces on a large scale.

Notes

1. Lathbury, Brigadier General, *British Army Review*, issue 79, August 1985.
2. Protheroe, Staff Sergeant, H., 1 Squadron, 1st Battalion GPR, by permission of *The Eagle*.
3. Protheroe, Staff Sergeant, H., 1 Squadron, 1st Battalion GPR, by permission of *The Eagle*.
4. Protheroe, Staff Sergeant, H., 1 Squadron, 1st Battalion GPR, by permission of *The Eagle*.
5. Lathbury, Brigadier General, *British Army Review*, issue 79, August 1985.
6. Protheroe, Staff Sergeant, H., 1 Squadron, 1st Battalion GPR, by permission of *The Eagle*.
7. Davis, Squadron Leader, P., 38 Wing RAF, diary extract 14 July 1943.
8. Wilhemsmeyer, W., *British Army Review*, Issue 79, August 1985.
9. Protheroe, Staff Sergeant, H., 1 Squadron, 1st Battalion GPR, by permission of *The Eagle*.
10. Protheroe, Staff Sergeant, H., 1 Squadron, 1st Battalion GPR, by permission of *The Eagle*.

11. Protheroe, Staff Sergeant, H., 1 Squadron, 1st Battalion GPR, by permission of *The Eagle*.
12. Atkinson, Warrant Officer 2, W., 1 Squadron, 1st Battalion GPR, by permission of *The Eagle*.
13. DFC citation, Barrie, Lieutenant, J., by permission of Mr M. Barrie.
14. *History of the Glider Pilot Regiment*, Pen & Sword Ltd, Barnsley, 1992, p. 65.

CHAPTER 17

The Phoenix Rising

This was a serious disaster

The swift withdrawal of 1st Airborne Division from Sicily to North Africa had always been part of the overall plan for Operation HUSKY, with 1st Airlanding Brigade and 1st Parachute Brigade being recovered, reorganised and reformed as quickly as practicable. Once ready for action again, the aim was that it could then either be redeployed again on Sicily or held in reserve for landings on the Italian mainland.

In the days following LADBROKE and FUSTIAN it was immediately obvious, however, that 1st Airborne Division would not be capable of mounting operations on any such scale for some time. Even before the 1st Parachute Brigade was committed to the Ponte di Primosole attack, serious doubts existed among the Allied hierarchy as to the viability of further large-scale airborne operations on Sicily. 1st Airlanding Brigade had suffered so many casualties, and lost so many gliders, that it was in no fit state to play any further part in the campaign.

In the days and weeks that followed the withdrawal of the division, small groups of glider pilots steadily found their way back to North Africa from Sicily, Malta and from the ships that had rescued them from the sea. Slowly the core of Nos 2 and 3 Squadrons were reforming into the semblance of their former selves.

These survivors were reinforced with the arrival from England of the balance of 1st Battalion GPR from Fargo Camp at Tilshead. This had left Liverpool in June under the command of the battalion's second-in-command, Major Maurice Willoughby. The journey on board the troopship *Samaria* had proved an uneventful one and the much-needed pilots arrived without incident in Algiers where they waited in harbour for two days. They had then been transferred to an American ship in which they embarked for Philipville. It was at this point in the journey, however, that Major Willoughby and his men went adrift. Having been disembarked at Philipville, they were moved to No. 5 Infantry Reinforcement Training Depot where they remained, seemingly trapped in a state of limbo. It took twelve days of frequent and increasingly frantic signals between Willoughby, Headquarters 1st Airborne Division and Allied Force Headquarters in Algiers before the glider pilots were released and transported onwards to 1st Battalion GPR and their respective squadrons. As a result, they did not arrive until a week after FUSTIAN and thus were too late to take part in the Sicily operations.

The reception that they received from the survivors of Nos 2 and 3 Squadrons was described by many as 'cool'. Those who had survived ditching in the sea or the battles inland were in sombre and reflective mood. Any atmosphere between the two different groups, however, soon cleared when conversion training on the WACO brought veterans and new arrivals together in the cockpit. Nevertheless, away from the airfields, the resentment and anger felt by the survivors of the LADBROKE lift towards their USAAF tug crews still had the potential to flare up and cause a damaging rift between the two Allied armies. Emotions were running high among the British, including the men of the 2nd Battalion The South Staffordshire Regiment who were effectively out of the campaign. Their anger over the unnecessary loss of so many comrades was close to boiling point. Sergeant Norman Howes, who with his fellow survivors had been confined to their tented camps in order to prevent any physical contact with the USAAF, later summed up the strength of feeling among the remnants of his battalion at the time:

> We went in with 800 men ... I think the statistics were, we went in with 800 men and we came back with 450, which is just under 50 per cent casualties and those casualties weren't prisoners of war or wounded – they were dead ... and we were feeling pretty badly about the Yanks.
>
> In fact we were kept at camp because the Yanks were ... there were some Yanks camped just over the hill and I think that we'd have lynched the bloody lot of them. We were so intensely angry at the way that they'd ... killed our men ... that was the feeling at that time.
>
> The General that was, I forget who it was then – Pip Hicks I believe was the Brigadier, 'Hoppy' was the Divisional Commander, and they brought some American Generals down to address us. We all sat down before this platform and they came forward and started talking to us and a little squaddie right in the front stood up and he took of his beret and he quietly started to sing the hymn 'For Those in Peril on the Sea' and we all joined in. And the Generals they turned around and ran, they left us ... There was no answer for what had happened to us.[1]

Lieutenant Colonel George Chatterton was very aware of the potential for friction between soldiers of the two nations. His own men were also confined to camp and he, like the other commanding officers in 1st Airlanding Brigade, received clear orders from Headquarters 1st Airborne Division:

> When we returned to the shores of North Africa I was met by a staff officer and told: 'On no account will you allow any of your officers and men to get into any argument with the Americans about this operation.'[2]

Having taken part in the operation and witnessed the fighting at close hand, he had his own experiences of the landing and the subsequent battle on which to reflect. He also had wider concerns about what impact the postoperational reports, and high casualty figures, would have on the future of The Glider Pilot Regiment and 1st Airborne Division as a whole. The casualty figures made sober reading, and the numbers recorded for 1 Airlanding Brigade were high:

Killed in action on land	61
Wounded	133
Missing	44
Drowned	252
Total	490

The casualty figures for 1st Battalion GPR were equally stark:

	Officers	Other Ranks
Killed	3	11
Wounded	4	25
Missing	6	52
Total	13	88

With his battalion scattered around the Mediterranean and a limited number of gliders and tugs available for training, Chatterton had ample time to consider what had gone wrong:

> I was under no illusions concerning the main reason for the near disaster. Whatever mistakes I may have made, and no doubt I did make many, what I could not help was the limited training and, therefore, the limitations of the glider pilots.
>
> As I lay in my tent I meditated on all that had come to pass and I was determined that I would get to the highest authority and put my point of view. By good fortune, just at that time I was informed that The Glider Pilot Regiment was temporarily to come under the command of the United States Army Air Force, and I realized that my opportunity had come. But what must I do was to get the right people to hear what I had to say about the state of the regiment. Then I remembered that, buried in the sand was a bottle of Johnny Walker Whisky – my

> monthly ration. I dug it up and decided to go down to the tent of the local USAAF commander, Brigadier General Ray Dunn. It was about seven in the evening and he too was lying on his bed.
>
> 'Good evening sir' I said politely.
>
> 'Oh hullo, Colonel. Come on in,' answered Dunn.
>
> 'Thank you, sir. Look I've got a bottle of whisky here. I thought that you might like a drink.'
>
> 'You bet I would.' he cried, and jumped off his bed. 'Come on. Here are two mugs and some water.' We talked of this and that and inevitably of the recent operations in Sicily. Gradually the bottle emptied and I said: 'Colonel, may I tell you what I feel?'
>
> 'OK,' he answered, 'Go ahead.'
>
> 'Well sir,' I continued, 'I am sure that a great deal of the trouble on this operation was due to the fact that those in charge had no idea what we were being asked to do.'
>
> 'Well, so what?' he said, rather unsteadily.
>
> 'I feel that before further mistakes are made through sheer ignorance and lack of training, the top people should be made aware of what happened.'
>
> 'How do you think that can be done?' he asked.
>
> 'Well, sir, I think that if you would send me to England I could do it.'
>
> 'OK, boy, you can go. I'll fix it. I think it's a good idea.'
>
> 'There's one thing, sir,' I said.
>
> 'Yes?'
>
> 'If I go, could you get me the backing of a very high general? I have had too much experience of trying to do it without any real power behind me.'
>
> 'Who do you want then?' he said.
>
> I took a deep breath and said: 'General Eisenhower, sir. Is it possible?'
>
> 'Boy, you shall have Ike himself.'
>
> We went on drinking and talking, I cannot remember what happened next, but I know that we parted very good friends.'[3]

It would seem that Chatterton had found a strong ally in Brigadier General Dunn. The commander of the 51st Troop Carrier Wing was as determined as his British counterpart that the lessons of the Syracuse landing should be learned, drafting his own post-operational report for the USAAF chain of command in October 1943 in which he pulled no punches about the conduct of his own aircrews during the Sicily operations. The following paragraph extracted from his report could hardly be more frank:

> There was no flak within several thousand yards of the actual glider release point, but there is no doubt that the tug pilots, due to their lack of battle experience, saw flak come up from other points and estimated

> that it was a lot closer than it really was. The tendency therefore was for them to swing out away from that fire, whereas they were not in any actual real danger at the proper release point.[4]

In spite of this apparent unity, there are conflicting and controversial accounts that suggest that below the surface there was bad feeling between the USAAF Transport Command and 1st Battalion GPR. Major Maurice Willoughby recounted a conversation that he had with Brigadier General Dunn, while undergoing his own WACO conversion, during which the American became animated and vented his own anger:

> We told you at the briefing that a thirty miles per hour headwind was blowing off Sicily and proposed that the release heights should be raised a further 2,000 feet, but your people wouldn't have it. Now we are being blamed for the fiasco.[5]

Other versions of this statement put the suggested release height at an additional 1,000 feet rather than 2,000. Willoughby tactfully refused to be drawn into a debate or argument about the conduct of the operation or the role of the tug crews in the events that had occurred out over the Mediterranean, pointing out that he had not been involved in any aspect of the operation. At the time of the conversation, Lieutenant Colonel Chatterton was still in North Africa and was closely involved in the board of inquiry held by Headquarters 1st Airborne Division into the reasons for the near failure of Operation LADBROKE.

In the absence of the Commanding Officer, the daily management of the battalion's training and reconstitution rested firmly in the hands of Willoughby. Determined to rebuild the morale of the LADBROKE survivors and to integrate them with those newly arrived from England, he initiated a robust training programme that involved the entire battalion. This included WACO conversion and consolidation, military skills training, and organised recreational time for swimming and sport. Lieutenant Robin Walchli was one of the Ponte Primosole veterans who benefited from this regime:

> After a spell in hospital in Subrata near Tripoli, a very dejected subaltern returned to the olive grove groves of M'saken. In the company of Bill Barrie and the reassembled remnants of the squadron, and aided by daily swimming, weekends in Tunis and squadron recreational breaks in Hammamet, I soon recovered the zest for adventure. I was appointed Divisional Baggage Officer when the time came to return to England. The excitement of bidding au revoir to the squadron and then waiting for a couple of weeks for the arrival of a very ancient freighter proved too much ... having seen the baggage loaded, I then retired to hospital with jaundice. I recovered in time to link up with Major Frankie Potter of Div HQ who was also in hospital and who just happened to have a

> Humber staff car complete with a driver. We toured the Atlas Mountains and the coast of North Africa and eventually arrived in Algiers to catch a convoy home.[6]

Many of the glider pilots, who just over a year hence were to escape from Arnhem in September 1944 by swimming across the lower Rhine, owed their prowess in the water to the regular swimming training organised for them in North Africa. The training programme initiated by Major Willoughby would seem to be a logical and effective course of action, but it led him into direct confrontation with his Commanding Officer.

After so many years it is difficult, if not almost impossible, to know exactly what followed and for what reason. What is known is that Willoughby and Lieutenant Colonel Chatterton were seen to have what was described as 'a blazing row'. It is thought that the latter perhaps felt that his position as Commanding Officer was being undermined by Willoughby's training programme, and his probing questions about the general conduct of the operation, and the decision on cast-off heights in particular. There are some clues about the undercurrents between the two men at the time in the following passage, written by Chatterton, referring to Anglo-US relations in North Africa immediately after the return from Sicily:

> There were many unpleasant rumours in the air that they let us cast-off too early, but I tried not to listen to them, for recriminations seemed useless. I even had trouble among my own officers, some of whom wished to make me the scapegoat for the fact that so many gliders had landed in the sea. In fact such an ugly situation arose that two officers had to be dealt with. Even today, one senior officer (who incidentally took no part in the operation) is a severe critic of mine.[7]

Major Maurice Willoughby was charged with undermining the authority of his superior officer and dismissed from the battalion. As was his right, he challenged the verdict and appealed to the divisional commander, Major General Hopkinson. The appeal was not heard as Hopkinson refused to see Willoughby and so, in company with Major T.R. Mordaunt-Hare, Willoughby was unceremoniously shipped back to England. His own version of events add more background to the reasons for the conflict:

> In fact we had kept what views we had to ourselves and had supported him at all times. We had told the CO that instead of sitting around doing nothing it was high time the pilots who had been on HUSKY should start doing some military training for the good of their own morale. This was met with a violent reaction.[8]

There were other incidents linked to the Operation LADBROKE landings that have caused some controversy over the years. One of which was the recommendation by the British of Flight Officer Samuel Fine for a gallantry award. A citation was drafted by Headquarters 1st Battalion GPR, recommending the American for the award of the US Silver Star. This was supported by several witness statements from British airborne soldiers. Brigadier General Harold L. Clark USAAF, the commander of 52nd Troop Carrier Wing dismissed the citation on the grounds that glider pilots were pilots, and therefore not eligible for gallantry awards reserved for soldiers.

At the conclusion of the LADBROKE board of inquiry in August 1943, Lieutenant Colonel Chatterton handed over command of the battalion to his newly appointed second-in-command, Major John Place, and then set off back to England to make the case for the retention of The Glider Pilot Regiment in the British Army's order of battle. He left North Africa with the blessing of Major General Hopkinson and Brigadier General Dunn.

Soon after Chatterton's departure, 1st Battalion GPR received new orders from Headquarters 1st Airborne Division. Secret negotiations between the Allied powers and members of the Italian government were very close to fruition, and the Italians were poised to surrender and join the war on the Allied side. The Allies planned to land on the Italian mainland 24 hours before the Italians capitulated, and 1st Airborne Division was earmarked to play a role in a subsequent operation that was codenamed SLAPSTICK. It was tasked with seizing the key Italian naval base and port of Taranto, but this would not be an airborne operation as the USAAF transport fleet had been withdrawn to support US airborne forces. The division would thus carry out a seaborne landing at Taranto.

Although gliders would play no part in the operation, 1st Battalion GPR would still featured in Major General Hopkinson's plans. The heavy casualties suffered by 1st Airlanding Brigade and 1st Parachute Brigade had not yet been replaced and so Major John Place received orders that he was to convert his battalion to the infantry role. The battalion, which now numbered 400 officers and senior NCOs, was to be employed as light infantry for the Taranto operation and Place had just 48 hours to reorganise and equip his men for their new role. The landing on 9 September 1943 was not expected to be opposed, the object of 1st Airborne Division's landing being to facilitate the escape of the Italian fleet from its anchorage at Taranto. The Italian Army had by this time surrendered but there was always the risk that the landing could be opposed by fanatical Italian troops or, worse, German forces. Major John Place later commented on the task given to him:

> I was given forty-eight hours to convert the battalion from a glider pilot unit of six squadrons into an infantry unit of four companies! I was limited as to the number of officers I took and the equipment to be carried with us. I was allowed only the bare essentials of cooking kit and the minimum of baggage, but I was required to work out a complete scale of arms and ammunition, as for a normal airborne battalion, or as

> near as we could get to it. But we were allowed no transport! Not even a Jeep. It was a terrific task but we managed it.[9]

The newly re-roled battalion moved by road convoy to Bizerta where it was ordered to embark on ships. The leading company, under command of Major G. Coulthard, was embarked aboard the cruiser HMS *Aurora* and was to act as an advance guard, therefore sailing first. The main body of the battalion meanwhile boarded the troopship *Princess Beatrix*. The crossing to Taranto passed without interference, the glider pilots witnessing the unusual sight of Italian submarines sailing on the surface toward Malta where they were to surrender to the Royal Navy. They were followed later during the crossing by the still formidable Italian surface fleet, also steaming toward Malta.

The leading elements of 1st Airborne Division landed unopposed at Taranto on 9 September, the first ashore being Headquarters 4th Parachute Brigade and 10th Parachute Battalion, which immediately moved inland to guard against any German counter-attack. The remainder of 1st and 4th Parachute Brigades then landed on the following day; it was at this point that tragedy struck when the fast minelayer HMS *Abdiel* struck a stray mine in the harbour and sank, taking with her 130 officers and men of 6th Parachute Battalion. The two brigades then moved through Taranto and deployed north of the city where they established defensive positions

Thereafter, 1st Airborne Division advanced northwards but as it did so encountered strong opposition from a strong German rearguard, comprising elements of 1. Fallschirmjäger-Division, which had established a series of ambushes and roadblocks to impede the British advance. One such roadblock, near the town of Castellenat, was attacked on 10 September by 10th Parachute Battalion. During the ensuing action Major General Hopkinson, who was observing the attack from nearby, was hit by a burst of machine gun fire. He died of his wounds in hospital on the following day, being replaced as divisional commander by Brigadier Eric Down.

Meanwhile, the pilots of 1st Battalion GPR had not been required to prove their mettle in the infantry role but were instead employed in a series of support roles in and around Taranto. Staff Sergeant Tommy Gillies had travelled aboard HMS *Aurora* with No. 3 Squadron. After witnessing the loss of HMS *Abdiel*, he and his comrades were soon involved in carrying out some of the secondary tasks allocated to them:

> We boarded the cruiser *Aurora* at Biserta together with a motley bunch of behind-the-lines combatants including the Phantoms and Popski's Private Army ... on arrival in Taranto hundreds of Italian sailors surrendered, and with Taranto having earlier suffered heavy bombing the town was in a state of chaos. Not knowing what to expect the Italians were terrified. At one time the squadron was given the task of

> manning the Taranto Bridge, which meant examining the papers of all civilians passing through. Having no Italian linguists, the examinations were to say the least cursory![10]

As the war moved further north, 1st Battalion GPR was concentrated at Putignano in Italy where it awaited further orders. In November 1943, a series of movement orders were received by the battalion headquarters that would split the now tightly knit unit. The bulk of the battalion was returned to Sousse from where it was then embarked on a number of troop convoys returning to England. The majority arrived back in England in December 1943 and January 1944.

The officers and men of No. 3 Squadron, however, received different orders. They were to remain in the Mediterranean theatre of operations under command of Major G. Coulthard, being redesignated the Independent Glider Squadron and attached to 2nd Independent Parachute Brigade. By the end of November 1943, the squadron was established alongside the US Airborne Training Centre on the airfield at Oujda in French Morocco. Here its pilots underwent refresher training on WACO gliders and prepared for their new role. Thereafter, the squadron returned to Sicily and continued to build up flying hours by day and, most importantly, by night. Its first mission, Operation BUNGHOLE, involved flying three Horsas, towed by C-47s of the 64th Troop Carrier Command USAAF, across the Adriatic into Yugoslavia. The gliders were loaded with supplies, weapons, members of the SAS and a Soviet Military Mission to Tito and his partisans. The mission was a huge success and the three crews returned to the squadron after weeks living with the partisans behind enemy lines.

The Independent Glider Squadron also took part in Operation DRAGOON, the invasion of Southern France in August 1944. Success there was followed by Operation MANNA, the liberation of Greece in October 1944, in which the squadron played a pivotal role in the timely delivery of elements of 2nd Parachute Brigade Group and its heavy weapons. This was the squadron's final operation of the war as it returned to England as part of 2nd Independent Parachute Brigade Group in June 1945.

At the same time that No. 3 Squadron was being redesignated and redeployed, another small group of glider pilots was told that it also would not be returning to England. Major Peter Stancliffe was selected to command the group that comprised four officers, a warrant officer and 25 senior NCOs. He and his men were then shipped to India where they would form the nucleus of the airlanding component of the newly established 44th Indian Airborne Division. Equipped with WACOs, this small group would ultimately develop into a glider force of five squadrons.

While the remainder of 1st Battalion GPR awaited embarkation for England, Lieutenant Colonel George Chatterton had already arrived there in August 1943. Armed with his letter of authority signed by Air Commodore Wigglesworth on behalf of General Dwight D. Eisenhower, he set about lobbying and educating senior officers and their staff officers on the planning considerations and technical requirements of glider operations. He gathered support among the higher echelons of the War Office, the Air Ministry and, most significantly, the RAF.

The newly promoted Colonel Chatterton, who now held the appointment of Commander Glider Pilots, then visited The Glider Pilot Regiment Depot at Fargo Camp on Salisbury Plain but he was far from impressed with what he found, the training regime being far removed from what he now knew was required to produce well-qualified glider pilots who were fully integrated into the RAF. The newly formed 2nd Battalion GPR, however, had adopted the same tough training regime as that implemented to create its predecessor: drill and physical training were very much the order of the day, with flying training on Hotspur gliders taking place at Netheravon Airfield.

Chatterton discovered, however, that critically the student glider pilots were kept well away from their aircraft and had little contact with their RAF tug crews. Their daily routine consisted of a drive in trucks from Fargo Camp to Netheravon, a march up to dispersal, flying training, and then a march back to the transport for the return to Fargo Camp. The painful experience of Sicily had taught Chatterton that this segregation would not produce the team mentality required to produce the strong bond of understanding between tug and glider crews that would deliver the latter on to LZs under fire. The concept of the Total Soldier had been proven on both Sicily operations, and those glider pilots who had reached their objectives had been required to fight, acquitting themselves well. It was however now evident that the focus of their training was unevenly loaded toward military skills rather than the ability to fly. Something had to change and it had to be done quickly. Years later Chatterton, by then a brigadier, would reflect on the situation:

> After Sicily it was realised that if it were to operate really efficiently, the glider force must undergo a radical change. From now on it should be 'blue printed' to the RAF. From now on, its home was the RAF hangars and airfields. It became a homogenous unit in that it had one controlling headquarters ... Naturally many people did not like it. But the main organisation remained the same: once he was on the ground, the pilot was an infantryman. He had to fight along with the rest of them.'[11]

In a few short weeks, through the autumn of 1943, a radical plan was developed to reorganise The Glider Pilot Regiment. Meanwhile the training of the 2nd Battalion continued at Fargo Camp and Netheravon, while in Italy the 1st Battalion was being misemployed at Taranto by the 1st Airborne Division.

The lessons of Sicily had also been identified by the higher echelons of the Allied command structure. General Alexander, the commander of 15th Army Group, felt qualified to comment on what was required in the future and with an eye on the invasion of Normandy, wrote a paper advocating the continued use of airborne forces. Critically, he too, stresses the need for dedicated transport aircraft and closer integration of airborne forces and the RAF;

> The recent operations have proved the value of airborne troops, and given us a peep into their great possibilities if they are properly organized and employed. I can say without hesitation that the early capture of Syracuse was largely due to the 1st Airborne Division which was dropped outside the town to seize the immediate approaches to the port, and later the important bridge across the River Simeto, south of Catania.
>
> The airborne troops themselves are excellent. Tough, fit, efficient and of high morale; I don't say that they haven't a lot to learn which can only be done by Training-Experience-Training. The outstanding weakness in the set-up is the lack of trained air force pilots to transport them. Through no fault of their own, they are untrained for and inexperienced in the job. The RAF must produce the pilots if we are to develop the arm, which I am convinced we must do.
>
> Personally, I believe that it is the best solution to the invasion of Europe across the channel – airborne troops in large numbers in conjunction with the attack on the coast from the sea. I look at the problem like this: Tactics are continually changing with the introduction of new weapons and new equipment. The side which can take advantage of this and develop its tactics accordingly before its enemy will keep the initiative and produce the new surprises – both battle-winning factors. The land defences have few, if any, open flanks to get round and turn but there is one flank (if you so term it) – the flank, or open door which is always there. It is there wide open for the side which has the air superiority. What an opportunity for us, if we can only seize it.
>
> Therefore, I repeat, we must at once raise, organize, equip and train an airborne force of parachutists and gliders – say a corps of two divisions. The RAF pilots, crews and machines must be made available and put aside for this corps with whom they must live, work and train to the exclusion of everything else.
>
> I know that the answer will be that it is quite impossible to afford the pilots and the aircraft. Well! it is a question of priorities and personally I firmly believe that with our growing air supremacy, priority No. 1 is for the Airborne Corps.[12]

The reorganisation of The Glider Pilot Regiment was very much in tune with the mood of the time. Such heavy losses were tragic and almost certainly unsustainable. Now Chatterton and his small headquarters staff set about remoulding the regiment. In order to ensure that he had access to the key RAF staff officers that he needed, Chatterton established his office in the cellars of Headquarters 38 Wing RAF. Although he and his staff were frequently covered in coal dust, this location gave him direct access to the headquarters that controlled the airfields and tug aircraft that he needed so badly and to influence in future planning. This key decision was to result in exactly the kind of relationship required between The Glider Pilot Regiment and RAF Transport Command. Using the authority of 38 Wing RAF, Chatterton carried out a programme of tours and inspections, visiting numerous airfields around England. The result was a plan for the co-location of Glider Pilot Regiment squadrons and their supporting tug squadrons, being interwoven with the RAFs own plan to expand 38 Wing to become 38 Group RAF and the formation of a second transport formation – 46 Group RAF. With airfields and transports promised or already in place, the restructuring of The Glider Pilot Regiment could also get underway.

The regiment's two battalions were formally re-titled as wings, each made up of squadrons. Four squadrons were grouped under No. 1 Wing GPR, commanded by Lieutenant Colonel Iain Murray MC, while Lieutenant Colonel John Place was appointed to command No. 2 Wing GPR, which comprised the three squadrons that had taken part in the Sicily operations. Each of the squadrons was made up of three to five flights of 44 pilots. Wherever possible, each squadron was to be located at the same airfield as its attendant RAF tug squadron, the aim being that the two units would over time build a close working relationship and an understanding of each other's requirements on operations.

The return of the Sicilian veterans, who embarked at Taranto on Christmas Eve 1943 and arrived at Liverpool in early January 1944, coincided with the reorganisation of the regiment, news of which did not do anything to assuage their feelings of neglect. The re-designation of the battle-proven 1st Battalion as No. 2 Wing GPR, with the newly formed 2nd Battalion being given the title of No. 1 Wing GPR, did not impress the veterans of Sicily who perceived it to be a slight on their reputation.

The reorganisation proved timely, however, as the summer of 1944 would bring another major airborne operation. OVERLORD, the Allied invasion of Europe, was now looming on the horizon and airborne forces were destined to play a critical role in it. Elements of The Glider Pilot Regiment were destined to be among the first to land in occupied France in what was to be one of the most complex operations in military history. The centrepiece of the British airborne landing would be the now famous gliderborne coup de main attack on the bridges at Benouville spanning the River Orne and the Caen Canal. The successful capture of the bridges by the men of the 2nd Battalion Oxfordshire & Buckinghamshire Light Infantry would be attributed largely to the pinpoint accuracy of the landings made by the crews of The Glider Pilot Regiment that night.

Many of the glider pilots and RAF tug crews who flew the coup de main force from England to Normandy on the night of 5 June 1944, and the gliderborne elements of 6th Airborne Division on the following day, were survivors of Operations LADBROKE and FUSTIAN. In so doing, they ensured that the mistakes made over Sicily less than a year earlier were not repeated and thus it can perhaps be said that the men of the British airborne forces who lost their lives on those two operations did not die in vain.

Notes

1. Howes, Sergeant, N., C Company, 2nd Battalion, South Staffordshire Regiment, by permission of John Howes.
2. Chatterton, Lieutenant Colonel, G., 1st Battalion GPR, By permission of *The Eagle.*
3. Chatterton, Lieutenant Colonel, G., 1st Battalion GPR, *The Wings of Pegasus*, Nashville, Battery Press, 1962, p. 107.
4. Interview with Dunn, Brigadier, R., Commander US 51st Troop Carrier Wing USAAF, 14 October 1943, ABFM.
5. Dunn, Brigadier, R., Commander US 51st Troop Carrier Wing USAAF, *Operation Ladbroke*, Woodfield, p. 107.
6. Walchli, Lieutenant, R., 1 Squadron, 1st Battalion GPR, By permission of *The Eagle*.
7. Chatterton, Lieutenant Colonel, G., 1st Battalion GPR, *The Wings of Pegasus*, Nashville, Battery Press, 1962, p. 105.
8. Willoughby, Major, M., 1st Battalion GPR, *History of The Glider Pilot Regiment*, Pen & Sword, Barnsley, p. 70.
9. Place, Major, J., CO, 1st Battalion GPR, by permission of *The Eagle*.
10. Gillies, Staff Sergeant, T., 3 Squadron, 1st Battalion GPR, By permission of *The Eagle*.
11. Chatterton, Brigadier, G., DSO. By permission of *The Eagle*.
12. Alexander response to Churchill August 1943 (PREMIER 3/32/5).

Appendix 1

Operation LADBROKE Post Mission Reports

Glider Chalk No.	Glider Type	Departure Airfield	Pilot 1/ Pilot 2	Unit Carried	Tug Aircraft/ Tug A/C No.	Pilot	Group/ Squadron	Comment	Released within 3,000 yards of land	Released more than 3,000 yards from land
1	Waco	A El Djem Base	RSM Archer/ S/Sgt Cram	'B' Company 2 South Staffords			60 Group	Landed in Sea		X
2	Waco	A El Djem Base	Lt Col Chatterton/ Lt Harding	Lt Col McCardie 2 South Staffords			60 Group	Landed in Sea		X
3	Waco	A El Djem Base	Major Murray/ Lt Brazier	Battalion HQ 2 South Staffords			60 Group	Landed in Sea		X
4	Waco	A El Djem Base	Lt Ellson/ Sgt Baxter	'D' Company 2 South Staffords			60 Group	Landed in Sea		X
5	Waco	A El Djem Base	S/Sgt Rodway/ Sgt J. Smith	'B' Company 2 South Staffords			60 Group	Made landfall	X	
6	Waco	A El Djem Base	Lt Barclay/ Sgt Owen	HQ Coy 2 South Staffords			60 Group	Made landfall		X
7	Waco	A El Djem Base	Lt G.C.P. Impey (2)/ Lt Robson	Battalion HQ 2 South Staffords			60 Group	Landed in Sea	X	
8	Waco	A El Djem Base	S/Sgt Dawkins/ Sgt Kelly	'D' Company 2 South Staffords			60 Group	Made landfall	X	

Glider Chalk No.	Glider Type	Departure Airfield	Pilot 1/ Pilot 2	Unit Carried	Tug Aircraft/ Tug A/C No.	Pilot	Group/ Squadron	Comment	Released within 3,000 yards of land	Released more than 3,000 yards from land
9	Waco	A El Djem Base	S/Sgt Mowatt/ Sgt Bell	'B' Company 2 South Staffords			60 Group	Made landfall		X
10	Waco	A El Djem Base	S/Sgt Andrews/ F/O Kyle	Battalion HQ 1 Airlanding Brigade			60 Group	Made landfall		X
11	Waco	A El Djem Base	S/Sgt Palmer/ Sgt New	Battalion HQ 2 South Staffords			60 Group	Made landfall		X
12	Waco	A El Djem Base	S/Sgt McConnell/ Sgt Fowell	'D' Company 2 South Staffords			60 Group	Unaccounted for – probably landed in sea		
13	Waco	A El Djem Base	S/Sgt E.B. Wikner (2)/ F/O Fine	'B' Company 2 South Staffords			60 Group	Made landfall	X	
14	Waco	A El Djem Base	S/Sgt J.B. Taylor/ Sgt P.A. Wilson				60 Group	Landed in Sea		X
15	Waco	A El Djem Base	Sgt Robertson/ F/O G.T. Petroulias (5)	Battalion HQ 2 South Staffords			60 Group	Landed in Sea		X
16	Waco	A El Djem Base	S/Sgt O'Donnell/ Sgt Walker	'D' Company 2 South Staffords			60 Group	Landed in Sea		X
17	Waco	A El Djem Base	Sgt Dowds/ Sgt Boyce	'B' Company 2 South Staffords			60 Group	Landed in Sea		X
18	Waco	A El Djem Base	Sgt Allen/ F/O Cugene				60 Group	Landed in Sea		X
19	Waco	A El Djem Base	S/Sgt L Turnbull/ Sgt Saunders	Mortar Platoon 2 South Staffords			60 Group	Landed in Sea		X
20	Waco	A El Djem Base	Sgt R.V. Brown (1)/ Sgt J. Church (1)	'D' Company 2 South Staffords			60 Group	Landed in Sea		X

Glider Chalk No.	Glider Type	Departure Airfield	Pilot 1/ Pilot 2	Unit Carried	Tug Aircraft/ Tug A/C No.	Pilot	Group/ Squadron	Comment	Released within 3,000 yards of land	Released more than 3,000 yards from land
21	Waco	A El Djem Base	Capt R.M. Hanson (1)/ Sgt East	'B' Company 2 South Staffords			60 Group	Landed in Sea		X
22	Waco	A El Djem Base	S/Sgt Mather/ Sgt Meakin	att'd 2 South Staffords 181 Field Ambulance			60 Group	Landed in Sea		X
23	Waco	A El Djem Base	Lt O.E. Mathias (1)/ Sgt D.N. Willis (1)	Mortar Platoon 2 South Staffords	C47 – #23471		60 Group	Unaccounted for		
24	Waco	A El Djem Base	S/Sgt Wallwork/ Sgt D.W.J. Richards (2)	'D' Company 2 South Staffords			60 Group	Made landfall	X	
25	Waco	A El Djem Base	S/Sgt Fairgrieve/ Sgt Lowett	'B' Company 2 South Staffords			60 Group	Made landfall	X	
26	Waco	A El Djem Base	S/Sgt Naismith/ Sgt Coppack	att'd 2 South Staffords 181 Field Ambulance			60 Group	Made landfall	X	
27	Waco	A El Djem Base	Sgt E. Barker (1)/ Sgt G.R. Barker	Mortar Platoon 2 South Staffords			60 Group	Landed in Sea		X
28	Waco	A El Djem Base	S/Sgt Glover/ F/O Bates	'D' Company 2 South Staffords			60 Group	Landed in Sea	X	
29	Waco	B El Djem No. 1	Sgt Wilson/ Sgt Pitcock	'B' Company 2 South Staffords			60 Group	Made landfall		X
30	Waco	B El Djem No. 1	Sgt Cato/ Sgt Cook	att'd 2 South Staffords 181 Field Ambulance			60 Group	Landed in Sea		X
31	Waco	B El Djem No. 1	Sgt Moorcock/ Sgt Mills	Mortar Platoon 2 South Staffords			60 Group	Landed in Sea		X
32	Waco	B El Djem No. 1	S/Sgt S. Howard/ Sgt D.J.V. Bennett (1)	'D' Company 2 South Staffords			60 Group	Landed in Sea		X
33	Waco	B El Djem No. 1	Sgt Davidson/ Sgt Langton	'B' Company 2 South Staffords			60 Group	Made landfall	X	

Glider Chalk No.	Glider Type	Departure Airfield	Pilot 1/ Pilot 2	Unit Carried	Tug Aircraft/ Tug A/C No.	Pilot	Group/ Squadron	Comment	Released within 3,000 yards of land	Released more than 3,000 yards from land
34	Waco	B El Djem No. 1	Sgt May/ Sgt Marshall	Signal Spares 2 South Staffords			60 Group	Made landfall	X	
35	Waco	B El Djem No. 1	S/Sgt Howard/ Sgt Tigar	Pioneer Platoon 2 South Staffords			60 Group	Made landfall	X	
36	Waco	B El Djem No. 1	S/Sgt Warburton/ Sgt Paynton	'D' Company 2 South Staffords			60 Group	Made landfall	X	
37	Waco	B El Djem No. 1	S/Sgt Crook/ S/Sgt Redknap	'B' Company 2 South Staffords			60 Group	Made landfall	X	
38	Waco	B El Djem No. 1	Lt Dale/ Sgt Baker	att'd 2 South Staffords 9 Field Company RE			60 Group	Made landfall	X	
39	Waco	B El Djem No. 1	S/Sgt Ainsworth/ Sgt Sibley	Pioneer Platoon 2 South Staffords			60 Group	Landed in Sea		X
40	Waco	B El Djem No. 1	S.S.M. Blackwood/ Sgt Silcock	'D' Company 2 South Staffords			60 Group	Made landfall	X	
41	Waco	B El Djem No. 1	Capt Plowman/ S/Sgt Feehily	'H' Company 2 South Staffords			60 Group	Returned not having cast off		
42	Waco	B El Djem No. 1	S/Sgt Bird/ Sgt Toller	att'd 2 South Staffords 9 Field Company RE			60 Group	Did not cross North African Coast		
43	Waco	B El Djem No. 1	S/Sgt D.H. Smith (1)/ Sgt S.A. Surry (1)	'E' Company 2 South Staffords			60 Group	Unaccounted for – probably landed in sea		
44	Waco	B El Djem No. 1	Sgt J. Harmer (1)/ Sgt W.R. Holland (1)				60 Group	Landed in Sea		X
45	Waco	B El Djem No. 1	Sgt Campbell/ Sgt McCuish	'H' Company 2 South Staffords			60 Group	Made landfall	X	
46	Waco	B El Djem No. 1	Sgt Dyer/ Sgt Maddocks	att'd 2 South Staffords 9 Field Company RE			60 Group	Made landfall	X	

Glider Chalk No.	Glider Type	Departure Airfield	Pilot 1/ Pilot 2	Unit Carried	Tug Aircraft/ Tug A/C No.	Pilot	Group/ Squadron	Comment	Released within 3,000 yards of land	Released more than 3,000 yards from land
47	Waco	B El Djem No. 1	Sgt Moore/ Sgt Garratt	'E' Company 2 South Staffords			60 Group	Made landfall	X	
48	Waco	B El Djem No. 1	Lt V. Whittington-Steiner (1)/ Sgt Wood	'E' Company 2 South Staffords			60 Group	Unaccounted for – probably landed in sea		
49	Waco	B El Djem No. 1	Sgt S.A. Maynard (2)/ Sgt Firth	'H' Company 2 South Staffords			60 Group	Made landfall	X	
50	Waco	B El Djem No. 1	Sgt Vickers/ Sgt Sutton	att'd 2 South Staffords 9 Field Company RE			60 Group	Made landfall	X	
51	Waco	B El Djem No. 1	Sgt James/ Sgt Beard	'E' Company 2 South Staffords			60 Group	Made landfall		X
52	Waco	B El Djem No. 1	Sgt Attwell/ Sgt Wakefield	'E' Company 2 South Staffords			60 Group	Returned not having cast off		
52A	Waco	B El Djem No. 1	Sgt Barnwell/ F/O Parks	'E' Company 2 South Staffords			60 Group	Made landfall	X	
53	Waco	B El Djem No. 1	Lt Grieve/ Sgt Lunn	'H' Company 2 South Staffords			60 Group	Landed in Sea		X
53A	Waco	B El Djem No. 1	Sgt Landadell/ 2/Lt Kinney	Simforce 2 South Staffords			60 Group	Landed in Sea	X	
54	Waco	B El Djem No. 1	Sgt Sands/ Sgt Jones	att'd 2 South Staffords 9 Field Company RE			60 Group	Landed in Sea		X
54A	Waco	B El Djem No. 1	Sgt J.A.A. Bennett (1)/ Sgt W.J. Morel (1)	Simforce 2 South Staffords			60 Group	Landed in Sea		X
55	Waco	C El Djem No. 2	Major Place/ Maj Gen Hopkinson	'C' Company 1 Border			62 Group	Landed in Sea		X
56	Waco	C El Djem No. 2	S/Sgt R. Dance/ Sgt E. Barker (1)	'D' Company 1 Border			62 Group	Landed in Sea		X

Glider Chalk No.	Glider Type	Departure Airfield	Pilot 1/ Pilot 2	Unit Carried	Tug Aircraft/ Tug A/C No.	Pilot	Group/ Squadron	Comment	Released within 3,000 yards of land	Released more than 3,000 yards from land
57	Waco	C El Djem No. 2	Lt Buchan/ F/O Rau	Battalion HQ 1 Border			62 Group	Landed in Sea		X
58	Waco	C El Djem No. 2	Lt M.B. Connell (1)/ Sgt H.D.J. Hill (1)	Battalion HQ 1 Border			62 Group	Landed in Sea		X
59	Waco	C El Djem No. 2	S/Sgt Barclay/ Sgt Shirley	'C' Company 1 Border			62 Group	Landed in Sea		X
60	Waco	C El Djem No. 2	S/Sgt J.A. Boorman (1)/ F/O Diewaltowski	'D' Company 1 Border			62 Group	Landed in Sea		X
61	Waco	C El Djem No. 2	Lt Iremonger/ Sgt Cole	'A' Company 1 Border			62 Group	Landed in Sea		X
62	Waco	C El Djem No. 2	Sgt Lee/ F/O Johnson	att'd 1 Border 181 Field Ambulance			62 Group	Landed in Sea		X
63	Waco	C El Djem No. 2	S.S.M. Masson/ Sgt D.L. Cason	'C' Company 1 Border			62 Group	Made landfall	X	
64	Waco	C El Djem No. 2	Lt Godman/ Lt Hayes (American)	'D' Company 1 Border			62 Group	Landed in Sea		X
65	Waco	C El Djem No. 2	Sgt R.R. Burton (1)/ Sgt E.D. Baker	'A' Company 1 Border			62 Group	Landed in Sea		X
66	Waco	C El Djem No. 2	S/Sgt T.G. Laidlaw (4)/ Sgt Simons	att'd 1 Border 181 Field Ambulance			62 Group	Landed in Sea		X
67	Waco	C El Djem No. 2	Sgt Battersby/ Sgt R.N. Clarke	'C' Company 1 Border			62 Group	Made landfall	X	
68	Waco	C El Djem No. 2	Sgt Ellis/ Sgt Bates	'D' Company 1 Border			62 Group	Landed in Sea		X
69	Waco	C El Djem No. 2	Sgt L.N. Ryan (1)/ Sgt C.J. Smith	'A' Company 1 Border			62 Group	Made landfall	X	

Glider Chalk No.	Glider Type	Departure Airfield	Pilot 1/ Pilot 2	Unit Carried	Tug Aircraft/ Tug A/C No.	Pilot	Group/ Squadron	Comment	Released within 3,000 yards of land	Released more than 3,000 yards from land
70	Waco	C El Djem No. 2	Sgt Dilnutt/ F/O A. Bordewich (6)	att'd 1 Border 181 Field Ambulance			62 Group	Landed in Sea		X
71	Waco	C El Djem No. 2	S/Sgt G.A.L. Reeves (1)/ F/O Daves	'C' Company 1 Border			62 Group	Landed in Sea		X
72	Waco	C El Djem No. 2	S/Sgt Hay/ Sgt G.A.V. Hill (2)	'D' Company 1 Border			62 Group	Landed in Sea		X
73	Waco	C El Djem No. 2	Sgt G. Scriven/ Sgt D.E. Witham (1)	'A' Company 1 Border			62 Group	Landed in Sea		X
74	Waco	C El Djem No. 2	Sgt Leadbetter/ F/O Dees	'B' Company 1 Border			62 Group	Landed in Sea		X
75	Waco	C El Djem No. 2	Sgt P. Mansfield/ Sgt R.A. McLeod	'C' Company 1 Border			62 Group	Landed in Sea	X	
76	Waco	C El Djem No. 2	Sgt Stewart/ Sgt Joyce	'D' Company 1 Border			62 Group	Made landfall	X	
77	Waco	C El Djem No. 2	S/Sgt P.L.G. Hampshire (1)/ Sgt J.E. Randell (1)	'A' Company 1 Border			62 Group	Landed in Sea		X
78	Waco	C El Djem No. 2	Sgt McLean/ Sgt H. Brown	'B' Company 1 Border			62 Group	Landed in Sea		X
79	Waco	C El Djem No. 2	Sgt L. Raggett/ Sgt H. Rossdale	'C' Company 1 Border			62 Group	Made landfall	X	
80	Waco	C El Djem No. 2	Sgt O. Morgan/ Sgt Russell	'D' Company 1 Border			62 Group	Made landfall	X	
81	Waco	D Goubrine Base	Lt I.A. McArthur/ Lt T. Breach	'C' Company 1 Border			62 Group	Made landfall	X	
82	Waco	D Goubrine Base	Sgt S. Peacock/ Sgt G. Cushing	'D' Company 1 Border			62 Group	Landed in Sea	X	

Glider Chalk No.	Glider Type	Departure Airfield	Pilot 1/ Pilot 2	Unit Carried	Tug Aircraft/ Tug A/C No.	Pilot	Group/ Squadron	Comment	Released within 3,000 yards of land	Released more than 3,000 yards from land
83	Waco	D Goubrine Base	S/Sgt S. Coates/ Sgt V. Percy	'A' Company 1 Border			62 Group	Returned not having cast off		
84	Waco	D Goubrine Base	S/Sgt Bridges/ Sgt D.G. Jones (1)	'B' Company 1 Border			62 Group	Unaccounted for		
85	Waco	D Goubrine Base	S/Sgt Stewart/ Sgt Guinan	'C' Company 1 Border			62 Group	Returned not having cast off		
86	Waco	D Goubrine Base	Capt T.D.M. McMillan/ Lt B. Halsall	'D' Company 1 Border			62 Group	Made landfall	X	
87	Waco	D Goubrine Base	S/Sgt A.G. Shepherd (1)/ F/O C.R. McCollum (5)	'A' Company 1 Border	C47 - #15540		62 Group	Unaccounted for – probably landed in sea		
88	Waco	D Goubrine Base	Sgt K.A. Evans/ Sgt R.E. Martin	'B' Company 1 Border			62 Group	Made landfall	X	
89	Waco	D Goubrine Base	Sgt H.J. Aylott (1)/ F/O Wilson	'C' Company 1 Border			62 Group	Landed in Sea		X
90	Waco	D Goubrine Base	Sgt J. Frampton/ Sgt P. Cooke	'D' Company 1 Border			62 Group	Landed in Sea		X
91	Waco	D Goubrine Base	Sgt Anderson/ Sgt Caslaw	'A' Company 1 Border			62 Group	Landed in Sea		X
92	Waco	D Goubrine Base	Sgt Hill/ F/O Gunter	'B' Company 1 Border			62 Group	Landed in Sea		X
93	Waco	D Goubrine Base	Sgt D.E. Kent (2)/ Sgt P.S. Purcell (2)	'C' Company 1 Border			62 Group	Made landfall	X	
94	Waco	D Goubrine Base	Sgt R.B. Hall (1)/ F/O K. Hollinshead (6)	'D' Company 1 Border			62 Group	Landed in Sea		X
95	Waco	D Goubrine Base	Sgt M. Pryor/ Sgt E. Rowbotham	'A' Company 1 Border			62 Group	Made landfall		X

Glider Chalk No.	Glider Type	Departure Airfield	Pilot 1/ Pilot 2	Unit Carried	Tug Aircraft/ Tug A/C No.	Pilot	Group/ Squadron	Comment	Released within 3,000 yards of land	Released more than 3,000 yards from land
96	Waco	D Goubrine Base	Lt Stevens/ F/O White	'B' Company 1 Border			62 Group	Landed in Sea		X
97	Waco	D Goubrine Base	Sgt W.J. Percy (1)/ Sgt Reddish	'C' Company 1 Border			62 Group	Landed in Sea		
98	Waco	D Goubrine Base	Sgt W.J. Sleigh/ Sgt D. Tasker	'D' Company 1 Border			62 Group	Landed in Sea		X
99	Waco	D Goubrine Base	Sgt V. Taylor/ F/O Samek	'A' Company 1 Border			62 Group	Landed in Sea		X
100	Waco	D Goubrine Base	Sgt Worley/ F/O G.V. Capite (5)	'B' Company 1 Border			62 Group	Landed in Sea		X
101	Waco	D Goubrine Base	S/Sgt Henden/ Sgt L. Turner	'C' Company 1 Border			62 Group	Landed in Sea		X
101A	Waco	D Goubrine Base	Sgt Jeavons/ Sgt Westerby	'H' Company 1 Border			62 Group	Landed in Sea		X
102	Waco	D Goubrine Base	Sgt Cole/ Sgt D.N. Willis (1)	'D' Company 1 Border			62 Group	Landed in Sea		X
102A	Waco	Goubrine Base		'H' Company 1 Border				Did not take off as no Tug available		
103	Waco	D Goubrine Base	Sgt A. Gillies/ F/O Browning	'A' Company 1 Border			62 Group	Landed in Sea		X
103A	Waco	Goubrine Base		'H' Company 1 Border				Did not take off as no Tug available		
104	Waco	D Goubrine Base	Sgt Turner/ Sgt Flanders	'B' Company 1 Border			62 Group	Landed in Sea		X
104A	Waco	Goubrine Base		'H' Company 1 Border				Did not take off as no Tug available		

Glider Chalk No.	Glider Type	Departure Airfield	Pilot 1/ Pilot 2	Unit Carried	Tug Aircraft/ Tug A/C No.	Pilot	Group/ Squadron	Comment	Released within 3,000 yards of land	Released more than 3,000 yards from land
105	Waco	F Goubrine No. 2	Capt Boyd/ Sgt Bannister	att'd 1 Border 9 Field Company RE	Albermarle/ P 1373	F/O Merrick	296 Sqn	Made landfall		X
106	Waco	F Goubrine No. 2	S/Sgt K. Cawood/ S/Sgt A. Holt	Battalion HQ 1 Border	Albermarle/ P 1518	F/O Scott	296 Sqn	Made landfall	X	
107	Waco	F Goubrine No. 2	S/Sgt J.C. Carr (2)/ S/Sgt Matthews	'A' Company 1 Border	Albermarle/ P 1434	F/O Boyer	296 Sqn	Made landfall	X	
108	Waco	F Goubrine No. 2	Sgt Douglas/ Sgt Donald	'B' Company 1 Border	Albermarle/ P 1521	F/O McCall	296 Sqn	Made landfall		X
109	Waco	F Goubrine No. 2	S/Sgt J F Wood (3)/ Sgt Isaacs	'H' Company 1 Border	Albermarle/ P 1382	F/O Cumberworth	296 Sqn	Made landfall	X	
110	Waco	F Goubrine No. 2	Lt Boucher-Giles/ Sgt Miller (?)	'H' Company 1 Border	Albermarle/ P 1389	S/L Bartram	296 Sqn	Made landfall	X	
111	Waco	F Goubrine No. 2	S/Sgt A. Prescott/ Sgt Scott	'A' Company 1 Border	Albermarle/ P 1516	F/O Horn	296 Sqn	Landed in Sea		X
112	Waco	F Goubrine No. 2	Sgt Bayely/ Sgt Linscott	1 Border	Albermarle/ P 1444	F/O Hamer	296 Sqn	Landed in Sea		X
113	Waco	F Goubrine No. 2	S/Sgt MacDonald/ Sgt Welsh	'H' Company 1 Border	Albermarle/ P 1435	F/O Lee	296 Sqn	Pulled Off immediately after take off		
114	Waco	F Goubrine No. 2	Sgt Struthers/ Sgt Southey	H' Company 1 Border	Albermarle/ P 1466	P/O Matheson	296 Sqn	Landed in Sea		X
115	Waco	F Goubrine No. 2	S/Sgt Ferguson/ Sgt Rye	Recce Platoon 1 Border	Albermarle/ P 1469	P/O Cholmondeley	296 Sqn	Made landfall	X	
116	Waco	F Goubrine No. 2	Sgt Sharpe/ Sgt V.C. Webb	'B' Company 1 Border	Albermarle/ P 1467	F/S Brydon	296 Sqn	Made landfall	X	
117	Waco	F Goubrine No. 2	S/Sgt Whale/ S/Sgt J.R. Wheatley (1)	H' Company 1 Border	Albermarle/ P 1512	F/L Sutherland	296 Sqn	Landed in Sea		X

Glider Chalk No.	Glider Type	Departure Airfield	Pilot 1/ Pilot 2	Unit Carried	Tug Aircraft/ Tug A/C No.	Pilot	Group/ Squadron	Comment	Released within 3,000 yards of land	Released more than 3,000 yards from land
118	Waco	F Goubrine No. 2	S/Sgt R. MacKenzie/ Sgt L.A.R. Webb	H' Company 1 Border	Albermarle/ P 1526	F/L Smulian	296 Sqn	Landed in Sea		X
119	Waco	F Goubrine No. 2	S/Sgt Waldron/ Sgt Harris	Recce Platoon 1 Border	Albermarle/ P 1553	P/O Hyde	296 Sqn	Landed in Sea		X
120	Waco	F Goubrine No. 2	Sgt Read/ Sgt W. Gill	'B' Company 1 Border	Albermarle/ P 1440	F/S Nichols	296 Sqn	Did not cross North African Coast		
121	Waco	F Goubrine No. 2	S/Sgt MacKenzie/ S/Sgt Edwards	'H' Company 1 Border	Albermarle/ P 1474	F/O Snell	296 Sqn	Did not cross North African Coast		
122	Waco	F Goubrine No. 2	Sgt Kendall or US WO Locart (?)/ Sgt G Patterson	'H' Company 1 Border	Albermarle/ P 1501	F/O Whitty	296 Sqn	Made landfall	X	
123	Waco	F Goubrine No. 2	S/Sgt Chapman/ Sgt Kelly	Recce Platoon 1 Border	Albermarle/ P 1517	F/O Crowe	296 Sqn	Made landfall	X	
124	Waco	F Goubrine No. 2	S/Sgt H.J. Iron (1)/ Sgt G.E. Nelson (1)	'B' Company 1 Border	Albermarle/ P 1525	S/L McMonnies	296 Sqn	Landed in Sea		X
125	Waco	F Goubrine No. 2	Sgt J.T. Braybrooks/ Sgt Atkins	Mortar Platoon 1 Border	Albermarle/ P 1439	F/O Jackson	296 Sqn	Did not cross North African Coast		
125A	Waco	F Goubrine No. 2	Lt W.J. Carn/ Sgt D.W.J. Richards (2)	Mortar Platoon 1 Border	Albermarle/ P 1437	F/O Buzeta	296 Sqn	Made landfall		
126	Waco	F Goubrine No. 2	S/Sgt Chandler/ S/Sgt Torrence	Mortar Platoon 1 Border	Albermarle/ P 1470	P/O Wylie	296 Sqn	Made landfall	X	
126A	Waco	F Goubrine No. 2	S/Sgt Nutton/ Sgt Davitt	Mortar Platoon 1 Border	Albermarle/ P 1468	F/O Kemais	296 Sqn	Did not cross North African Coast		
127	Waco	F Goubrine No. 2	Sgt Pavitt/ Sgt Boucher	Battalion HQ 1 Border	Albermarle/ P 1551	S/L Davis	296 Sqn	Pulled Off immediately after take off		

Glider Chalk No.	Glider Type	Departure Airfield	Pilot 1/ Pilot 2	Unit Carried	Tug Aircraft/ Tug A/C No.	Pilot	Group/ Squadron	Comment	Released within 3,000 yards of land	Released more than 3,000 yards from land
128	Horsa	E Goubrine No. 1	Lt J. Lockett/ Sgt Granger	'A' Company 2 South Staffords	Albermarle	S/L Wilkinson	295 Sqn	Landed in Sea		X
129	Horsa	E Goubrine No. 1	Sgt Guthrie/ Sgt Pearson	'A' Company 2 South Staffords	Halifax	W/C May	295 Sqn	Made landfall	X	
130	Horsa	E Goubrine No. 1	S/Sgt Armitage/ Sgt Calder	'A' Company 2 South Staffords	Halifax	F/O Norman	295 Sqn	Unaccounted for		
131	Horsa	E Goubrine No. 1	Sgt D.S. Wood (1)/ Sgt H.J. Woodland (1)	'A' Company 2 South Staffords	Halifax	F/O Muirhead	295 Sqn	Unaccounted for		
132	Horsa	E Goubrine No. 1	Capt J.N.C. Denholm (2)/ Sgt R.A. Knott (2)	'C' Company 2 South Staffords	Halifax	F/O Bewick	295 Sqn	Made landfall	X	
133	Horsa	E Goubrine No. 1	S/Sgt Galpin/ Sgt Brown	'C' Company 2 South Staffords	Halifax	F/Lt Grant	295 Sqn	Made landfall	X	
134	Horsa	E Goubrine No. 1	S/Sgt Watmough/ Sgt Miller (?)	'C' Company 2 South Staffords	Halifax	F/Lt Briggs	295 Sqn	Made landfall	X	
135	Horsa	E Goubrine No. 1	S/Sgt McDonald/ Sgt Hobbs	'C' Company 2 South Staffords	Halifax	F/O Cleaver	295 Sqn	Made landfall	X	
X	Waco	B El Djem No. 1	Sgt Mallinson/ Sgt Wright	att'd 2 South Staffords 9 Field Company RE	Albermarle/ P 1432	F/L Jamieson	296 Sqn	Made landfall	X	
Y	Waco	F Goubrine No. 2	Sgt Pearson/ Sgt Curry	att'd 1 Border 9 Field Company RE	Albermarle/ P 1557	F/O Whitehouse	296 Sqn	Unaccounted for		
Z	Waco	A El Djem Base	S/Sgt R. Turnbull/ S/Sgt Coulson	Simforce 2 South Staffords			60 Group	Made landfall	X	

(1) Cassino Memorial, Italy, Panel 12
(2) Syracuse War Cemetery, Sicilly, Italy
(3) Catania War Cemetery
(4) No Known grave - not on CWGC site but in books
(5) Tablets of the Missing at North Africa American Cemetery, Carthage, Tunisia
(6) Tablets of the Missing at Sicily-Rome American Cemetery, Nettuno, Italy

Outcome of Operation LADBROKE Glider Flights – by Glider Chalk Number

1. Very rough flight, visibility off Sicily negligible. Glider released 2210hrs at 1,800 ft, approx 2 miles off coast. Glider not able to make land, landed in sea ¼ mile from coast.
2. Good but bumpy tow. Glider almost uncontrollable for 5 min over MALTA owing to bad weather and steep turns of tug regaining position. Intercom u/s. Tug altered course near target area twice and flashed lights for glider to release at 2210 hrs at 1,800 ft too far out to sea. Glider just missed reaching land owing to 100 ft cliff which necessitated pilot turning to avoid it and landing in sea off CAPE MURRO DI PORCO
3. Good tow, but intercom broke during flight. Released as arranged at 2217 hrs at 1,900 ft approx 3 miles off coast, but owing to strong wind and distance off shore, glider was unable to make land and landed 1–2 miles off coast.
4. Rough but satisfactory tow. Too far off coast at release. Glider released at 2215 hrs at 1,500 ft approx 3½ miles off shore. Glider could not make land and came down in sea approx 1½ to 2 miles off coast SE of PUTA DI MILOCCA.
5. Rough but satisfactory tow. Glider released at 1,800 ft approx 2,000 yds off shore. Glider made successful landing on PUNTA DI MILOCCA. Crew and glider intact. Glider later burnt intentionally
6. Good tow. Glider released at 2215 hrs at 1,800 ft and approx 2 miles off shore. Pilot unable to recognise LZ and landed glider on CAPE MURRO DI PORCO, collapsed undercarriage on landing.
7. Good tow. Glider released at 2215 hrs at 1,500 ft approx 3,000 yds off shore. Owing to strong winds pilot unable to make land and landed in sea about 600 yds from coast.
8. **Statement by passenger:** Exceptionally bumpy flight, glider pilot released at 2215 hrs approx 1,000 yds off shore height unknown. Pilot did not know his location. Glider landed on MADALENA Peninsula where it hit a wall on landing. Both pilots broken legs.
9. Tug made first landfall North of AUGUSTA, glider pilot requested a second run in and tug then came in on correct point. Glider released one hour late at 2310 hrs at 2,900 ft approx 5,000 yds off shore and made successful landing ½ mile SW of LZ but hit a tree after landing – all passengers safe.
10. Tug made first landfall near AUGUSTA – turned and made correct run in. Tow fair until tug started evasive action from AA and S/Ls. Glider released on instructions from tug pilot one hour late at 2300 hrs at 2,800 ft approx 10,000 yds from shore, made successful landing 2 to 3 miles SW of LZ crew and glider intact (later burnt).
11. Extremely bumpy tow off coast of SICILY, Glider towed first to AUGUSTA in error, towed back to correct point and released one hour late at 2320 hrs at 3,000 ft approx 3 miles off coast, glider made successful landing on tip of MURRO DI PORCO.
12. Tug pilot stated released at 1,800 ft at St Croce 115502 at an unstated time. Missed SE tip of Sicily and hit coast at Augusta. Considered glider could make land. GLIDER MISSING.
13. Tug pilot stated released at 2212 at 1800 ft. **Statement by passenger:** Bumpy flight. AA fire encountered before release. Glider landed somewhere south of LZ. Pilot did not know where they were. One pilot wounded in shoulder as he left glider.
14. Glider pilot found difficulty on tow owing to excessive speed when diving during violent evasive action. Glider pilot was ordered to release at 2215 hrs at 1,300 ft approx 4 miles off coast. Glider unable to make coast and was landed in bay approx 1½ miles off coast.
15. Experienced mist between MALTA and SICILY, tug climbed to clear it. Tug A/C made diving turn to right near coast when flak came up, thus loss of height and lengthening necessary glide to coast. Glider released at 1,700 ft approx – 5 miles from coast, was unable to make land and came down in bay 3–4 miles from coast.
16. Most uncomfortable tow. Tug pilot ordered glider pilot to release at 2200 hrs at 1,800 ft approx 5 miles off coast. Glider unable to make land and came down in sea approx 3½ miles off shore.
17. Intercomn broke during flight. Glider released at 2235 hrs at 2,000 ft approx 5 miles off coast. Owing to distance off shore of release, glider was unable to make land and came down in sea approx 3 miles off shore.
18. Good tow. Intercomn unreliable. Towed past release point on first approach and glider released on second run in at 2235 hrs at 2,200 ft approx 3 miles off shore. Landed in sea about one mile from coast off PUNTA DI MOLUCCO. One man drowned.
19. Tow was good but weather very rough. Intercom was inconsistent. Tug appeared to miss release point on first run up and made a second circuit. Glider released at 2230 hrs at 1,900 ft approx 6 miles from shore and was unable to make land, came down in sea approx 2 miles off shore. One man drowned.

20. **Statement by passenger:** Bumpy flight – saw MALTA. Glider released over sea, distance off shore unknown. Landed in sea approx 3–4 miles off shore. All missing with the exception of two passengers.
21. Considering the weather, good tow up to release area. Tug then started weaving and made a 180° turn to right, then on making a left turn, tug cast glider off owing to a misunderstanding of tug pilot, at 2250 hrs at 3,000 ft approx 4–5 miles from coast. Glider could not make land and came down in sea 4 to 5 miles out south of MURRO DI PORCO. 2 men drowned.
22. Considering the weather, good tow until 20 mins before release when tug pilot turned off his lights and began to take evasive action. Tug pilot cast off glider at 2230 hrs at 2,000 ft approx 10 miles off shore. Glider could not make land and came down in sea off CAPE PASSERO.
23. **Tug pilot reports:** Lost glider over sea at 36°50′ at 1,200 ft. Time unstated. GLIDER MISSING.
24. Tug pilot made two approaches to the island. Glider pilot found difficulty in control when tug pilot made steep 360° turns. Glider released at 2240 hrs at 2,000 ft approx 500 yds off shore. Landed successfully near CAPE PASSERO.
25. Good tow. Glider released at 2230 hrs at 2,200 ft approx 3,000 yds off shore and made successful landing on land about 2–300 yds inland and one mile short of LZ.
26. Considering weather, good tow. Glider was cast off early by tug at 2230 hrs at 2,000 ft and approx 3,000 yds off shore. Glider made successful landing approx ¼ mile short of LZ.
27. Tow fair but formation too close. Glider released at 2215 hrs at 2,000 ft too far out to sea. Pilot was unable to make land and came down in sea about 2 miles off shore and about 1 mile south of Cape MURRO DI PORCO.
28. **Pilot reports:** Released at 1,850 ft at 2233 hrs at correct point. Glider landed in sea. Crew picked up and landed at SUEZ. Not returned at compilation of report.
29. After rather a bumpy tow and intercom going u/s, glider released at 2226 hrs at 2,200 ft four miles off coast. Glider landed on land approx 300 yds to right of correct landing lane.
30. Reasonably tow, but lost formation on approach to island. Tug released glider at 2,000 ft, 6–7 miles off shore and landed in the sea about 4–5 miles out from PUNTA DI MILOCCA.
31. Bumpy tow, lost remainder of formation at end of run up. Glider released by tug at 2228 hrs at 2,000 ft approx and 4 miles off shore. Glider unable to make land and came down in sea about 1–2 miles off coast and south of Cape MURRO DI PORCO.
32. Good tow, but formation too tight. Tug lost remainder of echelon and released glider without warning at 2230 hrs at 3,000 ft approx 5–6 miles off shore. Glider landed in sea off CAPE MURRO DI PORCO.
33. Normal tow, glider released at 2225 hrs at 1,800 ft approx 2,500 yds off shore and landed on land approx 2 miles south of LZ as pilot was unable to recognise correct LZ.
34. Good tow but formation considered too close for night flying. Very bumpy conditions. Glider released at 2227 hrs at 1,800 ft approx over the coast and made successful landing on DZ.
35. Good tow though failed to pick up MALTA. Glider pilot experienced difficulty in seeing coast line. Glider released at 2222 hrs at 1,800 ft approx 1,500 yds off coast and made successful landing 2 miles SW of LZ but struck wall at end of run – 3 men hurt.
36. Tow uncomfortable at low altitudes and when avoiding other formations. Glider released at 2225 hrs at 1,900 ft approx 2,500 yds off shore and owing to poor visibility landed ½–¾ mile SW of LZ.
37. Satisfactory flight, coast line difficult to identify. Tug pilot approached release point as arranged. Intercom u/s. Glider released at 2235 hrs at 1,900 ft approx one mile off shore. Glider made successful landing approx 1 mile SE of LZ.
38. Successful and correct tow under bumpy conditions. Glider released at 2230 hrs at 2,000 ft approx 1,000 yds off shore and made successful landing ½ mile east of correct LZ. Pilot hampered by poor visibility.
39. On the whole tow was good but formation too tight. Glider released at 2235 hrs at 1,700 ft approx 3 miles off coast and came down in sea about one mile south of PUNTA DI MILOCCA. 1st Pilot all right but others believed drowned.
40. Tow in formation as far as MALTA where tug did steep right hand dive and lost formation which was never regained. Given into wind release in area AVOLA-NOTO at 2255 hrs 1,500 ft approx ½ mile from coast. Glider landed some 15–20 miles south of correct LZ. Fuselage undamaged but wings and undercarriage damaged.

41. On second attempt failed to locate Malta and got completely lost. After approx 6 hrs returned to N African coast and landed approx 80 miles south of SFAX.

42. After take off car 5 cwt came loose in glider and pilot cast off and landed approx 60 miles from airfield. Slight damage to a/c. Insecure lashing of car 5 cwt.

43. Tug pilot reports: Glider broke loose 10 miles west of MALTA. GLIDER MISSING.

44. Known to have landed in sea. No report available. All but two believed casualties; those two in hospital in SYRACUSE.

45. Good tow, constant speed, too close formation. Steady evasive action at Sicilian coast. Glider released at 2235 hrs at 2,000 ft approx 2,000 yds off shore and made successful landing ¼–½ mile west of LZ. No injury or damage to crew or load.

46. Very good tow, fairly constant speed, too close formation to release point. Over MALTA plane crossed rope of leading combination. Glider released at 2235 hrs at 2,000 ft approx 2,000 yds off coast and made successful landing 3–400 yds short of correct LZ. Undercarriage damaged.

47. Tug pilot states glider released at 2254 hrs at 1,800 ft at correct point on second run up. **Statement by passenger:** Bumpy flight. Met AA fire as glider came in to shore. Glider landed on beach 50 yds from sea, close to enemy post. Ammunition handcart in glider exploded, believed caused by enemy grenade thrown into glider. 2 men wounded, 8 men missing.

48. **Tug pilot reports:** Released at 1,800 ft, at 2245 hrs at correct point, having gone off course and circled the release point. GLIDER MISSING.

49. Uncomfortable tow when flying low and avoiding other a/c. Glider released at 2235 hrs at 2,000 ft approx one mile off shore and made land. Overshot LZ and did 360 degree turn and finally landed in some trees about 2–3 miles SW of bridge.

50. Glider experienced trouble from slipstream from formation ahead. Intercomn went u/s after one hour flying. Flak was experienced from coastal batteries. Glider released at 2230 hrs at 1,800 ft approx 2,000 yds off shore and made successful landing on LZ but broke undercarriage.

51. **Statement by passenger:** Glider landed at 2300 hrs approx; crashed into orchard 10 miles south of LZ. First pilot badly injured.

52. Tug got lost and never located release area. Brought glider back to MALTA where glider made successful landing.

52A. Tug pilot states: released at 2245 hrs at 2,500 ft over Syracuse Bay. Statement by passenger: Fairly good flight, slightly bumpy. Glider landed 2½ miles from BILSTON, SW of LZ met light AA fire on landing 15 yds after landing glider hit wall. 2 hospital cases.

53. Good tow at constant speed. Tug made coast 15–20 miles south of correct area; Tug pilot convinced correct point. Intercom u/s and tug released glider at 2310 hrs at 2,000 ft approx 3–4,000 yds from coast. Glider landed in sea 500 yds off shore.

53A. **Tug pilots report:** Released at 2,100 ft at 2238 hrs at correct point. Landed in sea close to coast. All but 3 occupants survived.

54. Glider pilot found formation too tight. Intercom went u/s after ½ hour flying. Glider cast off at 2230 hrs; at 1,800 ft, approx 5 miles off shore and landed in sea south of ABOLA, about 2–3 miles off shore.

54A. **Statement by passenger:** Bumpy flight. Glider released at 2230 hrs at unknown height. Pilot said just after releasing, 'We are at 600 feet', next moment glider landed in sea about 8 miles from coast. All men got out of glider, but both pilots and 7 ORs missing.

55. On approaching coast of Sicily off CAPE MURRO DI PORCO, Pilot observed small amount of flak some distance away. Tug then turned south and a/c formation lights were extinguished. Glider pilot could no longer see tug, so cast off and landed in sea 2 miles off AVOLA.

56. Tug cast glider of at 2255 hrs, at 1,100 ft, approx 3 miles off shore. Glider could not make LZ so tried to make landing on Cape MURRO DI PORCO, gliding in at 75–80 mph. Could not make it, so landed in sea, just south of Cape. Considered cast off too far out. Intercom went u/s through tug taking evasive action, and snapping cable.

57. Glider pilot stated tug a/c made incorrect approach – not as planned. Intercom went u/s. Glider cast off at 2225 hrs, at 1,400 ft, approx 2½ miles off shore; could not make land and came down in sea approx ¼ mile off Cape MURRO DI PORCO.

58. **Statement by passenger:** Flight bumpy but uneventful until reaching Sicilian coast. At 2230 hrs and approximately 1,500 ft, when tug a/c appeared to sheer off to east, Glider was released about 5 miles off shore. Glider landed in sea about 3 miles SE of AVOLA. Both pilots missing, believed drowned.

59. Glider felt sloppy on tow and there was bad vibration. Glider released on order from tug navigator, at 2230 hrs at 1,450 ft, approx 4 miles out to sea, and landed in sea about 2 miles south of LZ.

60. **Statement by passenger:** Glider pilot cast off at 2215 hrs, about 1,400 ft, on seeing glider on left cast off. At about 400 ft, pilot gave the order for a sea landing and glider landed approx one mile off shore. First pilot failed to get out of glider and three more are missing, believed drowned.

61. Uneventful tow. Glider released at 2225 hrs, at 1,500 ft (Alt reading), approx 2½ miles off coast. Glider unable to make land and came down in sea approx one mile off shore. Altimeter was reading 300 ft on landing.
62. Glider pilot was ordered by tug pilot to release at 2230 hrs, at 1,500 ft, approx 2 miles off shore. Tug pilot had mistaken CAPE OGNINA for CAPE MURRO DI PORCO. Glider landed in sea, 100 yds short of CAPE OGNINA.
63. Good tow, but co pilot's left rudder bar came loose twice. Intercom went u/s after take off. Glider released at 2225 hrs, at 2,000 ft, approx 1½ miles off coast; Glider landed in area of LZ, but crashed into wall and a tree. Crew and passengers safe.
64. Very steady flight without incident. Glider pilot released at 2230 hrs, at approx 1,500 ft, about 3 miles off shore. Glider could not make land and came down in sea, approx 1½ miles off shore. 5 passengers believed drowned.
65. **Statement by passenger:** Glider was released, thought by the tug, at 2210 hrs; very low down. As soon as released, pilot ordered troops to prepare for sea landing. Glider made a bad landing in the sea, 6 miles off PORTO PALA. 2 missing, believed drowned.
66. Normal flight. Glider was cast off by tug a/c at 2230 hrs, at 1,100 ft. Approx 3½ miles off shore, made landing on sea approx 2–2½ miles off PUNTA DI NOLOCCA. 1st pilot drowned.
67. Very good tow, but approach to release point not as briefed. Glider released at 2245 hrs at 1,500 ft, approx one mile from shore. Glider landed in field adjacent to correct LZ, no casualties.
68. Good tow. Intercom failed on take off. Made incorrect landfall and glider was released by tug a/c on second run in at 2300 hrs and 1,600 ft approx 4,000 yds off shore. Glider landed in sea approx ¼ to ½ mile south of escarpment on Cape MURRO DI PORCO. Probably 6 drowned (Pilots report).
69. Very good tow. Intercom worked well all the way. Glider released at 2245 hrs at 1,500 ft about one mile off coast and landed in field next to LZ.
70. When approx off the twin headlands flak came up from there and CAPE MURRO DI PORCO. The tug a/c immediately made a 180° right hand turn and headed EAST away from land. Tug a/c then ordered release by signal then at 1,400 ft. After release glider glided at 75–80 mph in direction of nearest land, but was unable to reach it and came down in sea approx 4 miles off CAPE MURRO DI PORCO. Glider pilot was unable to recognise any point on land as tug flew eastwards out to sea prior to release.
71. **Statement by passenger:** Flight uneventful. Released at 2220 hrs at unstated height and glider landed in sea about 3 miles off shore. 1 missing believed drowned.
72. Approach was made too far out. Intercom faulty, visual signal was given by tug for glider to release at 2230 hrs at 1,400 ft approx 2½ miles off shore. Glider could not make land and came down in sea approx one mile off coast.
73. Tug a/c became lost in vicinity of release point and glider then cast off at 2225 hrs at 1,400 ft approx 2½ miles off shore. Glider was unable to make land and came down in sea approx 1½ miles off coast.
74. Tow uneventful. glider released too far off shore on signal from tug a/c at 2220 hrs at 1,400 ft approx 5 miles off shore. Glider landed in sea approx 2 miles from shore. Starboard wing damaged on landing.
75. Good tow and intercom. Glider released at 2225 hrs at 1,400 ft, approx 3,000 yds off shore and was unable to make land, came down in sea about ¾ mile south of Cape MURRO DI PORCO about one mile off shore. One or two killed by MG fire (Pilots report).
76. **Statement by passenger:** No information available about flight. Glider released at 2200 hrs at an unknown height close in to shore and landed 100 yds inland about 5 miles south of the RV. One officerr and 4 Ors injured in crash.
77. **Statement by passenger:** Flight without incident until experience of considerable amount of flak on coast of SICILY. Tug a/c appeared to turn to east and when glider released was going out to sea again. Glider failed to make land and came down in sea off shore. One drowned, one missing believed drowned.
78. Bumpy tow, at times out of formation. Whole element swung right on approaching bay and pilot could not see landmarks as briefed. Glider released 2220 hrs at 1,500 ft approx 4 miles off shore and landed in sea 2 miles off shore in the bay.
79. Tow successful. Glider released at 2330 hrs at 1,400 ft approx 500 yds off shore, made successful landing in an orchard 5–7 miles SW of LZ but crew safe.
80. Tug a/c lost bearing off SICILY and returned to MALTA where a night fighter was encountered. Made second attempt to reach release point glider eventually cast off at 2325 hrs at 1,500 ft approx 700 yds off shore and landed successfully on LZ.
81. **Statement by passenger:** Uneventful flight, no details available on release. Glider landed on land ½ mile SE of PACHINO. 2 wounded.

82. Tow successful. Missed release point and glider released near SYRACUSE at 2320 hrs at 1,800 ft approx 800 yds off coast. Caught by S/L and flak - 2 men killed, glider landed in sea about ½ mile south of SYRACUSE.

83. Tug appeared to make two attempts to find correct release point, but failed. Each time was approx 3 miles off shore. Tug eventually got lost and returned with glider to MALTA where it landed successfully.

84. Made four attempts at run in finally released over SYRACUSE BAY. GLIDER MISSING.

85. Tug pilot could not pick up release point after several attempts after which he insisted on bringing glider back to N Africa, rather than release. Tug ran short of petrol off coast near SFAX and ordered glider pilot to land on sea close to shore for safety. Glider slightly damaged on landing but personnel safe.

86. Good tow, intercom worked well all the way. Strong cross wind. Tug missed release point on first two attempts and glider released on third run in at 2340 hrs at 1,300 ft and one mile from coast. Glider landed in orchard 2–300 yds west of LZ. One man received broken leg.

87. GLIDER MISSING. Believed down at sea.

88. **Statement by passenger:** Flight uneventful but bumpy – glider hit telegraph wires on landing and crashed into wall 2 miles south of CAPE MURRO DI PORCO. 3 wounded.

89. **Statement by passenger:** Flight went well. Glider released at 2220 hrs at approx 1,400 ft, and landed in sea. Personnel picked up by HMS CARLISLE. One missing presumed drowned.

90. Developed tail flutter and cast off. Took off again new glider at 2007. Tug missed release point, glider cast off on return run in at 2245 hrs, at 200 ft approx 3 miles off coast. Glider landed in sea, approx 1–2 miles off shore, south of CAPE MURRO DI PORCO. One man drowned.

91. Observed 'flak' some distance off. Tug turned eastwards from coast and began evasive action. Tug pilot ordered glider to release at 2215 hrs at 2,000 ft somewhere over SYRACUSE BAY. Glider turned into moon and glided at 70 mph but could not make land. Glider landed in sea three miles off coast.

92. **Statement by passenger:** Glider landed in sea about 2230 hrs, approx 3 miles off shore. Three men and first pilot missing.

93. **Statement by passenger:** Glider just cleared the cliff and hit a wall. Crew surrounded by Italians after few minutes. 2 pilots killed, 6 wounded.

94. **Statement by passenger:** Bumpy flight. Flak about 3–4 miles off shore. Sudden release of glider and warning from pilot – prepare for sea landing. Glider landed in sea. 3 missing, believed drowned.

95. Tow uneventful. Approach too far out to sea. Glider ordered to release at 2250 hrs, at 1,700 ft, approx 2 miles off shore. Glider made successful landing on neck of PENINSOLA DELLA MADALENA.

96. Approx 10 miles from release point and ten miles out to sea, tug pilot released glider from tug end, pilot stating that that was the point. Glider landed in sea approx 7 miles from land.

97. Glider pilot states glider was 4 miles off shore and ordered to release at 2230 hrs, at 1,400 ft. Tug pilot ordered release and then dived off right without waiting for glider to release. Glider turned into moon and headed for land, but could not reach it and came down in sea, 2 miles off shore in SYRACUSE BAY.

98. Glider pilot instructed to cast off by tug pilot, at 2220 hrs, at 2,000 ft and approx 6 miles off shore. Glider landed in sea about 5 miles south of CAPE MURRO DI PORCO. 5 passengers were drowned.

99. **Statement by passenger:** Glider released about 6 miles off coast. Glider landed in sea about 4 miles off shore, hitting water hard and filled up immediately. 13 missing believed drowned.

100. On final run up to CAPE MURRO DI PORCO, glider was so far out to sea that pilot could not see coast. When at 200 ft, glider pilot was instructed by tug pilot through intercom to release. Glider turned to bearing 298 degrees at 80 mph; pilot could only see 'flak' in distance. Pilot could not make land and so landed glider in sea approx 2 miles off CAPE MURRO DI PORCO.

101. Pilot reported tow conditions good, but never passed over MALTA. Glider released at 2235 hrs, at 1,500 ft, approx 3 miles off coast, was unable to make land, so landed successfully in the sea 1½ miles off PONTA DI MILOCCA - One drowned.

101A. **Statement by passenger:** Consistently bumpy and men sick. First sign of approaching objective was 20 mm flak to port. A/C immediately appeared to swerve to starboard and glider was released at 2230 hrs, at approx 1,000 ft, about 3–4 miles off shore. Glider landed in sea off AVOLA. 3 missing believed drowned.

102. Tug a/c took evasive action, although clear of flak, then ordered glider pilot to release at 2240 hrs at 1,400 ft approx 4 miles off shore. Glider unable to make land and had to land in bay 2 miles off shore.

102A.

103. No details available but glider known to be down in sea.

103A.

104. **Statement by passenger:** Flight uneventful, landed in sea, all got out.

104A.

105. Satisfactory tow but intercom went u/s after MALTA. Glider released at 2240 hrs at 1,800 ft approx 3 miles off coast. Glider made successful landing but 6 to 7 miles from LZ near CASTIBILE.

106. Good tow. Intercom failed. Made first landfall north of SYRACUSE, turned and released on second run in at 2310 hrs at 1,500 ft approx 500–1,000 yds off shore. Glider landed in field next to LZ under power cables and hit a tree. All personnel except 1 officer and 1 OR were injured.

107. Good tow. Intercom went u/s half way over. Glider released on correct run in at 2240 hrs at 1,600 ft approx 400 yds from coast and landed successfully in field next to LZ.

108. Good tow until it became dark when tug lights hardly visible. Intercom failed on take off. At 2315 hrs and in very bad visibility glider released on orders from tug pilot at 1,500 ft about 3 miles off shore. Glider landed about 50 yds inland from coast about one mile north of AVOLA beach. 4 men had broken legs on landing.

109. Pilot reports a good tow but intercom was u/s. Port light on Albermarle was u/s from start. Released at 2345 hrs at 1,400 ft approx 500 yds off shore. Glider made perfect landing on LZ.

110. A first rate tow and navigation, but intercom went u/s. Glider released at 2240 hrs at 1,400 ft approx 1,200 yds off coast and made successful landing on LZ. One man injured on landing by gun load breaking loose.

111. Glider pilot reports a good tow with intercom working. Released at 2230 hrs at 1,800 ft approx 5,000 yds off coast, unable to make land so landed successfully in sea about one mile off CAPE MURRO DI PORCO.

112. Fairly bumpy, intercom failed after 30 mins. Made very wide sweep and did not see MALTA, later ran west and then NW and released at 2310 hrs on correct run at 1,400 ft approx 4–5,000 yds off shore. Glider could not make land but came down in sea approx ¾ mile from shore. No casualties.

113. Pilot reported glider nose heavy, it broke port wheel of undercarriage on take off. Pilot cast off just after take off and landed back on airfield – no one injured, unable to take off again.

114. Approach too far from coast to read map. Tug pilot ordered glider to release at 2236 hrs when at 1,400 ft and 2 miles off coast off CAPE MURRO DI PORCO, Glider could not make land and came down in sea approx ½ mile off coast. Faulty intercom.

115. Glider released at 1,400 ft at 2253 hrs approx one mile off shore and landed approx in correct LZ.

116. After a good tow, glider released at 2238 hrs at 1,500 ft approx 1,200 yds off shore. Landed ¾ mile SW of LZ. Glider hit tree and broke up. Two passengers slightly injured. Intercom went u/s.

117. **Statement by passenger:** Glider landed in sea within a few hundred yards of shore and drifted close enough for passengers to swim for the shore.

118. **Statement by passenger:** Uneventful flight. Ran into heavy flak near coast and went out to sea again. On second attempt, pilot released about 1,500 ft and glider landed in sea just in sight of shore. One missing believed drowned.

119. Uneventful tow as far as SICILY. Glider pilot then realised he was not in correct release area but intercom had failed, so he released when tug began to turn eastwards at 2235 hrs at 1,400 ft about 6½ miles off shore SE of PONTA DI MOLOCCA, glider could not make land and came down in sea 3–4 miles off shore.

120. Glider appeared right wing heavy just after take off. Pilot attempted to correct this and shifted the load to balance, but made little difference. Pilot eventually cast off and landed about 2 miles south of SAKEN after 20 minute flight. One casualty on landing.

121. Glider released at 2020 hrs just after take off, owing to starboard aileron going u/s. Glider on its side in slip stream and wing would not come up.

122. Timing did not work out owing to increased strength of wind. Intercom went u/s. Glider released at 2245 hrs at 2,000 ft 300 yds off shore on an incorrect signal from tug. Glider pilot mistook a flickering light for that of his tug. Glider landed on land approx 30 miles south of objective.

123. After a reasonable tow glider pilot released at 2240 hrs at 1,800 ft approx 500–600 yds off coast. Found it impossible to locate DZ landed glider on land approx 2 miles south of LZ.

124. **Statement by passenger:** Glider hit cliff and fell back into the sea. Severe crash into sea. 3 wounded, 9 missing believed drowned.

125. Tug a/c engine caught fire approx half an hour after take off. Tug returned to base and released glider near airfield. Sun dazzled glider pilot's eyes and he landed glider heavily near airfield – damage to glider but no personnel.

125A.

126. Good tow, intercom failed after 10 minutes flight. Glider released at 2310 hrs at 1,600 ft about ½ way across bay between PUNTA DO MOLOCCO and MURRO DI PORCO and landed about one mile SW of LZ. No casualties but undercarriage came through floor.

126A. Pilot cast off at 2100 hrs shortly after take off owing to aileron control becoming u/s. Broke undercarriage on landing. No one injured.

127. Pilot released immediately after take off as wheel came off on take off. Not able to take off again.

128. On beach 44 wreckage found. No details.

129. Good tow, intercom worked well all the way. Glider released on orders of tug pilot at 2155 hrs at 4,000 ft about 300 yds off shore and landed successfully about 1,000 yds short of correct LZ. Pilot states visibility poor owing to position of moon.

130. No report. GLIDER MISSING.

131. No report. GLIDER MISSING.

132. **Statement by passenger:** Glider crashed about 400 yds upstream from the bridge (objective). Burst into flames on landing. One officer and 2 OR injured, remainder killed.

133. A very good tow, intercom worked well throughout. Glider released at 2220 hrs at 5,000 ft approx one mile off coast, made successful landing on correct DZ.

134. **Statement by passenger:** Rough flight. Released approx 2215 hrs at 3,500 ft over land. Glider subjected to AA fire after release, heavy tracer, left wing hit. Flew over LZ. Glider landed 6–10 miles SW of SYRACUSE hitting a 6 ft wall. Left wing burning, also 77 grenades ignited inside glider. Thick smoke in glider and men trapped by ammunition panniers which began to explode. Intense heat and small arms fire made extrication of men difficult. 2 pilots and 12 ORs killed, 7 wounded.

135. Good tow as far as MALTA. Outer starboard engine of Halifax caught fire and towed on three engines for 40 miles. Certain equipment had to be jettisoned. On instructions from tug a/c, glider released at 2200 hrs at 2,000 ft over the coast. Glider landed 2 miles west of landing area, hit a brick wall, undercarriage knocked back and broke leg of passenger on rear seat. Compass in Horsa was not luminous and had to be read by torch.

X. Fair tow. Experienced flak near coast. Glider released at 2227 hrs at 1,800 ft approx correct distance from coast. Glider made successful landing to SE of LZ. Too dark for pilot to locate correct LZ.

Y. GLIDER MISSING.

Z. Good but bumpy tow, intercom went u/s on take off. Glider released at 2300 hrs at 2,000 ft over PUNTA DI MOLOCCA and landed in cactus hedge about one mile north of LZ. No casualties.

APPENDIX 2

Operation FUSTIAN Post Mission Reports

Glider Chalk No.	Glider Type	Departure Airfield	Pilot 1/ Pilot 2	Unit Carried	Tug Aircraft/ Tug A/C No.	Group/ Squadron	Comment
114	Waco	E	Sgt A. Goodall (2)/ Capt A.H. Kitching (2)	B Troop 1 A/L Anti Tank Battery	Albermarle/ P 1444	296 Squadron	Missing
115	Waco	E	S/Sgt J.S.A. Pattinson/ F/O T.B. Leckard	B Troop 1 A/L Anti Tank Battery	Albermarle/ P 1466	296 Squadron	A/C crashed on take off. Glider cast off, successful landing. Unable to take off again in time.
116	Waco	E	Sgt R.C.A. Vanassche/ F/O F.G. Martin	B Troop 1 A/L Anti Tank Battery	Albermarle/	296 Squadron	Successful tow but intercom u/s from take off. Released at 0111 hrs at 500 ft over LZ. Caught in S/L on release, starboard wing hit, side slipped and crash landed on outer defences of CATANIA Airfield where MG fire was experienced all round. Unable to unload gun owing to enemy activity.
117	Waco	E	Sgt W.J. Wells/ F/O Zaneby	B Troop 1 A/L Anti Tank Battery	Albermarle/ P 1469	296 Squadron	Good tow, intercom OK. Successful release but late at 800 ft above LZ. Successful landing north of LENTINI but undercarriage damaged – unable to release car 5 cwt which was jammed in. Glider landed within enemy Field Force.
118	Waco	E	Sgt R.W. McKay/ F/O C.A. Casella	B Troop 1 A/L Anti Tank Battery	Albermarle/ P 1474	296 Squadron	Cast off 2101 hrs near M'SAKEN - pilot found a/c uncontrollable.
118A	Waco	E	Lt J.B. Mockridge/ S/Sgt J. Bridge	D Troop HQ 1 A/L Anti Tank Battery	Albermarle/ P 1440	296 Squadron	Successful tow and released at 1,000 ft above LZ, but 87 minutes late. Glider made heavy landing on beach (9666) no casualties, but unable to remove jeep owing to angle of landing preventing the opening of nose – unable to cut it out owing to being in enemy defences.

Glider Chalk No.	Glider Type	Departure Airfield	Pilot 1/ Pilot 2	Unit Carried	Tug Aircraft/ Tug A/C No.	Group/ Squadron	Comment
118B	Waco	E	S/Sgt T. Montague (2)/ S.S.M.W. Atkinson	Battery HQ 1 A/L Anti Tank Battery	Albermarle	296 Squadron	Released over LZ 7 29½ minutes late. Glider fired on on way down by light flak but no hit observed. Nothing more heard.
118C	Waco	E	Lt N.V.M. Adams/ Sgt F.H. Street	Brigade HQ 1 A/L Anti Tank Battery	Albermarle/ P 1517	296 Squadron	Released over LZ 7 20 minutes late. Crash landed area SW of LZ (9266) – all personnel injured. Nose jammed preventing removal of jeep. No pilot's report as yet.
119	Horsa	F	Lt D.P. Gregg (1)/ Sgt R. Beddows (1)	A Troop 1 A/L Anti Tank Battery	Albermarle/ P 1551	296 Squadron	Released without warning to tug 2,500 ft 2 miles off coast. Nothing more heard.
120	Horsa	F	Lt W.N .Barrie/ Sgt I.N. Williams	B Troop 1 A/L Anti Tank Battery	Albermarle	296 Squadron	Good tow. Tow rope broke when circling and looking for LZ 7 at 0107 hrs at 1,600 ft. Glider made successful landing 2,000 ft west of LZ 8. Landed on skid. Gun and Jeep OK, unloaded in 3 hrs. Intercom OK up to coast but very weak after that.
121	Horsa	F	Sgt D. Craske (3)/ Sgt J.W. Jackson	B Troop 1 A/L Anti Tank Battery	Albermarle/ P 1521	296 Squadron	Tug missing. Nothing heard of glider.
122	Horsa	F	Lt G.T. Mills/ Sgt O. Boland	D Troop 1 A/L Anti Tank Battery	Albermarle	296 Squadron	Released over LZ 7 at 1,200 ft. Circled and landed NE of LENTINI (square 9358). Glider riddled with .303 and 20mm bullets, one casualty on landing. Successful landing on skid. Final position of glider made door unloading impossible – attempted to blow tail off with CORDTEX resulted in complete burning of glider.
123	Horsa	F	Lt Thomas/ Sgt McCulloch	D Troop 1 A/L Anti Tank Battery	Albermarle	296 Squadron	Successful tow. Intercom perfect, released at 0120 hrs approx 500 ft. Made successful landing in ravine 7 miles SW of LZ 7. Gun and jeep out in 30 mins.
124	Horsa	F	S.S.M.J.A. Preston (2)/ Sgt J.M. Broadhead (2)	D Troop 1 A/L Anti Tank Battery	Halifax	295 Squadron	Rope broke on cable – replaced and took off again. Released over LZ 8 at 700 ft. Nothing heard of glider.
125	Horsa	F	Sgt H.N. Winkle/ Sgt C.R. Holdren	D Troop 1 A/L Anti Tank Battery	Halifax	295 Squadron	Did not take off due to damage to glider on first attempted take off.
126	Horsa	F	S/Sgt H.G. Protherce/ Sgt A.M. Kerr	A Troop 1 A/L Anti Tank Battery	Halifax	295 Squadron	Released slightly past LZ 8 at 0045 hrs at 500 ft. Lights not visible. Perfect release, Made heavy landing on LZ, one casualty. Load unloaded without much difficulty in one hour. Intercom OK.

Glider Chalk No.	Glider Type	Departure Airfield	Pilot 1/ Pilot 2	Unit Carried	Tug Aircraft/ Tug A/C No.	Group/ Squadron	Comment
127	Horsa	F	Major A.J. Cooper (2)/ Sgt C.P. Morgan (2)	HQ RA, Battery HQ 1 A/L Anti Tank Battery	Halifax	295 Squadron	Tug missing. No pilot's report. Glider crashed NE of LENTINI (area 9159) complete write off. 4 killed (including pilots) 3 badly injured.
128	Horsa	F	Lt R.O. Wachli/ Sgt W. Mackenzie	A Troop 1 A/L Anti Tank Battery	Halifax	295 Squadron	Released 500 ft over LZ 8. LZ obscured by smoke and fire. Glider crashed in river by LZ 8 4 crew killed, 2 injured, 1 OK. No information available as to gun or jeep.
129	Horsa	F	S.Sgt D.A. White/ Sgt H.F. Webb	A Troop 1 A/L Anti Tank Battery	Halifax	295 Squadron	Released over LZ 8 at 1,500 ft, 27 mins late. Glider pilot reported he knew exact location because of flak. Made successful landing on road 100 yds south of bridge over river. No casualties, gun removed in 4 hrs and Jeep in 9 hrs. Intercom OK.

(1) Cassino Memorial, Italy, Panel 12
(2) Catania War Cemetery
(3) Salerno War Cemetery, Italy

Appendix 3

National Archive Source Documents

AIR 20/3151	North Africa: ferrying of gliders.
AIR 20/6040	Operations 'Beggar', 'Ladbrook' and 'Fustian': operational attachment to No. 295 Squadron., report by Flt. Lt. D.A. Grant.
AIR 27/1644	295 Squadron Operational Records Book.
AIR 37/253	Operation 'Beggar': movement of aircraft and crews to North Africa.
AIR 37/310	Operation 'Beggar': organisation; movement of aircraft and crews to North Africa.
AIR 37/311	Operation 'Beggar': organisation; movement of aircraft and crews to North Africa.
AIR 37/703	Operation 'Beggar'
AIR 38/88	Operation 'Beggar': despatch of gliders and paratroop aircraft to N. Africa.
AIR 8/1315	Operation 'Husky': airborne forces requirements.
AIR 8/1316	Operation 'Husky': airborne forces requirements.
CAB 106/687	Sicily: report on operations of 1st Airborne Division in operation 'Husky'; part I, preparation of the Division.
CAB 106/688	Sicily: report on operations of 1st Airborne Division in operation 'Husky'; part II, 1st Air Landing Brigade Operation.
CAB 106/689	Sicily: report on operations of 1st Airborne Division in operation 'Husky'; part III, 1st Parachute Brigade Operation.
CAB 106/690	Sicily: report on operations of 1st Airborne Division in operation 'Husky'; part IV, 2nd Parachute Brigade Operation; Control of Airborne Base.
CAB 106/691	Sicily: report on operations of 1st Airborne Division in operation 'Husky'; part V, lessons and conclusions.
CAB 106/692	Sicily: report on operations of 1st Airborne Division in operation 'Husky'; part VI, maps.

CAB 106/693	Sicily: report on operations of 1st Airborne Division in operation 'Husky'; part VII, appendices.
WO 106/3900	Operation 'Husky': planning.
WO 169/10182	War Diary 1st Battalion The Border Regiment.
WO 169/10299	War Diary 2nd Battalion The South Staffordshire Regiment.
WO 169/10341	War Diary 1st Battalion The Glider Pilot Regiment.
WO 169/10343	War Diary 1st Parachute Battalion.
WO 169/10344	War Diary 2nd Parachute Battalion.
WO 169/10345	War Diary 3rd Parachute Battalion.
WO 169/10346	War Diary 4th Parachute Battalion.
WO 169/10357	War Diary 21st Independent Parachute Company.
WO 169/10554	War Diary 1st Parachute Squadron, Royal Engineers.
WO 169/10576	War Diary 9th (Airborne) Field Company, Royal Engineers.
WO 169/8837	War Diary HQ 1st Parachute Brigade.
WO 169/8845	War Diary HQ 1st Airlanding Brigade.
WO 169/9639	War Diary 1st Airlanding Anti-Tank Battery, Royal Artillery.
WO 175/108	War Diary HQ 1st Airborne Division.
WO 201/659	Operations: 'Husky': 1st Airborne Division.
WO 204/10397	Operation Husky: diary of events and correspondence, planning.
WO 204/1072	Operation Husky: report on participation by 1 Airborne Division.
WO 361/494	Sicily: glider landings and missions; Casualty investigations.
WO 361/495	Sicily: glider landings and missions; Casualty investigations.
WO 361/942	Sicily: The South Staffordshire Regiment; glider operations; missing personnel.
WO 361/943	Sicily: Army Air Corps; Parachute Battalions and The Glider Pilot Regiment; missing personnel.
WO 361/944	Sicily: 1st Battalion The Border Regiment; glider operations; missing personnel.
WO 361/946	Sicily: Royal Engineers; missing personnel.
WO 361/952	Sicily: Field and Anti-Tank Regiments, Royal Artillery; missing personnel.
WO 361/969	Sicily: Airborne Units, Royal Army Medical Corps; missing personnel.
WO 373/3	Combat Gallantry Awards Sicily.

Bibliography

Andrews, A., *So you wanted to Fly, Eh?* ISTE, Burnaby, B.C. 1997.
Blackwell, I., *Battle For Sicily*, Pen and Sword, Barnsley, 2008.
Buckingham, W., *Paras*, Tempus Publishing Ltd., Stroud, 2005.
Chatterton, G., *The Wings of Pegasus*, Battery Press, Nashville, 1962.
Cherry, N., *Tunisian Tales*, Helion & Company Ltd, Solihull, 2011.
Cole, H., *On Wings of Healing*, Blackwood & Sons Ltd, London, 1963.
Dank, M., *The Glider Gang*, Cassell Ltd, London, 1978.
D'Este, C., *Bitter Victory*, Aurum, London, 1988.
Devlin G., *Silent Wings*, W.H. Allen, London, 1985.
Dover V., *The Sky Generals*, Cassell, London, 1981.
Eastwood, Gray & Green, *When Dragons Flew*, Silverlink, Peterborough, 1994.
Farrar-Hockley, General Sir A., *The Army in the Air*, Alan Sutton Publishing, Stroud, 1994.
Ford, K., *Assault On Sicily*, Sutton Publishing, Stroud, 2007.
Frost, J., Major General, *A Drop Too Many*, Buchan & Enright Publishers, London, 1982.
Fullick, R., *'Shan' Hackett*, Pen and Sword Ltd, Barnsley, 2003.
Greenacre, J., *Churchill's Spearhead*, Pen and Sword, Barnsley, 2010.
Harclerode, P., *Para! Fifty Years of The Parachute Regiment*, Brockhampton Press, London, 1992.
Heilmann, L., *Fallschirmjager auf Sizilien*, Unknown, 1959.
Hickey, M., *Out of the Sky*, Mills and Boon, London, 1979.
HMSO, *By Air To Battle*, London, 1945.
Junier, A. & Smulders, B. with Korsloot, J., *By Land, Sea and Air*, Sigmond Publishing, Renkum, 2003.
Kent, R., *First In!* Batsford, Trowbridge, 1979.
Lloyd, A., *The Gliders*, Arrow Books Ltd, London, 1982.
Lowden, J., *Silent Wings at War*, Smithsonian, Washington D.C., 1992.
Lynch, T., *Silent Skies*, Pen and Sword, Barnsley, 2008.
Ramsey, W., *After The Battle Magazine Issue 77*, 1992.
Miller, V., *Nothing Is Impossible*, Spellmount Ltd, Bury St Edmunds, 1994.
Mithcham, S.W. & Stauffenberg, F.V., *The Battle Of Sicily*, Stackpole Books, Mechanicsburg PA., 1991.
Montagu, E. & Cooper, D., *The Man Who Never Was*, Spellmount, Stroud, 2003.
Montgomery, B.L. Field Marshal, Memoirs, Pen & Sword Books Ltd, Barnsley 2005.
Mrazek, J.E., *Fighting Gliders Of World War II*, Robert Hale Publishing, London, 1975.

Otway, T.B.H., *Airborne Forces*, IWM, London, 1990.
Pack, S.W.C., *Operation Husky*, David and Charles, London, 1977.
Peters, M. & Buist, L., *Glider Pilots at Arnhem*, Pen & Sword, Barnsley, 2009.
Reynolds, M., *Monty and Patton*, Spellmount Publishing, Staplehurst, 2005.
Seth, R., *Lion with Blue Wings*, Gollancz Ltd, London, 1956.
Shannon & Wright, *One Night in June*, Airlife Publishing, Bury St Edmunds, 1994.
Smith, C., *The History of The Glider Pilot Regiment*, Pen & Sword Ltd, Barnsley, 1992.
Waldron, A., *Operation Ladbroke*, Woodfield Publishing Ltd, Bognor Regis, 2003.
Whiting, C., *Hunters From The Sky*, Leo Cooper, London, 1975.
Whiting, C., *Slaughter Over Sicily*, Pen and Sword, Barnsley, 2006.
Wood, A., *History Of The World's Glider Forces*, Patrick Stephens Ltd., 1990.
Wright, L., *The Wooden Sword*, Elek Publishing, London, 1967.

Unpublished sources

Brown, G.R., by permission of his widow Mrs Dorothy Brown.
Etherington, R., *My Overworked Guardian Angel*, 1996.
Howes, N., Interview transcripts by permission of his son, John Howes.
Wright, L., *Operations Turkey Buzzard and Elaborate*, 1988, by permission of MAF.

Museums & Archives

Bundesarchiv, Koblenz
Airborne Assault Museum, Duxford
Imperial War Museum, London
Museum of Army Flying, Middle Wallop

Index